DAWS

D A W S

A MAN WHO TRUSTED GOD

The Inspiring Life and Compelling Faith of
Dawson Trotman, Founder of The Navigators

BETTY LEE SKINNER

NAVPRESS
BRINGING TRUTH TO LIFE
NavPress Publishing Group
P.O. Box 35001, Colorado Springs, Colorado 80935

The Navigators is an international Christian
organization. Jesus Christ gave His followers the Great Commission to go and make
disciples (Matthew 28:19). The aim of The
Navigators is to help fulfill that commission by
multiplying laborers for Christ in every nation.

NavPress is the publishing ministry of The
Navigators. NavPress publications are tools
to help Christians grow. Although publications alone cannot make disciples or change
lives, they can help believers learn biblical
discipleship, and apply what they learn to their
lives and ministries.

Printed in the United States of America

17 18 19 20 21 22 23 24 25 / 99 98 97 96 95

It is not always given to the men of vision to perfect their dreams. As pioneers and pathfinders they map the country, prepare the plans . . . others must do the actual work of constructing.

— John S. Fisher in *A Builder of the West*

CONTENTS

FOREWORD

Many years have passed since Dawson Trotman drowned while rescuing another. He died as he had lived—for others.

I was one of those "others." I had been a Christian for about a year when Daws adopted me as his son in the faith—a relationship that continued until his death fifteen years later. This association included living in his home and spending hundreds of hours just listening to him and watching his life. It also included what seemed to me severe exhortation, yet I was always conscious of his love for me and of his desire to help me reach my fullest potential.

In the time since Dawson's death at the age of fifty, we who knew him find ourselves often referring to what he said and did. His recorded messages, such as "The Need of the Hour," always outsold the others in The Navigators' tape library. I am happy that many who did not know him can now have a deeper glimpse into the life of this extraordinary man.

Betty Skinner has thoroughly researched and carefully written this biography of Daws. For years God has been preparing her for the task, from her vantage point on The Navigators staff.

I, along with thousands of others, have eagerly awaited this account of a unique, gifted, and intense man of faith. May it have wide distribution and significant impact upon the lives of all who read it.

Lorne C. Sanny
President, The Navigators
1956-1986

PREFACE

As the motorcycle with its lone rider topped a small rise on the highway north of San Diego, the motor sputtered and died. Out of gas. He knew he could coast down the next grade for maybe a mile or more, but then what? *Lord, I need gas to get home.* He knew this territory, this corner of the U.S. between Los Angeles and Bisbee, Arizona, where he was born. The California sun shone warm but not oppressive in the wide, pale sky. The tall palms were stationed about like extras on a Hollywood movie set.

He steered the cycle down the hill and into a service station. It was closed. Just as well. He had no money. Quickly brushing back his hair on one side in a habitual gesture, he decided to wait and see how God would answer his prayer.

"Outa gas, fella?"

"Yeah." He tried to be casual. The driver of a gasoline truck had just finished filling the station's underground tanks and guessed the stranger's plight. He reached over and emptied what gasoline was left in the hose from his truck — enough to overflow the motorcycle's tank. The young man grinned, thanked him, then waited for the spilled gas to evaporate before starting his motor for the trip home. Another of the unaccountable ways the Lord had provided for him and protected him on the road, he reflected. There was the time he and Lewie were thrown off the cycle and pitched headlong, stunning him unconscious. Hearing the ambulance siren had roused him enough to protest, "*Me* in a ambulance? Get on this motor. Let's get outa here." Lewie had climbed on behind him as they sped off. The next day he could not recall the incident, leaving the astonished Lewie to realize he had been chauffeured through traffic by someone not fully conscious!

The motorcycle, leather jacket, whipcord pants, boots, and studied casualness of grooming might have stamped Dawson

11

Trotman as a member of the youth subculture a generation later. His steel blue eyes, jutting jaw, and sinuous neck topped off a lean, too-slight frame, giving the illusion of a much sturdier build. Above a wide forehead, the thick shock of reddish-brown hair seldom looked combed.

He intentionally cultivated the rugged, he-man image to counter the idea that Christianity was suitable only for women and children. He may also have been spurred by his lack of physical stature and his fear of an appearance of weakness or sissiness in any form. But in any case the point was made, as in his frequent witness to hitchhikers on the motorcycle. "Hook your chin over my shoulder," he would instruct the passenger. Then he would quote Scripture verses and explain the Gospel and the subject's precariously lost condition. Swerving around the winding roads through Sepulveda Pass while he reasoned of righteousness and judgment helped him convince the sinner of his need. Whether any "decisions" were made out of fright is not on record.

* * * *

In the quarter-century that followed, the course of church history was changed through the life of this young motorcyclist. The Navigators, the movement he founded while not intending to found a movement, spread to world-wide proportions. Beyond this, his influence is seen in countless other works and the church at large through men and women whose lives he touched and through principles of discipling he pioneered.

I came to know Dawson Trotman as a member of his postwar "crew" in the Los Angeles Navigators office. He had become more civilized than in the motorcycle days, but the excitement about living and serving God was still there. He liked to recruit staff members from different parts of the country, and he invited me from New Orleans, where he had previously come to speak at a Young Life-sponsored youth rally. At a time when I was asking God where to invest my life, The Navigators appealed to me — their initiative in personal evangelism, their strong reliance on the Word of God, their faith financial policy, and, of course, the contagion of Dawson's own dynamic purpose.

But even these high expectations did not prepare me for the immediate and loving acceptance by the Navigator "gang," most of whom lived with the Trotmans in the frame mansion in South Pasadena known as "509." This famous prototype of Navigator Homes was not so much a place as an experience: a warm, living fellowship of those who share and care in every detail of life and work together — details in which each exhorts the other to rejoice and to see God's hand at work for good.

There is an indescribable kinship among those who live in a Navigator Home, a community of shared joys and sorrows that is still unique on the Christian scene. That family mystique remains today, though the organization is in twenty-eight countries and has passed its fortieth birthday.

This book, a definitive biography insofar as space limitations permit, aims to present in true and balanced proportion Dawson Trotman's life as he lived it. People and events are seen through his eyes, his viewpoint expressed, with a minimum of author interpretation or comment. The reader is thus free to make his own observations and draw whatever lessons or challenges he sees in the life experiences, principles, trials, mistakes, and victories of this remarkable man of God.

A few who knew that Dawson Trotman was not perfect warned me not to canonize him in this book. The warning was unnecessary for one who worked with him long enough to know that he had faults and to be painfully aware that he knew mine. So both history and conscience have been looking over my shoulder to keep me honest.

Source materials were abundant. Although I had a certain grasp of Dawson's thinking and pattern of life firsthand, to avoid bias and broaden the view I have interviewed almost 700 people in the years since his death — some whose knowledge went all the way back to his childhood. The journals he kept carefully for some years were available, as well as his correspondence in Navigator archives. Lila Trotman's recollections helped immeasurably. Irene Mills, his teacher who figured in his conversion and early Christian growth, has been a great source. The Navigators' President, Lorne Sanny, Vice-President, James Downing, and other staff who worked beside Dawson for many years gave valuable information and insights.

Billy Graham called him "a man of great vision, courage, faith, and, above all, personal discipline . . . . How many lives he touched no one will ever know." A man with a touch of

genius and a reservoir of loving-kindness, immersed in the job
God gave him but always ready to clown and enjoy a practical
joke. Boasting shamelessly about his wife and children, yet
sparing no effort to help someone he scarcely knew. Claiming
whole continents for God in prayer, but insisting that he choose
the color of paint for his office shelves. You will find other
paradoxes in the life of this man sent from God to navigate
for fifty years on the planet Earth.

At an hour preset in heavenly councils, the work of Dawson
Trotman, pioneer and pathfinder, one who saw the world
through the individual, was finished. He lived every day to the
full, with his last moment typically devoted to saving the life
of another.

DAWS

I

The Making of a Man of God

1906-1933

(above) The Trotmans in San Diego—1914. Dawson (age 8) in foreground. Mildred was 11 and Rowland was 3.

(left) Dawson's teachers-counselors: Laura Thomas (left) and Irene Mills with a day's catch of fish.

Charles Hare Trotman was a loyal subject to Her Majesty Queen Victoria. A Sandhurst-trained captain in the British Royal Army, he was posted to India where he served as magistrate for several hill stations of Madras. There he met and married Adelaide Rowland, an English governess, who bore him two children and hurried back to England for the arrival of her third, Charles Earle, because of a whimsical wish to have one child born in her native land.

Soon afterward Captain Trotman was caught in a monsoon while traveling over his judicial district and died of pneumonia. His widow decided to stay on and rear her children in the land of teakwood and elephants. But when Charles was six years old, she married a British surgeon who took her and the young step-family back to England.

The well-traveled Charles set out again at eighteen, visiting his cousin's farm in another part of England, where he came to love cattle and the country life. This soon fueled his desire to travel again — to emigrate to America to be a cowboy. His trip financed by an aunt, he sailed in the summer of 1892 on a ship with 800 Jews fleeing czarist Russia for freedom in the New World.

After chugging across the country behind a wood-burning locomotive, the young adventurer reached the frontier West, where he planned to live and work with some fellow Englishmen on their ranch homesteads. His intense interest in every new acquaintance and his boundless enthusiasm for new experiences led him from place to place and job to job — ranch hand, cowpoke, paint store clerk, mule driver, miner, cook. He changed jobs not from boredom but for the lure of new adventures, and sometimes with enough money accumulated he simply gave his whole time to enjoying himself at dances, beaches, and the like. When he was flush, he traveled by Pullman and ate in the diner; then upon discovering he was penniless he would make his next trip as a hobo.

Hired to cook Thanksgiving dinner in the home of a Utah mining official (after asserting that cooking was what he did best), Charles Trotman parlayed the contact into a job in the mine. Later, a glowing report of copper miners' wages as high as $3.50 a day in Arizona Territory sent him on a hitchhiking odyssey by freight train through California and on to copper-mining Bisbee in Tombstone Canyon. As he rattled along the frontier rails sharing a boxcar with a load of warm, smelly sheep, the young immigrant might have seen the humor of his position in view of his distinguished heritage — a family tree heavily populated with Anglican clergymen, landowners, and barristers. The Trotmans had been English landed gentry, their coat of arms going back several centuries. The family had been established before the Conquest of 1066. If Charles thought of it at all, it was doubtless with the detachment of one totally savoring the here and now *joie de vivre* that the Great West offered hardy souls at the close of the nineteenth century.

He knew at once that Bisbee was where he would settle, find a wife, and establish a family. He began to attend dances and picnics, hoping to meet the girl he would marry. Instead, he met her in the waiting room of a doctor's office where he had come for treatment of an injured hand. He decided on the spot that she was the one.

Mildred Keller had heavy auburn hair, deep-set eyes, and an air of integrity and good breeding. As a child she had fallen from a horse, and for the rest of her life experienced excruciating headaches and nervous tension which left their mark of suffering in her eyes. Mildred's father, a ship captain, had quit the sea to bring his family to Arizona by wagon train. Soon afterward, however, he divorced his wife and returned to New England. Mrs. Keller had worked as a seamstress to support her growing tomboy daughter and now kept a rooming house. The lovestruck Charles Trotman promptly rented the only two rooms vacant at Mrs. Keller's to keep away any competition for Mildred's favor. In September 1902 they were married.

Dawson Earle Trotman, their second child and first son, was born March 25, 1906 in the home behind the general store from which Charles and a partner provided Bisbee with groceries, pack saddles, ladies wear, dynamite, and whiskey. Trotman named his son for Berkeley Dawson, an English immigrant friend. A premature baby weighing only two and one-half pounds, Dawson also had a heart defect which, although incorrectly diagnosed for most of his life, would vitally affect his career.

His first days were a struggle for existence. "We thought we'd never raise him," his father recalled. "He was such a delicate little fellow." He did not walk until he was two or three years old. His conscientious mother so sheltered him that a doctor once advised her to "Let him get down and play in the dirt. Let him get dirty."

When the general store burned, Charles Trotman opened a lunch counter business which flourished, then left it to run a restaurant which did not. So the restless optimist moved his wife, daughter Mildred, the frail seven-year-old Dawson, and a third child, Rowland, to a new promised land, San Diego, where he took a job driving a produce truck. Mrs. Trotman supplemented their income by one dollar a day earned at a five-and-ten store in order to provide music lessons for the children. Ten-year-old Mildred took piano lessons and was charged with the task of teaching her brother. Dawson timed his arrival home so as to be busy with his chores and piano practice at the precise moment his mother returned from work. The children, both quick-tempered, fought while she was away, often firing objects across the room at each other.

Mrs. Trotman's self-sacrifice for her children could not be faulted. Unfortunately, what they remembered most was her telling them about it repeatedly, emphasizing their lack of appreciation. For her part, the more she talked the more her headache tension built and the more often she lost her temper with the children, miserably condemning herself for it. Her husband, after three years' hard work in San Diego, returned to the Bisbee copper mines. His increased earnings there, combined with an unexpected inheritance, enabled him to buy land on the main avenue of Lomita, a small town near Los Angeles, where he had a fine three-bedroom bungalow built for his family.

*   *   *   *

"D'ya ever get in any fights at the shipyard, dad?" Eagerness shone in the face of twelve-year-old Dawson. He and his brother Rowland had felt so proud when their dad had been in a fistfight in the Bisbee copper mines. The drama of the incident still appealed to both father and sons, though a hostile or pugilistic strain was alien to their natures. When he had moved his family into the new bungalow in Lomita, Trotman easily found a job as riveter in a shipyard where they were building ships for the Allies toward the end of World War I. Lomita, one of the towns which dotted the harbor area of southern Los Angeles County, lay less than ten miles from the Pacific. Nestled in a valley of bean and melon fields, the community embraced some 3500 souls, many transplanted from the Midwest.

The family in the house on eucalyptus tree-lined Narbonne Avenue was not typical. The wiry English father who enjoyed people and new situations went from the shipyard to the foundry, then to sea as cook on a tanker, and back to land to read meters and repair pipelines for the local water company. The conservative New England mother, frugal, generous, and humorless, tended and fed her family well and would have died for any one of them, lecturing them all the while. The talented teen-age daughter, strong-willed, honest, and exacting, with her father's outgoing disposition, supervised her brothers' lives — an activity only Rowland appreciated. The enterprising Dawson, extrovert like his father, perfectionist like his mother, often stopped his bike on the streets to entertain young children with rhymes, limericks, and stories while he delivered daily copies of the *Los Angeles Express*. And the happy-tempered Rowland, age seven, felt secure in the extra mothering he received from his older sister. Dawson and his sister often clashed, but were fiercely loyal to each other.

When he was unable to dodge his mother's frequent calls to do some household chores, Dawson obeyed, muttering just out of earshot, "Nag, nag, nag. Work, work, work." His mother awed and impressed him, but he did not feel close to her. He was fascinated by his flamboyant father and rose at five every morning just to be with him at breakfast before he left for work. This habit of early rising gave Dawson incentive to use the time for his studies, once the ambition to excel in school overtook him.

The off-beat family circle was undoubtedly considered the norm by those within it. The Lord Himself must have been amused, however, at the rare combination of personalities and backgrounds He had brought together to produce a son who would fill a unique role in His kingdom. The disparate traits of the parents probably influenced and molded Dawson's life more than he realized, and God had added to the equation the quirky heart valve that pumped extra blood to his brain, giving energy and ideas faster than he could use them.

The sight of Charles Trotman making his rounds by motorcycle, his pet goat Nancy Hanks perched on a platform on the handlebars munching a lollipop, delighted the children of Lomita and embarrassed Mrs. Trotman. Her disapproval of his antics only egged him on and made her nervous condition worse. The two seldom went out together socially. He liked to go dancing, and she did not. He would not accompany her to church. Despite her conventional turn of mind, Mildred Trotman leaned toward Pentecostalism and became an adherent of the colorful evangelist Aimee Semple McPherson, founder of the new Foursquare Tabernacle in Los Angeles. Charles Trotman had been properly christened in the Church of England, but the influence of his atheist friend Berkeley Dawson had pushed God out of his life, and Mrs. McPherson did not help matters for him. His lack of domestic peace eventually polarized around religion and gave him a rationale for the divorce which came later. "Aimee Semple McPherson came between us," he said matter-of-factly, adding with unconscious irony, "she was too flamboyant."

Dawson was popular in school, his winning smile well known around town. He had his mother's inquiring mind, and though he possibly read more than average, people were his main source of learning. He was aggressive and people-oriented, known for his extraordinary kindness to younger children. His friends remarked his keen interest in them and their doings, one saying

that he concentrated so intently and asked so many questions
"you almost wished you had not brought the conversation up.
He would get all the details and facts and he would ask you
why. . . . He was always good for fun, too. You could depend
on him for something different going on."

This insatiable appetite to learn made school enjoyable. Irene
Mills, Dawson's general science teacher in ninth grade, found
he directed every class session by his leading questions. He
seemed to dominate any group with a naive charisma that won
over teachers and classmates, catching them up in the mood
he generated. He earned A's in his subjects, an achievement in
which substance was possibly aided by style.

Dawson joined the Boy Scouts, and at age fourteen joined
Lomita Presbyterian Church, where Miss Mills was his teacher
in Sunday school. He became a leader in Christian Endeavor,
which was the main social life of the small town. He and other
high schoolers in the church also met on week nights at the
home of Miss Mills and schoolteacher Laura Thomas for Fun
and Study Club. Bible study was sandwiched in with good fun
and keen competition at table games. Dawson's mother had
sensed that he did not favor the kind of church she attended
and generously asked the two teachers to influence and train
him in theirs, lest he be lost to the Christian faith altogether.

By his senior year in high school, life for Dawson had gathered momentum. Nicknamed Porky because his reddish-brown
hair resembled a hog bristle brush, he seemed to be everywhere
at once. He especially liked to drive his Model-T jalopy through
the streets, steering with his feet from the back seat to give
the appearance that no one was behind the wheel. He was
president of Christian Endeavor and took carloads of young
people to Los Angeles County C.E. conventions, driving properly and sanely on such occasions. Late in his senior year he
began escorting Louise to various events. She was a lovely
Christian girl with wavy blond hair.

Dawson's grade average remained high, making him valedic-
torian. He was student body president, chairman of student
council, and at ninety-seven pounds captained a basketball
team. He was editor of the school annual *El Eco*, in which
sprightly verse and cogent quips appeared under his byline, as
well as a serious article on how student government works.

Once while he was student body president his gift for leadership and inspiring others was put to a test when he was invited to a rival high school to demonstrate his success in conducting student body meetings. Tension between the two schools was traditional; every football game was a highly volatile affair, with police on hand to quiet any clashes among the ethnic factions. So when Dawson, half-pint representative from the enemy school, stood before the San Pedro student body, the air was charged with hostility. He looked out over the assembly and suddenly began to laugh, first in waves of chuckles and then convulsively. Caught off guard, the entire audience was soon laughing with him, and their antagonism vanished. His act had worked.

He was riding high, enjoying the pace, the popularity and success in school, and being leader of everything he was associated with — but a flaw in his character bothered him. His propensity for lying had continued since childhood. His sister, who was painfully honest, observed that he fabricated an elaborate lie when the truth would have been much easier and simpler. His mother warned him, "A liar is a coward." She told a friend, "I can't believe a word he says," yet his convincing manner disarmed her and she believed him against her better judgment. He suffered pangs of remorse over it, sometimes even scraping his knuckles against a masonry wall to skin them so that whenever he bent his fingers he would be reminded not to lie. Still he did it. He also stole things, a practice concealed ever since he had taken a dime from his mother's bank when he was ten. The fact that people liked him and trusted him made his duplicity easy to cover.

Dawson had made an apparent decision for Christ in C.E. when a guest speaker illustrated God's gift of salvation by offering his gold watch to anyone who would accept it. Dawson jumped up and went after the watch, and the speaker led him to commitment to the Lord. This commitment was a second one; he had earlier made a profession of faith with Misses Mills and Thomas at the time he joined the church. His reputation as a Christian was flawless. When he gave his valedictory speech titled "Morality Versus Legality," no one knew he had been stealing regularly from the school's locker fund.

He hated himself for the stealing and lying which he seemed powerless to overcome, and the hypocrisy ate like acid through his conscience.

Charles Trotman, still a favorite of the town children, often gave them rides to and from school in his water company vehicle. One of his special friends was third-grader Lila Clayton, child of a Tennessee family who had recently moved to Lomita. He entertained Lila and her girl friend with songs and told her in proud-father fashion about his son Dawson, the high school senior. And he carefully made a point of telling his son of the girlish charms and virtues of the nine-year-old Lila.

On graduation night Dawson dropped Louise, went out with the boys, and got thoroughly drunk. When he woke it was afternoon, his suit was ruined, his mind blank. Along with the defeat in his first encounter with liquor came the end of the hypocrisy he had been living. *It's just not in me to do right,* he concluded. *I'm a loser.* All the skinned knuckles in the world couldn't keep him from lying or stealing. And all his churchgoing had not kept him from getting disgracefully drunk. All right, he'd go that way and quit trying to live a double life.

In the mid-twenties, the red Buick touring car with its tan top and big headlights was a familiar sight, roaring through Lomita and neighboring towns. Dawson liked to stunt drive it as he had done his jalopy, steering with his feet as he ducked his body out of sight, so that the car looked driverless. Or he and a buddy would change places at the wheel while barreling down the street.

Dawson's attendance and leadership in C.E. and Fun and Study Club had dropped off soon after graduation. A jaunty pipe completed his man-of-the-world image, and his little black book began to fill with names of girls he had dated. A meticulous diarist, he nearly always recorded which girl he took out and where they went. He was a regular at the little dance halls that had sprung up during those prohibition days and usually spent Sundays at the beach.

His need to excel seemed to be fulfilled for the moment by no greater achievement than piloting his Buick with precision skill and driving his Ross Luther lumber carrier like a race car at the lumberyard where he worked. This dexterity carried over to other things, too. When he and a friend took a pair of walking canes onto a golf course one morning to look for lost balls and drive a few, he made his first hole in one — using a cane!

He also became a pool shark. "I had to get him away from the pool hall," Charles Trotman recalled. "He was a good player and won some prizes. He won a five-dollar gold piece and a gun and came home and showed them to us. His mother didn't like it at all." Whether the "prizes" were payoffs on bets is not clear, but by this time Dawson was an obsessive gambler, willing to bet on anything and everything imaginable. His employer finally warned him he would be fired if he was seen again with dice on or near the job.

Though an honor student in high school, Dawson apparently had given no thought to further education. Or if he had, the idea was dropped along with his shattered moral facade after graduation night, when he gave up all pretense of being able to do right. A corresponding drop in self-esteem followed the realization that he could not gain mastery over lying and stealing. He would have no second-rate morality; it was all or nothing. His disillusionment with himself left a vacuum that he tried to fill with pleasure-seeking. Thus, the buoyant vitality pulsing through his slender body was wasted on things of no profit. An entry in his journal just before his nineteenth birthday betrays his restless lack of purpose:

> *Sherman and I went to Frisco. Two guys with a pull to look for us a job. Went show, smoke in it. Back O.K. Took cousin to skatin rink. My pal and I met two girls, mine the cutest. Take home, make date.*

Always on the move, never really happy. Dawson's old friends watched his sunny good humor fade and his famous smile go flat. His short temper on the job and his expertise in profanity were well known; it was evident that his bluff exterior masked an inner guilt. When Misses Mills and Thomas passed him on the street, his big black pipe in his mouth, he did not look up or acknowledge their greeting. In the tree-shaded home on Narbonne Avenue his mother prayed for him and worried about him. But he came in too late each night for her to see him and discover he had been drinking.

He had wasted three whole years since high school. Dawson, with his boundless energy, his ability to influence people, his facile gift for achievement and thirst for knowledge, had squandered those years in aimless carousing.

Whenever things began to catch up with him, often in the form of a policeman who found liquor in his car, Dawson quickly called on God for help. Then when danger passed, so did his prayer. At this point it would not have helped the miserable young man or kindled in him much pride of heritage to know that a number of his forebears had been vicars in the Church of England and that another ancestor was niece of the William Tyndale who was martyred for translating the Bible into English. And he would have scoffed at the notion that God planned to use him, Dawson Trotman, as a special instrument of change in the direction of Christianity in his century. The Hound of Heaven was pursuing him, but at a distance.

One escapade came near frightening him back to God. With a buddy and two girl friends, Dawson went to a mountain lake resort for the weekend. Soon after they arrived, while swimming across the lake, Dawson's girl was unable to reach shore; his attempt to rescue her was a struggle that left them both bobbing under once or twice. The other couple came along in a boat at that moment and fished them out. During the incident Dawson felt this was God trying to get his attention. Arrow-like, he shot a prayer heavenward. *God help me, and I'll do what You want.* Help came, but he forgot his promise.

A month later he had reason to recall it. Arrested near the Long Beach Pike amusement beach, too drunk to find his red Buick or remember where it was, Dawson sensed this was it. Again he sent an SOS. *O God, if You get me out of this, I'll do whatever You want.* His mother, still in frail health, had said, "Son, if I ever hear you are in jail, I'll die." Now her threatened heartbreak seemed imminent, and Dawson wept.

The big cop talked to him like a father. "Son, do you like this kind of life?" "Sir, I hate it," the young man answered, leaving unsaid the certainty that he was powerless to quit. The policeman left him on a bench in Virginia Park for three hours to sober up, then returned his car keys in exchange for his promise to do better.

Dawson didn't go to the Silver Spray dance hall that night, the first night in a long time he had turned in before 2:00 A.M. Nor did he go the next night to the pool hall or to Long Beach to have fun. He was shaken. However, it was beginning to wear off.

Whether the officer had notified Mrs. Trotman, or whether she discovered it another way, she knew. Sobbing, she telephoned her friend Cora Lewis, a Christian neighbor. "Pray for Dawson," she begged. "He's in terrible trouble. He's been picked up by the cops. Please pray the Lord will get hold of him."

Mrs. Lewis called her the next day. "We spent the night praying," she said. "And the Lord showed me a vision of Dawson holding a Bible, speaking to a large group of people. And the burden has lifted. Don't worry about Dawson any more."

Miss Mills and Miss Thomas had also prayed often for the young man who had been such an active Christian witness in high school years. They prayed that he would be convicted of sin and brought back to the Lord.

*   *   *   *

Sunday evening, two days after his encounter with the police, Dawson glanced quickly toward the pool hall, made sure no one was watching, then bounded toward the Presbyterian Church. Two of his old high school friends were team captains for an attendance contest in C.E., and both Johnny and Alice had tried to recruit him. Alice won. Whispers of "Look, there's Porky" probably buzzed through the group of astonished regulars.

One of six ways to gain points for the team was to memorize Scripture — five points each for ten verses. Dawson quickly accepted the list of ten verses on salvation and learned them by the following Sunday. And he found he was the only one who did learn them. That week there were ten more verses, this time on Christian growth, prayerfully selected by the group's sponsors, Misses Mills and Thomas. Dawson learned these too and his team won the contest.

Somewhat reassured now that he was an active churchgoer, he went back to his dance hall-pool hall routine feeling much less guilty. The promises he had made to God at the mountain lake and in Long Beach had not changed him — neither had attendance at C.E. He felt better; he felt respectable. But he knew he was the same sinner underneath.

However, during the third week the power that could change him did. The verses of Scripture he had diligently memorized, not for spiritual profit but for the sake of competition, took root. The prayers of a mother, a neighbor, and two concerned teachers could be answered now that the Holy Spirit had wherewith to work — the incorruptible seed.

Dawson was walking to work, lunch pail in hand, along the familiar path beside a slough when suddenly the words of one of the twenty verses he had memorized blazed in his consciousness. *Verily, verily, I say unto you, He that heareth my word, and believeth on him that sent me, hath everlasting life.*

Why, that's wonderful, he thought. *Hath everlasting life.* For the first time in years he prayed when he wasn't in trouble. "O God, whatever this means, I want to have it." As if in telegraphic answer, the verse John 1:12 flashed on his mental screen: *But as many as received him, to them gave he power to become the sons of God, even to them that believe on his name.* His response was immediate. "O God," he said simply, and meant it, "whatever it means to receive Jesus, I want to do it right now."

He walked on. Visibly, nothing had changed. Yet everything had changed. He would look back on it as his Damascus Road, his new birth, described in the verse following the one he had acted upon, John 1:13: "Which were born, not of blood, nor of the will of the flesh, nor of the will of man, but of God." If he recalled the decisions made in his teens, he probably discounted them as part of his pattern of self-deception during those years. If indeed one of those earlier occasions had been the time he passed from death to life, then this was the referee's whistle calling time on his living for self and turning him to follow Christ completely. One vital difference marked this decision: it sprang not from impulse, face-saving, or self-effort to do right, but from the living Word planted in his heart. Whether the earlier or later time was his real conversion, the prevenient grace of God had brought him to the point of commitment this June day in 1926 when he yielded his autonomy to the lordship of Jesus Christ. He would be God's son and servant from that day forward.

Mrs. Trotman telephoned her friend Mrs. Lewis. "Guess where Dawson is," she exclaimed. "He is up praying in the Palos Verdes hills! All by himself!"

After his meeting with God on the path by the slough that day, Dawson went on to work where the reality of his new birth was evident. He heard a man tell a dirty joke, and he did not enjoy it. He swore, out of habit, and was immediately ashamed. He learned the truth of another verse he had memorized, 1 John 1:9: "If we confess our sins, he is faithful and just to forgive us our sins, and to cleanse us from all unrighteousness." He made use of the promise now, and often.

Suddenly, at age twenty, Dawson's interest locked in on a new target. He was amazed at his changed outlook, unaware that this greening new life was the harvest for which his mother and others had long prayed.

None of his many friends in Lomita were left in doubt about Dawson's conversion. Mrs. W. G. Hammack, who was then a teen-ager, said, "The whole town knew it. He told everyone he saw. He would corner you anyplace and say, 'Have you heard what's happened to me?'"

At the lumberyard where word spread among the workmen that "Pork's got religion," it wasn't so easy. A first hurdle was mustering courage to bring out his New Testament and be seen reading it. The next was identifying himself with the man who came over from the mission each Thursday to preach the Gospel to the men who sat around eating their lunch. Dry but sincere, this man faithfully delivered his weekly talk while much of his audience moved out of earshot. Dawson listened eagerly, strangely warmed by the preaching of the Word, whereas before this he would not have stayed for a moment. *I'd better step out and shake hands with him*, he thought — *but imagine what the fellows will think. No, I have to do it.* He strode up to the man, shook his hand, and acknowledged that he, too, was a Christian. "Good," said the evangelist. "I'll expect to see you here every Thursday. Bring some of the boys."

The next test soon followed. "How about getting up here and giving your testimony next week?" the mission man asked one day. Ouch. This was even tougher than having to step forward and identify himself with the preacher. Yet he had promised the Lord he would do anything to please Him and had prayed that the men in the lumberyard would hear the Gospel. He dared not refuse.

"All right, I'll do it." The decision did not seem momentous, but he later looked back on it as an important step of obedience to God — a test he might have failed. A small step, but a step that God honored.

Dawson confided to one or two friends that he would be speaking the following Thursday, and the news crackled along the grapevine. Up on the company bulletin board went a sign: "Pork's Gonna Preach." On Thursday the entire work force of some 200 turned out. Dawson's initial fright soon passed, and flailing away on the sensational topic of hellfire and brimstone, he made up in forcefulness what he lacked in rhetoric and syntax. And the workers listened. In the weeks following, this paved the way for personal conversations with men he would not have dared to approach coming to ask him questions.

Those twenty verses of Scripture he had memorized fed and guided his new life from the first day, encouraging, instructing, and correcting him. If twenty verses could be so vital, he reasoned, why not learn twenty more, or a hundred? He started at once to learn one new verse every day, usually choosing those which met his immediate need, answered a question, or built on a particular truth.

Some he witnessed to brought up questions he could not answer, and he went to his pastor for help. "Son, the Bible has an answer for every excuse a man can give for not coming to

Christ," the pastor told him. Dawson determined he would not be caught twice without the Bible answer to any question. At lunchtime he read books on doctrine; as he hitchhiked to work he memorized verses, then sped up a nearby hill to pray before the workday started. His resolve not to be caught a second time without the answer hardened into a related life principle: *Never make the same mistake twice.*

He learned much from the "personal work" demonstrations Misses Mills and Thomas conducted at C.E. This kind of step-by-step instruction in leading a person to Christ was rare at a time when evangelical churches were content to teach fundamentalist doctrine and let it go at that.

But Dawson's witness at the lumberyard was hindered by one thing — his quick temper, which flared all too often. This eventually cost him his job when a boss saw and heard him take out his anger on a machine on which he was working. Even though he soon found another job, he felt compelled to go back and make amends. It was different since his conversion. Sin still fought for the upper hand, but he now saw the Holy Spirit equipping him to fight back with new weapons from God's Word.

Gambling, too, was a persistent holdover from the old life. It was in his blood to wager; he found it impossible to pass a dice game without stopping to roll a few. He had often gone with a group of cronies on a fishing boat to Catalina where, once outside the three-mile limit, they could gamble to their hearts' content while bootleg liquor flowed freely. Only once after the day of his decision by the slough did he give in and go on the Catalina trip. He did not drink with the men this time, but he felt uneasy about gambling with a New Testament in his pocket and was sorry he went. When the trip home over the choppy waves made all hands seasick except "Pork," he took it as God's signal that all was forgiven.

Another longstanding problem plagued him, and he went to his schoolteacher friends for help. "Pray that I'll conquer this terrible habit of lying," he asked them with desperate frankness. "Y' know, the trouble with lying is that when you tell the story to a second person and then a third, you forget how you told it the first time. Then you hafta tell a big lie to get yourself out of all the others." The women added this item to their regular prayers for his spiritual growth.

His worst battle, however, was with smoking. He knew, without anyone mentioning it, that he must quit. But the struggle lasted for months, and he lost as many rounds as he won. Several times he threw his cigarettes away, and each time he could not hold out. In desperation he walked through the fields near his home, praying that God would wrench this habit from his life for good. The promise of 1 Corinthians 10:13, which he had claimed so often, flashed across his memory again: *There hath no temptation taken you but such as is common to man: but God is faithful, who will not suffer you to be tempted above that ye are able; but will with the temptation also make a way to escape. . . .* Here was his answer — the habit could be broken because God said it could be, and he would believe that Word. Now after the sixth try he quit, the desire left him, and he had won. Victory! He looked back on the experience as invaluable in helping him identify with and help others in similar kinds of bondage.

Less than a year after his conversion, Dawson and Graham Tinning, the pastor's son, organized an intercommunity Easter sunrise service, a first for the Harbor area. They advertised it widely, arranged for Boy Scouts to direct traffic, and made a large cross of flowers on the hillside. Early Easter morning they were amazed to see hundreds of people streaming in from the area. The sunrise service became an annual affair in which pastors and churches of the region cooperated.

Driving his carrier around the lumberyard, Dawson went over and over the verses whose references were neatly printed on cards in his pocket. Fellow worker Jim Cullen saw his lips moving and asked what he was doing.

"Reviewing Scripture."

"Well, it looks crazy," Jim said.

Days later Dawson asked him, "How'm I doin'?"

"Good."

"Here's one for you. Look it up."

The next day Dawson bought a New Testament and inscribed it "To my pal Jimmy." Jim was touched by the gift. After that, every day as he drove by on the carrier, Dawson tooted the whistle and reached down a stick with a verse card wedged in the end of it. One day he missed, and Jim asked, "Where's my verse?"

Some time later Jim had a verse to give Dawson. It was 2 Corinthians 5:8 — "We are confident, I say, and willing rather to be absent from the body and to be present with the Lord." Daws read it, swung quickly back around the corner of a lumber pile, and asked, "What do you mean? Have you found the Savior?"

"Yes," Jim replied. "After you took me to the Easter sunrise service I went home and that night my wife and children and I all accepted Christ." Dawson had won his first soul at the lumberyard. There were others, but he would always remember the joy of this first. Seven of the twelve bosses for whom he prayed also became Christians, though not all through his own witness.

Dawson found it as difficult to witness for Christ at the bungalow on Narbonne Avenue as at the lumberyard. His brother Rowland was indifferent. His sister Mildred, married and living in Whittier, haughtily declared that "my reasoning powers will not let me believe." Dawson was embarrassed that his mother, the only other Christian in the family, had so alienated his father he was unwilling to talk of spiritual things.

"Dad, I've accepted Christ as my Savior," Dawson ventured bravely one day, "and from what I observe of your life, you have not. I recommend that you do."

"Son, when I'm ready to talk about that I'll let you know," his father answered. Many years afterward he would ask, "Did I say that? I've been waiting for you to talk to me." All those wasted years, Dawson felt, because he had not learned as a young Christian to witness to his family by a changed life before speaking to them directly of their relationship to Christ.

Mrs. Trotman's zeal for her church's emphasis on the charismatic gifts led her to urge this teaching upon her son, supporting her case with Scripture which he looked up in the new Scofield Bible she had given him. His pastor at the Presbyterian church gave him other passages which counterbalanced hers, and Dawson sought the Lord for an answer. As he prayed, a breeze fanned the pages of his Bible and John 7:17 caught his eye: "If any man will *do* . . . he shall know. . . ." Another puff turned the pages back to John 5:39, "Search the Scriptures. . . ."

Rising early as he had during school years, Dawson spent time each morning searching out every reference in Scripture to the Holy Spirit. Later he realized he had used one of the best methods of finding the truth concerning any doctrine, the one the Bereans used as they compared Scripture with Scripture to find the truth. He selected some sixty passages on the Spirit's work in relation to believers and memorized them. The result was a set of firm convictions on the doctrine of the Holy Spirit that he believed were in balance with the whole testimony of Scripture. In later years he recommended this same approach for getting a balanced grasp of a teaching and avoiding tangents.

Dawson had found Eber Hazelton, a Christian youth at the lumberyard with whom he could share the things of Christ. The two of them asked Miss Mills to teach them public speaking. The patient lady coached them as they stood at one end of her living room preaching and leading singing with purposeful vigor. The topic of Dawson's first sermon: "The Seven Churches of Revelation"!

Dawson's desire to witness for Christ and learn more of Him was fulfilled when he discovered the Fishermen Club. This group had begun in Los Angeles in the early 1920s with the aim of making practical the promise of Jesus, "Follow me, and I will make you fishers of men" (Matt. 4:19). On his first visit to the Long Beach club Dawson was thrilled to discover forty to fifty young men, teen-age and older, learning from Dr. Vernon Morgan to "fish for souls." Each week the young men gave testimonies of their witnessing experiences, then heard a Bible message and instruction in soulwinning from Mr. Morgan.

Fishermen Club immediately attracted Dawson by its emphasis on the Word and personal evangelism. Mr. Morgan's message this first night was on getting a burden for souls. Dawson was so moved by the challenge that he and his friend stopped on the way home, knelt under a tree, and prayed, "God *give us a burden for souls,* one that will last until we die!"

God did give Dawson a burden for souls, and he began look-ing for opportunities to witness. Traveling home from a club meeting he picked up a Mexican lad. On the way to the place where Juan said he lived, Dawson shared the Gospel with him and asked if he would accept Christ. He would and did, then said he wanted to go back to Wilmington. "Why?" Dawson asked. "I came to rob my brother tonight," Juan confessed. "He lives here. He's on vacation. But now I want to go back home." Dawson was glad for this evidence that his first con-vert was genuine.

A year after his conversion Dawson was a personal worker at an evangelistic campaign in Lomita. He found his high school buddy Walt Stanton in the audience and stepped down beside him to urge him to decide for Christ. "I wasn't ready," Stanton recalled, "but his real concern made him ready to be a fool for Christ's sake. Right there he bowed and prayed for my soul. It made a great impression on me. Later Miss Mills led me to the Lord."

Walt became an enthusiastic Fisherman Club member and joined Daws on "fishing" trips. He was somewhat dazzled by Dawson's high-powered presentation of the Gospel to hitch-hikers. "Within two minutes he would be witnessing, and everyone he picked up accepted Christ in the car," Walt said. Dawson's sincere interest and concentration on the person to whom he witnessed doubtless led to some decisions just as sincerely made but without the stamp of the Master Fisherman.

Christian Endeavor also claimed Dawson's interest. He was president of his society and early in 1928 became prayer meet-ing chairman for the Centinella Division. Finding in the C.E. manual that his duties included organizing gospel teams, he issued a call for volunteers from the division's thirteen societies to join him in a gospel team.

Six young fellows volunteered, and they began to take part in meetings in various places. Dawson noted that their testimonies were of the "Jesus saves, keeps, and satisfies" style, containing no Scripture — an omission he tried to correct by assigning them verses to memorize as he was doing. Each week he assigned new verses and heard the team members quote the ones they had learned. Soon they asked to continue on their own, choosing and learning new verses. But when the assignments stopped, the memory work stopped. Through this experiment Dawson observed an important principle that would influence all his future ministry: that human nature tends toward inertia in spiritual things and needs a prop, a stimulant — the stimulant of other persons to prod and encourage them to continue, and the convenience of methods which make it as easy as possible to follow through.

An associate from C.E. days, Cecil Jeffery, remembers Dawson's "terrific smile" and his unorthodox mode of dress. "I used to work him over about his clothes," he said. "The whipcord pants and loud shirts. But he was an up-and-going guy. He'd move, a bundle of energy. In a meeting he'd be in and out of the room a dozen times. He was always on the go."

Reading missionary biographies recommended by Mr. Morgan at Fishermen Club greatly influenced Dawson's thinking and spiritual development. David Brainerd kneeling in the snow to pray for the salvation of the Indians. Dawson knew no such hardship but felt he could at least spend time out in the Lomita hills praying for the lost. George Muller's thrilling experience of faith, seeing God provide in answer to prayer, was an example he determined to follow, along with that of Hudson Taylor, whose remarkable trust in God underwrote his venture of founding a pioneer mission in China. He also was challenged by reading about the famous prayer meetings of the Haystack Group in the early 1800s, with which Adoniram Judson and others launched the American student missionary movement.

"Dawson had all sorts of spots in the hills and parks where he would go and pray," Walt Stanton said, "early on Saturday or Sunday or other mornings. He was always trying to get other young fellows to pray with him. Most of them lasted a few days or weeks. Then they would get tired. He would come to my house and throw a rock in the window to wake me up so I would go pray with him. One morning I threw the rock back out and went back to sleep. This was the only time I saw him disgusted because he believed so definitely in Matthew 18:19, the power of two praying together."

The statement of D. L. Moody often quoted, that "God has yet to show what He can do through the life of a man who is wholly yielded to Him," drew from Dawson the inevitable response: *O God, let me be that man.* This was his heart's desire — until long afterward when the truth dawned upon him from Colossians 1:28 that God wants not one but many such men. In fact, He wants "every man" to be "that man."

The Fishermen Club, which had given Dawson his momentum to win souls, became the main vehicle for his early ministry. For more than three years he attended and taught Fishermen Clubs, always challenging young men to "get into the Word" and get out and fish for souls. Dr. Eugene Nida of the American Bible Society, then a Long Beach Fisherman, remembers "Dawson would bring fellows into that meeting that he picked up on the street. Sometimes they couldn't walk straight. His zeal meant a great deal to me."

A quartet called Fishermen Four included Dawson and Lewie Coates, who became his constant companion, disciple, and assistant. The Fishermen Four would roar off on motorcycles to sing and give testimonies at church meetings and youth groups. They often held "light tackle meetings" in churches, where they explained the work of Fishermen Club and sought to stir church people to witness for Christ.

Fisherman L. E. Knowles recalls Dawson as "forceful, a dynamic personality. In giving his personal testimony, I can never remember when he did not fix the attention of his hearers. He had that ability to move to action. He could make you feel uncomfortable if you were not proceeding along the lines he indicated — which is the height of dynamism." The forcefulness, the rugged motorcyclist clothes, and his rough-and-ready appearance may have been part of Dawson's attempt to squelch the impression of sissiness that some associated with evangelical witness. He also made an effort to lower the tone of his voice to project a more manly image.

Image-building was not his chief concern, however, as he continued to spend much time alone with God in the Word and in prayer. According to Cecil Jeffery, the outstanding thing was "the obvious first place Jesus Christ had in his life. You always thought of him as a Christ-one. Usually when you said good-bye after a visit there was a Scripture verse."

Jeffery was impressed by the intensely practical way God used Daws and the Word he had memorized. "In prayer times he'd say, 'Lord, we're just reporting for duty. We don't know who we'll meet today or what their need will be, but give us the right word for them.' Later in the day he'd listen sympathetically to a man telling of his burdens and troubles; then he'd say, 'Well, brother, you're a Christian. Let me give you 1 Peter 5:7: *Casting all your care upon him; for he careth for you.*' Afterward he'd say, 'Where'd I get that verse? I haven't read 1 Peter for a long time.' Then we'd remember we had prayed and asked the *Lord* for the verse. It was all so practical. To Daws every verse was an arrow pointed at somebody's heart."

While Dawson was soaking up Mr. Morgan's messages and reading Hudson Taylor, he was also developing his own theology of the Word of God. He was drawn less to objective analysis of its doctrine than to serious acceptance of its direct meaning to him as a personal message from God. With imprecise regard for context, he believed God was promising *him* or commanding *him* or speaking to *him* through a given text. Though the notes in his Scofield Bible defined the successive dispensations, Dawson felt free to take personally a promise or command intended for one of another era in God's timetable.

He was deeply impressed by Morgan's series on Genesis which stressed Abraham's claiming of God's promises. As he kept his prayer appointments in the hills, Dawson began to look for promises God would give to him. His faith in the Word was being strengthened, and there was growing reality in his relationship with the God who spoke and it was done, who commanded and it stood fast.

His literal approach to the Word placed upon Dawson the demand for literal obedience. This in turn meant personal discipline, which cost him considerable effort since he had no special share of this trait by nature.

"I thought he was one of the craziest guys I'd ever met," a friend said of him. "Who wants to go out on top of a small hill and pray at five or six in the morning?" Dawson's naturally buoyant spirit and the extra mental energy produced by his circulatory system could not account for it. His chief motivation seemed to be simply a loving desire to please God by obeying His Word.

"His discipline was basic to everything," says Dick Hightower, who met him a few years later. "First just disciplining himself to get up. To get the Word into his heart, to take the time to do it. Discipline to meet the Lord in prayer — and it takes real discipline to get up at four or five in the morning and get out in the cold hills to pray."

*   *   *   *

As junior department superintendent of the Presbyterian Sunday school, Miss Mills asked Dawson early in 1928 to take a class of boys. The first Sunday he taught, the boys did not listen, as they had not listened to their previous teachers. Dawson prayed about the problem. *Lord, You made little boys. Give me an idea that will help me hold their attention.* If God wanted it done, there must be a way to do it. The requested idea came: talk to each boy individually. "Jack," he explained to the chief offender, showing him from Mark 4 how the devil snatched away the good seed before it could grow, "the devil did not need to be in class last Sunday. You helped him. You took the other boys' attention away from the Word of God so they didn't hear what God had to say to them." Jack was properly impressed; so was the second boy to whom Dawson talked. The following Sunday the boys were angelic. Dawson learned from those interviews how much more could be accomplished in one-to-one conference — a discovery which may have helped to shape his future conviction on the value of man-to-man ministry.

Dawson and the boys soon found the class period too short. "We couldn't finish the lesson so I had them over to my home on a week night to teach them." He also learned of the plan for Junior Fishermen Clubs for junior high school boys and soon had his Sunday schoolers rounding up other boys to become Junior Fishermen. Then Prospectors Clubs, so named to indicate digging for nuggets from God's Word, started for grammar school boys.

He visited Don Milligan's junior high clubs in nearby Placentia and attended Milligan's training classes for boys club leaders. He was fascinated with the array of membership cards, ranks, and systems of graded Bible lessons and memory materials Milligan used. Starting with these ideas, he added, adapted, and expanded in great detail and soon had clubs going in Lomita. Club songs, salutes, pins, and rewards were all part of his program.

Lomita businessman Norge Cook recalls that "joining Prospectors Club was like joining the Boy Scouts. We got prizes for memorizing Scripture. Got New Testaments and diamond-shaped blue-and-white felt badges to sew on our sleeve. At our first meeting in the old building behind the Presbyterian church, he gave an invitation to anyone who wanted the Lord as Savior, and half a dozen boys stood up.

"He had two rubber stamps. One was an arrow he used to stamp the verse to memorize. If you memorized it the next week, he would stamp a star on the verse. He was very intent on our memorizing. Once when I was sick I heard a knock on the door and quickly started a mental review of my verses. I knew he would be asking me to say them.

"He would take us home and would have some good thing to say about every boy he dropped off. I thought, 'I hope he says something nice about me when I get off.'

"At our meetings the way we took the offering was to throw it at a little washtub in the middle of our circle. That was a lot of fun. He called it 'hitting the bucket.' We had a lot of activities too, like going up in the hills to play Capture the Flag. Our Lomita club grew from fifteen to fifty at least."

Four Japanese-American boys came to the club. A little grandmother stopped the Model-T bus one day to bow and, pointing to her grandson, say to Dawson in her limited English, "T'ank you . . . George . . . t'ank you . . . George . . . t'ank you."

In summer Dawson had opportunity to help Misses Mills and Thomas with daily vacation Bible school, umpiring the baseball games, teaching the children choruses and keeping things moving. The boys club ranks swelled as those who attended Sunday school and C.E. also joined the clubs.

In teaching his Junior Fishermen the verses which explained the plan of salvation, equipping them to "fish for souls," Dawson applied his belief that "there's a way to do it — find it." He found it, as he had in his first Sunday school class and would thereafter, by praying for an idea. To help the boys turn to verses in the right order, at the top of the margin of their New Testaments he stamped a red arrow pointing to the first verse, and just below it an arrow aimed at the second verse, and so on through the sequence of Gospel verses. When witnessing to someone, the boys could easily find the verses by following the arrows down the margin.

But he needed another idea. Although the boys had learned the books of the Bible, they were slow in finding verses he referred to as he taught the lesson. One day he noticed that the edge of his own Bible was smudged where the book opened to the Psalms because he turned there most often. Why not mark the edge of the pages to show where the Gospel of John was? By drawing a series of fine lines across the page edges at regular intervals and initialing them to indicate book names, he had the answer to quick location of verses which added efficiency — and a dash of glamour — to club Bible studies.

The ingenious margin index designed for the boys clubs and widely used today has not been improved upon as a means of opening a Bible quickly to within one or two pages of a given reference. Referring to the idea once in a message challenging his hearers to think, Dawson asked, "Isn't that marvelous? No, it's just a few little lines. Any person could have thought of that. Don't always be waiting for someone to set the pace for you. See the need and do something." Do something, that is, after praying, "Lord, give me an idea."

The boys' New Testaments were getting dog-eared from being carried to school in hip pockets and from sliding into third base on the ball field. Discovering that a Testament would fit neatly into a Prince Albert tobacco can, Dawson had the boys collect cans around town, which when boiled in lye solution came out clean and shiny. Soon boys by the hundreds were carrying their New Testaments to school in "converted tobacco cans." Evidence that the Word was also in their hearts and daily lives prompted the Roman Catholic principal of Narbonne High School to speak to Dawson. "Whatever you are doing with these boys, keep it up. I have never had so few discipline problems. And their grades are better too." At one point the entire football team had come to Christ. They prayed for their games and for the salvation of family and friends. The local movie theater lost business as so many of its young patrons were busy with club activities.

Two years after his conversion Dawson felt he needed Bible training to equip him for whatever service God had for him. He quit his job at the lumberyard and in the fall of 1928 enrolled in the new Los Angeles Baptist Theological Seminary, where a high point was Charles E. Fuller's class on Romans and Ephesians. "It seemed to come at a time when he wanted some method of digging into the Word," Fuller recalled. "He was a great personal worker. He often referred to the first chapter of John and how the disciples found their brothers. And he urged people to memorize Scripture and hide the Word in the heart."

To an unusual degree Dawson did recognize the memorized Word as a Christian's vital source of power. His conviction was strengthened by the example of lay minister Tom Olson, who often spoke at Fishermen Club meetings. Olson's mastery of the Word had come largely through memorizing it. Dawson's own store of the Word hidden in his heart had greatly enriched his life, and he noticed how often a verse of Scripture came seemingly out of nowhere to answer a problem of the moment or a question raised in witnessing. Memorized Scripture had brought him to Christ, and he was convinced it was a must for the would-be soulwinner.

Being a compulsive sharer, he decided to publish a course that he could use to help others get started hiding God's Word in their hearts. He had found with the C.E. gospel team that a person is not likely to memorize on his own initiative. A personal challenge and example would help, but a convenient system for doing it might make the difference. So he designed an attractive four-by-three-inch booklet with Psalm 119:11 handlettered on its cover: "Thy word have I hid in mine heart, that I might not sin against Thee."

The booklet gave encouragement and directions for memorizing a verse a day, then a statement for the recipient to sign pledging his best efforts to hide the Word in his heart as directed. Sixty-two single or double references appeared on the following pages, with their texts on the back of each page: verses on the Gospel, the greatness of God, the Christian walk and warfare, assurances of answered prayer, comfort and help, and warnings against disobedience. On a back page potential distributors were asked to reclaim any books from users who were not making progress.

Investing a small fortune of sixty dollars in this first attempt to "sell" Scripture memorization added incentive for Dawson to see it succeed. The booklets were given away free, mainly to youth leaders in the thirteen C.E. societies of Centinella Division. When a later survey showed that only one of the first 100 to take the book was continuing to memorize, Dawson's disappointment was keen.

There's a way to do it — find it. He tried another method. To any who showed interest in memorizing, he gave a pack of blank cards in a holder with printed instructions for choosing and writing out verses on the cards. This brought a slightly higher rate of success.

New Testament Greek was a struggle. As Dawson put three hours a day into study for this class, he wished he had given more attention to basic English fundamentals in high school. However, the fundamental of spending much time in prayer stayed with him. Reading such assigned books as E. M. Bounds's *Power Through Prayer* fired him anew to seek God early and earnestly. He was distressed to find he had the school's prayer room virtually to himself in the early mornings, as most of the students appeared heavy-eyed at 6:15 just in time for calisthenics. Returning to Lomita on weekends, Dawson met his friends Walt Stanton, Jim Cullen, and others for prayer early Saturday and Sunday mornings.

During the school year Dawson continued Fishermen Club activities. He was delighted that his sister Mildred, whose decision for Christ he had witnessed a year or more after his own, accompanied the Fishermen Four quartet on the piano and sometimes sang duets with him at their meetings in churches. Mildred also prepared and served the dinner for their weekly meetings of twenty-five or more Fishermen.

Dawson still taught his Sunday school class and the boys clubs, using every resource at his disposal to establish them in the Christian life and get them memorizing and witnessing for Christ. At one time he was asking parents to check the boys' memory verses and sign a statement that they had quoted them correctly and were doing their best to live up to them. This also served to expose parents to the Word and to encourage boys to "live the life" at home.

Teaching his boys week by week, Dawson used the familiar illustration comparing the Christian life to a three-legged stool, the legs representing the Word, prayer, and witnessing. One missing leg would cause the stool to collapse. But the more he thought of it, the more he disliked it. The Christian life was too exciting and dynamic to live sitting down. *Lord, give me an idea.* The idea he was given was a wheel, denoting forward motion. The Word, prayer, and witness would be spokes of The Wheel, but he felt another element was necessary to the Christ-centered life. He had observed that it was possible for one to be nominally taking in the Word, praying, and witnessing and yet fail to exhibit Christ in daily life. So he called the fourth spoke "living the life," representing the Christian's total conduct toward God and man. Later the "living the life" spoke was renamed "obedience," having the same meaning.

Dawson believed that The Wheel, which in final form showed Christ as the hub with the four equal spokes connecting the Christian with his source of life and power, was a graphic model of the kind of disciples God wanted. If it was truly God-given, it would stand the test of time.

As the school year continued, Dawson took stock. Study was tedious, though he was conscientious and made high marks. Greek study took the best hours of his day, however, and it seemed his spiritual life was suffering. He decided to end his seminary career at the end of the year.

One area of Dawson's life had changed abruptly after his conversion — girls. His nightly appearance at the dance halls ceased, and the red Buick he had acquired with girls in mind was now dedicated to the Lord. He purposed to look up each one of the many girls he had dated and tell her about his new life in Christ. Somehow during all this time he had remained sexually pure. He now saw it as the grace of God to him and was profoundly thankful.

Once the decision was made to cut out girls completely, he was lonely. *Lord, can't I have one girl friend?* Scanning the old list in his little black book, he suddenly saw Louise's name. Louise, the Christian girl from high school days! Surely she was the one God had meant for him all the time. Tracing her whereabouts, Dawson found to his dismay that she was engaged to be married. He was stunned. Louise of the blond, wavy hair, the gentle disposition, the wholesome country-girl qualities and steady Christian walk *had* to be his girl. Again he prayed, "Lord, please break this up."

His next shock came when three weeks later Louise's fiance died. Dawson called to offer his condolences and soon was seeing her often. There was no doubt about it; he was in love. They were both twenty-one and she was the ideal girl. Why wait? So one evening he said, "Louise, I want to ask you something." "All right." Silence. He could not speak. Terrified, he suddenly realized he had not prayed about this. He sent up a silent SOS. *Lord, if this isn't Your will, please stop me.* Long moments passed. The words stuck in his throat.

Finally Louise asked what he wanted to say. "Oh nothing," he muttered. "We'd better go home." Answering Dawson's quick prayer, God kept him from contracting a marriage that would have limited the work he was destined to do for Christ in years ahead, for Louise did not have the physical stamina for the load Dawson's wife would be called upon to share.

Dawson, still puzzled by his quick change of heart, invited Louise to go with his family to Yosemite. While spending days together in the outdoor beauty, he tried to recapture his feeling for her. But love had vanished. He confessed to her that he had intended to propose marriage but could not after praying about it. Louise was hurt but responded graciously.

After this experience Dawson resolved to forego the idea of girls and marriage completely for the time and devote himself to serving God single if He required it. He adopted such an impersonal attitude toward girls that Misses Mills and Thomas felt free to give him the responsibility for transporting all the unescorted girls to and from C.E. The women were sorry the romance with Louise had died; she was the only girl on the horizon who had seemed worthy of Dawson.

Driving carloads of girls to and from C.E., Dawson saw to

it that no girl sat beside him twice consecutively. He took a different one home last each time in order to talk to her about her relationship to Christ. After one incident he learned to let the girl out of the car before such discussion. On this occasion the perfumed blonde girl beside him shattered his defenses, and under the spell of the moment he found himself kissing her. He was horrified. "Get out!" he reacted suddenly, "that's sin! Get out!" Not a little surprised, she got out. Dawson was sorry he had been cruel, but thankful for his narrow escape.

Late in 1927 one of the new girls in C.E., Lila Clayton, had won an award, and Dawson was asked to drive her up to Olive View Sanitarium to receive it. As they rode along under the sunny California sky, Lila was singing "O Little Town of Bethlehem." Dawson looked over at her and saw an angel. He was in love again. *This,* he told himself, *is it.* He had given this area of his life to the Lord, and now the Lord had honored his act of faith.

Overwhelmed, he asked suddenly, "Lila, will you be my sweetheart?"

"If it's all right with you, I'd be tickled to death." The pact was that simply made, and sweethearts they were for more than twenty-eight years.

Dawson did not remember that his father had told him about this young lady years before when the Claytons had just arrived from Tennessee. But she clearly remembered seeing Dawson roar around town with the big pipe in his mouth.

"What grade are you in?" Daws asked his new sweetheart. "Eighth," she replied smartly. Taken aback, he demanded, "How old are you?" "Thirteen." He was robbing the cradle! Oh well, she'd grow up, and he could wait. Lila would be worth waiting for.

A few weeks earlier, Dawson had given her a ride home from Sunday school. "Why don't you come to Christian Endeavor?" he had asked her. "I have no way." "I'll pick you up along with the rest," he promised. Taking her home last after C.E. meeting, he let her out of the car, then asked, "Are you a a Christian?"

"I've gone to church all my life," she answered without hesitation. "I didn't ask are you a churchian, but are you a Christian?" he replied. "Well, I was baptized," she said, a little less confident. Opening his New Testament, Dawson explained verses describing the salvation Christ offers without conditions to those who receive Him. "Don't go to sleep tonight until you have settled it," was his parting word.

Settle it she did. At 2:00 A.M. Lila Clayton knelt beside her bed and became a new creature in Christ. She was a quiet, sensitive girl with many warm friendships at school. She was active in athletics, average in studies, and a good sport. Her parents were loving but strict. Dad Clayton, in good Southern fashion, kept a tight rein on his three daughters and a slack one on his three sons.

The day of the Olive View trip, Dawson said, "Just take your turn with the others sitting in the front seat." Lila did not like the idea but was too dazzled to object. Soon, however, everyone knew the front seat was hers and that she would be escorted home last.

Buddie, as Dawson called her, became as much his disciple as his girl friend. She regarded him as her spiritual teacher, accepting with mixed awe, love, and loyalty the disciplines he prescribed. She remembers eagerly doing her daily reading in Proverbs and memorizing new verses and that "on almost every date we would get back to Isaiah." Riding in the car, Dawson liked to redeem the time by memorizing a Scripture passage while she checked it for him. Their once-a-week dates were trips with gospel teams to hold services in jails and rescue missions.

When Lila was fifteen and finishing ninth grade, they became engaged. Some weeks later Dawson wrote in his journal:

> *I thank my God for a sweet and humble girl like Buddie. She makes mistakes, but she's glad when counseled with. We are both determined by the grace of God to show ourselves "examples of the believer."*

About the time of their engagement Dawson wrote in Lila's high school annual, encouraging her devotion to Christ and sharing his dreams for their life work.

> *. . . Buddie, my hearts desire for yours and my life is that we might labor, pray, and live such lives as would result in winning the greatest number of*

*souls possible.... Shall we not accomplish the most
for or rather through Him as we labor among
young lives, boys and girls, young men and young
women, and shall not we, Buddie, as we are yet
young and flexible, yield our lives in loving obedience to the Lord Jesus Christ.*

At age twenty-three, the dominant theme of Dawson's life
was prayer. Prayer alone, with another, or with a group. Prayer
early and late. His journal for one week in 1929 reflects its
importance to him:

*Saturday, August 24 — We had a wonderful meet-
ing at San Pedro. 20 Navigators (boys) and Jr.
Fishermen, 5 Sr. Fishermen. Afterwards Ed, Bill,
Jim, Walter, and I had a prayer meeting lasting
until about 11 o'clock . . . Jim, Walt and I continued all night in prayer to God.*

*Sunday, August 25 — At 6 a.m. we were met by
five others and had a prayer meeting on the hill.
Preached . . . at Harbor City Methodist Church.
Evening, led young people's meeting at Wilmington
Methodist Church.*

*Wednesday, August 28 — Had a talk with Miss
Mills after prayer meeting....*

*Thursday, August 29 — .... Then a prayer meet-
ing on the hill — alone with God.*

*Friday, August 30 — I went to the old church
about 9 o'clock p.m. and prayed until I could stay
awake no longer and laid down on the floor and
slept until daybreak, at what time I again poured
out my heart before the Lord.*

The October 13 entry shows the pattern continuing:

*Eight of the small boys met with Jim, Walt, and I
at 6 a.m. on the hilltop for prayer. Wonderful faith
being shown by these lads.... Jim, Walt, and I*

*have been meeting at 4 a.m. Sunday for about two
months.*

On January 11, 1930 he refers to the different subjects for
prayer:

*I rejoiced in the Lord as it suddenly dawned on me
that I was privileged by having Miss Mills and
Miss Thomas to pray with concerning our church
and its condition. Walt and I could pray for the
Fishermen's Club. The younger fellows meet to
pray for the boys' work. Harold Chrisman and I
meet twice a week at 4:30 to pray for school.
In my private devotions I could pray for missionaries, friends, loved ones, power, understanding,
courage, etc. The lie the devil has been whispering
in my ear has been revealed, and I can rejoice in
the Lord that He has given me so many real prayer
companions and so much time to pray.*

Eighteen months later a recorded exception only emphasizes
his rule:

*Slept till 7 o'clock (shame). Because of this I must
begin the day with but a few minutes of prayer.
This is sin.*

On the previous day he had written:

*I find the hardest thing for me to do is to get to
prayer. God is able to make me a man of prayer
if it pleases Him.*

Dawson's compelling drive to spend time in prayer might
have appeared legalistic, but his journal from that period reveals
his motives: the joy he found in spending time with his Lord
("Rose early to meet with Him whom my soul loveth. He
thrills my heart."), and his deep conviction that God worked
only in response to prayer. He fervently wished to be a usable
instrument in "the Lord's work — that wonderful work of
winning souls." With this goal in mind, prayer was power, not
a ritual; he would discipline himself to pray, whether the in-
clination was there or not. And the Word of God was indispensable both in the making of a man of God and in any ministry done in His name.

Journal entries such as one for July 18, 1931 suggest that discipline did enter into keeping his trysts with God:

> *Spent 3 or 4 hours (with Henry and Walt in a quiet rendezvous in the hills) with God. God has never yet failed to bless such a season to the quickening of the inward man, and striking some needed blows to the carnal man.*

He also needed discipline in his relentless memorization of Scripture, though he so enjoyed it ("prayer and God's Word are my delight") that this kept him at it most of the time. For a while he was memorizing as many as two new verses a day and reviewing those previously learned. But no matter how willing the spirit, self-assignment still helped shore up the flesh. At the Bible Institute of Los Angeles, where he had enrolled in September following the year at seminary, he sometimes found on returning late at night that his day's memory work was not finished. So he would turn and walk in the opposite direction until he had learned his verse, then review it as he walked back to the school.

Discipline helped, too, in applying the Word to combat temptation. As he sped on his pre-dawn rounds delivering newspapers, one of his several part-time jobs while in school, Dawson passed by a certain provocative picture in a downtown office building each day. About the third day, he decided to be preoccupied with meditation on the Lord and His Word at that point in his route.

He was learning that discipline insured his obedience, serving as a bridge between knowing what he should do and doing it without fail. But persistence in any one activity did not come easily to him, for new interests constantly vied for his attention. He had plenty of enthusiasm and momentum, and his perfectionism made him insist, to himself and all others, that anything worth doing was worth doing well. But these qualities usually applied to the matter immediately at hand. So the ability to discipline himself to continue anything over a period of time could only be a work of God in his life, honoring his desire to do at any cost what God wanted him to do.

Appearing younger than his twenty-five years, his boyish exuberance leading others to go along with a continuous stream of new ideas, Dawson held to his consuming purpose to become a man of God, a man of prayer. He felt he did not qualify as a man of prayer in the mold of Brainerd and Hudson Taylor. Yet in looking back later, he had little doubt that his disciplined practice of prayer during the first five years of his Christian life laid the foundation for all his subsequent ministry.

The year at Biola upped the tempo of life for Dawson, adding classes and ministry assignments to his involvement with boys clubs, the Fishermen, C.E., and the Presbyterian church, where he was unofficial assistant pastor. His extensive prayer times now included early mornings at the school, where he again found the prayer room empty as he had at seminary. He eagerly soaked up the expository teaching of men of God on Biola's faculty and took reams of notes. These he later sifted through, carefully distilling their essence for his edification and use in the Great Business of Winning Souls.

Some classmates remember Dawson's indulgence with them in daring pranks. Grant Whipple, director of The Firs conference grounds in Washington, recalls how they would get a running start on the roof of the thirteen-story building, jump to the waist-high ledge rimming the roof, and from there to the roof of the Mayflower Hotel. Dawson liked to spring from a long jump to perch on these ledges; later he concluded the trick was too foolish and stopped it.

Others felt the pressure of his hard-sell persuasion to memorize Scripture. Dick Hillis, converted a few months after enrolling at Biola, was standing on the curb when Dawson roared up on his motorcycle reviewing his verses. "What verse are you workin' on today, pal?" he asked with a grin. Hillis obviously wasn't working on any verses. He decided not to be standing there on the curb again when Daws came by. Years later when Hillis was returning from missionary service in China, he still dreaded meeting Daws and being prodded about Scripture memory. Finally they met, and there was the same question.

"All right, Daws, I surrender," Dick said. They met at five the next morning. "For two or three wonderful years we met every week, and I am a better man for it," Hillis said.

Going out with a Biola student team to speak in churches, Dawson usually spoke on The Wheel, with a challenge to Christians to dig into the Word, memorize it, and apply it to life. He also led "shop teams" and "jail teams," preaching the Gospel to captive audiences. But his prime interest was still individuals. A fellow student said, "You had the feeling that *all* his spare time he was down on Skid Row working with bums. He was tremendously admired and loved in the student body, and was always one of the first to pop up with a testimony or to stop and talk to anyone."

When witnessing, Dawson seemed gifted in penetrating the defense of the most difficult person, and people responded to him who would not respond to the average witness. This led to opportunities to teach some of his classmates to "fish," a challenge he enjoyed as much as winning one to Christ himself. He had launched his buddy Lewie Coates on his first witness experience by putting a tract into his hand and shoving him smartly downhill toward an unsuspecting prospect as they walked through a park. Thus committed to battle, Coates made good. On occasion Dawson and Lewie boarded a trolley to distribute tracts, one of them speaking to the conductor about Christ while the other engaged the motorman.

Once a student body leader dropped into Dawson's room to ask for help in learning to win souls. The help he received was unexpected. "How's your prayer life?" Dawson asked abruptly. It was not good. "Get that straightened out and then we'll talk about winning souls," was the terse prescription. But the student took it and did learn how to win people to Christ — by praying first.

On a fishing trip with his friend Harold Chrisman, Dawson asked a young man in Pershing Square if he were a Christian. After the usual "I didn't ask if you were a churchian . . . ," Dawson asked if he was a sinner.

"Oh no," the lad answered.

"Harold, come quick," Dawson called. "I found one!" He continued, "The first one I have met in my whole life. Wallace here says he's not a sinner. Wallace, this man is president of his class at the Bible Institute. He is a sinner. He has lied and stolen."

The enlightened Wallace said, "Oh. Oh, I am a sinner." He listened while Dawson explained the Gospel and made his decision within the hour. Dawson marked three verses in a Gospel of John for Wallace to memorize, encouraged him to witness and to pray, and took him along to school to give his testimony at report hour next morning. Such an example was great encouragement to other students to venture out in personal witness.

His own tenacity in going after a decision shows in one account from his journal:

> *October 9 — I met a sailor and dealt with him for about half an hour. He failed to see why he should accept Christ when he had no inclination to, although he acknowledged that he was a sinner. Name, Beckrow.*
> *October 10 — 7:15 I again dealt with Beckrow. At 7:40 he said he had to leave in a hurry to make his ship. After breakfast I strolled through the park around the library and to my amazement I run on to Beckrow. He had lied — imagine his feelings. We read Isaiah 53 — John 1 — Prov. 27:1 — Prov. 29:1 — Luke 12:19, 20 — I Tim. 6:6, 7. After another half hour I left, and although he made no confession of Christ, he knew plainly the way of salvation, of his being a sinner under condemnation, and certainly from his actions he was under deep convictions. My God is indeed able to finish the work and save his soul — John 6:44, Phil. 1:6.*
> *October 14 — What do you know, I met the sailor boy of Wed. night and after much persuasion managed to get him to come to Fisherman Club, where a definite appeal to the lost was given. He rejected the offer of God.*

Impressed by the example of a man who prayed that he might lead one person to Christ each month, then one each week, and finally one a day, Dawson tried it. *Lord, let me win one soul for You each month.* Then one soul a week. God answered. Then a week passed, and a second, without fruit. During the third week he came down from his rooftop prayer room to find waiting for him an offer of a part-time job managing The Green Frog, a miniature golf course. This answered his prayer, for in order to bring in business he would invite a group of high schoolers in for a free game as starters. Afterward he presented the Gospel to them and easily got enough decisions to catch up on his quota.

But though decisions increased, something did not seem right. Dawson withdrew his request for one soul a week until God should lead him to ask again. God never did. The Green Frog experience was the dawn of change in Dawson's thinking, a realization that decision is not the goal but only the beginning, that an unsatisfied barrenness still haunted one who brought new souls to birth and left them there.

Dawson was president of the Student Missionary Union that year, investing much prayer in choosing speakers, planning programs, and building attendance to the 100 mark. He had volunteered for India shortly after his conversion when he heard a missionary present the need of that land. Now as he heard other missionaries speak and as he read Hudson Taylor and missionary biographies, he was moved by the need of each field. He continued to pray that God would focus his vision on a particular one. Yet every field seemed important, and were not the lost in Los Angeles as needy as those of a faraway land? Better than a missionary vision for one needy field would be a burden and vision for the whole needy world. He would volunteer for the field which seemed the most daring or difficult, but thus far he felt "called" to no one area.

As he waited on God, however, a doctor's exam ruled out foreign missionary service for him. He was disappointed, but was able to submit to God's control over the matter. *Lord, if I can't go to India, let me send men*, he prayed.

Dawson limited his time with Lila, now a high school sophomore, to one evening a week. He wrote in his journal on November 16:

> *I must not forget to say I see my 'Buddie' nearly every Friday night. A delight indeed. She is growing in grace. I have been trying to help her memorize God's Word more.*

And this thought immediately follows:

> *Definite memory of Scripture — definite continual reading of Scripture — builds the prayer life, which growing makes the working, vital Christian, indeed fruitful. Think!!*

Saturday mornings Dawson spent gardening and doing odd jobs for Misses Mills and Thomas at their home in Lomita. Then over lunch he asked their counsel on his work with the boys or whatever was on their hearts to share with him. Seeking personal counsel from older Christians may have set the pattern for his lifetime emphasis on counsel as an important element in building disciples.

A monthly subsidy from Miss Mills helped finance Dawson's schooling and gave him extra time for ministry. For his occasional need when funds ran short, he determined to follow the example of George Muller and Hudson Taylor, trusting God to supply through prayer.

Two days later the decision was tested. Due to lead a boys club in Torrance, he needed carfare — forty cents for the train and ten cents for the connecting bus. He prayed, sticking to his resolve rather than asking one of his schoolmates for a quick loan. Eleven minutes before train departure time he started walking to the station. Dashing around the corner of the building, he met Mr. Hale, the superintendent of men, who tossed something into his coat pocket. Dawson dared not look until he was a block away. Then he reached into his pocket and there it was — a half-dollar engraved with the words "In God We Trust"!

He was overjoyed with the precision and timing of such answers, for they proved that the communication lines to an omnipotent God were open both ways. At Biola and the adjoining Church of the Open Door, offerings were taken regularly for visiting missionary speakers. With just six dollars in his pocket and five dollars rent due at Biola next morning, Dawson reached into his pocket for the one-dollar bill. Or should he give the five and trust the Lord to replace it by morning? Perhaps the Lord would provide for the missionary and Dawson should keep his five. After a brief struggle he gave it. Next morning before daylight he was up on the roof where he usually went to spend time with the Lord, and there lay a five-dollar bill He had caused someone to drop in Dawson's path. His pre-Christian gambling held no thrill to match this.

Opportunities for ministry multiplied, some of which Dawson found next to impossible to refuse. He had added the pastoring of a small church in Manhattan Beach to his responsibilities and tried to figure a way to make up a half-hour each day to provide the three hours a week needed to take on another club of "sixteen fine boys" at Pico. He always seemed pressed for time to do all he wanted to do, and now again he must reevaluate.

Some faulted him for abandoning established interests for new ones; he had dropped Fun and Study Club and left seminary after a year. Now he was deciding to leave Biola, though this would require courage in view of opinion which would be against it. He was getting good grades and was blessed by what he had learned, but faced the fact that for him full-time schooling would no longer be warranted. So he finished the school year and left Biola, planning to give himself more fully to work with boys. He commuted to Los Angeles to audit certain classes at Biola during the following year, but his attention was now on boys clubs in Lomita and neighboring towns.

Each club had its own lore, insignia, salute, and its Bible study plan and projects. Dawson's shrill, piercing whistle was a well-known rallying signal. The boys also enjoyed his stunt songleading when he pulled them to their feet like puppets on imaginary strings, using hand signals to seat or draw them up instantly or in slow motion. He often took the club boys and the Sunday school junior department on Saturday outings, for ball games and wiener roasts.

Main emphases in all the clubs were Scripture memory and witnessing. Dawson's new ideas for getting the boys to do their assignments were sometimes superimposed on previous ideas. But no intricacy of method could dampen the boys' sense of the importance of club nor blunt the feeling of transgression when, as one of them might confess, there was a lapse in living the Christian life such as attending a movie.

Dawson started a card record of each boy's progress, noting one week in early 1931 that 141 boys attended clubs, adding laconically, "Reason: the Word." His belief in the power of God's Word to change their lives was absolute.

During this period Dawson learned much by trial and error that further shaped the principles he applied in later ministry. One such lesson was learned through the regrettable error of a church split in which he and his boys were involved. There had been an undercurrent simmering in the church as factions built along modernist-fundamentalist lines. Some twenty years earlier a series of booklets called The Fundamentals had been published to combat the erosion of faith caused by biblical higher criticism — faith in the inspiration and authority of Scripture, the virgin birth of Christ, His atonement and resurrection, the necessity of new birth, and Christ's imminent return. Churches and individuals holding these doctrines began to be tagged "fundamentalist." "Modernist" labeled the then sophisticated notion that modern science destroys the credibility of biblical miracles, the virgin birth, the infallibility of Scripture, and the Second Coming.

This ferment had been in the Lomita church since Dawson's high school days, when Misses Mills and Thomas were relieved of their leadership of the young people because of their fundamentalist doctrine. They returned to the church during Mr. Tinning's pastorate, but after he had gone, the liberal element again reacted, especially to the obvious success of Dawson's evangelical ministry among boys and in the community as a whole. His persistent emphasis on the Word and the power of Scripture memory also produced a backlash from some who may have been convicted of their negligence in this area.

The condition Daws saw as worldliness in the church — probably a combination of its disregard for the Word and the fact that its officers had not quit smoking — led him to announce that he planned to leave the church, taking his four boys clubs elsewhere. He wrote: "I state my purpose and reason in church — Bombshell!" That week the session asked Misses Mills and Thomas to leave. Dawson wrote, "Group of those dissatisfied with worldly condition of church meet and plan new work." A few days later, "C.E. is being drawn into Modernism. God must it seems provide something to take its place."

The little band of dissenters pooled their faith and launched the new church on a rainy April Sunday in 1931 in a rented hall on Redondo Boulevard. Dawson noted that 126 turned out for Sunday school. "A most glorious atmosphere pervaded the room as well as our hearts. The Holy Spirit was there." Morning and evening services, an afternoon prayer meeting, and evening youth meeting were well attended. Dawson found ways to help the church get going, submitting a visitation plan, painting a sign on the roof, mimeographing invitations, mobilizing his club boys to canvass some 350 homes inviting kids to daily vacation Bible school and inviting their parents to church. The clubs met week nights in homes, and many of the boys, especially the older ones, followed Dawson to the new church. In August the clubs joined in an effort called Booster Band to promote a three-week evangelistic campaign in South Lomita Church. Dawson promised the Boosters they would have a group picture taken when attendance reached 300. In the second week of meetings they reached 299 and got the picture.

Directing an evangelistic campaign was another first for Dawson. He began by inviting a pastor friend, Irwin Moon, to preach the first two weeks. Moon had never given an evangelistic series, but brought along some of his congregation who rented a house in Lomita and made an event of it.

Fishermen Club's Mr. Morgan was evangelist for the third week and was called as regular pastor of the church. The campaign was judged a success, decisions for Christ resulted, and the church flourished. But in later years Daws looked back at the breakaway church as a mistake. It never became the lighthouse for truth it was meant to be. And though most of the older boys moved to the new church, many others quit church altogether and dropped out of club as well. Parents forbid their boys to return to club, calling Dawson a church-splitter.

"I had failed to recognize," he said in retrospect, "that 2 Corinthians 6:17, 'Wherefore come out from among them, and be ye separate, saith the Lord,' applies to separation from unbelievers, not believers with whom you disagree. The command in Romans 14 is to make allowances for imperfect believers — we're all imperfect in one way or another."

For at least two years Dawson had felt sure his life work would be with young men. He now found himself looking to the Lord to confirm this and to give him direction. He did have certain guiding principles settled in his mind. He wanted to live by faith, trusting God to supply his needs in answer to prayer. He was also convinced that a fruitful servant of God must be a man of much prayer and must saturate his life with the Word — conditions he found great joy and difficulty in meeting. He was determined to invest his efforts in a part of the vineyard where laborers were truly few; having heard a church official say that 300 ministers of his denomination in Los Angeles were without pulpits, he felt he was not needed in the pastorate. He took as one of his life mottoes, "Never do anything that someone else can or will do, when there is so much to be done that others cannot or will not do."

The word from God commissioning him to a life work with young men is recorded in his journal early in 1931, a time when the boys clubs were thriving. His stilted, self-conscious prose hints at the significance he attached to this occasion, as he wrote on March 17:

> *While waiting upon the Lord and reading His Word, He speaks to me very definitely. I was reading II Sam. the first 7 chapters. I was strangely aware that God was nigh unto me. God was ... with David for His people, Israel's, sake. II Sam. 5:10-12. David enquired many times of the Lord. I am and was then peculiarly and especially aware of mine own insufficiency and dependence upon the Lord. Chapter 7, wherein David was promised what God should verily do, burst with special significance before me. While reading the second time Hebrews 6:16-18 flashed into my mind; not knowing what it was I looked it up. I cannot explain how definitely the Lord spoke to me in view of the boys' work in the light of America's, yea the world's need. O, but that through Chapter 7, also Isaiah 41:10 and Hebrews 6:16-18, Romans 4:20, 21 He did speak. I am as sure as that Carey the missionary knew. I trust God, His Word, not myself nor my feelings.*

Late in April Dawson and a buddy, Louie Bardwell, rode up into the Sierra Nevadas and camped out for nine days in Rock Creek Canyon, spending much time in the Word and prayer. "I am memorizing 7 passages a day," he noted in his journal.

"Louie and I are eating only two meals a day to the end we might have more time." Isaiah was the book he was most drawn to. "Wonderful blessings. Can only be known by them who read much of God's Word."

Three weeks after the Sierra trip a prayer meeting began which lasted some forty days and in Dawson's mind was a foundation stone for his later ministry. "Prayer is God speaking things into existence through human lips," he had written in his Bible by 2 Samuel 7. He asked Walt Stanton to join him at five every morning to claim the promise of Jeremiah 33:3. "We are praying for a revival," he wrote.

"It took him a couple years to get anyone to the place where they would pray that long, but I was ready to go on," Walt recalled. "He had in his mind the background and outline of the forty days probation period" [of Mount Sinai].

Riding out every morning to the "L" Canyon at the edge of town, the two walked a quarter-mile to the dead end of a dry wash with sloping sides; this was their chosen prayer spot under a big pepper tree. There they built a fire as protection from the foggy chill sweeping in from the Pacific and knelt for two hours to pray before they went on to work. Dawson's knees soon tired, but Walt, a plumber used to working on his knees, did not notice. They prayed for the boys in their clubs in Lomita and other towns, and soon they were praying for young men in more distant towns throughout Southern California. As their faith increased, they began to ask God to use them in the lives of young men across the U.S., naming each of the forty-eight states before the Lord. Then toward the end of the time they took a map of the world up to their prayer hideaway and, touching Europe, Asia, Africa, Australia, and the Pacific islands, they asked God to use them to reach men for Him there.

Finally they quit — perhaps because Daws felt their mission was accomplished or because his physical endurance ran out. But he did believe God had heard and would answer. "He not only believed the Bible was true, but that the promises were true and he could apply them to himself," Stanton said. "God could do great things through the apostles and prophets, and he had faith God would do them through him. . . . Anyone can see now that he was a great person even then."

Looking back at the forty-day marathon years later, Dawson analyzed the protracted time in prayer: "We couldn't have prayed the first week for those little islands and countries you had to look close to see. I don't think the amount of time you spend in prayer has much to do with whether God hears you, but I do believe time has something to do with your faith being built up as you pray and as you ask."

Dawson may have seen the loss of the younger boys through the church split as an indication that God was leading him to concentrate on high school age and older. In the fall he enrolled in five subjects at the high school for a month or two — "a wonderful opportunity to keep in touch with my boys."

In November, while taking time out to recover from poison oak, he found God renewing to him many previous promises for his life work. His conviction was deepening that the Word was far more than an inspired record: it was the living, present voice of God. With due respect to dispensationalists, he still did not feel Scripture should be apportioned to certain peoples for certain times exclusively. In the margin above Jeremiah he wrote, "Is it possible that God wrote this whole Book to one small people, or did He, knowing the end from the beginning, write to others herein." And beside Isaiah 58:12, "Given many times when praying about my life work." Why should Christians who claim God's promise of peace from Isaiah 26:3 or forgiveness of sin from Isaiah 1:18 consider the promise in Isaiah 58:12 off limits? Even Isaiah 58:11 "And the Lord shall guide thee continually . . ." was commonly claimed and quoted. Telling later of God's promises to him from Isaiah for his life work, he explained with a light touch, "Some say the Book of Isaiah is for the Jews. Well it's full of promises, and as I looked around, I didn't see the Jews claiming them — somebody should be using them!"

Dawson felt strongly that the more Scripture one memorized, the more channels of communication the Lord had at His disposal. During the poison oak experience he wrote of one such instance:

> *Again waiting upon God with the Book before me, and after speaking to God about certain things, within the space of ten seconds four verses flash before me — I Pet. 2:25; Heb. 10:20; Heb. 11:6;*

> Rev. 3:7, 8. *In the light of my prayer to God, no*
> *message could be more significant and real. Blessed*
> *be God.*

He knew now what his life work would be. He saw how
God had been leading and preparing him through the years —
including the recent forty-day prayer meeting with Walt — for
a work with young men, a ministry of training spiritual guer-
rillas, Christian soldiers who would give no quarter in battle
for their Commander in Chief. At the moment the Fishermen
Clubs seemed to be the agency through which to work. He
asked Mr. Morgan to get permission for him to organize a team
to work under International Fishermen Club, reviving and
building up existing clubs and starting new ones. He would
choose his team members with care. Walt was the first, and he
was ready to go. Lewie Coates too was enthusiastic, as was Louie
Bardwell.

"The good hand of our God is upon us," Dawson noted
when he had presented his plan for an IFC team to six young
men and all six responded. It was exhilarating to be on the
verge of something big that God was going to do. He was not
certain *how* He would work, but felt no presumption in believing the God of Abraham, Moses, David, and Hudson Taylor
would make good His promises to Dawson Trotman, promises
burned into his heart through prayer.

Not that he saw himself as different from others. But he
saw God with such clarity and believed His Word with an
immediacy that compelled him to act on it. And he would
allow no mediocrity in himself or others; anything done for
God must be done well. Therefore, in forming the IFC team
and in all future undertakings he would search for the best
men and the best ways to get the job done. If God wanted the
world reached, no effort was too elaborate and no sacrifice too
great. So while devotion to the Lord and the power of His
Word pulled Dawson along toward fulfilling the Great Commission, the added force of rigorous discipline pushed him.
Getting up to pray at 4:00 or 5:00 A.M. wasn't enough — the
new team would meet at an early morning hour to pray together.

Detailed minutes kept by Coates record the team's activities
from February 1932 to June 1933. Several times a week they

would participate in a Fishermen Club, speak or sing and give testimonies at young people's meetings or church services, and plan strategy and team "business," usually including a "wonderful time in prayer."

The team set themselves rigid disciplines, seven items at first: 1) one hour of prayer daily, 2) daily Bible reading, 3) touch one soul a day for God, 4) one fishing trip a week, 5) teach a boys club, 6) always be equipped with New Testament, Gospel of John, tracts, and Fishermen Club information, 7) memorize one verse a day. These standards, called the TNT (for "Trust 'N 'Tackle," possibly also for their explosive power), they occasionally revised, usually by adding to them. The TNT for a sample week was 1) memorize Isaiah 53, 2) pray one hour a day, 3) touch three every day, 4) read Nehemiah, 5) memorize a verse a day. They continually fell short of meeting their standards, but when the team met to take stock and reconsider, they ended with an assignment as heavy or heavier than the one before. In his drive for excellence, Dawson could not yet brook the notion that human performance tends toward mediocrity. He learned this in time, when the disciplines proved too much for all of them, including himself.

But the team members were in it to win. At a February 1933 meeting they concluded that though their team standards had grown to a daily dozen, varying from memorizing Scripture to keeping personal files, the personal checkup was vital to their success in these disciplines. They voted to continue the checkup "as unto the Lord and not unto men." They roared over Southern California on their motorcycles, winning people to Christ, organizing new Fishermen Clubs, challenging one and all to memorize the Word and win souls. They started a Fishermen Club school in Long Beach, enrolling young men from seven towns for classes in Scripture memory, Bible study, and public speaking.

At an all-night prayer meeting the team found themselves making some momentous requests:

> *We considered the future work of the F.C. and realizing the great need of a great work done for God, in His power, and for His glory, we asked Him to touch two million young people through us. In considering the boys' work, we saw that count-*

*ing all Prospectors and Junior Fishermen possible
we could account for only 200 in clubs. This led
us to ask for one thousand.*

The faith to ask for two million young people doubtless grew out of the forty-day prayer meeting. The answer was years in coming.

The team members dubbed themselves Minute Men after the volunteers of the American Revolution, clerks, farmers, and blacksmiths ready any moment to grab their muskets and go out to fight for their country. These modern Minute Men were armed and instantly ready to do spiritual battle for the Lord.

After another all-night prayer meeting the team felt certain God was going to expand their ministry. They were leery, however, of growing into a large organization with the attendant risk of infection by worldliness and modernism. If each club were organized as a separate entity, they reasoned, they could avoid big organization and the work would be less vulnerable, the clubs more likely to stay true to the Word. Also, what about their association with IFC? "Daddy" Horton, the godly Fishermen Club founder, had died. What if future leadership of IFC changed course? So after a year of representing IFC, the Minute Men sent a courteous letter of resignation, though indicating they hoped to continue as individual members. Their work was growing, more Minute Men were joining the team, and it would be simpler to function independently with freedom to establish new clubs in their own format. Probably underlying other reasons was the one Stanton observed, that "Dawson always had to build on his own foundation."

The Minute Men aimed to be sharp, alert businessmen for God, a goal they furthered by their small pocket notebooks with separate cards for prayer lists, business lists, personal duties, and club business.

Dawson's diligence in notebook-keeping went back to the time Miss Thomas had asked him, "Where are the little cards you used to carry in your pocket to help you remember things?" "Oh, I graduated from that," he had assured her. "I just depend on the Holy Spirit to bring them to my remembrance." "Well, it hasn't been working. I notice you've been forgetting a number of things." He went back to the cards.

Inspired by their team leader's persuasion and example, Minute Men kept their notebooks as religiously as their devotional times with God. The system was the forerunner of many versions which evolved through the years in Dawson's search for better methods — smaller notebooks, larger ones, more elaborate systems, simpler ones. His pursuit of the perfect notebook was in line with his goal expressed in a favorite slogan: "Accomplishing the greatest possible amount in the shortest possible time in the most effective way."

Dawson found his own struggle for discipline increased with time. His exuberant devotion to the Lord helped sustain his habit of meeting the Lord early each morning. But he was twenty-six, well past the magic years around age twenty when one may freely squander his capital of physical strength. (He learned later that his prayer heroes such as Hudson Taylor who rose so early to pray also retired much earlier at night than he did.) He had been burning both ends of the candle and was beginning to notice it.

Having to set the pace for the Minute Men added an incentive for personal discipline. And having to report to one another in weekly meetings gave extra stimulus to succeed. Still, what helped him most with the dead weight of human inertia and the daily struggle with temptation was the strength he drew from the Word and the special joy he felt in being God's servant. Obstacles and temptations were just part of the battle he was sent to win.

Touch a life a day for God. Dawson had just climbed into bed when he realized he had not talked to anyone about Christ. Well, what if he spoke to two tomorrow? It wouldn't do, he decided. Rather than fail his week's assignment, he dressed and clattered off in his Model-T to find a listener. After several miles he saw a man with a briefcase who had just missed the train to Long Beach, and Dawson offered him a ride.

"You may not believe this," he began after introductions, "but I got out of bed to come down here. It's a rule of my life never to end the day without sharing with someone the most wonderful thing in life. I am a Christian."

The passenger heard the story of God's love in Christ, then said thoughtfully, "Son, twenty years ago I started to search for God. I've gone to church nearly every Sunday for twenty years. Tonight you have told me about what I've been looking for." If going out to witness that night instead of the next day merely to check off his daily chart was legalistic, it was legalism in the providence of God, for the next day he would not likely have crossed the path of the man who that night ended his long search for peace with God.

No matter how often Dawson witnessed, it was never without fear. He once gave this analysis: "I realized that fear was a little flashing red light to remind me it was 'not by might, nor by power, but by my Spirit, saith the Lord.' You never get to the place where you can do it on your own. You need Him." Once he stopped the Model-T for a traffic light, after he had prayed for opportunity to witness, and tried to ignore the rough, burly hitch-hiker standing there. He seemed a most unlikely prospect. But the man would not be ignored, so Dawson took him aboard and handed him a gospel tract.

"What do you think of it?" he asked when the man finished reading.

"I think it's wonderful," was the startling answer.

"Oh, you're a Christian!"

"No, I'm not. I've been goin' to some tent meetings down here every night for two weeks, but I can't get through."

"Get through?" Dawson stopped to explain how Someone had already "got through" for him. Dawson felt rebuked for his fear and for prejudging a man's interest by his appearance.

The Minute Men had their secret team signals. "7:7" (for Matt. 7:7) meant prayer. When eating at a restaurant, if someone said "6:6" (Matthew) it meant grace would be said silently. "12:11" (Romans) indicated a need to shape up. Other references were equally cryptic. The team's journal records some ways God provided for their meager ministry needs:

April 4, 1932—We ... praise the Lord for His careful provision for all our needs. ... One week ago to get to Whittier one of the team members sold 20c worth of stamps for which he had no immediate need, then was given 5c and in searching around the house found five pennies. On the way to Whittier the lights burned out and another had some money with which to buy new ones, just leaving enough money to get gasoline to ride home the following day.
May 21, 1933 [after ministering to a church C.E. group]—God surely supplied the financial need as we were given two dollars.

The Minute Men's strategy was to "take" one city at a time — Whittier, then Pasadena. Traveling by motorcycle or Dawson's Model-T, they ministered in the main churches, teaching classes and challenging church people to memorize Scripture and win souls. Whether or not they saw results in the congregations, they were encouraged by the response of one or two young men they were able to recruit in each place. When the one or two had grown to a dozen or more, a club could be started. Dawson began to think and pray about Fishermen Clubs for girls, but they did not materialize. The Minute Men also had opportunities to speak in high schools and junior colleges.

On Pastor Tinning's recommendation, Dawson was invited to lead a boys group at Hollywood Presbyterian Church and possibly be called as part-time boys worker. The idea drew a strong reaction from Henrietta Mears of the church staff. "Oh, no! He'd never fit in Hollywood!" And with good reason. The Hollywood sophisticates were not ready for the likes of Dawson at his current cultural level.

After about nine months the team had "taken" three cities. In Long Beach, Whittier, and Pasadena clubs now flourished and choice young men were "getting into the Word" and learning to witness. But at this rate how long would it take to reach the nation — how much longer to reach the world? Pondering this question brought Dawson a step nearer to his lifetime conviction about God's plan for getting His message to all the world. He thought of his promises from Isaiah 43, such as verse 4: "Since thou wast precious in my sight, thou hast been honourable, and I have loved thee: therefore will I give men for thee, and people for thy life." He had prayed for laborers for God's harvest. Now he began to see the vast difference between a mere believer and a laborer, and to see the need to concentrate on building laborers on whom God could depend. He began to preach that "God can do more through one man who is 100 percent dedicated to Him than through 100 men who are only 90 percent."

About that time he wrote in the margin of his Bible, near the Isaiah promises, this request: "That God will soon bring us into touch with a mighty band of young men, strong rugged soldiers of the cross, with an eye singled to His glory." Something had happened over this last half-year. Dawson's goal had been changing from winning souls to building strong disciples and recruiting laborers for God.

Coinciding with this change in his thinking was a shocking discovery. Dawson picked up a hitch-hiker whose speech indicated he was not a believer. Within moments he discovered this man was one of his "converts" of the previous year whose decision had not been followed up and who had virtually died on the vine. Shaken, Dawson reasoned that there must be countless such persons who had sincerely, perhaps with tears, called on the name of the Lord, but whose lives had not been changed. What was wrong?

From that time on Dawson resolved to follow up anyone he led to Christ — a work more difficult than soulwinning — and to encourage others to give their converts their rightful opportunity to grow in Christ. The truth had come into focus, and he made an axiom of it: "You can lead a man to Christ in twenty minutes to a couple of hours, but it takes twenty weeks to a couple of years to adequately follow him up." The hitch-hiker convert startled him into realigning his ministry — less emphasis on getting the decision and more on growing up into Christ.

The conviction of the need to build laborers and the conviction of the imperative of follow-up for the new Christian began to shape the course of Dawson's ministry and figure prominently in his preaching. He became a pest on the subject until follow-up became a staple of Christian ministry.

"*Don't* bring spiritual babes to birth and leave them to die for lack of nourishment," he exhorted his audiences. Giving them a Bible was not enough. They must be fed. "Don't just set the baby in the pantry with a can opener. Mix his formula and heat it to the right temperature; then hold the bottle for him." The hit-and-run evangelism he and others had practiced for years, resulting only in the "survival of the fittest," he now condemned as dead wrong.

The junior high school girl Dawson had led to Christ was now a mature young woman, a product of that rare home where both love and discipline prevail and the father's authority is never questioned. Dad Clayton, a massive man, son of a southern preacher, was unconverted. He could use language similar to that used on his job as dock superintendent for an oil company to describe his feelings about his daughter's engagement to a religious fanatic who would probably let her starve to death. But she was eighteen now and knew what she wanted, and there was nothing he could do.

Dawson and Lila quarreled only once in the three years they were engaged, and that was when she broke a promise and had her hair cut short. To Dawson the perfectionist this could only mean calling off the wedding. If her loyalty to him was so fragile before marriage, what would it be after? But when he heard that one of his boys club leaders had gone to the hills to pray God would bring them back together, Dawson remembered his own shortcomings and quickly forgave Lila.

Afraid to trust himself, and with so much at stake for the future, Dawson set puritanical standards for their courtship. Lila was not to sit too close to him in the car, and his letters to her during his year at Biola were more pastoral than romantic. One evening a week was allowed for dates, often involving a mission meeting or other ministry. He knew a false move in the marriage department could be catastrophic to God's plan to use him to raise up foundations of many generations. Mindful too of his parents' home life, he wanted nothing short of God's best for his and Lila's.

"Those first six months of 1932 were important in our lives," Lila recalled, "when we were established as to what God would have us do. Dawson wanted to be sure my position in the home was clear — one that would free his hands for the ministry God was giving him. He constantly took me back to 1 Samuel 30:24: '... as his part is that goeth down to the battle, so shall [her] part be that tarrieth by the stuff....' "

Millie Dienert, a friend in later years, was struck by the unusual way Lila looked to Dawson as her spiritual teacher who had taught her to find in the Word its personal meaning for her. "He was definitely a teacher, and she was his most apt pupil.

When I had opportunity to talk to Dawson over a cup of coffee, I found him using God's Word, a verse or portion in every attitude — toward a vision, a person, a desire, a plan. . . . I do not converse with many people who apply God's Word to every phase of their lives. But everything they feel and do is wrapped around portions of God's Word, and they have stood upon that."

To Lila, the great driving force of Dawson's life was that he believed God. "Lila, you have to believe God," he told her, a simple premise they would test countless times. That spring they claimed the promise of Isaiah 60:11 for their home: *Therefore thy gates shall be open continually; they shall not be shut day nor night; that men may bring unto thee the forces of the Gentiles, and that their kings may be brought.* In the margin of his Bible Dawson pledged, "Our home — always — God willing."

On July 3, 1932, a month after Lila's high school graduation, they were married in the second floor storefront South Lomita Bible Church. Misses Mills and Thomas outdid themselves decorating the drab hall with ferns and flowers, and Pastor V. V. Morgan officiated. Reluctantly, the Claytons gave a garden reception at their home. The wedding trip was a happy foursome, as best man Walt Stanton and his bride accompanied the couple by boat to Catalina.

Opportunity to believe God began at once. The day before the wedding, a missionary couple called to offer their North Long Beach home to the Trotmans for two months while they were away. Dawson's job at the lumberyard had been cut back, and until then he did not know where they would live. Money for groceries was provided when his mother pressed upon them a twenty-dollar bill, money it had doubtless taken her months to save.

Dawson and Lila moved six times in their first year of marriage, remembering from the start their Isaiah 60:11 pledge of hospitality and ministry. For a few months they combined households with the Irwin Moons, an adventure both couples fondly recalled later.

Moon had preceded Dawson at Biola, where his handstands on the flagpole staff were a legend, as were some of Daws's stunts. Now pastor of Montecito Park Church, Moon did research in astronomy as a hobby.* Dawson helped him build his ten-inch telescope and helped in ministry to the church young people. Moon's salary in that Depression year was twelve to fourteen dollars a week. Carrots at a penny a bunch were often on the menu, and Thanksgiving dinner featured rabbits they had shot.

The two-family arrangement was enjoyable, but built-in stresses made it less than ideal for very long. So in January Daws and Lila moved to Lomita, and a month later to a four-room furnished house in Whittier which they rented for twelve dollars a month.

It was a time of transition and learning for Dawson. The Minute Men had just decided to break away from IFC and minister on their own. Two minor accidents at work that winter and early spring laid Dawson aside with foot injuries for about two months, giving him much opportunity for prayer and reflection. He wrote in his journal:

> *This noon while beginning to read Hudson Taylor for a little, I asked God to direct where I should read. I was led to read the chapter which told of his being stricken to his bed during a most busy season, through the wisdom and providence of God. About 2 p.m. I was thinking of the possibilities of being stricken for a season to enable me to have time for God to speak to my soul. Not many minutes after the drive shaft broke loose, striking my left foot. I will be unable to use it for at least a week. I thank God, who works all things purposefully, wisely and to His own glory. A good deal of pain.*

Back to work at the lumberyard on April 12, Dawson recorded an important lesson learned: God enables His laborer to accomplish His work with or without a salaried job. He purposed to serve wherever God directed without thought of remuneration. He would make no connection between ministry and income and would expect God to provide finances through whatever channels He chose.

*Moon's hobby of scientific research led to a world-wide ministry through his Sermons from Science and later Moody Institute of Science films.

Dawson's doctrinal persuasion seemed to be a combination of Presbyterian and Methodist. Along with a settled sense of destiny and of God's immutable purpose, he held an equally firm duty to obedience and good works, as though all depended upon him. It was a strong but compatible mix, one he kept and propagated throughout his life. The parallel truths showed up in such notations in his journal as the one for January 2, 1933:

> *At club (Pasadena) only those were there whom God wanted. Two young fellows . . . [who] are strengthened and helped through considering plan of victory as shown in the Word.*

Certain content of his teaching had taken shape. "His life centered around the Word," observed Charles Vanian, a Pasadena Fisherman, recalling the set jaw and the steel in Dawson's challenge to young men to get into the Word. "Just to know the Word and to obey it in discipline." The Wheel was becoming the foundation of his teaching — an urgency to give oneself to prayer and to the Word, especially study and Scripture memory, to witnessing and wholehearted obedience. Dr. Sam Sutherland of Biola spoke of his "constant nagging on memorizing Scripture" and admired his dogged determination to get the message across.

The direction his ministry would take was less clear. Living in Whittier, he assumed he should minister there, so started a group in his home for boys thirteen to sixteen. With the Minute Men he continued to speak in church services, youth groups, high schools, and junior colleges around Southern California. Horton MacDavid, one of the team, recalled unusual opportunities to speak in modernist churches. "Some enthusiastic youth in junior college would invite us to speak in one of the big churches. They would get a big bunch of youth together and we would give them the Gospel. That was in the time of extreme modernism." There was still a blunt directness in the team's style. A sailor who came to Christ at a Minute Men church meeting in San Diego was told his Christian life would be useless until he quit smoking. The next day he returned with his decision to quit.

The Minute Men often met at the Trotman home, their minutes duly noting Lila's graciousness as hostess at dinner.

The team had gained new members and lost some, their momentum and ambitious plans unhindered by their frequent failure to chalk up perfect records on the daily dozen. They now planned three Sundays a month for church meetings, one day for prayer, and one for Minute Men business, in addition to week-night meetings with Fishermen Clubs. On May 30, 1933 they celebrated a year-and-a-half of colaborship with an elaborately planned day of fellowship and recreation.

With increased opportunities — boys work in several towns, Minute Men activities, church youth groups, individual contacts — Dawson decided to go to a four-day work week, with three days for ministry. Even so, he felt he must give top priority to prayer, and though his journal shows five times in one week of June spent with the Lord in the hills or the park, he exhorts himself on the subject:

> *Had a truly blessed time alone with the Lord. Early this morning. Again have I had the matter of prayer brought definitely to my attention as being vitally connected with accomplishing much business for God. I set my face again to pursue and persevere in habits of much time with Him. Truly our most difficult work, as refreshing and as wonderful as it is — Prayer.*

This sensitivity born of much prayer helped him not to miss an important contact that opened the door to a whole new field of ministry.

Spencer. Les Spencer, fireman third, U.S.S. *West Virginia. Father, be with Spencer today. Help him to grow in the knowledge of Christ.* . . . Dawson flicked the page of his notebook to other requests. His prayer time over, he went on to work, still thinking about Spencer. How would God answer his prayer? He telephoned Trona Field and radioed a message to the ship. MEET ME FIFTH STREET LANDING FOUR THIRTY. LOOK FOR LIGHT PANTS DARK COAT. TROTMAN.

Spencer was there, looking freshly scrubbed, his wheat-colored hair showing at the edges of his squared sailor's hat. Dawson took him home to a chicken dinner prepared by Lila, then suggested they spend some time in the Word and prayer in the Palos Verdes hills. Parked by a schoolhouse, they were poring over the Scriptures when a security guard approached and asked what they were doing. "Reading the Bible," Dawson answered, and seized the opportunity to witness. The three went inside, where Dawson turned from one passage to another to explain the Gospel and answer all the defenses of the hapless guard, who now wished they would move on. Spencer watched, impressed by Dawson's skill in using the Bible.

On the way back to the landing he said, "Boy, I'd give my right arm to know how to use the Word like that." "No you wouldn't," Daws baited him. After a brief exchange the sailor insisted, "I would. I mean it."

It was the response Dawson wanted. "All right, you can. And it won't cost your arm, but you'll have to be willing to dig in and study and apply yourself. I'll give you all the time you'll take."

Back aboard ship, Spencer woke his buddy Gurney Harris. "Boy, I met a real man of God tonight. He really knows the Word and knows how to use it." From then on Spencer was at the Trotman home whenever he had liberty, and he invited Dawson aboard on visiting day. Daws was fascinated as he toured the big battleship, a whole city in miniature. But he was deeply excited about his discovery of one man among its crew who was eager for all the training he could get in serving Christ — an excitement not reflected in his laconic journal note of April 30, 1933, "Spencer to become a MM." He sensed during those months that God was about to do something important in His work, and while he did not see the full significance of his meeting with Spencer, this was undoubtedly the "something," a historic beginning.

On trips to San Diego, Dawson and the Minute Men often contacted and gave a hand to Helen Rittenhouse, a former Biola classmate who opened her home to servicemen for weekly Bible studies. Helen called her work the Service Men's Bible Club and adapted her studies from those of Milo Jamison's University Bible Club. They followed a three-point pattern:

1) What does the Bible say? 2) What does the Bible mean? 3) What am I going to do about it?

Christian sailors, a tiny minority in the pre-war Navy, welcomed the help and fellowship at the Rittenhouse home. However, Helen did not feel a woman should head such a ministry, and she went up to ask Dawson to come to San Diego and take it over. "I remember Dawson out in that little Ford praying for every ship in the harbor," she said. Dawson considered it. San Diego was a training point where most men spent only a short time before assignment to ship or shore duty elsewhere. Spencer was one of these whom Helen had referred to Dawson to ensure that his commitment to Christ would grow. Dawson's burden to reach servicemen led him to make frequent trips to San Diego to lead the Bible class at Helen's home. But he found men contacted at San Pedro more available for training because of their liberty schedules and the fact that ships home ported there gave longer continuous contact with them.

The circumstances of recruiting Spencer to Minute Men confirmed Dawson's growing conviction that more could be accomplished for God by building in depth in one life than by scattering shot in all directions, ministering to groups only once or occasionally. He had copied a quotation in his Bible: "Emotion is no substitute for action." He now added: "Action is no substitute for production."

At the same time he was learning another lesson. The rigid twelve-point standards Minute Men were required to follow often led to failure and a guilt syndrome. And though confessions and resolves cleared the books for a fresh start, over a period of time the total effect was negative. Dawson later learned that discipline imposed from the outside eventually defeats when it is not matched by desire from within. But now he knew only that he should scale down the requirements so as not to discourage the person of average ability and desire. He noted in his journal,

> *Changed many plans today. Cut MM duties to a happy medium which will both keep stronger Christians busy and will yet make it possible for new or weaker Christians.*

Spencer and those after him started on this reduced schedule, benefiting also from Daws's conclusion that he could lead a man to more solid discipleship by spending more concentrated personal time with him rather than by heavy written assignments. He began to see his ministry as two-pronged, extensive and intensive. He would sow beside all waters, teaching a YMCA group or Fishermen's Club, witnessing to a hitch-hiker, leading a couples' Bible study or a student group on campus. And he would spend countless hours with one man, teaching and challenging him over the months toward investment of his life for God. He found endless opportunity for extensive ministry — so much so that he was restless sitting in the pew in a church evangelistic service with so much to be done. As for intensive ministry, the fewer opportunities, the more effective he could be. And through this ministry God could fulfill His promises to "give men for thee, and people for thy life" and to "raise up the foundations of many generations."

Dawson and Lila on their wedding day, July 3, 1932.

II

"They That Go Down to the Sea in Ships"

1933-1937

THE WHEEL

CHRIST supplies the Power in a CHRISTian life, as does the Hub in the Mechanism of a Wheel in Action.

"All power is given unto ME in Heaven and in earth." (Matt.) "I AM the Vine, Ye are the branches   Without Me ye can do - - -   - - - nothing. (John).

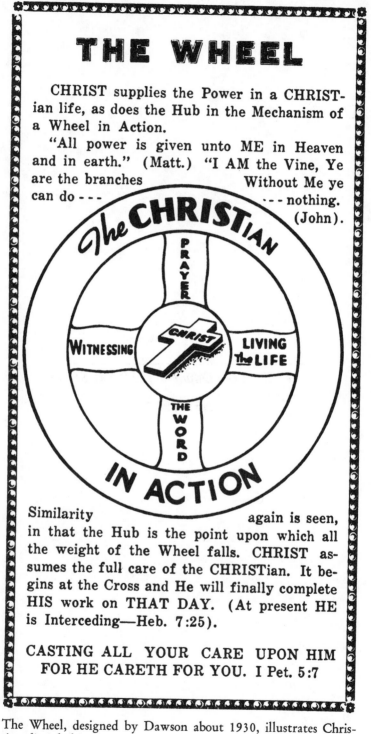

Similarity   again is seen, in that the Hub is the point upon which all the weight of the Wheel falls. CHRIST assumes the full care of the CHRISTian. It begins at the Cross and He will finally complete HIS work on THAT DAY. (At present HE is Interceding—Heb. 7:25).

CASTING ALL YOUR CARE UPON HIM FOR HE CARETH FOR YOU. I Pet. 5:7

The Wheel, designed by Dawson about 1930, illustrates Christian discipleship.

It would have been easy to settle down in Whittier. Daws and Lila called their first real home their honeymoon cottage, as it met all the requirements of a dream home. Yet they shared it freely with others, as his journal reveals:

> *I truly thank God for the little home He has given Buddie and me for a place to serve Him. The home is open to all — nothing hinders meeting oft to pray.*

A couples Bible study group met in the home one evening, the Whittier Fishermen Club another. Minute Men gathered here to plan strategy and pray, and the church youth leaders came to plan with Dawson for their Bible conference. When Spencer's ship was in, Dawson had him over every free evening for time in the Word or out in some ministry, driving him the thirty miles back to the ship in time for duty next morning.

Here in this home Dawson set up his first serious follow-up effort after the shock of meeting a former "convert" who showed no evidence of life. He was impressed by such verses as Colossians 1:28, "Whom we preach, warning every man, and teaching every man in all wisdom; that we may present every man perfect in Christ Jesus," that a decision resulting from his evangelism-on-the-run was only the beginning of a job God expected him to finish. He set up a card file, recruiting Lila to help him record names, addresses, and other information on every life he had touched in some way, and he began a feverish campaign of letter-writing and record-keeping to try to make up for past failures. Though many previous contacts could not be salvaged, he aimed to do all possible to follow every one, writing letters and cards to encourage those he could find and sending helpful literature.

This new grasp of his responsibility as a spiritual parent to the new Christian did not slow his constant drive to "touch lives." On one day he noted he had "dealt with" two people and witnessed to four others. He discovered that one young hitch-hiker was meeting with a group of a dozen fellows in a neighboring town for prayer every morning, so joined them next morning to see what God was doing there. He found among them two who would like to become Minute Men. Every person he met was important to him, opening a potential new adventure for God. But the added dimension of follow-through on each contact began a gradual shift in his objective from "touching lives" to seeing lives grow to fruitfulness for Christ.

He soon found follow-up took more time and effort than he had to give, though he had not yet reached the inevitable conclusion that his involvement in greater depth with people would have to mean fewer people. Instead, he worked harder and longer, trying always to make better use of the time, so that a two-hour siesta he took one day was such a novelty he recorded it in his journal, justifying it by adding, "Though it seems I begrudge the hours spent in sleep, a rested body serves the Spirit more effectively and more readily."

As new activities snowballed — ministry with boys, couples, Minute Men, church young people, San Diego servicemen, and strangers he met on the road — Dawson did turn some of them over to others, invoking his motto: "Never do anything that someone else can and will do when there is so much of importance to be done which others cannot or will not do." Still his pace continued to be heavy. Getting his vital prayer times alone called for iron discipline of his will, battling fatigue and enemy resistance to the powerful weapon of prayer.

Spencer was getting his spiritual sea legs as he spent hours with Dawson in the Minute Men disciplines, learning to memorize and study the Word and use it in witness, and learning to pray with purpose. A Christian since age eleven but with little opportunity to grow, he now showed a Scots-Irish steadiness in applying himself to everything Daws taught him. He shared enthusiastically with shipmate Gurney Harris and encouraged him to visit the Trotman home.

"Daws, I'd sure like to get Gurney over here to learn what you're teaching me," he once remarked.

"Sure, he can come," was the answer. "But why don't you get him started? Just pass on to him what I'm givin' you."

"I haven't had the training," Les objected.

"Doesn't matter." Dawson looked him in the eye. "If you can't teach him what I've taught you, I've failed."

Gurney, an easygoing, soft-spoken Arkansian, had joined the Navy to save money for seminary. When he first met Spencer, Harris's Christian life was none too visible, but the warmth of their fellowship revived him. He began to hide his cigarette whenever Spencer came around. He was challenged by Spencer's obvious growth and wanted to get the same help. But before he could make contact with Trotman, their ship sailed for Bremerton for dry dock.

Dawson kept in touch with Spencer by mail and was delighted to hear of a Bible class started on the ship and a gospel team with several fellows in Bremerton. His letters encouraged his young disciple in the life principles he had taught him, and he prayed often for Spencer, that he would become God's man to touch other lives on the *West Virginia*.

In the hills above San Pedro harbor, he prayed for men on every ship he saw anchored there. *When there's so much to be done that others cannot or will not do.* Was it possible God was giving him the job of reaching these men, just as He had sent him in answer to his own prayer for Spencer that morning in April? It was possible. Who else would reach them? Servicemen were an untouched field, and he had found in his San Diego contacts men hungry for spiritual reality. Sadly, Navy men of the 1930s did not enjoy the social acceptance they did a decade later. A posted notice "No Sailors or Dogs Allowed" reflected too well the community's regard for the white hats. And though many sailors, like Spencer, were merely small-town boys in uniform, the stereotype in the public mind was a drunk staggering along the street with a cheap girl on his arm.

Active Christians in uniform were nil. In a half-dozen years around San Pedro-Long Beach, Dawson had heard only one Navy man give a testimony — an old chief who always reeled off the rote "He-saves-He-keeps-He-satisfies" with none of the Word on his tongue or in his hand. If the Navy were to be reached for Christ, Daws reasoned, it would certainly not happen through the empty witness of an old chief who did not even carry a Bible or quote a single verse of Scripture. It would be through men like Spencer — strong, rugged soldiers of the cross, schooled in prayer and skilled in using the Sword of the

Spirit. Men who could and would nurture a convert to productive maturity in Christ.

I will give men for thee, and people for thy life. . . . thou shalt raise up the foundations of many generations. The promises burned a holy restlessness into his heart. He felt God was signaling the next step: concentration on the men on these ships in the harbor, and thus on the men they would reach.

The decision was made. Before their first anniversary Daws and Lila would move once more, leaving their Whittier honeymoon cottage to move nearer the harbor and the sailors.

> *June 24, 1933 — We move today to Lomita. Under the guiding hand of God dear Buddie and I move, knowing that God is leading. I ofttimes think God has kept us on the move in view of future labour (that we might be ready). From all indications God is going to do something soon. I really believe some outstanding events with reference to His work will take place soon.*

Such eager optimism could only spring from strong faith. The conditions into which they moved surely did not warrant it, for they were sketchy, if not depressing — a one-room cabin in a motor court with a two-plate burner for cooking, and a garage behind a Texaco service station two miles away where the men could meet for Bible study and bunk overnight. For a man to whom God had promised great things, the outlook was not promising. But David in the Cave Adullam never forgot that he was already anointed king of Israel. And Dawson, at twenty-seven, anticipated God's working with a confidence that bordered on presumption.

Another apparent setback was a blessing in disguise. The Minute Men team dissolved as suddenly as it had begun a year and a half before. One member went to seminary to study for the pastorate, another to prepare for missionary service, a third to a civilian work camp, while a fourth dropped out in order to work longer hours. The remaining men were unable to take over the team's full ministry schedule. So with Minute Men disbanded, Dawson was left with several evenings free to invest in the servicemen. God had simply cleared the decks for action.

*　　*　　*　　*

He stood waiting, white hat tilted just right of square, brown eyes scanning the docks where lumber was stacked for shipment. A big lumber carrier thundered up to stop beside him, and the driver wearing a Mexican sombrero landed cat-like on the dock. With a grin that squinted his eyes to narrow slits, Dawson Trotman held out his hand. "I suppose you're Gurney." The awestruck sailor confessed he was, standing under the gaze of the man who had taught him for three months through his shipmate Spencer.

"Les wrote that you'd be over even if he had the duty. So the *Weevy's* in," Daws made it sound like the kickoff for third quarter. "Tell you what. Bring the gang, the Christian guys, and we'll meet at 1800 at the station. Here's the — here's how you get there." Another penetrating look, a "praise the Lord," and he was off, rumbling down the dock on his mechanical monster.

Every afternoon the liberty boat dropped several *West Virginia* sailors at the landing, and they immediately headed for the garage behind the service station. Here Dawson spent long evenings with them around the Scriptures. Their sense of need had grown since Seattle, where they had tried to witness as a gospel team and found their knowledge of the Word limited. Too, they had become involved in Oxford Group teaching while there, as Dawson soon discovered. Spencer recalled later how timely Dawson's guidance was at that point, as he tactfully showed them from Scripture the error of this cult.

Spencer remembers the main emphases of those evenings of Bible study and instruction were from The Wheel — "personal witnessing, a consistent prayer life, a regular intake and application of the Word, and the importance of living a dedicated Christian life before the world." At the dinner hour a Model-T Ford would rattle up to the station with Lila at the wheel, bringing pans of hot baked beans, rolls, and potato salad she had prepared for them at the motor court two miles away. "Lila was a lovely lady; even as a girl nineteen years old she was very sweet and a lady in every sense of the word," Gurney said. "She was on the road quite a lot preparing food and serving it to this gang of sailors."

Spencer and Harris, both athletes, began to bring their friends to the garage Bible study evenings. Les was halfback on the ship's football squad, and Harris had won honors in all-Navy swimming competition. John Dedrick was the team's 220-yard man, and Ed Goodrick had won medals for clipping eleven or twelve seconds off the all-Navy 440-yard swim. At the close of Bible study one evening the fellows were sharing testimonies. Goodrick, not sure what to say, began, "Well, I'm happy in the Navy." Pause. "I have a good billet and have had lots of honors." Then he pointed a finger at Gurney and said, "But this fellow has something I want."

Dawson explained that it wasn't some*thing* but Some*one* Gurney had and Goodrick needed. He received Christ soon afterward, the first fruits of Spencer's and Harris's witness aboard ship.

Dedrick took his time. Night after night he listened as the group searched the Scriptures and shared their experiences of walking with Christ. "As a thickheaded unbeliever I didn't hear nearly as much of what Dawson said as I saw of what he was," Dedrick said later. His father had told him "there is no contact with God," and he clung to that denial. But Goodrick's conversion shook him, and the Word finally penetrated his defenses. "If God can do it for Goodrick, He can do it for Dedrick" he concluded. Alone in his hammock, he surrendered to Christ.

Dawson's schedule was again overcrowded. In addition to the sailors, he had the Pasadena club, boys at Camp Bethel, San Diego servicemen, and other groups in churches and out. He decided to leave the lumberyard and manage the small Texaco station in front of the garage where they met.

On August 29, 1933 he wrote, "I take this step wholly because of the Lord's work. I must have time to work, plan; and I must be able to get off whenever I need to for His sake." Income from the station was around two dollars a day, a sum which bought a respectable quantity of groceries. Gurney remembers that all the sailors would rush out to service a car, clean the windshield, check the oil, then get back to their Bible study in nothing flat.

Through summer and early fall Dawson taught the four men, imparting along with the basics of a dynamic Christian life his fervent desire to reach the world for Christ. He shared the Isaiah promises and challenged them to be part of the fulfillment of that vision.

The bleak surroundings in this garage, with a handful of sailors sitting on the edges of bunks studying the Bible, praying together, eating Lila's baked bean dinners and planning to reach the world for Christ, did not strike Dawson as incongruous. He knew God was at work to fulfill His plan. He would live to see Spencer establish Sunday schools and rural churches across America, Harris become a missionary leader in East Africa, Goodrick a pastor and Bible school teacher in the Northwest, and Dedrick a translator in Mexico giving an Indian tribe its first written language and the New Testament in that language. And hundreds — thousands — would follow them.

* * * *

The balmy August landscape was airbrushed with soft haze and cooled by ocean breezes. Stately palm trees lined the highway at intervals from San Diego to Long Beach, an occasional eucalyptus grove scenting the air with its pungent leaves. Across these clean, scarcely used coastlands, the hour after sunset seemed suspended above reality or passing time.

Chugging along toward home in the Model-T Ford, Dawson and Lila talked of their weekend in San Diego. She listened to his enthusiastic account of time he had spent with servicemen aboard ship, in church, and at the Rittenhouse home. He was delighted with her oneness of heart with him and her involvement in the ministry God was giving them. Nor had she ever complained of the cramped inconvenience of living in the motor court. Her high-spirited cooperation in doing her part in this work, her modest, discreet manner, and her warm personal interest in the fellows who came regularly to the Bible studies were only a few of the qualities he appreciated in this woman God had fashioned for him.

He looked across at her and remembered the day six years ago when he first knew he loved her . . . her steady growth in the Lord and love for Him . . . her self-assertion on occasion and her willingness to learn . . . her incredible adoration of him and the feeling he could do no wrong . . . her constant efforts to please him. "My darling wife and mother-to-be — so sweet," he mused. She was a woman now, though not yet twenty, with handsome patrician features, hair drawn close and coifed at the back of a shapely head, gray-blue eyes that twinkled halfway between mischief and laughter or softened to express the warmth of a loving welcome.

"Thank you, Father, for the priceless gift of this girl," Dawson prayed silently as he reached for her hand. "We truly are in love. I could not have selected from a million one more suited than Buddie."

* * * *

Spencer and Harris decided they had prayed long enough. "Dawson," one of them said, "we believe the Lord would challenge you with the idea of being our full-time missionary to the fleet. Several of us are ready to chip in on rent and expenses if you and Lila will move to San Pedro near the Navy landing where we can bring more fellows we're trying to win to Christ. That way you could give us more time and sort of train us on the job in witnessing."

"We'll pray about it." Dawson was overjoyed at this evidence of growth in the men — their hunger for the Word and further training. Their willingness to give out of their meager Navy pay to support a home base was a big step of faith. Yet he knew also that the sailors would discover later that rent and other expenses would be more than their combined efforts would cover, so it would be a new exercise in faith for Lila and him as well. They expected their first child in a few weeks, a new responsibility. But Hudson Taylor and George Muller had trusted God for provision, and they would too.

"Lila and I are willing to put ourselves in the Lord's hands," Daws told the men. "Let's do it."

The sailors found an apartment with an ocean view on Point Fermin and on November 20 moved the Trotmans into the first real Navigator Home (more than a year, however, before the name Navigators was adopted). Lila's diary reflects her enthusiasm for the new home and records that "as yet we had not moved in, but we had several here for dinner." The following Saturday she wrote, "The *first* meeting of the fellows in their new home." The main Bible study to which men were brought was on Saturday evening, and those who could stayed overnight.

Lila named Helen Rittenhouse and her mother among the nineteen present for dedication of the home. "We had a bit of refreshment, then gathered around the fire and had a few

songs and prayer and testimonies. Daws brought the message."
From the first it was a busy place. A young woman had come
to help Lila with cooking and housework. Dawson asked former
Minute Man Horton MacDavid, now in college, to live in the
home and help in the ministry. From one to six guests — sailors,
friends, relatives — joined the four for dinner most evenings.
If the strain on the food budget was a concern to Lila, she did
not show it. Her diary listed dinner guests and visitors and
spoke of good times of singing and praise to the Lord in evenings around the fireplace. "Truly He is wonderful!" she
added after listing five different sets of guests entertained one
Friday.

Expenses soon mounted above income, though the sailors
shared generously of their limited means and the service station,
which Dawson and Horton tended on alternate days, brought
in a little. With a wood-burning pencil and a can of shellac,
Dawson began making plywood wall mottoes with Scripture
texts, selling them for a few cents more than the materials cost.
The former Minute Man who taught him this process also
helped him design and produce silk-screened mottoes ornately
lettered in color on parchment paper.

But with all this, the prayer for daily bread was still a daily
matter, as an incident typical of those days shows. With the
apartment full of sailors, some sleeping on the floor, Daws and
Lila had gone to their room and prayed before retiring, including a request for food for the morning. After midnight a knock
on their door brought an apologetic sailor who handed Dawson
a dollar. "Sorry I forgot to give you this. I'll be leaving early
in the morning for mess cooking." Waiting until all hands were
asleep, Dawson slipped out, pushed the Model-T downhill to
avoid waking anyone when he started it, and went shopping.
At an all-night market he bought enough bacon, eggs, bread,
and margarine for breakfast for the unsuspecting group at Point
Fermin.

Dedrick, who as second class petty officer was the group's
first rated man, was also a natural fourth for a quartet including Spencer, Harris, and Trotman — waggishly described as
two tunas, a barracuda, and a bass. There was much singing in
those days, the fellows often harmonizing for their own enjoy-
ment. Gurney remembers enjoyable times of singing and praise

to God in the car on the way to meetings. "Dawson was always happy, always talking about the Lord, praising the Lord for what He had done, and stimulating our vision to trust the Lord for our lives in the future." Soon they were being invited to sing and hold services at Montecito Park Church and at other churches, youth groups, and the local radio station. The novelty of their testimony as Navy men prompted a feature story in the Long Beach *Press Telegram* of March 22, 1934 headed "Bluejackets Enjoy Bible Study."

As new men were brought to the Home, those with interest kindled in spiritual things returned. Virgil Hook, a sandy-haired sailor with wry speech and a twinkle in his Scottish blue eyes, was one who soon became a family regular. Others came and went. After three months of crowding into the apartment for meals, Bible studies, and overnight stays, the fellows again decided they needed a larger place. So in February the Trotman household, now including a firstborn son, moved to 33 Surfline, a house at the water's edge in Long Beach, a block from The Pike amusement strip. The larger place would be better, they reasoned, for more sailors could be reached, especially at such a convenient location.

The move to 33 Surfline was an advance in the ministry, though mainly as a means of learning and growth for Dawson and his young disciples. Many more sailors did come to the new Navigator Home near the beach. But it was soon apparent that increased numbers did not increase effectiveness, since they were not getting the concentrated nurture in discipleship that the original half-dozen had enjoyed, both from Dawson and through cross-pollination of their own experiences. Spencer's protest about lack of formal Bible training when Dawson first charged him to "teach Gurney what I'm teaching you" had proved invalid when Gurney in turn began to share with Dedrick, Goodrick, and Hook the things he was learning from both Lester and Dawson. So through the months the little group encouraged one another to fight the good fight of faith, to resist temptation and opposition to the Gospel, to strengthen their dedication to Christ.

Now with the influx of many half-committed or uncommitted men, the group's impact was diluted. Without the intensive personal help the first men had received, with spiritual nourishment served more in buffet style, some grew nominally while others withered on the vine or drifted away. A few took hold and survived.

The close-in group at Surfline could learn practical lessons of faith. Gurney, helping Lila prepare dinner, recalls being sent out the back door to buy chicken turnovers for the last ten men who arrived unexpectedly.

"Daws set an example for us in the life of faith," he says. "Though we shared the burden, it was a challenge to see how he cast himself on the Lord continually for every need and how the Lord came to our aid financially to secure things necessary for this Nav program."

Dawson's journal reflects this. On one July day he noted "Many in home today," then listed activities and plans made with evident disregard for their financing, then a postscript, "We have one penny." A few days earlier: "Horton & Lois MacDavid drop in for the evening. Our food is low, yet we have enough. We have no money nor do they. We plan to take them home but do not know how. Just as we leave Lester has us follow him and fills our gas tank." The plan to do what the Lord led him to do was usually made before His provision was in sight. Small stakes, to be sure, but repeated exercise of faith as the evidence of things not seen served to reinforce a habit that could lead to larger ventures of faith. The impact was not lost on the little band who watched life lived in intimate openness before God and themselves.

Lila, along with Dawson, earned their admiration. "Through all these experiences Lila was a jewel, working faithfully in the background, keeping house, preparing meals, preparing lunches for outings," Spencer says. "She was a genius in operating a home so efficiently on a very small budget. Her testimony before the men as a Christian wife and homemaker and colaborer was magnificent. A difficult role to play, but she did it well with the Lord's help and strength."

Dawson's early morning prayer times with the fellows built into their lives more than a message on prayer could have done. Gurney recalls vividly one such pre-dawn meeting in the hills above Pasadena, when a handful of men prayed until daylight. "Then we read the Word together, and Daws opened his heart and told us something of his missionary friends on different fields. He opened a big map, and we pointed out where they were and prayed for them individually. I began to reexamine my childhood commitment to the Lord concerning missions, and my mind and heart turned toward what the Lord wanted me to do in the future. I'll never forget poring over that map there under the trees and praying for different people. Dawson was a very practical man and a pacesetter in prayer."

Inhaling deeply, Dawson felt the searing freshness of mountain air, its scent of evergreen carrying a mint cleanness to his very soul. Among the trees on the slope above Big Bear Lake in the Sierra Madres he walked, sang, prayed aloud, and read from the travel-worn Scofield Bible he carried everywhere. These special times alone with God exhilarated him, filling his heart with praise and firing his zeal to new highs. Invited with Lila and six-month-old Bruce David to a Bible conference at Big Bear, he took the opportunity to regroup physically and spiritually after the fast pace of the last months.

The fleet had steamed out on cruise through the Panama Canal to the East Coast, to be gone until fall, taking along the men whose discipleship would now be tested under pressure of shipboard life. A cynical gob had stood beside Dedrick watching the harbor recede.

"Well, John, there goes Long Beach and there goes your religion. When you come back you won't have any." John knew he was right — except for one thing. Dawson had given him Philippians 1:6 to stand on and had challenged him to continue memorizing the Word as his defense against temptation. And the reports had been good.

Dawson saw in himself the same failure-prone law at work. He knew firsthand the truth Paul recorded in Romans 7:18, "For I know that in me (that is, in my flesh,) dwelleth *no good thing. . . .*" In recent weeks especially he had known such fierce temptation that it seemed the enemy was making a concerted effort to bring him down. God had used him, he knew, as evidenced in the lives of these beloved men into whom he had poured time, prayer, and effort for many months. Yet, looking inward, he wondered. The weakness and vulnerability he saw frightened him. He must turn, as he had a thousand times, to the instant refuge of memorized Scripture. "Now thanks be unto God, which always causeth us to triumph in Christ, and maketh manifest the savour of his knowledge by us in every place (2 Cor. 2:14)."

Never had he been more convinced of the indispensability of the Word for his own survival and for the protection and growth of the young Christian. Jesus had prayed concerning the men He had nurtured, "I have given them thy word." Daws found comfort in this as the lads navigated spiritually dangerous seas during the next months.

The life principles contained in The Wheel, which he had proved in his own experience and with boys clubs and Minute Men, were rooted as deep convictions as he discipled these sailors, teaching them to know the Book, to move God's hand in prayer, and to live the life before their shipmates and try to win them to Christ. He realized The Wheel had become his main message, along with Scripture memory, whenever he spoke to church groups. Recently at Montecito he had used for the first time an Old Testament verse which seemed to illustrate the four spokes in the life of Ezra (7:10): "For Ezra had prepared his heart to seek the law of the Lord, and to do it, and to teach in Israel statutes and judgments."

If diligent application of these truths was so clearly the secret of centering one's life in Jesus Christ, why was it so easy to slip away from them? In his own case, he had let himself be drawn into busyness, the constant ministering to others, along with the ever-present resistance of the flesh to things of the Spirit. Now was the time to get back to the basics. For openers, he would review 100 of his verses that day and witness to at least one non-Christian before he left Big Bear. On the last night of their stay, Dawson remembered he had not carried out his purpose. Slipping out of the meeting, he walked two or three miles, saw a man walking alone, and started a conversation. The man offered him a drink; Dawson offered him the water of life and told of his conversion. Though not convinced, the man was interested and gave his name and address for further contact.

Dawson had anticipated more time for study and prayer during the half-year the fleet was gone, but other ministries crowded in on him. In June he recruited a dozen leaders and managed a boys camp for his friend Bill Graves, with ninety-five boys of sixth grade through high school age spending eight days at a "ranch" in San Dimas Canyon. Some thirty-five made decisions to receive Christ, and thirty-five more acknowledged Him as Lord.

For the same camp the next summer, Dawson had every moment preplanned. Each of 175 boys arriving at Camp Bethel was given a pass stick with his name burned on it and space for his achievement and conduct records. A mimeographed program showed him the schedule of track events and swimming meets. Meetings would be announced by a bugle, meals by a bell, and recreation by a whistle. There was a song sheet with choruses to sing and a list of fourteen camp rules. ("No fighting or wrestling in cabins. Absolutely no loud hollering during meals. At meetings no sticks, knives, lighted flashlights, throwing of anything, moving around.")

Total participation by everyone in everything was the order of the day. Competition was keen, and the timid or sissified were scorned as "mama's boys." Any rule violator must surrender his pass stick and could not join in activities till he appeared before kangaroo court to receive justice. Some penalties were worked off on the "rock pile," resulting in rock pathways built to beautify the camp.

One of the camp speakers objected to the strict discipline.

"You're forcing those boys to follow rules, and we want to win their hearts." But Daws's belief that discipline would help win their hearts was vindicated when sixty-nine boys who had not already done so accepted Christ as Savior early in the week.

Dawson had tackled boys camp with his usual energy and perfectionist standards. It was the spirit shown in his first responsibility of ushering at church, when he decided to find a way to seat worshipers in the forward pews, and in his memorizing the entire chapter for the Sunday school lesson before teaching his first class. He despised mediocre effort, admired Spencer's I'd-give-my-right-arm response to the challenge to get down to business, and praised Dedrick's determination to memorize all 105 verses without missing a week.

The 33 Surfline home was used, as the sailors had hoped, in ministry to civilians. Night after night they came — relatives, friends, young men with their girl friends, and strangers brought in to hear the Gospel or enjoy Christian fellowship. A Wednesday Bible class for young people majored on how to witness. A Monday personal work class for nine high school boys included prayer, singing, checkout of memory verses, sharing of witness experiences, instruction from the Word, and critique of a live demonstration. Dawson also held a week's evangelistic meetings in a nearby church, regularly taught a Sunday school class, and wrote many follow-up letters to the servicemen.

Lewis Coates, soon to wed Helen Rittenhouse, had gone to help in the San Diego servicemen's work that Helen had once asked Dawson to take. Perhaps encouraged by Helen, an assertive and determined young woman, Lewis expressed his desire for an independent ministry after years of working in Dawson's shadow. Dawson persuaded him that what he called domination was merely leadership, but agreed Lewie was now ready to go out on his own.

Six weeks later Lewie and Helen, on a visit to 33 Surfline, met with Daws and Lila to form a Service Men's Bible Club council, with Lewie elected president for the year, Helen secretary, and Dawson treasurer. Stated purpose of the council, to include the Long Beach and San Diego homes and any others opened later, was "not building an organization, but bringing individual servicemen to know Christ and teaching them to win others." It should also answer those who felt the work should legitimize itself as a ministry sponsored by a church. Minutes of their meeting listed methods of reaching the objective, the word "Bible" prominent in each one: 1) Bible teaching in SMBC homes; 2) mailing Bible studies; 3) distributing books, pamphlets, and Bible study helps; 4) Bible study and prayer groups on ships and shore stations.

Dawson now broached an idea he had considered for the past year. Why not open an evening school for servicemen here at Surfline? He listed nine possible courses: Personal Work, Memory and Use of the Word, Boys Clubs, Homiletics, Public Speaking, Doctrine, Science and Theology, Prophecy, Salvation. The school did not materialize, but a week-long Bible conference planned for the servicemen during their Christmas leave undoubtedly grew from that idea.

A joyful family reunion followed the return of the fleet in the fall. Dawson noted tremendous growth in Dedrick and Goodrick and learned that Virgil Hook had led two men to Christ. Spencer and Harris had finished their Navy hitches and enrolled at Biola, leaving nine men to form the core of the shipboard work.

One sailor who had gone through basic training with Spencer was now on the cruiser *Cincinnati* at San Diego. Texas-born Dick Hightower, called simply R. W. until urged by the Navy to choose a name, met Dawson after hearing him speak at a church in San Pedro. Les introduced him. To Dick, the Bible Dawson carried looked bigger than a dictionary. "He stuck his face in mine and said, 'Are you a Christian?' I was so backward and self-conscious he almost scared me out of my wits."

Dawson started Dick in Bible reading and memorization that day and followed him up with the persistence of an encyclopedia salesman, encouraging him to bring his contacts to Surfline and to Camp Bethel weekends.

Within a few months Dick had led two shipmates named Fred and Red to Christ. This news Dawson had hoped for as a result of tenaciously building disciplines into the easygoing Hightower's life. Now he would include instruction on following up his spiritual babes. Dawson's letter of November 21, 1934 reveals both his detailed thoroughness in this effort and his intense interest in a lad some might have undervalued as just one of many.

Dear Dick —

Great! I Cor. 16:13! Surely glad you will be coming up with the Gang. If possible bring blankets.

Glad you have finished assignments. I am sending your book "All About the Bible." Now this book covers more territory than would be needed to gain knowledge on the study "How to prove the Bible is the word of God." However as I look over it I do not believe you had better skip any of it. Your future assignment will be to read this book through once thoroughly, not hastily. Then browse thru it and note chapters or pages that are valuable for use, then go through and underline each line you believe you will use in the future, then read all lines underlined. By then you will be ready for the next assignment which is to go to Fred (he likewise is to come to you) [Margin note: Fred should buy one of these immediately] and attempt to prove to each other verbally that the Bible is the word of God. In the meantime, be reviewing in your mind each point that you believe points to the truth of the Word. The balance of the assignment is to keep a handwritten record of every outstanding proof you learn of. Don't become frightened with this hard "set up." Just dig in and the first thing you know you'll have it. It is better to master a little than to be semi clear on a lot. The world takes note of a man who speaks with authority and you are learning these to use in convincing men.

Stay with the memory work. Be careful to let no verse you have learned become stale.

Keep looking for Gregory's "Seven Laws of Teaching." Review your poem now and then. Above all II Tim. 4:1, 2 —

Love in Christ
Daws

P.S. Of course study the book "Can a Young Man trust his Bible." Greet Harry, Red, Fred.

It is safe to assume Hightower showed up at the Christmas conference not only bringing blankets but bringing Fred and Red.

The week before Christmas was a high point in the 33 Surf-line ministry. Dawson had invited beloved Daddy Hale of Biola, Long Beach pastor Louis Bauman, Irwin Moon, radio Bible teacher Milo Jamison, and Lewie Coates as speakers. Sailors were sardined into the Home and the extra second floor rented for the month to accommodate them. It was a time of feasting on the Word by the hour, of singing and fellowship, of prayer by twos and groups, of enjoying meals served by the radiant Lila — with Dawson amid the three-ring confusion, his finger on every detail.

At four Wednesday morning, a phone call brought Dawson word of the tragic death of his brother Rowland, whose battered body was recovered from the foot of a cliff. Hiking in the mountains at Big Pines with others from his church youth group, twenty-three-year-old Rowland had seen his fiancée's foot slip at the top of a steep incline. He quickly reached out and pushed her in the direction of safety, losing his balance in the process, sliding down the 100-foot incline and dropping fifty feet over the cliff to his death.

Dawson gripped the phone as he stood in the pre-dawn light among the sleeping forms of sailors on the living room floor. Instinctively he prayed, giving thanks as God had schooled him to do in everything, realizing he would see his younger brother again, pleading for strength to break the news to his mother, his sister, and to dad who now lived with Mildred in Whittier.

It would be hardest for mother. Since her husband's departure from the household years before — their divorce would become final this month — Rowland's cheerful presence had been her last refuge from loneliness. She was still devoted to her family and nursed a self-sacrificing love for Dad Trotman, even while he was "keeping company" with a widow he wanted to be free to marry. Dawson felt sorry for his mother. He appreciated her gifts of food and funds to his ministry, but took them as the Lord's provision, returning little real warmth of love and feeling no remorse for his detachment from her orbit since his adolescent years. He had effectively sealed off from his otherwise warm and generous heart a relationship marred by her early preachments to a precocious son. It remained a blind spot with him the rest of her years. He made weak attempts to obey the command to "honor thy father and mother," writing to her when he was away on a trip, but to the end he treated her with polite deference as to a stranger.

The funeral was large. "The funeral parlors were packed out, with people standing out in the street — so many young people," Miss Mills said. "I was praying these friends would be touched for the Lord." Rowland's engaging personality had won him countless friends, and many were touched by his heroic sacrifice, by the fact that he knew his quick-witted move to save the girl would cost him his own secure footing on the mountainside. "He died like a man (as he laid down life) and with love," Dawson wrote. "I thank God for my dear brother whom I shall see soon after I see *Him*."

Rowland had worked with Walt Stanton as an apprentice plumber. His indifference to the Gospel had helped Dawson learn that aggressive witness to one's family was not as effective as "living the life" before them, waiting and praying for the right time to talk about their relationship to Christ. In Rowland's case that time had come three weeks before his death. Dawson discovered in conversation with his brother that he had only recently made a commitment to Christ and was beginning to grow. Knowing this had made it inexpressibly less painful for Dawson to put down the phone that early morning and do what he must do.

* * * *

While Daws seldom thought of finances, either their lack or their necessity, he did record with praise that they could enter 1935 debt free, thanks to Mother Trotman's gift of an eight-year-old Chevrolet coupe and a portion of Rowland's insurance which cleared outstanding bills. Daws and Lila purposed not to incur debts again if it was in their power to avoid them. A ledger kept at 33 Surfline showed the servicemen who gave regularly how expenses stood at any time. Monthly expenses included: rent $25, utilities $8, milk $3, laundry $2, telephone $2, eggs $1, newspaper $1. Dawson had given up the service station, and occasional gifts from friends, from the Montecito Church, and sales of silkscreened and woodburned wall mottoes combined with the sailors' subsidies to keep the ship afloat. They rejoiced in God's provision.

There were other reasons to rejoice. Goodrick had just won his first man to Christ. Men in various stages were growing. That spring, two years after he met Spencer, Dawson could list twelve "foundation men" in the work, two of them in Biola and ten in uniform, and four young Christians coming along. Good reports from the *West Virginia* in Bremerton included the conversion of the square-jawed Jim Downing, a prove-it-to-me Missourian, through his shipmates' prayers and his study of the Word. Jim had visited the Home at Point Ferman more than a year before, noting in his diary that he "got quite serious in discussing my soul's security and Dawson made me a wonderful exposition of the only important thing in life." The sincerity of Christian fellowship impressed him, but he concluded that it was more for homesick boys than for his kind of tough-fibered fighting man. Now that would change.

Dawson's follow-up letters to the men whenever ships were out were laced with hard-fisted challenge. One mimeographed epistle read:

> *My heart is thrilled as I read of the struggles that come your way and which you are fighting like real men. A battle is on, more fierce and more subtle than any physical combat, "for though we walk in the flesh, we do not war after the flesh (for the weapons of our warfare are not carnal, but mighty through God to the pulling down of strongholds)" (II Cor. 10:3, 4). We read in Psalm 108:13 "Through God we shall do valiantly; for He it is that shall tread down our enemies." Certainly this must be an important truth — Through God — the same meaning as "In Christ" (Phil. 4:13, II Cor. 2:14, II Cor. 5:17). When we are in*

Christ, Through Him stumbling blocks become stepping stones in this most wonderful life of being a Christian.

The near obsession with the value of time and the disdain for laziness which made Dawson bound through life as if he had not a moment to lose showed up in these early letters to the men:

> *The Lord Jesus Christ in a parable told of a Nobleman who entrusted his servants with a certain amount of money and exhorted them saying, "Occupy till I come." The story went on to tell how the Nobleman commended and rewarded those servants who obeyed him. Time is short men. The sun is hardly risen before it once again vanishes out of sight, days become weeks, weeks become months which slip into the past with alarming rapidity. Opportunities fade into the past and become but a haze in the memories of those who failed to heed their knocking. What shall we do. By the Grace of the Living God let us shake from every fibre of our being each tendency to be lazy, every temptation to waste time, and heed the Word of God as expressed in Phil. 3:13, 14; Rom. 12:11. Someone has said and rightly so — "The greatest waste of time is the waste of time in getting started." Another has summed up a valuable truth in the words "A minute saved is a minute earned." There is plenty to do for the man who is willing, and remember, dear fellow soldiers, that the business of living before and witnessing to men is the greatest business in the world, bar none.*

In the same letter he named seven cruisers which had no contact and exhorted the men to break through barriers of indifference and fear to reach men on these ships.

Dawson demonstrated his own sense of the value of time by never quitting. Driving to Los Angeles one March evening with fourteen-month-old Bruce, he was hit by an oncoming car which threw them both out on the road. He was grateful for God's protection from worse injury and that a few stitches taken in a Long Beach hospital, plus the other driver's insurance, settled the matter with little loss of time. Next day he wrote in his journal, "Find it hard to work but speak at C-E in Eve. Am helped."

Time, he felt, was to spend with the Lord or invest in other people. About a week after the accident Dick DeLong, a sailor from the *Texas* who had come to the Home two months before and made a decision to again walk with the Lord, brought a sailor friend for Dawson to "deal with." DeLong was growing steadily on the Minute Men disciplines of "verse a day, life a day, hour a day." Dawson spent two hours with the friend in the afternoon and another in the evening, then from 10:00 P.M. until 1:30 with the hungry DeLong sitting across the table, the open Bible between them. At one point while he expounded the Word, Dawson's chin sank to his chest and his voice trailed off. DeLong gently nudged him awake. "You were right there," he said, pointing to the place on the page where his teacher had stopped.

*   *   *   *

"My son, keep my words, and lay up my commandments with thee." The Bible, flopped open to Proverbs 7, lay limp across his palm as Dawson quoted from memory, eyes on the Saturday night circle of sailors at 33 Surfline, his voice driving each word home separately as if nailing them to the wall. "Bind them upon thy fingers, *write them upon the table of thine heart.*" Pursuing what one friend called "his one idea of getting ahead with the training of the fellows and his insistence upon pure Christianity," Dawson emphasized by turns such issues as systematic Bible study, consistent prayer life, living witness to Christ's power, and sensitive obedience in everyday life. But no one present would deny that the topic he harped on most often was Scripture memory. Not only had it been crucial in his own conversion, but decisive in his walk with the Lord in obedience and victory and his main equipment for witness and counsel. He had reason enough to be fanatic on the subject.

The sailors got his message, though not many responded with the tenacity of Les Spencer, who could say thirty-five years later that "the habit of memorizing the Word which was started then by the use of the card system is still in practice . . . an untold blessing and spiritual help to me down through the years."

Dawson's love of the unadorned Word also led him unwittingly to apply a principle of meditation that psychologists would later stress as an important influence on the mind — the purposeful use of the subconscious, the theory that the last dominant conscious thought will inevitably simmer in the unconscious mind during sleep. Dawson's habit, on a camping trip or even at home, was to say when conversation ended and lights were out, "All right, H.W.L.W.," after which a passage of Scripture would be quoted without comment as the last word spoken. The H.W.L.W. habit — His Word the Last Word — was popular on early Minute Men trips, but Daws and Lila continued the practice through the years, as did others, as a way to end a day with thoughts fixed on the Lord.

But the current need was to find a way to train the men in memory. Not since the failure of the 1928 booklet system and the blank-cards-in-packet attempt had there been a workable system. He had given the first few sailors handpicked verses to list or mark in their Bibles, but as the number increased he saw they needed a better method. Oscar Lowry, who along with Tom Olson inspired him by their belief in memorizing Scripture, had published a card memory system which some of the men used. Dawson liked the card idea and felt with verses better selected for the men's specific needs he could enthusiastically sell them on its use. Analyzing his previous memory systems, he formed a conclusion that might have been a Parkinson's law: *Systems don't work by themselves; they must be made to work by personal effort.* That effort he was ready to give.

Starting with The Wheel, he chose the three best verses on the Word, prayer, living the life, and witnessing to be printed on twelve cards. To engineer the card size he borrowed a sailor's blue regulation jumper and measured the depth and width of the pocket often used for cigarettes, then tailored the cards so that a pack of them would fit neatly into that pocket. The reference was printed on the back of each card, the verse on the front.

Jim Downing recalled how one afternoon at Surfline Dawson and Lewie Coates hotly debated the selection of the remainder of thirty-five topics pertinent to the life of a young

Christian* and the three best verses for each topic. "I'm glad it was the Word they were arguing about," he said. Final selections for that 105-verse *Topical Memory System* were remarkably practical for the growing Christian, in effect pioneering the concept of learning relevant verses for specific personal use.

Another flash of inspiration led to awarding a leather pack to anyone who learned the first twelve Wheel verses, building incentive into the early part of the course. In time "the pack" in the Navy jumper pocket became a universal symbol of a man "down to business" in the Word. For those on deck when the course was new, there was little choice. "I was given the 105 and told to get cracking," Dick Hightower says. Dedrick accepted a challenge to learn three a week straight through and did it, though he reported to Dawson he had to hang from the rafters once or twice to stay awake and finish. The memory system would be revised and redesigned repeatedly, but for now Dawson was delighted with this new tool to help "get the job done." In his April newsletter to the men he reported that fifty persons, mostly civilians, already had memory sets.

Dawson's search for efficiency in doing business for God led to devising a simple filing system for quotations, clippings, and study notes. Then in true form as a compulsive sharer he noted, "I should have had this five or six years ago; in other words, I shall do all possible to see that other young Christians learn about how to use such files."

Preparing Bible study helps for the servicemen also concerned him. A man could do his reading without helps, could hear the Word at church and from Bible teachers at the Home, and could get the benefit of the study of other men of God through good books. But Dawson saw a need for written study helps, especially for those just beginning. As he often did, he began with someone else's idea, improved and adapted it, then applied his own genius to enlisting everyone within reach to do it. He worked over Helen Rittenhouse's beginning study which she

---

*Topics following the first four were: Sin, Penalty, Atonement, Appropriation; Christ the Way, Christ in You; Victory, Holy Spirit, God, Praise; Second Coming, Judgment, Reward, Separation; Obedience, Fruit, Faith, Love, Peace, Patience, Hope, Trust; Assurance, Forgiveness, Giving, Power, Guidance, Tongue, Fear, Temperance, Temptation.

had sent out in three parts: first week, the Bible; second week, how to become a Christian; third week, what to do about it. Whether Dawson's mimeographed study evolved from this or was completely new, "The Christian's Salvation" based on 2 Corinthians 1:10 dealt with verses on deliverance from sin's penalty through Christ's death, deliverance from sin's power, and future deliverance from sin's presence. The study was widely used, and other courses were in the mill, but nothing of substance was produced until years later when servicemen were given the inductive Bible study plans he had worked out for civilian Bible clubs, along with question-and-answer studies by Keith L. Brooks.

M id-Depression 1935 was a time for conservative second thoughts on any project requiring finances. Except for Dawson Trotman, whose God wasn't limited by tight money. That spring the idea took shape for a gospel team tour across the U.S. with Spencer and Harris, Dedrick, who was still in the Navy, Dawson, and John Visick, a civilian friend who could accompany the quartet's singing in meetings. It would be a pioneering venture in a day when traveling gospel teams were non-existent.

The trip would have three purposes: to contact servicemen and perhaps establish ministry bases at Norfolk, Philadelphia, New York, and the new Great Lakes Training Station in Chicago; to visit the homes of some of the servicemen; and to hold meetings in their home churches, challenging young people with the possibilities of the dynamic Christian life. Les, Gurney, and Daws had talked of such a trip for a year. Helen Ritten- house objected, however, giving the ultimatum that while their work shared the same name — Service Men's Bible Club — there would be no trip until local bills were paid. But the idea persisted, the debts were paid, and Home expenses current. Acquisition of a 1927 Buick was among the circumstances causing Dawson to write the servicemen that "in no uncertain way God has led us to definitely plan the tour." No funds were in sight for the trip, but God would provide as they had seen Him do before.

Mailing a mimeographed map of their tentative route, Dawson asked servicemen who wanted the team to visit their homes or churches to put them in touch. Lewie Coates, still nominal director of Service Men's Bible Clubs (No. 1 in San Diego, No. 2 in Long Beach), offered to man the Home in Dawson's absence. Lewie and Helen had been married six months and were continuing the San Diego ministry. Horton and Lois MacDavid also offered to help.

The quartet, Daws wrote, would be billed as Service Men's Bible Club Minute Men. The colorless label Helen originally put on her Bible studies merely for identification had by default become the name of the work in two ports. Then Milo Jamison objected to the obvious similarity to his University Bible Clubs. Dawson, therefore, considered "The Navigators" and late in 1934 had stationery printed with that name, the subtitle being "A Bible Club for Service Men" and the motto "To Know Christ and to Make Him Known." The sailors were unenthusiastic, perhaps associating the name with Dawson's former Navigator clubs for small boys.

But the Service Men's Bible Club Minute Men who set out June 30 for 12,000 miles and two months of meetings found the unwieldly name too heavy to tote. They probably worked over the idea as they chugged across country. Dedrick, the phlegmatic, unschooled intellectual, had studied navigation and knew the terms. They began to find parallels to spiritual navigation. All men were out on life's sea, some adrift without rudder or compass, others with no captain or home port. A Navigator was under way with Jesus Christ aboard as Captain of his salvation, the Bible as his chart and nautical almanac, and the Holy Spirit as his compass. Once a man learned to navigate, demonstrating these principles in his daily life, he could steer another on a true course and teach him in turn to navigate with Christ as his Captain. The name Navigators sounded better all the time, and by the end of the trip it stuck.

Dawson could not have foreseen that the Navigator name, like The Wheel and the memory verse pack, would become symbols of a way of life, denoting not so much association with a group as a distinctive spirit and quality of Christian living. The Navigators would remain a durable name for a world-wide movement, not forced to change as the work became international, as the names of some missions had changed to fit expansion to new fields. The motto "To Know Christ and to Make Him Known" continued from that day to fit the spirit and purpose of the movement which began with making Christ known to one man at a time and teaching that man to disciple another.

The '27 Buick took the team to Dedrick's hometown in Texas, Harris's in Arkansas, and Spencer's in Illinois, then east to Philadelphia and New York, down the coast to Norfolk, back across the heartland to Salt Lake City, and down to Long Beach. Ministering in churches, witnessing to individuals, singing and giving testimony by radio, the Bible-centered Navy men were a curiosity, for it was at least seven years before every family would be sending a son to serve in World War II. The neat, laconic Spencer, warmhearted Gurney, brainy Dedrick, talented Visick, and tireless impresario Dawson, brought the Gospel to many a town in a form it had not yet witnessed. The team enjoyed the warm hospitality of Christian families and unforgettable fellowship in the car as they traveled. Doubtless more than once the day ended with one or another declaring "H.W.L.W." and signing off with the quoted Word of God.

B y the end of the year the Long Beach Navigators had moved to an eight-room house at 1114 Pacific, the $65 rent two and one-half times that of Surfline. Dawson and Lila brought to the new Home faith for the larger budget and their promise of Isaiah 60:11, gladly sacrificing their privacy for the joys of the ministry God gave them. Not that everything was roses. There were probably still those such as Dawson once mentioned in his journal: "2 or 3 of the fellows . . .

who cause our hearts to sink upon their arrival each time. But God be thanked. Jas. 1:2-4."

But contrasted with the two or three were the men with whom the bond of love and fellowship was closer than blood ties. And always there was an aura of joy and camaraderie at the Home — with an impartial welcome for all who came. Navy custom crept in, as in the shipboard routine of port side personnel standing watch one night and starboard side the next. Goodrick was in charge of the port watch for dishwashing and another man the starboard watch on alternate nights. Dedrick, the only Navigator petty officer, tossed in his entire pay check to support the Home after paying his insurance and withholding a pittance for pocket money. This covered probably half the monthly overhead.

At a December business meeting with a few key servicemen and the Coateses, now San Diego Navigators, Dawson was elected director and Dedrick secretary-treasurer. A plan was made to issue printed receipts to acknowledge contributions and to have annual meetings in December to report on finances and handle business. Key servicemen would represent ships and stations where the work warranted it — they now numbered eight — at special meetings whenever called. But by next December Coates seemed to be ministering more to collegians than to servicemen, and it did not occur to Dawson that his own term of service as director had expired.

"I have a surprise for you," Lila had written Dawson during the gospel team trip. He was thrilled when his first daughter, Ruth, arrived, two days before his thirtieth birthday. Dawson was extravagant in praise of his son ("I love him a million times a million," he confided to his journal), but when his blue-eyed, curly-haired daughter took her place in the family, his expressions bordered on the fatuous. "Ruth, ah what a beauty . . . peaches and cream complexion . . . million dollar smile . . . she never cries. . . ." And she didn't. Bruce had cried so long and loud his first few weeks that Dawson decided to train Ruthie not to cry. He tried his idea beginning in her sixth week, and six weeks later she had learned.

Hightower, Harris, and other regulars learned much about training children by observing how Dawson and Lila handled their children, a process complicated, Gurney said, by all the sailors "who wanted to spoil the baby." One tenet firmly applied was Ecclesiastes 8:11, ". . . sentence against an evil work . . . executed speedily. . . ." Hightower recalls Dawson driving him to the dock, with the children in the back seat of the car. When Ruth accused Bruce of a minor misdemeanor which he admitted, Dawson reached back and spanked his hand without stopping the car or waiting till later.

Insisting on obedience was another cardinal principle. "Let's see who can pick up the most toys," Lila cajoled Bruce once when he had ignored her first plea. Of course she won the race. This method was discontinued when the other parent overheard and required his son to pick up all the toys himself — and promptly. Stern measures were balanced with great quantities of loving attention, assuring the children of their importance to the household. As they grew older they sometimes resented the severity of their father's discipline; the sailors, too, felt the imaginative penalties he levied were often harsh. In later years, however, the children's resentments had eroded, and they expressed thankfulness that he was strict with them.

Those who came to the Home saw an attitude between husband and wife that was rare even in Christian homes. "They were sweethearts all the time," said an intimate friend. "Our entire married life was colored by Daws's and Lila's respect for each other. Loving kindness. Never a snide remark or bringing up some idiosyncrasy that should not be aired." And no press agent could have done a better promotion than they each did for the other — to any audience.

The new Home was roomier than Surfline, and sailors came in numbers, especially on weekends — twelve for breakfast, sixteen for dinner on a typical Sunday — though the location did not make it convenient just to drop in for a snack. Dawson began to compare the ministry at the two Homes and concluded that very few sailors who had dropped in at 33 Surfline had followed through in discipleship. Of possibly 200 men touched, where were they? The food and recreation approach had not paid off. He felt that to many of them the presentation of eternal matters had been too easy, lacking the teeth of price-paying discipleship to which Jesus referred when He told a prospect that "foxes have holes, and birds of the air have nests; but the Son of Man hath not where to lay his head." The men who had grown in discipleship were mainly the inner core — members of the Nav family. Dawson began to see that the Navigator Home was unique in its possibilities for a ministry in depth in the most natural of settings. Having begun by using the home for ministry merely as a resource at hand, he now felt God had led them to discover an invaluable medium for the special work of disciplemaking.

The fleet was out for much of 1936, the first full year at 1114 Pacific, but not all ships at once, with the result that Dawson found he could give more time to individual men. He noted that although a solid work was under way on only three ships, there were down-to-business men on a dozen more. Contrasting the oak tree's slower growth and its permanence with the mushroom's overnight perishability, he was reassured that the slower growing shipboard ministry showed signs of enduring.

True, his efforts were scattered during the year with other side ministries, but he had kept close touch with the sailors by mail and concentrated time on key men and groups from ships when in port. In fact, the frequent sailings pressed him to give priority to developing key men able to head the work on their ships while at sea. Jim Downing was now leader on the *West Virginia*. Goodrick, Dedrick, and Hook, with Hightower and others, had followed their shipmates to Biola. (Dedrick, ineligible for Hebrew and Greek courses because he lacked academic background, audited the classes and passed the examination with the highest grade in the class.)

John Streater, who had gone through the 105 verses in less than a month, was key man on the *Mississippi*, teaching the Bible class and leading its gospel team services ashore. The Gospel team of the *West Virginia*, dry-docked three months in Bremerton, held many meetings in churches, gaining confidence in winning people to Christ and following them up. Monday nights were for work aboard ship, with Bible study and memory work often running till midnight. There was a Sunday Bible class on board, a Tuesday night class, and a daily prayer meeting with the chaplain in his office. Bill Goold, a *West Virginia* transplant, led the *New Mexico's* Bible study in the conning tower, a meeting place secured by their chaplain.

Daws could count one or more growing Christians on twelve ships where there was not yet a strong work. His goal, to see a key man on every battleship by year's end, fell short by four ships — the *Arizona*, the *Tennessee*, the *Oklahoma*, the *Idaho*. But he was not discouraged; God had fulfilled His good promise in the lives of stalwart men, and he could only rejoice. This he did in a style reminiscent of Queen Esther, dispatching mimeographed letters at Christmas to those scattered abroad, with a special Scripture promise and challenge for each ship.

The usual pattern was Bible study on board ship, with time at the Home given more to meetings to hear Bible teachers, and the key men getting personal time with Dawson. Whenever he spoke at Friday and Saturday night meetings, he dwelt at length on one of The Wheel basics, such as importance of Bible study, until he sensed everyone had heard him, then went on to memory, prayer, and so on, singling out certain men in the room as examples of success or failure in these things. Since the crowd often included new men, he was prone to repeat, as his aim was to move every man present to the point of conviction and decision. So by the time the last man had got the message, boredom set in for the others. The *West Virginia* men called Dawson aside to protest. His messages lacked spiritual power, they told him; they lacked a freshness that seemed to betray lax study and prayer habits. After all, Trotman had instilled in them the principle of pacesetting — that life only comes from life and that it is useless to challenge a man to do something one is not doing himself.

Soon afterward Jim Downing exhorted Dawson about his stewardship of time and talent. As he saw it, Dawson frittered away time designing notebook prayer pages and memory folders and doing household chores that he could better use in systematic prayer and study of the Word. His messages were long and rambling, seemingly unprepared.

This kind of rebuke Dawson could have resented and sharply rebutted, for as Hightower observed, "There were many instances in which Daws wasn't willing to admit he had made a mistake or would make one." Accepting reproof was most difficult, especially from these his younger brothers; but he respected them and knew they were right. Any defense he made — such as his having to spend time repairing old cars and do shopping for Lila when she was ill — would not pass muster with these men close enough to the situation to see it as an excuse. He purposed some immediate reforms in his schedule, especially to get more time with the Lord.

He had memorized Proverbs 17:10, "A reproof entereth more into a wise man than an hundred stripes into a fool," and the time had come to apply it. But apart from the embarrassment of admitting failure to his juniors, Dawson must have been gratified to see these men he had brought up in the faith grow in responsibility and zeal for Christ to the point where they could and would reprove him. Their spiritual insight and courage were in fact a tribute to his ministry, for which he could thank God.

In his journal Daws recorded the incidents briefly, but entries made in following weeks evidenced his change of heart in humbling himself before God's reproof. Much more time spent in study and memory of the Word. New programs laid out for prayer. He and Lila reading the life of D. L. Moody.

> *For the past weeks God has been dealing with me.*
> *The Lord is working something in my heart that*
> *is more than ordinary. Oh that His name might be*
> *glorified through my life whether by life or death.*

The next day,

> *I am strengthened as I realize that others whom*
> *God has used have had the same heart struggles*
> *that I have . . . . It has been so long since my heart*
> *condition has moved me to tears, but these came*
> *as I saw the sinfulness of my life in view of the*
> *Holyness of God and the preciousness of souls.*

*   *   *   *

Maintaining certain disciplines was a lifelong struggle for Dawson, with sustained victories dwindling often to defeat. Yet failures never dampened his enthusiasm for new beginnings, which dot his journal like mileposts — a new schedule for morning prayer, for Scripture memory and review, for study, with no shade of doubt that he would follow it through indefinitely. He often encouraged Lila to get on a schedule. She followed with the willing spirit of an obedient wife and with as much conviction as she could muster along with her exhausting pace and work load with the Home and family. Every few months he referred to her starting on a diet to lose weight, which was a constant problem. Swimming and tennis were also pursued by turns, semi-faithfully.

Late in 1936 Dawson felt the Lord would have him revive the Minute Men program. "Upon investigation into the hearts of the Minute Men it is found that each one needs very definitely the help that this plan will generate." He had given the plan to individual servicemen, but it had been every man for himself with no coordination as a group. Now he sent a letter to the ten men on the "set up," naming January and July as the months each would report his progress, reports to be in a record book open to all of them.

Self-checking without reporting would be done other months. Assignments were not the identical "daily dozen" of earlier Minute Men but were based on The Wheel, with such added projects as writing a statement of faith or explaining the Gospel. Dawson challenged the men to "put our shoulders to the 'Wheel' and carry out the plan as given to us by Him."

Besides the ten Minute Men, including those who began in the Navy, four new men were candidates and ten were being considered. Although the plan was available to any who requested it, Dawson's promotion of it as an exclusive privilege put heavy compulsion on a recruit to follow through; one not likely to "tackle the set up" was simply not offered it. "I wasn't interested in regimentation," recalled a UCLA student whose roommate was a Minute Man. "I am sure Daws sensed my unwillingness to go 100 percent and did not approach me. He was cordial but busy . . . devoting his time to those who were ready to go."

The men using the checkup system probably had a normal dislike for the everydayness of the discipline. Yet they testified to their need for such a program to corral the perversity of the flesh. The fact that some failed and dropped out led to the broad conclusion that discipline imposed from outside doesn't work. Whether those who continued in the program would have been as effective for the Lord without it is not known. Lois MacDavid observed that she had never met anyone with the fiber and character of these men. Indeed, the evidence is that imposed discipline does not work without an inner response of desire to match it. There is also strong indication that those who do desire to follow Christ rarely develop to their full potential as disciples without some form of discipline to draw them toward excellence. The so-called mechanistic regimen could not be held responsible for destroying those who lacked inner motivation to follow Christ, but it can be justly credited with contributing to the growth and development of those who did have desire.

"An important meeting and day of prayer is called for Sunday, January 3. We shall have breakfast and then adjourn for The Business," Dawson wrote the Minute Men. "I would like to suggest you spend the first day of the year alone with the Lord. 1937 must see the bulwarks of Satan crushed beneath the all-powerful arm of the Lord. We shall ask God to make every day a day of victory for Himself. The time has come to get up off our faces and meet the enemy of the Lord and of our soul as we have been commanded. Take heart, fellow laborers. He hath said, 'I am the God of all flesh and there is nothing too hard for Me.' "

Helen Coates asked Dawson to consider making the Minute Men plan available to young women. He purposed to do that.

A spring Sunday evening in San Juan Capistrano. Lights shining from church windows. Inside, more than a hundred souls listening to a half-dozen Navy men speak by turns from the pulpit. Each brief message spoken with conviction in crisp, straightforward style, buttressed by Scripture quoted from an open Bible. Yet each was different — one a personal story of decision to give his life to Christ, another a testimony to the power of prayer or the value of the Word of God in daily living. The service was planned to balance testimony with presentation of the Gospel and of victory in Christ.

They were Navigators of the *West Virginia* gospel team, invited through their chaplain to Community Presbyterian Church. Their leader, the ramrod-straight Jim Downing, now gunner's mate third class, spoke last, ending with an invitation for those wishing to decide for Christ to come forward. Though the team had earnestly prayed the meeting would honor Christ, they were totally surprised to see how many responded. Downing stationed team members in corners of the room and formed waiting lines of inquirers for individual counseling. "It was a revival!" they reported to Dawson very late that night back in Long Beach.

The *West Virginia* and *Mississippi* gospel teams that spring of 1937 were made up of sailors established in their faith and trained in leading others to Christ. Men from other ships joined them on occasion for ministry ashore at Long Beach, San Francisco, or Seattle. During ten weeks in Bremerton the *Mississippi* team held twenty-three meetings and turned down as many more invitations — meetings in churches and youth groups, at a merchant marine mission, a guard house, a conservation camp, and sometimes a radio broadcast.

On the *West Virginia* men from all over the ship squeezed in among the gears and machinery in the anchor windlass room for the Tuesday night Bible class where Downing taught an evangelistic lesson. Other nights the smaller group met there or in the ordnance tool room for prayer and advanced Bible study or work on memory verses. Downing was a gifted teacher, willing to fill every evening with a class assignment on his own ship or one nearby. In time the *West Virginia* had a Bible class almost every night, either doctrinal, topical, or analytical, so that long before Pearl Harbor it was dubbed "The Floating Seminary."

Downing, seen as a disciplinarian, a man of strong faith and zeal to know the Word — qualities not surprising in one whose pre-conversion ambition was to be president — was described by a shipmate as "the only man I ever met who was totally committed to what he believes twenty-four hours a day." By example and some pressure he led men to center their lives in Christ and live a life that attracted friends they could win to

Christ. Radioman Larry Dundon of the admiral's staff came to the anchor windlass room class. "I got interested because I liked the fellows personally," he said. "I began to read the Word. Then one night after Bible class I went up on deck and suddenly realized this was what I wanted more than anything — this feeling of security in Christ that they had. I just opened my heart and the Lord came in." Many others came to Christ through such friendship evangelism because they "liked the fellows personally."

Daws saw great potential in Downing, not yet two years old in the Lord. "Downing surely gives evidence of wonderful growth. I verily believe this man will really be a power in the Hand of God," he wrote in his journal. And later: "Jim and I have had increasingly blessed fellowship and the Lord has used the time to the edification of both of us. Espec to me. . . . He is demonstrating, I believe, what God can do through a man that is fully yielded."

Dawson came to regard Jim as his deputy in the work and his stand-in for weekend meetings at the Home when he was away. His confidence in Downing was shown by his acceptance of the younger man's "exhortation," as the straightforward method of dealing with faults was called. He had mentioned in his journal Jim's word about "things in my life" and steps taken to correct them. He tried to remedy complaints about his long messages by extra study and preparing compact presentations of subjects he regularly preached on. (Sincere as this effort was, rambling length remained a lifelong mark of Dawson's messages; though audiences were locked in rapt attention and often convicted, he continually ran overtime.)

But "exhortation" was a two-way street. Later in the year Dawson spent time with Downing "talking of things that might help Jim in his life." This practice of man-to-man admonition among Navigators became a normal element of discipling, in obedience to their Lord's command. Yet it was not common practice outside Navigator circles, nor has it been in large measure since. It remained a distinguishing mark among these men in whom obedience to God overcame fear of man and whose bonds of love in Christ would bear the risk of lost friendship. The practice has contributed much through the years to building stalwart soldiers of Christ.

Downing kept close to Dawson in the ministry, sending reports when his ship was out. Yet he held different views on how the ministry should be conducted and dared to assert them. Doubtless he could have profited from being more teachable and less independent, but Dawson was willing to let him learn on his own terms.

One point of difference was that Downing ran a taut ship, giving men the Gospel and the requirements of discipleship on a take-it-or-leave-it basis, while feeling that Dawson wasted his time on third-team men. Dawson, willing to spend more time on a man and with as much desire to see a less likely Joe come through for Christ as a more promising one, spread a wider net. But, Jim reasoned, why use Saturday afternoons playing volleyball at the Navigator Home with men not interested in getting down to business, when that was the best time for evangelism aboard ship? So the *West Virginia* men, infused with Jim's philosophy that the ministry is on the ship, spent less time than others did at the Home. Jim made this point again in a letter to Dawson after the ship had put in at New York and the gospel team had been kept busy ashore. "As we received more than a hundred recruits aboard just before leaving, we have open doors for service traveling with us which is no doubt a greater field than we left behind."

Jim also disagreed with Dawson on the importance of follow-up. Downing believed that if necessary the Holy Spirit could see to the follow-up once a man was converted, but thought Trotman doubted a man should lead another to a decision for Christ unless he was prepared to adequately follow him up. Dawson's drive to help *every* man make it, even if it meant fanning into life a very small spark of desire, may have reflected his need to do everything well or not at all. It did demonstrate his individual interest in every person, evidenced by warm attention to that person's spiritual need at whatever level he found it. All resources must be focused on the other fellow.

So the *West Virginia* under Downing steered its own course, and the key men from other ships tied in more closely to Dawson's direction. There were times when Daws wished the *West Virginia*ns would stand up and help work with the unsaved and young Christians from other ships, instead of heading back to the ship after a meeting.

At one point that year Dawson abruptly replaced Jim on the Navigator business committee and as key man on the ship on the grounds that he had been hitting it too hard and needed relief from responsibility. True, Downing had driven himself too hard, but the move also aimed to bring the maverick leadership under Trotman's control. Though he delighted in the spiritual growth and development of his men, he paradoxically but humanly enough reacted when one rose to challenge his own leadership. It was an unrecognized chink in his armor that plagued him and cost him in later years.

For months his newsletters reported doings of the *West Virginia* and other ships without prominent mention of Downing's name. But their relationship returned to even keel, Downing was still de facto leader in the fleet, and the "demotion" was forgotten.

The twenty-four-hour servicemen's retreat at Camp Bethel had its problems. Dawson was unable to get two of the speakers he wanted, and another speaker arrived almost too late for his meeting. Transportation for the men from Long Beach and San Diego was difficult. He had to estimate by faith the number expected, coming within one of the final count of sixty-three. And the key man from the *Texas* brought a number of non-Christians, for whom the retreat was not geared. Yet Dawson recorded the affair with typical buoyancy.

> *The first comers have a dandy ball game.... After supper we sing out under the trees. Up to the big Log Cabin for the meeting and we have a very wonderful time. The testimonies are real and the message by Art Ward is just right. No decisions were made in the meeting for the Lord but after the meeting there were a couple .... Downing gave a fine message on the Anchor, Heb. 6 [and] spoke again at the morning Church Service .... Had a fine time of recreation ... and then a good dinner just before we leave .... The trip was a*

real blessing but would have been better if there
had not been so many unsaved. The tone of the
Camp was under par.

The necessity of shaping the program to the newcomers'
needs had short-changed the down-to-business men, Dawson
felt, especially when these weekend retreats at the family-run
Camp Bethel were planned for their fellowship and spiritual
feasts in the Word. But he concluded God had overruled for
His purposes, and that was enough.

*   *   *   *

For nearly four years of Navigator ministry Daws and Lila
held to the practice of not mentioning financial needs and
trusting God to provide. Without self-pity, in a spirit of ex-
pectancy they marveled at the ways He did it. So regular was
His supply that even critical victories were recorded in Dawson's journal as routine. A check came in time to cover the
utilities bill. A serviceman handed him money that bought
gasoline, groceries, and postage stamps. A sailor asked Lila for
a complete shopping list and brought back groceries in time
for company dinner that evening. The driver of a milk truck
which had broken down knocked at the door asking if they
could use a large quantity of milk that would have spoiled.

Once on a trip to Pasadena Dawson noticed the car was
nearly out of gas. "I don't have any money, do you?" he asked
his friend.

"Yeah — but what about this faith business? What would
you do if I weren't here?"

"All right, keep your money and let's just see what happens."
Moments later a flat tire or some circumstance made it necessary to move the seat cushions, under which they found
enough coins to buy gasoline. Dawson had known God would
provide; now his friend knew.

But faith fixed in the Lord did not presuppose faith in a
certain method of provision. So when Dawson observed finances
running behind early in 1937 and he felt the Lord would
either provide or indicate a move, he was not too surprised
that He signaled the latter. Not only a move in location but in
finance policy. Dawson asked Lt. Emil Pearson, the one commissioned officer involved in the work, what he thought of

informing some of the inner circle that the ministry needed their financial support. Pearson strongly recommended giving them opportunity to know and share in the needs and volunteered to increase his own monthly gift.

His courage bolstered by Pearson's advice, Dawson talked to the few anchor men from each ship, getting an enthusiastic response out of all proportion to his reluctance to present it. One man probably expressed it for many — he was thankful to know the financial facts as he had thought the work was underwritten by a church. Once the anchor men were told, albeit apologetically, Dawson would resume the no-mention policy, determined there would "never be a plea for finances. Only those intimately connected with the active work will have the matters set clearly before them for careful and prayerful consideration."

"In those days when finances were an unmentionable subject, it was almost anathema for anyone to mention the matter," recalled Floyd Robertson, Spencer's contemporary who later became an officer. "Dawson was convinced the Lord was leading that way. Then when the day came [that] the needs were made known, *that* was the Lord's leading. To some that would be difficult to understand. But to me there is no inconsistency. The Lord led one way in the beginning and another way later. That reflects spiritual maturity rather than inconsistency." But though Dawson felt the Lord led, his strange diffidence on the subject stayed with him through the years; it was never easy to ask people to give. For him it was more blessed, in the extreme, to give than to receive.

Lt. Pearson further suggested that the Navigators buy or build a home, offering a $500 down payment himself so that the $65 now paid in monthly rent could be applied toward an equity. Dawson decided, since the fleet would soon leave on a three-month summer cruise, to give up the Home at 1114 Pacific, store the furniture, and move to Camp Bethel for the summer where rent would be only $10 a month. The $55 a month saved this way — an amount not in hand but considered so — could be used to buy a car! Through a friend's good offices Dawson purchased a 1929 Packard for $150 and made the move, planning to buy a home in the fall.

*　　*　　*　　*

At Camp Bethel during the first week Daws noted that "the relaxation of these few days has certainly put new vigor into my blood." He set up a woodburning workshop under a large oak tree and made mottoes. Lila was enjoying the cabin life, and the two children played barefoot under the trees. The scent of orange blossoms from a nearby grove wafted on the fresh, dry air. Clear sunrises vied with moonlit nights to highlight the semi-arid beauty of the low hills. Dawson was glad for the building and repair chores around camp that tired him physically. Work with his hands was therapeutic, and the weeks of renewing in the outdoors timely.

He wrote many letters to men on the ships that summer and spent hours in the Word, reading long portions, memorizing and reviewing verses, and praying unhurriedly. He treasured these times alone with the Lord. Yet they were somehow different from the protracted love feasts of former days. Now after only an hour or two in the Word and prayer he was restless, wanting to be back among people to whom he could minister. *Had his earlier pure devotion to Christ dimmed?* he wondered, as he found himself seeking His fellowship more from keenly sensed need for the Spirit's guidance and as a catalyst for his ministry. He pondered it briefly, as one does who is not given to introspection. He *did* love Christ with all his heart, God knew. But perhaps there were stages in one's relationship to Him and the rapt devotion of courtship had now given way to the business of living and working together, with his attention naturally dominated by desire to be about his Father's business. So much God wanted done in the world and so few ready to do it. He had no alternative but to throw himself into the breach as if he were the only one God had called to carry out His purpose.

He knew, without presumption, that God had called him to a special work related to His program for reaching the world. The Isaiah promises had been renewed to him over and over again. How they would be fulfilled or what directions he would be led to go, he did not know, but his blood raced with enthusiasm. He had been too busy doing the thing at hand to plan long-range strategy. God would reveal that in time. For now it was enough to know He was working out His sovereign plan. The glory of Christ alone was worth investing all he had, his time and effort, his family and home and privacy. Of this and some other fundamentals he was certain, whereas others were more fluid.

One certainty was the life principles of The Wheel. The Word, prayer, witnessing, and living a Christ-centered life were as essential as food, oxygen, rest, and exercise were to the body. He noted that the *West Virginia* men had printed their own edition, using a helmsman's wheel, with one-line instructions for living the Christian life: "WORD — at least fifteen minutes each day. PRAYER — morning, noon, evening. LIFE — live to make Christ attractive. WITNESS — contact one weekly for Christ."

Follow-up was also basic, as he had learned early through seeing the fruit of his own evangelism wither on the vine from neglect. Though he hoped his keen desire to win men from darkness to life in Christ would never dim, he knew follow-up would always be a life line in his ministry and an emphasis to all God allowed him to influence. So, too, Scripture memory, an imperative in his conversion and his entire Christian life. And personal discipline — he meant to emphasize throughout his ministry some means and ways to defy inertia and strengthen the willing spirit against weakness of the flesh. Inconsistency was a dragon he fought in his own life, and so he felt sure it was a problem for others..

The outlines of his future ministry were not yet clear. He saw no boundaries or horizons and did not feel he must confine his efforts to Navy men or businessmen or boys — God's hand had been on his work with these groups and with others. Nor was he locked into specific methods. He had experimented with study plans and produced a card system for Scripture memory, but much more was needed in development of materials. How the work would be supported financially was still an open question, though his conviction was unshakable that God would supply.

Also firm in his thinking was the unique worth of the Navigator Home as a base for ministry. He had found the home, with Lila so ably filling her role in self-denying service, a vital resource for discipling men for God — a resource virtually unused in Christendom so far as he knew.

He had reached a conclusion, evolving from the necessity

of follow-up, that obeying the Lord's command to get the Gospel to all the world meant not only thorough discipling of individuals, but training an army of leaders in depth — men who could be trainers of others. The vast size of the task demanded it. How to do this without neglecting individual attention in favor of work with larger numbers and groups he did not know, but it must be done.

He rose and paced slowly along the stream, head down, Bible clutched in one hand with a finger in the Gospel of John where he had been reviewing verses. He knew he needed these times to give him fresh perspective on the job ahead, to renew his physical reserves, and refurbish his spirit. Yet it was hard to be out of circulation even temporarily; he longed for contact with lives waiting to be influenced for Christ. The constant stream running through his mind found its way again into his mimeographed letter to the servicemen from Camp Bethel:

> *Time is short. Even God cannot bring back lost opportunities and precious hours. We read in the Word that we are to redeem the time because the days are evil . . . and to "awake to righteousness and sin not for some have not the knowledge of God, I speak this to your shame." Oh, if we could only get a glimpse of the wonders of heaven and Life Eternal and the contrasting view of a lost soul . . . without hope, we might take this business more seriously. There is hope for men, and it is our blessed privilege to tell men of the way of escape God has made through the atoning death of His only begotten Son. Whatever you do, don't let the Thief of time rob you of the Joy of leading precious souls out of Darkness into His Marvelous light.*

West Virginia Gospel team—1937. Jim Downing, center back, John Prince, front left.

First Navigators met in this garage behind the service station, 1933.

III

Training Trainers of Men

1937-1942

Daws and Lila enjoy Christmas with Bruce, 4, and Ruth, 2.

1940 Navigators Gospel team was guided around the big city by New York businessman Robert Swanson. From left, Vic McAnney, Ken Watters, Swanson, Trotman, Gordon Taggart, Oran Bell.

The crisp tang of fall was in the salt breeze blowing across Ocean Boulevard a dozen blocks away. Lights from windows of the bungalow on Sixth Street, set between the Colorado Lagoon and the golf course, told neighbors the residents again had something going on. At least three evenings a week they saw a stream of sailors in blue and a few civilians stop to greet the three-year-old, curly-haired girl and her five-year-old brother playing and arguing over a tricycle on the sidewalk. Those who came earlier played spirited volleyball with their host, using a net stretched across the end of the street.

Now they crowded around the lengthened table inside for a Saturday night dinner of hamburgers, baked beans, and chocolate pudding, liberally seasoned with banter, laughter, and talk. Lila sat at one end of the table, rising to pour coffee or refill a serving bowl. Her calm radiance and occasional hearty laugh pervaded the scene with warm hospitality and harmony, reminding some sailors of their own homes across the U.S. and showing others a dimension of the term "home" that they never knew existed. Too much their contemporary to allow them to regard her as "mom," Lila nonetheless provided the spirit of welcome and Christian love that made the Navigator Home, as one non-Christian sailor called it, "a welcome place to go."

Dawson, at the head of the table, dominated the conversation, embarrassing newcomers by deftly jamming their thumbs in the butter as he passed the plate or by some other well-used trick. "I never embarrass anybody a single time," he bragged, "always twice or more." No one felt safe, knowing he might be the next victim of a practical joke or be singled out to quote a certain verse or answer a question.

On this evening Dawson called for verses quoted around the table. A sailor reddened, confessing that he did not know one. "You don't *know* any *verses?*" Daws feigned surprise. "Ruthie, dear, you go over and teach him a verse."

127

Ruthie, feeling important, left the table to huddle with her student and soon returned with the mission accomplished. After sharing of verses and a moment of prayer, the port or starboard watch attended to kitchen cleanup and readied the place for the evening meeting.

Saturday meetings, which were evangelistic, drew the most newcomers, with touch football, volleyball, croquet, and Ping Pong in the afternoon. Friday nights were for Bible instruction for Christians, Wednesdays for a popular personal evangelism class attended about equally by sailors and business and professional people, with Dawson teaching the doctrine of salvation and assigning practical exercises in leading people to Christ. Those who had liberty stayed overnight Friday and Saturday, some taking Dawson's suggestion and getting time alone with the Lord out in the park and going out to churches on Sunday. Radioman Larry Dundon says, "I never saw so many fellows sleeping in one place." Four men bunked on sofas in the living room, more in the den, some on cots in the garage, and six or eight in the loft above it. The four Trotmans slept in one room on mattresses spread on the floor until beds could be purchased.

The plain, three-bedroom house, nicknamed "4845" by street number as Navigator Homes came to be called, had no extras in decor and furnishings but was tasteful and spotlessly kept. Lt. Pearson's down payment had made it possible to move in at the end of the Camp Bethel summer, with monthly mortgage payments similar to their previous rent. A second payment of $300 due three months later was met by $100 gifts from three Navy men, none of whom knew the others were giving the balance.

An accounting for December 1937 showed $201 received and $201 spent. Seven shipboard groups, eight individuals, and one church had given toward that total. Pearson designated his monthly gift for personal needs of the family. Dawson continued the policy of instructing a few key servicemen in the responsibility of supporting the work, and some gave regularly. Yet this did not replace faith and prayer for supply of specific needs, nor guarantee a surplus at any time. A $20 gift from a serviceman came the very day a $20 tax bill was due. A trip to the hospital by Lila would have necessitated borrowing $50 from another fund, but the doctor told Dawson an unnamed person had paid the bill. The afternoon mail might bring a blue postal money order on a day when nothing was on hand.

These continual answers to prayer were great adventure, and Daws and Lila wanted no more security than God's promise of provision. "Philippians 4:19," he once wrote to the men, "is just as fresh and powerful as the day the promise was given through the Spirit-moved lips of the Apostle Paul."

Even with the emphasis on discipling Christians, evangelism was prominent in the ministry at 4845. Gospel meetings were on Saturdays, but non-Christians who came other nights were given priority. "A great number of servicemen have found Christ as their Saviour in the last few weeks or months," Dawson wrote Lt. Pearson. Frequent notes in his journal confirm it. "Tonight we have some 26 over to the home. Two of these men accept the Lord." One who found Christ was Al Inglis of the *Texas,* who became a pastor in Seattle and a national leader in the field of education. Another was F. E. Lance, later a Wisconsin businessman, who came with a buddy to the Home, "where week after week we studied the Bible, which resulted in my acceptance of Jesus Christ as my personal Saviour." Dawson and Lila were not able to keep track of the host of men from many states who came to Christ one at a time at the Home — direct answers to forty days of prayer over a map in a canyon less than a decade before.

But Dawson's consuming desire was to see men grow into effective servants of Christ, and he aimed every effort toward that goal. Watching his children grow as they graduated from milk to solid food, he wrote, "Oh if Christians would just grow with the same steadiness that humans do. I thank God however for the marvelous way many of these Christian servicemen have grown." He brought in Bible teachers and missionaries to speak to the men on Friday nights; sometimes he taught them himself or took them to hear a special speaker at church. Once when Dr. Herbert Lockyer of England spoke at the Home, Dawson rigged a loudspeaker — still a novelty in the 1930s — so the message could be heard in the next rooms.

His challenges to the men to "get down to business" varied in form. One might be instruction on how to pray, including confession, thanksgiving, praise, intercession, and petition. Another time he would explain a plan for chapter study or review of memory verses, encourage them to persist in getting time with the Lord each morning, or give practical help in getting victory over sin.

The men knew he preached nothing he himself did not have to apply, for he shared their battle against the world, the flesh, and the devil. He had long since acknowledged his vulnerability to temptation and a weakness of will in areas of discipline, confiding to Downing that he knew the leadership in the work God had given him was not because of any personal virtue or holiness and that whatever spiritual fruit resulted would be undeniably the work of God. Yet he followed hard after God and shared with all he met whatever practical means he found that helped him in his pursuit.

Some exhortations to "walk in truth" he shared in his long mimeographed letters ("Greetings in the ever-precious Name of Christ our Saviour and Lord. How goes the battle?") and detailed personal letters to men at sea. All of this helped assure each man he was an important member of the family, a fact reinforced by the royal welcome he received on returning "home" to 4845.

To Dawson and Lila such open-heart, open-home policy was well worth the sacrifice of privacy and leisure for its dividends of love, fellowship, and spiritual harvest. Yet there were always things to try their faith and fuel their prayers. Besides the very few sailors who polluted the pure waters of hospitality with their boorishness, there was the chiropractor from upstate who, after dabbling in several of the cults which flourish in California, was impressed by Navigators and moved his house trailer in behind 4845. Hungry for reality in the things of God, he fed on the Word. But his physical diet was eccentric: he drank only vegetable juices and thought aluminum was toxic, so promptly disposed of all of Lila's aluminum pots and pans and laid in a store of tinware. Another rare guest at 4845 was the fiancée of a Navy chief in the Pacific. Not until the chief came into port did the Trotmans discover she was an impostor, living on funds which had mysteriously disappeared from the home operation. Such incidents were soon forgotten, however, and do not even appear in the record of those days.

Men from more and more ships began to head for "Navigators Club Headquarters" when they were in port. Ball games, Bible studies, meetings, convivial mealtimes, and relaxation in a home atmosphere all became treasured memories. But one activity least conspicuous and most significant at 4845 was man-to-man ministry. Dawson was uniquely gifted for this custom-tailored counsel to men, and he enjoyed it. His heart toward them was expressed by Paul: ". . . we exhorted and comforted and charged every one of you, as a father doth his children, that ye would walk worthy of God. . . ." (1 Thess. 2:11, 12).

"He never allowed the tremendous load of outside duties to interfere with his man-to-man ministry," Floyd Robertson said. "He loved individuals so much that he became all things to all men . . . transferred himself to their position. The man knew he understood him and was genuinely interested."

Daws's early desire to be "that man" D. L. Moody referred to had matured to the conviction that *every* man had the potential to be "that man" God could use, if only he would yield his life to the discipline of obedience to Christ. And he found the area of immediate need for help and growth differed with the individual. "Christ was to be honored and glorified above anything else," Dedrick said. "I thought of him as 'a man after God's own heart,' and he stimulated me to want to be that kind of man."

The spirit of all-outness seen in what one described as "his insistence upon pure Christianity" focused on any life he touched. This devotion to excellence left him open to the temptation to criticize those he felt were giving the kingdom of God short shrift, and would have alienated more than a few if it were not for his personal charisma that drew people to follow his leadership. The limitless potential under God that he saw in each individual made him impatient with those who failed to develop it.

"Daws was very aggressive," Hightower says, "and to me he was hard and harsh. But he was trying to instill discipline, and he wasn't demanding any more of us than of himself. Some resented it and left, some weak Christians particularly. But it was the thing I needed. I wanted to know the Lord, and I felt Daws had something I didn't have. I knew Les had it — a definiteness and purpose. There would not be any Navigators today if discipline had not been part of it."

"I think one of the reasons for his metallic exterior was tenderness underneath," a friend observed. "I have seen him weep." Dawson's bluntness was sometimes meant to jar the subject to action — and perhaps to bolster his own courage to speak out.

Those who saw both hardness and loving-kindness in him did not think it incongruous. More often than not, a display of wrath was calculated in the interest of the individual in question, for whom his love was genuine. His sensitive radar told him what degree of both elements was appropriate and the timing for administering them. One sailor, slated for rebuke, got it from the whole committee: "Ed, John, Les and Gurney and I deal with L--- and tell him whereby he has become a problem — particularly selfishness. He takes it O.K. and makes definite changes." The sailor survived, continued to reach men aboard ship, and after discharge went on to Biola.

Nor was a public meeting a place to hide. Seated on the platform before a youth convention in a San Diego church, Dawson heard their desultory singing of "My Jesus I Love Thee." As he stood to speak he said, "Just a moment. How many know what song you sang five minutes ago?" Two out of some 200 raised their hands.

"He was able to connect the experiences of people with Scriptures," observed John Newman of the *New Mexico*. "The vivid thing was application of the Word. He helped people face issues. Any saying or action in his life or the lives of those around him which didn't ring true to the Scriptures would become a subject of examination and possibly admonition."

And his capacity for insight was undisputed. Dr. Gordon Hooker of Biola felt it was a gift of discernment. "He could look a fellow over and see the potential in him." Floyd Robertson said, "Regardless of who my friend was, a new Christian or older one, a skeptic or agnostic or indifferent, I could introduce him to Dawson without getting him off to the side to explain the situation . . . never feared the wrong approach would be used. Dawson spoke as the Lord led him. The most simple-minded, uneducated person was never made to feel inferior, yet Dawson could meet the best intellect on his own level."

Speaking "as the Lord led him" must describe his encounter with young Jim Vaus, whom he handled with less than diplomatic finesse. Vaus, with a mixed quartet from Biola, sang and gave testimony at a meeting at 4845. Afterward Dawson took the hulking youth aside. "Jim, those others gave testimonies tonight that glorified Jesus Christ. *You* glorified Jim Vaus . . . you're a phony!" Jim, a preacher's son who passed for a Christian in most circles, smoldered over this for ten years until his conversion at Billy Graham's first Los Angeles crusade.

Dawson's magnetic leadership and almost naive belief that anyone would be glad to follow the truth once he knew it gave force to his challenge that attracted some and repelled others who were less motivated. Larry Dundon felt "Dawson had the personal attraction, the type of character that makes a man want to know him better. A dynamic individual who nevertheless could put you at ease. And he could on short acquaintance take a man apart personality-wise. There was no set pattern in the way he handled men. He always handled me with kid gloves because of my Irish ancestry. I admired him for that."

He frequently comforted one who was remorseful about some personal negligence by reminding him that ". . . all things work together for good to them that love God . . ." and that His purpose was undoubtedly being fulfilled even through the error. Dawson quickly sensed, however, when a person was trying to use this Scripture as an excuse.

> *March 27, 1938 — Speak to G--- about [his negligence] and make sure he does not lay his own failures on the Lord and Rom. 8:28. This he is apt to do as he has shown already and this is a thing many Christians today do. One of the causes that the Lord's business is so often behind is that Christians are careless about it. Oh that there was such a heart in all of us that we would do His business as efficiently as the world does their business for the sake of making money.*

A ministry of wise, godly counsel, as he had seen in older

saints like Charles Fuller and "Daddy" Moon, Irwin's father, was something Dawson had prayed he might have without waiting for the gray hair that seemed to go with it. God had answered, though Dawson lacked the mellowness that tempered the counsel of older men, giving a hard edge to his pronouncements which at times obscured his deep concern for the person's welfare.

In later years he would be mellowed through suffering, which itself was an answer to his prayer.

The hundreds of men who came to 4845 in its more than three years as Nav headquarters spanned a wide spectrum in personality and background. Among those who followed through and learned to navigate, the diversity remained, providing over the years an astounding variety of men known in the fleet as Navigators. But their common denominators — the Bible clamped firmly under arm, the memory pack in jumper pocket, the businesslike way of using time profitably — made it possible to identify a Navigator almost on sight.

Their first reactions to Dawson's uninhibited dynamism were mixed. Very few were bothered by his lack of polish, the high slang quotient of his small vocabulary — dinner was "grub" or "chow" — and his take-charge command of the situation. They were more impressed by his vital interest in them, and the reality of his touch with God.

The most colorful sailor at 4845 was Mexican-American Tony Trevino, designated by Dawson "the only Navigator we ever allowed to ignore the word-perfect rule in memorizing Scripture." Tony could write his name and he could lead men to the Savior. "The Lord is mightily using this man," Dawson wrote after spending time with him. "Not much in the way of tact but is led by the Spirit . . . I have found the Lord can steer a life better when it is moving. So often . . . doing things in a tactful way leads to doing nothing at all. I prefer the former, but why not allow the Lord to lead through both." Dawson labored at teaching Trevino to match his zeal in winning men with efforts to follow them up, giving them at least a chance to survive. Years later a degree of success was evident as Tony added a step to his usual procedure. As soon as his man said yes to the appeal to receive Christ and Tony had had a brief prayer with him, he handed him pen and paper. "Now here, you write-a Dosson Trotman an' tell him you want the help."

Another fascinating personality was an uncultured young sailor, John Prince. One Saturday Jim Downing had invited the blond, self-assured youngster from the radio gang to the Home. Prince wasn't much interested. "He imagined himself a great intellect in radio," Downing said, "so when I explained a great scientist was going to speak he agreed to go." That night after Irwin Moon presented the Gospel, Prince indicated a desire to receive Christ.

While not the intellect he fancied himself to be, Prince would later become an example of what God can do through a man wholly yielded to Him. Transferred out of the radio gang because he could not learn the code, he also had great difficulty learning his first verse of Scripture. But he did learn it, and learned many more. He became so absorbed with his new Lord and Master that he dared to witness where others feared to tread and displayed a rare, unquestioning faith. As the sailors prayed about transfers to other ships for ministry, the *West Virginia*ns decided Prince should transfer to the *California*. But when he returned from making his request he told Downing dejectedly, "I opened my mouth to say *California* and *Idaho* came out." Downing reassured him the Lord had undoubtedly led. Prince did not know the *Idaho* was one of four battleships Dawson named at the end of 1936 as not yet having a key man.

Prince boarded the *Idaho* on an October day in 1938 and his heart sank. There on deck was a seaman who had called the Christians fanatics and vigorously opposed their witness. Prince sent up a silent prayer. *Lord, either win this man or put him out of the way so he cannot hinder Your work on the Idaho.* That night the seaman borrowed four dollars from Cecil Davidson, a Christian on radio watch, went ashore and quietly dropped dead in a Long Beach bar.

In his first days on the *Idaho,* Prince purposed to do as he was counseled — live the life before starting to witness — though it was difficult to keep quiet. During his first week aboard, the *Idaho* sailed. A sharp pain in his side sent Prince to sick bay for an appendectomy. Since surgery was done at sea only in emergencies, Prince's misfortune was a headline event. The captain left the bridge to visit him. Prince's testimony to the doctor that he had peace because of the promise of Philippians 4:6, 7 now set the stage for his witness to all comers. Several were reached for Christ through the incident and a Bible class started on the *Idaho.*

The growing Navigator ministry needed extra hands. Occasionally a Navy wife volunteered to help with correspondence. An off-duty Marine who was a college graduate also did yeoman service, turning out great batches of letters. Dawson found him "a wonderful gift to the work." Daws also invited Lester Spencer and his bride Martha, who had lived in a California valley town since Biola graduation, to live at 4845 and join the ministry. This they did for several months, Lester also taking charge of Sailors' Rest Mission in San Pedro. It was an experiment without precedent, another pioneer move in a pioneer ministry. The arrangement worked, but haltingly, the wives particularly uncertain how to divide their responsibilities. So when Spencer was called to labor with the American Sunday School Union in rural Colorado, it was recognized by all as God's leading.

Early in 1938 Dawson conceived the idea of forming the eight ex-servicemen at Biola into a Gospel team. This would be a way to continue building in their lives while they gave valuable help in ministry to the fleet. With a candid note of caution in his journal — "I am waiting on the Lord. . . . I know if *He* leads there will be something permanently done. So many times I have started things which *He* never led in and they came to an end" — he spoke to Hightower and later to Dedrick and Harris. Along with Virgil Hook, Dick DeLong, Goodrick, and others, they responded to the idea of a team effort to contact men on ships, each man taking a ship for his parish. Dawson felt keenly the need for contact with the few battleships and most of the cruisers which had no key men, as well as the need to follow up men on these ships who had come to the Home once or twice. Civilian access to ships was limited, but these ex-Navy men could go aboard freely. They also had the advantage of immediate rapport with the men, having been in uniform.

The *West Virginia* and *Mississippi* gospel teams were well received on other ships, one Christian officer on the carrier *Saratoga* noting that instead of going ashore on Sundays the men stayed aboard if they heard the team was coming to hold chapel services, and many non-Christians attended. The Biolans made fifteen contacts their first Sunday visiting the ships, meeting afterward for reports and prayer. Dawson found this an excellent time to minister to team members, "laying things needful before them." That year Harris headed the work on battleships and Hightower on cruisers. Besides visiting ships, the team held meetings at the guardhouse and mission.

How to "get the job done" was the question always on Dawson's mind these days. The Great Commission was worldwide and therefore required a work of depth and quality in each life laboring to fulfill it, beginning with his own. He had concluded the basic resources needed for the job were men, time, and methods or tools. He was thankful God was giving men — like those in Biola, and Downing, Goold, and Newman on the ships — men of stature and conviction who were reaching out to evangelize and teach other men. He must hold before them the task of producing quality laborers for the Lord's harvest, each beginning with his own life as a tool in God's hand. He also wanted to foster in them the vision of the job world-wide as he had done by such excursions as taking a busload of sailors to the dock to meet and fellowship with Eber and Anne Hazelton returning from eight years' missionary service in China. Hazelton was the first man Dawson had helped at the lumberyard.

Any discovery, however small, of a way to redeem the priceless resource of time by using it double was important. A hundred daily shortcuts could be found. Reviewing a Scripture verse while waiting for a bus or in line at a service counter. Or plugging in his razor to shave while he drove from Long Beach to Los Angeles. This could make a passenger nervous, as John Newman commented, "He would shave and drive and talk and even let go the wheel and turn to a Scripture and say, 'Look at that.' "

Methods, too, were vital to getting the job done, so his search for system and efficiency was constant. The system of carrying memory cards in a leather packet that fit in a jumper pocket meant the difference between success and failure to many a man memorizing the Word. Gospel tracts Dawson printed on a friend's press were good conversation openers for witnessing and something to leave in a person's hand. The marked New Testament also helped, with arrows pointing to crosses and anchors beside verses for the Gospel and Christian living. A new index system the fellows gave him for Christmas was a time-saver in collecting and finding reference material to use in messages.

And now he had designed a new tool, an aid to personal efficiency — The Wheel check chart. Mimeographed on a 6"x3½" notebook page, it provided a reminder and spiritual inventory at the end of a day or week, a reliable gauge of weak places to shore up in one's life. A person could check his daily progress in Bible reading and study, in memory and review, in prayer time alone and with others, in witness by word and life. Dawson found it a great improvement over the early Minute Men chart.

"I am not making 100 percent in my daily checkup but am doing ever so much better and see the way clear to victory where before it was all fogged up." He started a few servicemen on The Wheel check chart, giving them also a Chapter Conquest Bible study plan by Bible teacher Earl Edwards. The more he worked with these men, the more he saw the necessity for providing tools to help carry out their decisions to follow Christ.

*　　*　　*　　*

The October sun set early in the canyon, its last long rays tipping the Santa Monica Mountains. The air was scented with autumn, and dried leaves crunched underfoot. From the rustic tabernacle at the Pacific Palisades church camp in the secluded canyon rolled the deep, rich sound of singing men. The few singing off key were absorbed by the robust melody of the rest, fewer than fifty men who sounded like a hundred. It was the opening of the second annual Life Triumphant in Christ conference, a special event to which Dawson invited down-to-business men from all the ships and a few civilians.

He had scheduled frequent weekend servicemen's conferences

at Camp Bethel and at least one at 4845, housing the men at homes of friends nearby and having some meals and meetings in the park. These come-one-come-all weekends included a few non-Christians along with believers and had been effective in recruiting and evangelism as well as building. But he envisioned Life Triumphant as a time for hand-picked Navigators to feast and surfeit on the meat of the Word ministered by top men of God. Because the Word was indispensable to the success of God's men, he determined to force-feed these growing disciples. It was the one conference of the year, he explained to the key men, for which "we aim to get the most outstanding speakers, the spiritual giants."

Some men could not get leave for the conference, but those who did moved heaven and earth to get there. Their arrival was marked by shouts, backslaps, and bear hugs as they greeted comrades in arms from other ships. The spirit of brotherhood and unity that weekend in 1938 was unique, heightened by the scarcity of men in uniform who loved Christ and lived openly for Him. Each man received a neat mimeographed booklet blazoned with *Life Triumphant in Christ* and key verse 2 Corinthians 2:14: "Now thanks be unto God, which always causeth us to triumph in Christ. . . ." A two-page challenge to live in victory by God's power was followed by pages for notes on messages by ten speakers, their topics listed with the hour they were to speak. There was one of the new Wheel check charts, a page for memory verses, and song sheets with words to favorite songs and choruses.

Charles Fuller, by this time a well-known radio evangelist-Bible teacher, was keynote speaker as he was year after year. "Daddy" Moon closed the meeting Sunday noon, speaking on "More Than Conquerors," following others' messages on prayer, personal evangelism, giving, and the Holy Spirit.

Life Triumphant conferences grew in size and significance for five successive years until Pearl Harbor scattered participants to the far corners. Later years featured both outside speakers and staff men giving "Navigator" messages. As time passed they trended to more Navigator speakers and fewer general Bible teachers, reflecting Dawson's thinking that the objective would be furthered by emphasizing New Testament principles which turned hearers into doers. No matter how wonderful the feast in the Word, he reasoned, conferees could easily go back to a life of passive uninvolvement; whereas if they were taught to use the tools for searching the Word themselves, the prospect for getting the job done was improved. So Navigator conferences gradually changed. But many who attended one of those first Life Triumphant events from 1937 to 1942 cherish fond memories of a high festival that nothing can tarnish.

"The Lord is mightily laying the work of boys and young men on my heart these days," Dawson wrote in March 1938 after a time of prayer in the park. This desire had simmered in his heart for months. His main ministry was with the Navigators; yet with the ships out often and for long periods, he felt he could give himself to boys work. And the Lord had not called him exclusively to servicemen, but to work with young men anywhere who could become laborers for Christ.

Not since Lomita had he had a full-scale work with boys, though he had directed the Bill Graves summer camps, had taught a Sunday school class at Church of the Open Door in Los Angeles, and had kept his hand in with a score of nine- to eleven-year-olds in weekly Regular Fellows Bible Club led by a friend. Spencer also helped with these boys. But now Dawson felt it was time to seriously consider a work with older boys. A few weeks earlier a high school senior had asked for help in his witness at school. This triggered the start of the first high school club which Dawson called Dunamis, from the Greek word for power in Romans 1:16, "... the gospel ... the power of God...." With six charter members, the club soon grew to eighteen or more. "Dunamis is fairly well attended," Dawson noted in April. "Really dig into First John using 2 Cor. 13:5 ... as a trowel to dig into the rich soil of this blessed book."

In May he convened a meeting of Greater Los Angeles boys work leaders, some of them associated with Fishermen Clubs, some in other ministries. The more than twenty leaders had opportunity to report on work being done and to outline plans. Out of this grew a committee for coordinating efforts, with clubs planned for all age groups, grammar school through college. The Biola ex-servicemen were involved in this as well as their ministry on ships. Dawson assigned Jim Hayden, who had helped him in summer camps, to spend half time in boys camp and club work. Jim's methodical attention to detail pleased Dawson, whose swift inception of new ideas made him no less insistent that every procedure already in force be carried out precisely. At Forest Home conference center for a personal prayer retreat, Dawson drafted a "first ever" plan for boys work that he felt could become a format for wide use.

To find qualified club leaders early in 1939, Dawson interviewed selected students at Biola, gaining faculty approval of club leadership for student ministry assignments. Bible clubs were launched with different notebooks and materials for each age group. Junior high schoolers were in Conquerors or Junior Dunamis Clubs. Grammar school boys had a simple Bible study called the Point Blank which folded and fit into the verse packs and used simplified forms of older club methods, memorizing and studying one verse each week. But these younger clubs soon faded out as Dunamis became the main vehicle with junior high boys growing into the Dunamis high school clubs. Dunamis also included college age.

In Dunamis Dawson was again pioneering; there was no Young Life or Youth For Christ precedent to follow. In the clubs he tested some firmly held principles, learning much from the boys' response. He discovered, for instance, that teens would accept a challenge to serious discipleship. Dead set against the "take-it-easy" philosophy, he purposely laid out a stiff program for them after making it a distinct privilege to be in the club.

Marshall Wilgus, who with his twin Morris wangled an invitation to join, remembers the conditions: "Daws said, 'I'm glad to have you boys come out, but we mean business in Dunamis club. You memorize two verses a week, summarize your chapter, put down your difficulties, your spiritual application, and do a weekly project and come back Tuesday with that all complete.' We'd study our heads off and of course Daws expected it word perfect. He got on us pretty hard, but really it was the making of us. We did not know the Bible at all. Had a general idea from Sunday school quarterlies but never any practical study. My brother would say, 'I am never going back. I'm not going to take that from anybody.' But we always went back.

"What squared me away more than anything is memorizing the verses," Wilgus says. "The verses I memorized then I use with people today as vice-moderator of the board of deacons. Last year we had over 150 accept the Lord in our church and we deal with everyone who comes forward. I practically wore out the Gospel verses and The Wheel Daws gave us." One of many devices Dawson tried was printing references on the face of an old wrist watch, pointing out to the boys the scriptural charge to "bind them . . . upon thine hand."

Dunamis meetings included hearty singing of choruses, oral check-out on memory, and reports on the weekly assignment, called TNT for Trust 'n Tackle. Reports could be only "complete" or "failed" with no partial successes acknowledged. Then followed a Bible study discussion and a challenge by the leader, sometimes a personal evangelism clinic, the meeting ending with a salute "All for Christ!"

Long Beach high schooler Bob Hopkins, led to Christ by two Navigator sailors, was invited with his brother Will to join the club. "Mom thought we were pretty radical, getting up early in the morning and spending time in the Word," he said. "The five of us from our liberal church really started to grow when we got into Dunamis club. We were starved and went to every meeting. But a bunch of kids from another church where they heard the Word all the time gradually dropped out of club." This confirmed to Dawson the truth of James 1:22, "But be ye doers of the word, and not hearers only, deceiving your own selves." His requirement that the boys apply Scripture they memorized was more than a notion; it was essential for survival.

"Daws had these early prayer meetings in the park, and asked if anyone wanted to join him," Bob said, recalling the air of privileged camaraderie that made it unthinkable to miss a meeting. "Will and I and the twins came every Saturday at six and sometimes a serviceman would join in. We read the Word and Daws made comments and threw out prayer requests. We prayed for many things." Wilgus added, "He always said

'Ask for big things. Take God at His Word and ask big. Attempt great things for God; expect great things from God.' "

The boys work flourished in the two years the fleet was out. Dawson had responsibility for the 1938 summer camp as Bill Graves had bowed out, so the hundred-plus junior and senior high boys who rallied at Camp Bethel included the new Dunamis clubbers with laymen Paul Walker and Norman Crider's Fishermen Club boys, the Regular Fellows Bible Club, and others. Dawson's father, Charles Trotman, reveled in his role as chef for the week, and Daddy Moon was again a favorite speaker. The camp was as frenetic as other summers, yet with a bit more style. Goodrick again coached track and swim meets with awards given for events. Jim Hayden planned the program and helped administer it.

The next summer sixth- and seventh-grade boys returned to Camp Bethel. High school and junior college campers were invited to Catalina. Milo Jamison had leased the Boy Scout camp for a month, with Dawson taking one week of it for Boys Bible Clubs and filling it far in advance with more than 100 eager lads who met for a pre-camp rally at the lagoon near 4845. Navigators Downing, Prince, and Goold were among the leaders and counselors for Catalina, with the Biola ex-servicemen and others of the boys work committee. Dawson named a few spiritually advanced campers as assistant leaders, which served two purposes — a high ratio of leaders to campers and the opportunity to train leaders. Any such endeavor with dual or triple function pleased him immensely. Catalina was judged a success with 85 percent of the boys evidencing decisions to receive Christ or to yield their lives to serve Him.

With the Navy work steaming along on course and Hayden and others helping with Boys Bible Clubs, Dawson now saw another potential labor pool. In summer of 1939 he met with a couple Long Beach businessmen to launch a Christian Business Men's Committee. The group soon grew to a dozen as their friends responded to the idea. With keen interest they "dug in" on Scripture memory and began witnessing to business associates, some for the first time, with the help of their arrow-marked New Testaments. CBMC luncheon meetings were spiced by Hayden's reading of minutes of previous meetings which inevitably revealed shortcomings of some members to the delight of the rest.

"Three or four of us who were doing the work went to Trotmans' for breakfast on Saturdays," one man recalled. "Before that I never had any regular Bible study. The thing that impressed me was the way he knew the Word. I had never heard anyone quote the passage and give chapter and verse like he did. Ezekiel 22:30 was one verse he used often: 'I sought for a man. . . .' Five of us went fishing one time and coming home Dawson recited the whole Book of Philemon."

* * * *

Daws was glad to see the sailors involved in the boys work in addition to their outreach aboard ship. Some had traveled from a distance to help at Catalina; they had also given heavily toward expenses of the camp and the boys work. He called a caucus of key Navigators in port, polling others by mail, to ratify his call to Hayden as half-time boys worker at $25 a month.

A secretary also joined the staff that summer. Dawson had opened a small Los Angeles office next door to Biola early in the year and spent two days a week interviewing those interested in boys clubs and club leadership. Once when he declined Goodrick's request to go on a camping trip with some boys because of a heavy work load, Goodrick promptly recruited fellow student Marjory Thomson of Seattle to help with correspondence. Her afternoon-a-week grew to two, and after graduation to full-time. She came to live and work at 4845 at a salary of $5 a week when it was available. It never was, but she found her needs were always supplied. Dawson's unconventional work habits included his famous sweatouts in a hot bath, during which he shouted dictation through the transom to Marge and Lila taking notes outside the door.

A Christian Girls Bible Club — later named Martyrus, then Martures from the Greek word for witnesses — was now under way, including Lila, Marjory, Biola students Georgia MacDavid and Vivian Fusby, and others. Individually they did the weekly TNT assignments of Minute Girls, which some had done for two years or more, a regimen patterned after Minute Men featuring chapter analysis Bible study and memory work. Soon girls from Whittier who attended the Long Beach club asked for a Martures group of their own. Mainly in their twenties, the girls wanted it for their spiritual growth, but also for their training as leaders of high school Martures Clubs. Georgia, who spent afternoons at the Los Angeles club office, was soon besieged with requests for high school clubs in many places.

The year which Dawson began with a resolve to concentrate on boys work was a year of discovering principles of discipling he would use in future ministry with Navigators and others. One such discovery was that a combination of required performance by the individual and inspiration of group fellowship brought better results than did either one alone. He concluded that every person in club must be expected to do a specific assignment tailored to his age level and, in addition, be encouraged and challenged by others doing the same things. The Minute Men, whose assignments were most demanding, had usually lapsed when group fellowship was neglected. Now they were enjoying more success as they scheduled an all-day or half-day meeting every three months, held the Sunday before the month for which they were to turn in written reports. Better follow-through was assured too by the fact that Dawson gave the Minute Men setup only to those with keen desire for it.

Minute Men meetings, in addition to business and planning, included a challenge to read biographies of God's great men and seek to follow their hard-driving discipleship. A favorite poem frequently surfaced in Dawson's messages to Minute Men and Minute Girls:

> *Be strong!*
> *We are not here to play, to dream, to drift;*
> *We have hard work to do and loads to lift.*
> *Shun not the struggle, face it, 'tis God's gift.*
> *Be strong!*
> *It matters not how deep intrenched the wrong,*
> *How hard the battle goes, the day, how long,*
> *Faint not; fight on! Tomorrow comes the song.*

With enough rallies and conferences scheduled to meet the need for group activity, Dawson turned his attention to refining individual assignments and finding ways to ensure success in completing them. As he had learned years before that evangelism could be salvaged from virtual fruitlessness by adequate follow-up, he was now convinced that the gap between desire and fulfillment in the lives of many who sincerely wanted to grow in Christ and follow Him could be bridged by simply giving them the tools for success and teaching them to use them.

A system for memorizing Scripture had proved helpful; now a workable plan for prayer was needed, and a method of personal daily Bible study. There was a need for a way a man could measure his progress and check on daily disciplines. This would not only show how but would ensure getting Bible study in on a busy day.

As he prayed for ideas, lights flashed on his mental console. The acronym STUDY could be the outline for a new five-part chapter analysis plan. For the "S" section a person would write a one- or two-paragraph summary of the chapter or shorter passage assigned for the week. For "T" a title for the passage. "U" would include "uplifts," truths the student could apply to his life, "D" the difficulties or questions raised in his study, and "Y" — "your key passage," the verse which best represented the content of the chapter. STUDY, thereafter labeled STS No. 1, was artistically printed on $3\frac{1}{2}''$ x $6''$ folded notebook paper, with "Study to Shew Thyself Approved Unto God" on the front and carefully plotted spaces inside for sections of the study, and distributed for use by the clubs. Dawson saw it filling a significant need — the need for a student to discover Bible truth by his own investigation rather than being fed exclusively by a class teacher or leader. His personal findings would be more important to him, even if not as theologically advanced as those of the teacher.

Dawson designed notebook pages for business items, for prayer lists, for daily checkup. Hayden helped him produce notebook materials on $3''$ x $5''$ pages for the junior high boys in clubs named Conquerors, and the girls' counterpart, Victory Bible Clubs. Younger boys still met in Regular Fellows Bible Club. Volunteers who gathered around the 4845 dining table to punch and assemble notebook pages could expect Dawson to charge in and immediately single out for correction the only one punching holes slightly off center.

Dunamis and Martures clubs became more numerous, both groups using the new materials Dawson prescribed for them. Dunamis fellows tackled a seven-week TNT assignment for

Marksman, a scaled-down set of Minute Men disciplines. From this they advanced to Sharpshooter rate, then to Expert, terms familiar from the rifle range. Martures girls advanced through parallel rates: Single W (for Word), Double W (Word, Walk), and Triple W (Word, Walk, Witness), with assignments increased at each level. No technical discovery was too small to be seen as a spiritual victory if it contributed to the overriding purpose of bringing young people into intimate daily fellowship with Christ.

Testing the new Dunamis materials on selected servicemen and civilians, Dawson watched for ways to improve them for use in the clubs. He urged Minute Men and Minute Girls to do the Dunamis work and learn how to use it and decided to give Dunamis as a qualifying step to prospective Minute Men.

Spencer, now a rural missionary, took back to Colorado the format for starting Conquerors and Victory Bible Clubs with his youngsters. Hightower and Harris, just graduated from Biola, gave themselves to the boys club work while preparing to leave for missionary service in Africa. Clubs started as far away as San Diego, making someone's gift of a 1928 Ford coupe, promptly christened Dunamis Jalopis, an important addition to the work. A student bound for Wheaton College asked for Minute Men work for himself and planned to form a committee at school to organize boys clubs there. The boys club movement was under way. And though Dawson found his time taken up with developing and testing materials, recruiting and coaching leaders, and related business, both the materials and the principles he was learning would be of value in his future ministry.

Again his energetic spirit drove him harder than his body could afford. His working hours grew longer and later and his rising hour for prayer earlier. He began to lose weight. In the afternoon he might be found, Bible in hand, dropped off to sleep in a chair. His doctor suggested he slow down.

Late in December of 1939 Dawson called together key men from the ships in port for a policy conference at Big Bear Lake

— Downing, Vic McAnney of the cruiser *Astoria,* Newman and Goold of the *New Mexico,* Oran Bell of the *California,* men from the *Pennsylvania* and carrier *Saratoga.* Through the year he had written the key men, instructing them in discipleship and ministry. He also felt it important to stimulate their prayer interest in Navigators on other ships. In fact, encouragement to keep in touch with one another was first on the agenda for this conference.

Dawson was cheered by evident progress the sailors had made this year under leadership of Downing and other maturing key men. This reinforced his belief that the health of the flock would depend greatly on the training given their shipboard leaders, and he determined to do more such training.

Some 130 servicemen and civilians had attended this year's Life Triumphant in Christ conference with Charles Fuller again a main speaker, at the close of which the Navigators gospel team took the Sunday evening service at Church of the Open Door. Broadcast on a local radio station, the dynamic testimonies of men living for Christ in the Navy evoked a large response from listeners who had sent sons to the Armed Forces. Dr. Louis Talbot, the pastor, invited the Navigators back for another evening service two weeks later. Downing, heading the gospel teams, dispatched sailors in dress blues for as many as five or six services a Sunday when they were in port. Their testimonies highlighted victories Christ had given them by means any interested listener could follow — regular Scripture memory and study, a disciplined prayer life, positive witness — spokes of The Wheel on which each man had cut his spiritual teeth.

The sailors' influence was spreading to new ships as well. Already, two years before U. S. entry into war, destroyers were being recommissioned and other ships manned, calling for a dispersion of experienced Navy personnel. Prince and other key men were thus transferred to new fields of ministry. Chaplains were still few in the fleet; usually only the big battleships rated one. Dawson noted as an answer to months of prayer for the Lord to do a work on other ships that "the Lord has transferred some of our fellows to recommissioned destroyers . . . each has accepted this as the call of God." He observed too that some men actually had contact with several destroyers as they usually tied up together, four to a division.

Some Navigators moved onto cruisers which had no key man aboard. John Tinkle reported sixteen to twenty men, from nearly every division, attended Bible class on the *Indianapolis*. Regulars in the class took prayer responsibility for those who showed even casual interest. The contact on another cruiser was no less ecstatic about his one man. "Great news, Daws," he wrote. "Remember the fellow with me last time I was over? He and I have been the closest friends the last few months and now that tie is bound for eternity. He accepted Christ last Saturday. We've started regular fellowship and study. I can feel my faith being strengthened and my courage lifted." Meanwhile the established Bible classes on seven battleships* flourished.

Dawson had counseled men to go slow in starting a new "work" on a ship, feeling slow growth would be more stable. This too was a topic of concern at the Big Bear Conference. "Just get together by twos and threes on the ship for prayer," he advised the men, "and wait on the Lord before starting anything like a Bible class." This applied also to choosing leadership for the class. If there was not a mature leader whom the Lord had chosen or if the class was not one directed by the chaplain, the Bible discussion could degenerate into argument. And there were other reasons for caution. On the *West Virginia* the chaplain had promoted and led the group in its ministry, but another chaplain unacquainted with Navigators might feel a subversive organization was extant. And there had been instances of a young Christian's zeal for evangelism outrunning his tact and his deference to the chaplain's professional function aboard, causing some chaplains to attach a caution signal to the name Navigator.

While stressing the need to take responsibility for the ministry aboard their ships, Dawson also shared with the men at Big Bear his burden to see branch Navigator Homes open in strategic ports and reviewed his efforts toward that goal. For several years layman Jim Forster had ministered to the men when the

---

*Battleships were easy to identify by their names of states, cruisers by names of cities, destroyers by names of famous men, and submarines by names of fish.

ships were in Bremerton, taking them to church and to his home and holding a weekly Bible class at Navy YMCA. The fact that Navigators Bible class was the only servicemen's Bible class in any YMCA anywhere occasioned a formal publicity photograph for that institution. Forster kept a careful record of the men's spiritual progress and faithfully served them. By 1938 he was official Navigator contact in the area. He also put the sailors in touch with saintly Louella Dyer, state secretary for Christian Endeavor, whose home was open to Navigators for many years.

In Oakland, Harold Chrisman had offered early in 1937 to open his home and teach a week-night Bible class for Navigators as a sideline to his work with American Sunday School Union. This ministry began but was short-lived. Dawson had also discussed with Harold DeGroff, a Baptist minister going to Honolulu, and another missionary headed for China the prospect of colaborship in ministry to servicemen in these outposts, and all agreed the Lord was in it. The China arrangement did not work out, but DeGroff made his home Navigator headquarters in Honolulu, ministering to the men a type of conventional Bible teaching consistent with his background. Downing and others from the ships carried the main line Navigator ministry there as more and more ships tied up at Pearl Harbor for longer stays.

In San Diego, which had no Navigator Home since the Coateses turned to other work, there had been more lessons to learn. Art Ward, enthusiastic young Christian and favorite speaker at boys camps, went with Dawson on a foray to San Diego and immediately accepted his call to work there. Daws was elated with God's apparent leading:

> *I am happy to find this man of God who is so yielded to the Lord. I find it so hard to find the right combination of things in men these days, men on the job in personal work, men of prayer that use the Word of God much, men that really hide the Word in their hearts, interesting and use plain but up-to-date language. This man Art has all of these plus a very pleasing straightforward way.*

He installed Art and June Ward in the San Diego Home and helped launch their ministry, rallying support from local friends and offering generous encouragement. Ward sent glowing reports. More than forty men decided for Christ in the first fourteen weeks, most of them at the Home. "Is He wonderful! Two more boots for Him today!"

But problems developed which Dawson failed to foresee in his high enthusiasm for Ward, whom time had not yet matured. Within a short time Art displayed an autocratic independence that sought no counsel but demanded loyalty, alienating such staunch friends as Mother Rittenhouse, Emil Pearson, and Floyd Robertson and trying to lead the servicemen into a local sect he had joined. In August 1938 Ward resigned. Dawson noted in his journal, "I truly believe God called Art there. Just what has happened I am not yet sure of."

Reviewing this for the key men, Dawson observed the urgent need for a Navigator Home in San Diego and for one on the East Coast — more than simply an open home. He discussed an eight-point list of "Qualifications for Nav Home" which specified that the couple in charge be able to meet the spiritual needs of men and help them grow, be willing to sacrifice personal time and possessions, and be willing to cooperate with Nav headquarters. Such a couple was hard to find, unless they had grown up in it. Goold, for instance, now engaged to Dawson's secretary Marjory, would be ready to man a Home after his upcoming discharge, for he had been trained at 4845, and Marjory was being trained specifically for a Nav Home ministry. Marge helped Lila part-time, learning not only her housekeeping standards and how to make those ingenious tuna casseroles that always stretched to feed one more, but lessons of faith as she watched Dawson pay the checker at the grocery with money a serviceman had handed him while they were filling the basket; lessons of patience and cheerfulness from Lila's own overflowing life; of discretion as the two of them often went out for bike rides so that Dawson could speak to the men with greater freedom in their meeting. Bill and Marge would be ideal for a home; Dawson wished he had a half-dozen couples like them.

After his recent radio contact with Honolulu, Dawson considered the possibility of connecting various Nav headquarters by short-wave communication. He also planned to take flying lessons with a view to possible travel across country in Navigators and boys work.

The omnipresent late spring sun shone on the wall across the narrow court. In the old building between Biola and the Los Angeles public library Dawson pushed open the long window of his office and inhaled the freshness. Looking up at the familiar pale, vacuous sky, he wondered how many paused to appreciate God's lavish gifts of warm sun and tonic fresh air, of a glass of pure cold water or the cheery warble of a songbird. *Thank You, Lord.* He returned to the armchair behind his desk and to his interview with the pert young lady seated across from him. She spoke with purpose, the assurance of well-directed energies, her quick smile seeming to add flashes of light to her cinnamon hair, her total presence unmistakably feminine. Morena Holmes, chosen women's speaker for her graduating class, was one of nineteen Biola girls in Martures work whom Dawson planned to interview to find out how they were using the system and what they would be doing for summer ministry.

"Martures has helped me in my devotional life," she said. "Just the definiteness of it helps me be sure I get that time with the Lord in the Word and in prayer that might otherwise be crowded out, even by good things like Bible study for classes." Daws listened, relishing her enthusiasm. "It helps me get organized too," she continued, "in memory, for instance. I always intend to do a lot of things, but the specific assignment to learn those new verses by the end of the week and check off a certain amount of review every night means I can't put it off like I tend to do, planning to do a lot of memory and review 'when I get time.' And sure enough, doing that little bit every single day probably adds up to more than I'd ever get around to doing without a definite system."

Her interviewer agreed. "That's exactly the way I am. If I *hafta* meet a certain deadline, I'll give it the old effort. But if I wait until a convenient season so as to accomplish a great amount, it's too hard to find a season convenient enough and time slips by. Y'know, I think that's just human nature. We all need that extra push and the challenge of something to aim for to get us to do what we know we ought to do but can't on our own.

"I learned my first thousand verses by just having a goal to learn one a day *every* day. I'd never have done it if I hadn't pushed for that old 100 percent record. Same with witnessing. The early Minute Men had a goal to touch one life a day, and I'd rather do anything than hafta check that I failed. So even if it meant going out and hunting for a soul to talk to before I went to bed, it worked. And we reached a lot more people than would have heard if we didn't have that goal. It's human nature to be lazy, isn't it? But the Lord knows that and He's given us a brain to figure out how to overcome any obstacle the enemy puts in our way to keep us from carrying out His orders."

Finding the student an eager listener, Daws went on to share from his philosophy and vision. "About nine years ago I was waiting on the Lord about my life work. I said, 'Lord, I'll do anything, I just wanta carry out Your orders. Let me win souls for You and bring them to know the joy of walking with You.' And as I prayed I kept comin' back to Isaiah. No matter which Bible I used it was Isaiah, along from chapter 40 to the end, especially 43, 44, 45, and over in 58. As time went on I knew beyond any doubt that God had given me these promises and would make them good if I'd only obey Him and believe Him. And in 1936 when the Nav work was about four years old I began to see some of them fulfilled.

"Listen to this." The Book lay limp on his hand while he read the phrases slowly, dramatically. *"But now thus saith the Lord that created thee, O Jacob, and he that formed thee, O Israel, Fear not: for I have redeemed thee, I have called thee by thy name; thou art mine. When thou passest through the waters, I will be with thee; and through the rivers, they shall not overflow thee: when thou walkest through the fire, thou shalt not be burned; neither shall the flame kindle upon thee. For I am the Lord thy God, the Holy One of Israel, thy Saviour. . . . Since thou wast precious in my sight, thou hast been honourable, and I have loved thee: therefore will I give men for thee, and people for thy life. Fear not: for I am with thee: I will bring thy seed from the east, and gather thee from the west; I will say to the north, Give up; and to the south, Keep not back: bring my sons from far, and my daughters from the ends of the earth; Even every one that is called by my name: for I have created him for my glory, I have formed him; yea, I have made him.*

"At first I thought yeah, but, Lord, 'bring my sons . . . *and my daughters'?* I was working with men. Then when the girls came around and wanted the Bible study and the memory work, and before long we had Minute Girls and Martures clubs — and the Lord knew that, see, from the beginning. *Thus saith the Lord, which maketh a way in the sea, and a path in the mighty waters.* This bothered me too. I said, Lord, what do You mean by 'path in the waters'? Here I had these 200 boys in clubs and was going around speaking in churches and working with the Minute Men. Then Les Spencer and High-tower and Gurney got goin' on the *West Virginia,* and Good-rick and Dedrick and Hook and Downing came along, and fellows were transferred to other battleships and we got men on cruisers and destroyers and they went all over witnessing for Christ and living the life on the ship, doing their work and helping the other guy, and so now on maybe fifty ships and stations men are down to business for Christ — that's making a path in the mighty waters! And the Lord knew all that when He gave me that promise.

"*Remember ye not the former things, neither consider the things of old. Behold, I will do a new thing; now it shall spring forth; shall ye not know it? I will even make a way in the wilderness, and rivers in the desert.* The first Navigators were second class seamen, and they thought you couldn't reach a man with the Gospel after he made petty officer. Well, we did reach some and later we got some commissioned officers and men of all ranks. God just fulfilled this promise." He flipped the page but quoted from memory: "*And they that shall be of thee shall build the old waste places: thou shalt raise up the foundations of many generations; and thou shalt be called, The repairer of the breach, The restorer of paths to dwell in.*

"You saw those twenty sailors get up and give their testi-monies at Church of the Open Door. These men, I believe, are part of the foundations of many generations the Lord promised way back there." The girl nodded. "They remind me of a verse in Song of Solomon."

"In Song of Solomon?"

"Yes. Song of Solomon 3:8. *They all hold swords, being expert in war: every man hath his sword upon his thigh because of fear in the night.* They're all so strong in the Word. When you see a Navigator sailor, he has his Bible clamped under his arm, a weapon of war ready for combat." The analogy pleased Dawson. "I'd never thought of that verse, but it's true. They're warriors. They know how to use the old Sword of the Spirit to defeat Satan. And they know how to get their orders from God directly in the Book, through study and hiding it in their hearts, and then go out and fight the good fight of faith."

Daws paced to the window and back, then jabbed a finger toward the Bible. "I know that regardless of what I say or do, God is going to make good on these promises. *Yea, before the day was I am he; and there is none that can deliver out of my hand: I will work, and who shall hinder it?* I wrote down six prayer requests at the bottom of the page and all but one have been answered already. One of them was 'That God will soon bring us into touch with a mighty band of young men, strong rugged soldiers of the cross, with an eye singled to His glory.' I've already seen that, Morena, the Song of Solomon 3:8 men. Strong rugged soldiers of the cross who are raising up more like themselves, becoming a mighty band.

"The one request I haven't seen yet is this one: 'That God will give two million souls to be saved in the U.S.A. through the efforts of this work.' And we'll see that too. Just think of having Dunamis and Martures clubs all over the U.S. in every high school and college in America, with fellows and girls digging into the Word and memorizing it and learning to witness to their friends and fathers and mothers and being real soul-winners! If we can get them into this Book and get the Book into them," as he tapped his chest with a forefinger, "there'll be no way to stop it." He paused, reflecting on that eventuality.

"But what we've got to do is not just give 'em a dozen verses and tell 'em to go get 'em. We've got to raise up young men and women who will yield *everything* to Him, who are willing to go all out like these guys on the ships. Then we've got to feed 'em and train 'em and give 'em time to grow till they have the Word so deep in their lives it will be like fire in their bones and they've got to give it out. We'll have to help them with their little problems and teach them how to look to the Lord for wisdom and guidance and everything else they need.

"One of my problems on the ships is that one or two fellows get things started too soon. They start a Bible class before they have the maturity and understanding to handle it, and it does more harm than good. I have to keep warning the guys to take it slow and get one or two men really grounded and disciplined in the Word and prayer and witness by life before they do a lot of talking and organizing Bible classes. We have to fight for thoroughness and depth. We have to fight to keep small instead of fighting to grow. Sounds crazy, doesn't it? But if you're gonna have foundations of many generations, you've got to have foundations that don't buckle under pressure, huh? I'm praying that God will raise up a key man for every ship in our Navy, and I'm praying we'll reach a good number of men who'll form the new Air Corps. But where your key man is going to be responsible for a whole ship or a base, we've got to make sure he's trained and ready to let God use him in a real way.

"It's the same with Dunamis and Martures clubs. If we're going to see this take hold all over the United States, we have to train leaders who are solid enough in their own lives in the Word that they can impart it to other faithful men who can teach others. That's what Paul said in 2 Timothy 2:2. *And the things that thou hast heard of me among many witnesses, the same commit thou to faithful men, who shall be able to teach others also.* The things that you, Timothy," he said, grasping his middle finger, "have learned from me, Paul," grabbing his forefinger, "the same commit thou to faithful men," — ring finger — "who shall be able to teach others also" — little finger. "From now on, Morena, I've got to concentrate on training Timothys and Timothettes who will be able to commit to faithful men and teach others also. That's the way I believe God is going to use us to reach young men and women across America who will glorify His name."

Morena walked back to class, her heart pounding as she thought of the vision Daws had shared in terms that made it seem not only possible but inevitable. His goal was clear. He was uniquely ambitious for the will of God and yet in a strange way detached from personal ambition. God was real to Dawson. Whatever happened, Morena decided, she wanted to be part of it; she felt privileged to be one of the nineteen at Biola who stood a good chance of being involved in this work. "His sense of the reality of the Lord awes one," she wrote in her diary. "How very near the Lord seems. What a vision and what a life! His life reminds me in many ways of Hudson Taylor's."

"Man, Daws, you know last night you took me to the landing and I missed the boat? Well, it was really of the Lord." The sailor, a regular at 4845, was elated. "A fellow saw my Bible and we got to talking and he accepted the Lord. Here's his name. Will you get in touch with him?"

"What are *you* planning to do for him?"

"Well, I — I dunno."

"Listen, Mack. You are going to look him up, write him a letter, and see that he is taken care of and begins to grow. You are his spiritual dad and he's your responsibility. No, *you're not gonna park your baby on* my *doorstep.*"

The 4845 living room was crowded on meeting nights early in 1940, even with some ships gone to Bremerton and others detained in Honolulu. But in spite of increased numbers of contacts, Dawson spotted a weakness he must correct — a lack of emphasis on follow-up. Men, even key men, were winning sailors to Christ and teaching Bible classes but neglecting individual care of their babes and their needs for growth.

"George, let me see the names of your men," Dawson asked. George opened his notebook. "Tell me about them — are they growing?" "Well, this one, he seemed sincere when he made his decision, but he doesn't come to Bible class. I don't see him much. This one sort of avoids me; I think he may not want to give up some things. I guess none of these nine are really down to business, Daws," he admitted finally.

"Well, George, Philippians 1:6 just isn't working, is it? You know why? I don't think it's your life. You're living the life, I know that. But this verse isn't working because you're not giving it a chance. In the very next verse after '. . . he which hath begun a good work in you will perform it until the day of Jesus Christ,' Paul says, 'Even as it is meet for me to think this of you all, because *I have you in my heart.* . . .' He looked after his babes, loved them, prayed for them night and day, wrote and encouraged them, helped with their problems. The last thing Christ told Peter, He told him three times: Feed My sheep, Feed My lambs, Feed My sheep."

So follow-up became Dawson's message that year, along with the challenge to memorize and the continuing sermon on The Wheel. He realized that what he had learned the hard way about follow-up he must continue to teach to these whom he had taught evangelism; it was not an inherited conviction or skill. Nor were the results of the hard work of follow-up as readily visible as a first-time decision for Christ. He drummed into the sailors the need to get their converts memorizing and studying Scripture, get them witnessing, praying, and applying the Word. In doing so Dawson felt he was following the pattern of 2 Timothy 2:2, committing to faithful men things they would teach others. But it would be a full five years before further maturing of vision revealed he had applied only half the verse.

Yet to him 1940 was a year of such progress in the work that he could look back six years to the filling station and 33 Surfline and declare God had done exceeding abundantly above all they had asked or thought. At least two reasons for the banner year were evident. For one, Dawson's move to major on training leaders who could carry a complete ministry on their own was beginning to pay off. Even with contacts snowballing and ship gospel teams holding meetings in a half-dozen or more ports, he was assured of the leadership of the key men in charge.

"Many of them are capable of . . . handling the work of the Lord on their own ship [and] helping train others," he wrote to a friend. "We do not care to prophesy growth. We are careful about growing and desire quality rather than quantity, but . . . I think in another three or four years the work will have trebled. The Lord is building and with Him nothing is impossible." In the work with servicemen as with students and the clubs, he felt the Great Commission would be fulfilled only by training many laborers to send into the harvest.

A second reason for the prosperous year was that a dozen or more key men had reenlisted in the Navy for the purpose of ministry. The discharge of the early Navigators had left a leadership gap which God was now filling. Dawson thought Downing, however, whom he often consulted and had kept informed of all decisions and plans the past two years, should get out after his current enlistment, take charge of the Bremerton Home, and be deputy director of The Navigators. Jim was praying about this and about Dawson's suggestion that Morena Holmes was the girl he should marry. (Daws also confided to Morena, first asking if she had any current romantic interest, that after prayer he and Lila had concluded she was the girl for Jim.)

One who reenlisted as a Navy missionary was John Prince. The artless Prince's acquaintance with logic or efficiency was remote, yet he seemed so attuned to the Spirit's leading that he could report as matter-of-fact the kind of experiences others would call remarkable. From Puerto Rico where his destroyer was docked Prince wrote:

> Last night after prayer went to Scout meeting and to my surprise they had a council meeting of all the troops—over 500 Boy Scouts. The way was opened to speak to them . . . around a big campfire. I used the twelve Scout laws (A scout is trustworthy, loyal, etc.) and proved as you once said, that no one could keep these unless he was a born-again Christian. Today the Executive called me in and handed me a letter [from an official of the Puerto Rico Council]. It read: "Last Friday evening we had the honor of having at our campfire a member of your crew, who brilliantly spoke to the boys. We wish you to extend to him our most sincere thanks. This letter is addressed to you as we neglected to ask his name. I would be very glad to be of any assistance to him while he is staying on our island and in case he can accept any invitation, please have him call me at my office or home." All the officers seemed very interested and many questions were asked. Before this they were critical of what I was doing ashore in different places. Now they seem very cordial and treat me differently.

Dawson grinned. God's hand was on Prince, all right. In

another letter he had told of giving a Gospel of John to a fire-man on the ship who promised to read it. That night Prince heard a splash and a shout, "Man overboard!" He ran over to see two men in the water between ships that were moored to-gether and, unmindful of danger, jumped to their rescue. He and one of the men were pulled out, but the body of the second man was not found till the following day. It was the fireman. "I believe God gave this boy his last chance when he read the marked Gospel," Prince wrote. "But he went ashore and got drunk. Upon returning he and another drunk got in a fight and fell between the two ships. . . . His death had a real effect on the men."

Prince reported that after the Boy Scout episode in San Juan "services opened up so fast we couldn't fill all of them. Twice I spoke over the air. Most of my ship was listening. Also spoke through an interpreter at the prisons, three or 400 attending. The way was opened to speak in the schools using Job 38 as a scientific basis to present the Gospel." Thus were a city and a ship's crew evangelized when a Spirit-led sailor prayed and went ashore to a Scout campfire.

*　　*　　*　　*

Much as Dawson wanted men to stay in the Navy for ministry, it delighted him even more to see men going out into home and foreign missions. So intent was he on missions that he was soon laying serious plans for a Navigators missionary society. Virgil Hook was graduating from Biola and going to Tibet with China Inland Mission. Spencer was in Colorado, and Hightower was going to Africa as soon as sailing permitted. Goodrick would teach at Westmont College; Dedrick would work in an Indian tribe in Mexico with Wycliffe Bible Trans-lators. Harris departed for the Congo just before German in-terference with U.S. shipping caused the State Department to cancel missionary sailings. Dawson and Downing had encour-aged some of the Navigators to underwrite half of Gurney's support and sent him off with a dinner rally at Clifton's in Los Angeles, presenting him with a sheaf of letters for the long voyage.

A further plan to see Harris off from New York spawned a cross-country gospel team trip like the one in 1935. The itinerary would include hometowns of four sailors who took thirty-day leaves to go — Oran Bell, an amateur boxer, lean, hard, elemental; Gordon Taggart, affable, easygoing Missourian; Kenny Watters, a year old in Christ, his Iowa-farm-boy face topping an athletic frame; and Victor McAnney, with the clean-cut look of a Navy recruiting poster.

Dawson saw the trip, to be made in late February in the 1931 Packard, as an opportunity for these men to see how God would supply their needs through prayer. He found on the eve of their departure, however, that Downing was taking each serviceman who came to the Home across to the park to pray for finances for the trip. Not surprisingly, each man later slipped Dawson some money. After several such gifts, Dawson sniffed out the plot and asked Downing to desist. He did, though his feeling about telling of financial needs was not so strict. Once when he had asked Dawson's counsel where to give some money he had accumulated, Daws advised him to give it to a missionary then ready to sail, not mentioning a definite current need in the Navigators work.

The vibrant testimonies of the Scripture-quoting sailors traveling across the U.S. startled their audiences no less than they had five years before. But this time they touched an open nerve as the Armed Forces had reached into thousands of homes and the spiritual needs of men in uniform were a live issue. Many contacts resulted with Christians in the service who needed fellowship — men like Gordon Gustafson on the *Tennessee.*

"I was weak and desperate and looking for Christians," Gus said. "Had had good Bible teaching at home but didn't know how to feed myself. Or help others. A fellow in Chicago heard the Navigator team and wrote me. Bell was the one I remembered. I looked him up, and he introduced me to the others. It seemed I had bumped into supermen."

One objective of the trip was different from that of 1935. With Dawson's vision focused on training leaders, he aimed for the training centers — Dallas Theological Seminary, Columbia Bible College, Wheaton College where Lewie Coates and another student had men under way in Dunamis — as well as ports where servicemen were stationed. The team made a visible impact, as noted by George Cowan of Wycliffe, then at Dallas.

"Each fellow took a part of the meeting," he said. "I remember the hard-hitting, hard-punching attack on things. Everything was laid down neatly and outlined — so businesslike but warm-hearted. To us at seminary it was a real challenge. You can get sloppy and lazy there, and here were these fellows who had a terriffic punch and impact." Thomas Petty of CBC recalled that President Robert McQuilkin appreciated Trotman's emphasis on the Word. "We were also impressed," Petty added, "that we were in the presence of a man who had a plan, and he was working that plan. The center of the plan was Christ, the center of responsibility obedience to Christ."

Back in the Los Angeles office a regular secretary was essential now to handle the volume of mail. So Martures girl Vivian Fusby, a senior at Biola, became headquarters "anchor man," relaying to the team daily reports of happenings and taking care of business for them.

In New York a packed schedule of meetings and appearances awaited the team, arranged by Robert Swanson, a businessman whose extraordinary hospitality included rooms at the YMCA, personal gifts of money, and even a new set of tires for the Packard. Swanson, whom Prince and Downing had met on earlier stops in port, was a guiding force in New York's new Christian Business Men's Committee, active in Pocket Testament League and Gideons, interested too in the evangelistic work of a businessman, Jack Wyrtzen, who was just starting youth rallies in Times Square. The ubiquitous Prince had met Wyrtzen by walking into a street meeting some businessmen were holding in front of city hall and giving his testimony. He later brought Downing and then Trotman into touch with the men.

Swanson and Wyrtzen recognized in these sailors and their leader a contagious enthusiasm for Christ that was rare indeed. The urbane Swanson, exact opposite of the rough-hewn westerner with a slang-salted vocabulary, was drawn by Dawson's joyous fervor for the Lord to become a permanent friend and a promoter of Navigators.

"New York turned out to be the highlight of our cruise, and the Lord used you in bringing this about," Dawson wrote him. "We have relived those precious hours a score of times. One of the fellows will say, 'Boy, wasn't that great riding around in that 1940 Cadillac with old Bob telling us those stories?' And another, 'Yeah, and how the Lord worked to get the Packard fixed for the rest of the trip . . . and weren't those swell kids, and wasn't Mrs. Swanson a peach!' The thrill of seeing the mighty New York skyline . . . opportunity to serve in Jerry McAuley's Mission with five or six precious souls finding Christ . . . witnessing at Flushing Presbyterian Sunday school . . . the New York Christian Business Men . . . besides getting to see old Gurney off, our first missionary. It was the good hand of our God upon us."

He told how God had supplied the remaining $140 needed to get home, plus $5 he had purposed to send Lila. An extra gift of $27 puzzled them, until a tire blew out on a lonely road. They bought a tire ($25) and paid $2 to the motorist who ferried them to town for the purchase. A spiritually needy motorist of course, to whom they ministered.

Swanson and Trotman wrote often, relaying names of servicemen to contact or Christian businessmen's groups interested in the work. But when Swanson asked him to send information about The Navigators to several wealthy men of his acquaintance, Dawson demurred. "It has been our policy never to mention finances. In remarkable ways our Lord has laid upon the hearts of servicemen the need at the right time," he wrote, indicating also that control of the budget through the flow of finances was one way the Lord could direct their activities. "I have always made it a point never to give the slightest hint to men of means. I think so many invite a man like L - - - not because he is a dynamic man as we know he is, but that he might do something for them. I trust you will understand our position, Bob. Be assured we desire to please Him alone." Swanson agreed heartily. "You display wisdom, Dawson, when you explain the way you handle 'men of means.' The Lord will honor you for this."

In April 1940 the entire combat fleet except the ancient U.S.S. *Utah* left for maneuvers near Hawaii. This and the Navy's rapid growth persuaded Dawson that it was time to visit the Honolulu Navigators. Sailing on the *Matsonia* April 18, he and Lila arrived six days later for a busy two weeks in the Islands. His heart sank as he saw the lack of preparation there for increased ministry as the fleet poured in, and the tone and quality of the work at the Honolulu Home.

"Find work in sad state," he confided to his journal. "Not truly a Navigators work, although going by that name." His desire for excellence only sharpened his disappointment at the sight of countless opportunities slipping away. "What a place and what a burden a fellow gets," he wrote to a friend, "to see the great mass of men gathered here — 40,000 officers and enlisted men on ships lying at anchor in Pearl Harbor (here on maneuvers). Besides a great host of soldiers — of the 30,000 in the Islands, 28,000 are here on Oahu."

With typical optimism Dawson plunged into meetings with the Christian men and spent time instructing DeGroff, the local representative, in making the work more "Navigator." DeGroff was teaching the Word, but the training man-to-man was missing — instructing, assigning studies, and coaching them in their labors on base and shipboard mission fields. It was there they would stand or fall before enemy attack and would win and train other men. Dawson noted that thirteen men who found Christ on the *West Virginia* during the month of April had each been led to Christ by a man on the ship, and would thus be personally followed up by the same man.

He was encouraged to see McAnney, Taggart, and other key men helping in the ministry, men in whom he and Downing had invested heavily. "Our hearts burn within us as we fellowship together almost for the last time now for many months," he wrote in his journal. "These men are ready to go to battle for the Lord. In fact, they are already in the battle. We can see an attempt of the enemy to disrupt — but God!" Seventeen meetings crowded into fourteen days in Honolulu, three of them gospel team meetings, the rest groups of ten to fifty servicemen for Bible study, testimony, and challenge to discipleship. A gathering of twenty, thirty, or even fifty Christians out of so many thousands seemed but "the small dust of the balance," but, he reflected, "they're pure gold dust."

On the ship returning home he found a quiet spot for many hours of fellowship alone with the Lord. Reading Hudson

Taylor was a fresh boost to his faith, and he claimed anew some of God's great promises for the servicemen's work. *Enlarge the place of thy tent, and let them stretch forth the curtains of thine habitations: spare not, lengthen thy cords, and strengthen thy stakes; For thou shalt break forth on the right hand and on the left; and thy seed shall inherit the Gentiles, and make the desolate cities to be inhabited. . . . The Lord God hath given me the tongue of the learned, that I should know how to speak a word in season to him that is weary: he wakeneth morning by morning, he wakeneth mine ear to hear as the learned. For the Lord God will help me; therefore shall I not be confounded: therefore have I set my face like a flint, and I know that I shall not be ashamed"* (Isa. 54:2, 3; 50:4, 7).

Pearl Harbor was now home base for the fleet. Downing commented on this in a letter to Dawson on the Honolulu visit: "I have never seen you finer and more productive under the sustained power of the Holy Spirit for that time in Hawaii. In light of the change of schedule, it certainly is all the more evident that you were to go to Honolulu when you did."

*   *   *   *

That spring an idea simmered in Dawson's mind for a newspaper with items of interest to all hands. Meanwhile a club leader suggested Young Men's Bible Clubs needed a news medium. The resulting four-page slick publication devoted half to club news — *Timely News Tips* Full of Dunamite — and half to *The Navigators Log*, mainly excerpts from servicemen's letters, was launched in June 1940. Dawson was now a publisher. Entire cost of the first issue, including postage for some 1000 copies, was $40. Dawson saw the *Log* as God's special provision for the men at sea, since June was the first month that fleet movements and ship locations were kept secret, making contact by mail suddenly more important. The *Log* tried hard to be a monthly, but often two months crowded into one issue. Then it became quarterly, and finally occasional.

Widened fleet activity, with ships visiting more ports for extended periods, made it urgent to Dawson to establish Navigator Homes in at least six or seven strategic ports. But his experience to date, including Honolulu, reinforced his belief that couples in charge should first be trained in Navigator ministry. Mindful of the warning to "lay hands suddenly on no man," he was reluctant to put an official Navigator stamp on a work, preferring instead to keep a loose connection of fellowship with those who generously offered their homes for hospitality. In Bremerton, Jim Forster was still faithfully on the job helping men. Besides the Home in Long Beach, there was the one in Honolulu and a missionary in Manila who provided a haven of Christian fellowship for those stopping in. But Dawson was most delighted that San Diego was reopened with seasoned Navigator Hightower at the helm, available because of delay in his sailing for Africa. Seven strong Navigators were stationed in San Diego, including Ken Watters in Navy service school and Bill Goold now assigned to a destroyer. This would give the port a solid operating team and contribute as well to the work in the fleet.

Dawson's only difference with Hightower was on financial policy. A man had inquired about financial needs, and Dick had willingly informed him. "That's not of the Lord, Dick," Dawson reproved. "When you start telling man your needs instead of making them known to God and waiting on Him to supply, you're walking in the flesh." The spunky Hightower wasn't convinced. "Well, that may be the way the Lord leads you, Daws, but I don't think you're the only one who has His leading in this matter, and I believe this is the way He wants me to do it."

Dawson was hurt by his disciple's departure from his training in this vital area of service. It seemed imperative that a co-laborer embrace his philosophy completely. Yet Hightower was a good man, and though it galled him to have such deviation from his policy, he would have to live with it.

San Francisco also needed a Navigator headquarters. In September Daws visited the Bay area, where his old friend Irwin Moon had packaged his scientific demonstrations as "Sermons from Science" and was using them effectively in evangelism at the world's fair. He had asked Daws to come to the fair and help follow up those making decisions, among them many Army and Navy men. Dawson was stirred when he saw Irwin reaching these men from all across the U.S. — a further answer to the prayer of nine years ago for boys from each of the 48 states to be reached for Christ. While he continued his efforts to establish a local Navigator work, Dawson was most thankful for Moon's ministry there.

By midpoint the year had gained a momentum that exhilarated Dawson, kindling the volatile sense of hurry that for him was a basic personality trait. "These are the busiest days of my life so far," he wrote Emil Pearson, "but oh how I love it. I am happiest when I am the busiest." Since the eastern and Honolulu trips his main work with servicemen was by correspondence — running to 150 or more letters a month — and frequent visits to San Diego. He was editing the *Log* and meeting at least monthly with Long Beach CBMC. Adding co-workers to his growing staff. Recruiting and training club leaders and leading some clubs. Planning monthly Dunamis-Martures or Conqueror-Victory club rallies. Planning and running summer camps and leaders retreats. Planning for separate Dunamis and Martures teams to travel in order to establish new clubs. Helping find the right homes for San Diego and Los Angeles headquarters. Designing better materials for Bible study and club use and supervising every detail of production. Checking out new mechanical ideas like plane travel or the possibility of a fleet of cars to use in the work.

There were also one-time opportunities: to give an evangelistic message at a conference; to help a high school group with a noonday Bible study; to join in fervent prayer with God's servants in a church and exorcise a demon from a tortured man; to encourage and promote the work of visiting missionaries.

Much as Dawson loved the diversity and volume of his activities, he also savored the idea of perfecting the quality of each experience. Rather than slide superficially over any duty, he handled it as meticulously as if it were his only concern. Every "i" must be dotted, every "t" crossed. It would seem inevitable that such an approach would lead him to bog down in details and lose sight of the objective, but it did not; he was steadily driven by a fixed and growing vision. His goal of bringing a man into the fellowship of Christ and teaching him to lead another into that relationship was as unshakable as his conviction that The Wheel, with special stress on the Word, was the high road toward that objective.

"In Christian warfare," he wrote in the *Log*, "the soldier of Christ needs two weapons above all others — the weapon of defense (the shield of faith) and the weapon of offense (the sword of the Spirit). Both these weapons . . . are one and the same: God's Word."

In Dunamis, as it evolved, Dawson believed he had something that would work anywhere. The plan was an example of his search for ways to plug efficiency gaps, whether in details of everyday living or in the great business of serving the King of Kings. He could see a tremendous potential for Dunamis-Martures clubs to multiply across the land in high schools and colleges, among servicemen and businessmen, now that pilot groups had proved successful.

Adding a new dimension to his zeal was his view of the whole world not only as a mission field, but as a vast labor pool. The personal interest he had shown in each individual from earliest days, which had impressed so many and discomfited a few, now focused on that individual as a potential laborer to help in discipling others for Christ. Dawson felt he should invest his best efforts in recruiting and training such leaders. This led him to the Big Idea of the Year — a Dunamis-Martures Seminar, a six-month training school for a dozen or more selected workers.

Meeting four days a week in concentrated class work and close-range fellowship, they would also act as a research laboratory for developing materials and methods Dunamis could use world-wide. Each trainee would lead two or three high school or collegiate clubs where he could test the theories and report back to the seminar from live experience.

In September the D&M Seminar began. Four girls just out of Biola moved into 4845, while one or two fellows bunked over the garage and others commuted. Classes ran all morning two days a week at the Home and two days at the Los Angeles office. Afternoons and evenings the trainees scattered across L.A. County to lead clubs for some 200 students who carried Bibles and black notebooks.

The seminar had one hour daily for a Bible message by a guest speaker. Other hours were workshops on club leadership, prayer, Scripture memory, STS Bible study, use of checkup and discipline. "Materials are just tools, remember," Dawson reminded them. "If they're not used, they rust. But if they are designed exactly right . . . they will be used. And the reason for finding better ways to do it is not some gimmick, but in order to help some fellow or girl *build in* to his life the strength and devotion to his Lord that will stand the test. So we want the very sharpest, most efficient tools possible. And why? Because whatever we do, whether we eat or drink, it should be unto the Lord, so let whatever we do be intense, clear, sharp, good quality, the best — for His sake."

So the group, joined by new club leaders during the six months, spent much time refining the STS study and prayer pages, the club check chart, and memory and review techniques. Trainees were assigned to write papers on each main subject studied by the seminar's end in March.

"Some splendid work," Dawson summarized in a letter to Downing. "This has been a terrific job, but one I enjoyed very much. Valuable information has been discovered which could never have been done without class debate, pro, con, etc."

One result of D&M Seminar was a new Scripture memory course to replace the old 105-verse, all-at-once pack in use for the last five years. Together they selected "forty-nine verses every new Christian should know," and the forty-nine became the standard memory work for Dunamiters, Navigators, and anyone else. Six verses, called the Initial Test, were the trial packet which qualified the user to get the whole pack. This bite-size incentive was one of several innovations the seminar produced. Another was the "fore 'n aft" principle in learning verses. Remembering references seemed to be a chronic problem in all the clubs but one.

"My kids don't have trouble with references," one leader reported. "Why not?" "Well, we found by saying the reference first when reviewing a verse, then saying it again at the end of the verse, they just remember it." "All right," Daws decreed, "let's try that in all the clubs and see if it works." It worked.

Details of method, such as the seminar concentrated on,

drew criticism later from those who contended that the work of the Spirit cannot be mechanized. "True," said Dawson, "but if methods can help a person reach his own goals in memory or study or effective prayer, the Spirit's work in his life can go forward." And what if mechanical means were used to hide the Word in the heart? From then on it was there for the Spirit of God to use for spiritual ends. Methods and materials could turn failure toward success in the real objective — knowing Christ and making Him known — and Dawson made no apology. He was merely packaging a product for which there was both need and demand.

More than spiritual technology, the seminar produced some unscheduled lessons in human relations and realistic missionary training. Before long the lack of privacy in the close quarters at 4845, the inconvenience of waiting until the living room was clear and sofas made into beds before anyone could retire, the varied preferences in rising times in the morning, and the division of household chores among them, began to fray the tempers of these girls whose Christian lives had never been on twenty-four-hour display. The very leadership qualities for which they were selected were squelched by what they saw as autocratic harshness in Dawson, restricting their free expression except in the open forums. Only acceptable opinions were to be spoken or even thought, they complained, feeling guilty as they did so. The girls were also critical of Dawson's strict discipline of the three children and his occasional word of correction to Lila.

For his part, Dawson was nonplused to find that girls could be so different. Instead of the free and open fellowship he had shared with the family and men who lived in the Home, he saw the girls taking their little matters underground, bickering in dark corners by flashlight, and building silent tensions toward him and each other. He did not feel he was dictatorial, but rather reasonable and open, willing to teach as freely as he had always done with the men.

"Who fixed this grapefruit?" he asked abruptly at breakfast. "Here, lemme show you the way to cut grapefruit," and proceeded to show the embarrassed girl before everyone, never dreaming her humiliation would be long remembered. To him, Proverbs 18:15 — "The heart of the prudent getteth knowledge; and the ear of the wise seeketh knowledge" — meant she would be glad to learn.

Except for his easygoing secretary Marjory Thomson, this was Dawson's first experience of having girls live in the Home, and he learned his ministry of reproof and correction required a different approach than with men. True, Lila had been much easier to train than these girls were, but Lila had come under his influence at age thirteen. The fact that he usually *was* right and he *did* know a better way, being as one said "a man of very few inabilities," was to the feminine mind irrelevant. But the fact that his forthright dealing with them, whether on spiritual or practical issues, was out of genuine love and interest served to heal most minor cuts and bruises the relationship suffered.

"A great warm heart and at the same time a disciplinarian," Wheaton President V. Raymond Edman described him. "Deeply interested in the welfare of each Navigator, yet there could be no slovenly habits or carelessness. He was disciplined, so he demanded discipline on the part of everyone and rightly so." One seminar girl later understood it. "He wanted to hold each one of us to the highest. He was brusque, but later learned to be more skillful in making people over."

The seminar thus unknowingly pioneered a phase of missionary preparation which mission executives have since grappled with — helping their young recruits through the inevitable personality clashes before they reach their field of service, where failure in human relationships is often fatal to a missionary career. But the friction which Daws identified as "attacks of the enemy" was not the dominant theme of those eventful months. The prevailing mood was of light-hearted good times: a comradeship of shared times of Bible study, prayer, and thanksgiving to God.

Lila's buoyant spirit made each mealtime a celebration and extra guests a blessing. She performed her home tasks unobtrusively, accepting the unexpected as God's will, struggling with her attitude only when she heard criticism of her husband.

Every member of the group except Dawson came in for a share of good-natured teasing. And in a swift change of mood Dawson might ask each one at the table to quote a verse on victory, on God's greatness, or on prayer. Always, and unselfconsciously, the Word was given preeminence. Upon parting at a street corner or bus stop, club members or leaders would say, "Let me give you a verse," and quote a specially chosen Scripture. Irwin Moon could not recall that Dawson ever failed to leave him with a verse — "always something appropriate, something precious, new and wonderful." The Word in the heart, on the tongue, and in the Home was the great sustainer of faith, giving instant assurance that the Lord was in charge, whatever the circumstance.

A move to a new Navigator Home ended the year 1940, as Long Beach and Los Angeles households traded homes. Daws and Lila's special promise for the new Home at 175 South Virgil was Haggai 2:9, *The glory of this latter house shall be greater than of the former, saith the Lord of hosts: and in this place will I give peace, saith the Lord of hosts.* The roomy two-story dwelling so conveniently located was the kind of exceeding abundant provision everyone had come to expect. Ideal base for the club work and for seminar classes, with access to the athletic field of Westmont College, 175 had no drawback except its distance from the Navy landing, a forty-five-minute ride by Pacific Electric red car for the sailors. But Dawson was happy to find that even this was no hindrance. On weekends when two or three ships were in port the house filled with twenty to twenty-five men.

New Year's Eve was one such occasion recalled by Vivian Fusby, Dawson's new secretary. "The house was full of sailors — the *California* was in and everyone was there. Jim Downing and Morena announced their engagement. We had a watch-night service and were up to the wee hours. And Daws took Lila clear to Long Beach to the hospital to deliver Faithie and just made it." The multiple activities, the hair-breadth timing that called for his race driver skill in traffic — Dawson loved it all. And Lila, good sport to the end, thought it was great adventure. It was not inconsistent that they named their fourth child and second daughter — who came an hour after midnight — Faith.

With the new Home, the growing club ministry, printing and office expenses for Navigator correspondence and materials, and the seminar group living mainly on pooled funds, Dawson was startled by the size of the budget at year's end. He liked to think about money only when he looked in his wallet for a handful of it to give to a co-worker in need. He still held to the Hudson Taylor faith principle — with rare exception, such as writing a letter asking servicemen to help with last summer's Bible camp deficit, a project to which they responded generously.

The prudent Downing, self-appointed finance minister of The Navigators, argued for a receipting procedure for gifts, which would not violate the faith principle and would assure the men their gifts were getting through the mail. Dawson resisted the practice on grounds that sending a receipt was an implied request for another gift. The men were generous and willing to give, Downing countered, but usually gave where they knew of a need, be it the Honolulu Home or whatever need was visible at the moment.

"You're right, Jim," Dawson admitted. "The needs of people with whom I'm not in close touch tend to fade. I've been encouraged, too, to hear later of the need that was met by some gift I've given, and this in turn has stimulated my desire to give." It made sense to him that those who gave should be made aware of current needs, but he determined that financial information on the work should reach only those who "should know." Strangely for a man of foresight, Dawson would not face the fact that he was indeed building an organization and would have to be involved in its financial matters, not only letting the right hand know what the left hand did but keeping an orderly record of both for government and public scrutiny.

It would be years before he would accept — and then unwillingly — the idea of balanced books and orderly use of funds from separate accounts. Until then he would be independent of such restrictions and enjoy the heady informality of seeing God rain down money in amounts needed. A journal notation during Boys Camp bears witness: "Run completely out of money.

The Lord sends $5 through one of His servants, just today from an unexpected source."

Dropped off at the train depot for a trip to the Valley, Daws found he was without his checkbook and dashed outside to hail those who drove him to the station. "The Lord had just enough change on the persons of those in the car to make possible the trip one way. It will be for Him to supply in His own wonderful way to come back." He made the return trip with a man driving to Los Angeles, to whom he presented the Gospel on the way.

Two days later he noted: "We have just passed through . . . several days like most of the former days of our work, in which we need to figure from meal to meal and from one need to the next. His gracious way of providing cannot be excelled." Not having had to spend "the $6 in the bank" for his train trip, Dawson found it was just the amount a Christian worker friend needed for his own travel expense. Next day he wrote, "One of the servants of the Lord . . . hands me $90 today. This is most timely." A month later, "Obligations today come in for $39 and something, but in the same mail a $40 money order." And the next day, "We are to meet a payment of $40 today, also a telephone bill of $8. Does the Lord supply? A man brings us a $51 check to the home."

That evening Dawson prayed for the privilege of giving sacrificially. Stopping at the home of some friends, he gave them what money he had and discovered it would be used to buy their breakfast. The following day two gifts totaling $15 met the day's needs, including a doctor's appointment for Lila, and allowed another small gift to this couple.

Again Daws wrote: "It is rainy weather and I need a car. Henry's is provided as he is away. It is quite noticeable that although I do not have a car, the Lord has supplied whenever it has been necessary. . . . The Lord laid on my heart to give the Packard to Hayden to sell toward clearing up his debt. I am more convinced as each day goes by that as each need arises, God will supply in one way or another, mostly in another. He so often does it in the way least expected. This is a great delight to the soul."

When tempted to feel deprived of time with his family whom he dearly loved, Dawson resolutely refused the thought, assured that if he put God's business first as he was called to do, God would care for his family; and he knew Lila was with him in this conviction. An evening at home with the children — ages six, four, and two — was rare enough to mention in his journal: "First time in a long time for evening home with kids. Bunch of cute clumsy clowns." And after Faith joined the little company: "I certainly love and enjoy my family. What a thrill it is to tear in and out, kiss them going and coming. They are lined up when I come in and I kiss the three and tear up to see my little Faith Arlene."

He loved to take quick shopping trips and bring home clothes for each of them and sometimes a toy. Lila approved of his selections and enjoyed having the children see him as the one who provided these things for them. It was always a highlight when they all went to visit Dawson's father and his new white-haired wife Sally on their small acreage in El Monte that included a vegetable garden, fish pond, rabbits, and a berry patch.

"Don't call me grandpa. Call me Dan," he ordered his grandchildren, clowning absurdly to prove his youthfulness. They squealed with delight when "Dan" accidentally swallowed a tiny frog he had popped into his mouth to entertain them.

God was using the children in the lives of Lila's parents. Though a minister's son himself, Dad Clayton personally received Christ only after hearing Bruce and Ruth at ages five and three quote Scripture much as other children quoted nursery rhymes. Now he had taken hold, attended CBMC meetings, and made a trip back to his boyhood home to witness for Christ among his kinfolk. Mother Clayton had lacked assurance, but her faith was strengthened through the little ones. Once at 4845 Ruthie quoted John 3:16 when her turn came in the after-dinner fellowship around the table, emphasizing "whosoever," a word she had mastered with effort. The sailor sitting next to her heard the familiar verse as if for the first time, realizing *he* was the "whosoever." Five days later he accepted the Lord.

Bragging about his family was an incurable habit which

Dawson's friends indulged good-naturedly. In letters or conversation or a conference message he would manage a reference to the "best-looking kids on either side of the Rockies and the smartest in either hemisphere" or the mock-serious statement that "other people think their kids are exceptional but mine really are." He appreciated the children's special place in the work, their contribution to the sailors' lives and what the men added to theirs. And Dawson freely taught the fellows what he was learning about training children. He had admired his sister Mildred's example in training her son with strict insistence on obedience, and he decided to use some of her methods. Now, Mildred thought he was more strict than she had been.

Obedience was his emphasis. "Daddy only wants one thing — that you do what he says," was a maxim they soon learned. They knew that though he would tolerate no exception, his love for them was strong and his praise lavish.

And Lila. His feeling for her demanded he describe her excellence to any who would listen. A romantic idealist whose spirit matched the age when gallant knights jousted for their ladies, Dawson could convince total strangers that Lila was indeed the fairest among women. He wrote an essay expressing his thanks for her, burning its letters on a wood plaque for Dad Clayton's birthday.

> . . . *In the little church in Lomita, you gave her to me. Abraham's son, Isaac, gave "jewels of silver and jewels of gold" for the hand of Rebecah. Jacob served Laban 14 years for the hand of Rachel his daughter. I just barely said thanks, I was so absorbed . . . . She's a Wonderful Girl, Dad, pure Gold and worth Billions. God made her and directed our paths together I know, but you and Mom are the ones who for 18 years cherished and cared for her, and you're the one who OK'd it and it cost as much as she's worth, I know!* . . .

His custom-made Valentines, which Lila treasured more than expensive gifts, were extravagantly sentimental. The two of them often staged mock arguments over which one loved the other "most," thus "Love you most" became their standard way of saying good-bye.

Not that Dawson's romantic view of his wife dimmed his

insight or kept him from holding her to a high standard. He was remarkably realistic in detecting her spiritual need or shoring up a weak place in her relationship with the Lord. He once admonished her for saying "I wish" this or that, since it signaled discontent with circumstances the Lord had allowed or sent. He later noted that "her life is much more of a testimony" and that she was tackling a new schedule. "Lila has certainly been growing in her ability to fill the place of a wife and mother," he wrote, "and as the one to do the many things that need to be done in such a work as the Lord has called us to." On one occasion he reproved her for putting the Sunday paper ahead of her time with the Lord. He kept after her, too, about losing weight, perhaps with less understanding than if he had ever had the problem himself. He was embarrassed by her appearance when she was both overweight and pregnant; it did not occur to him that his intolerance should have embarrassed him far more.

But Dawson's predominant thoughts of Lila were loving adoration and thankfulness for her. He saw how her whole purpose was to make things easy for him and stand by him in complete loyalty. He appreciated the warm, impartial hospitality she showed to all, knowing she had learned well the lesson of responding positively without hesitating when unexpected guests arrived. He knew that often she did not feel well but went right on efficiently running the household, submerging her feelings in a show of cheerfulness. Her faith had grown steadily, helping her accept her frequent illnesses and surgery among the "all things" a loving God caused to work for good.

One of the greatest virtues Dawson saw in Lila in relation to the Lord's work was an enthusiasm and love matching his own for the crew — their expanding household and circle of colaborers. A Biola girl who typed letters for Dawson part-time was amazed to find she was "one of the family," welcome to dinner any time. Lila preserved for the 175 family a warm atmosphere of acceptance that endowed each one with personal worth and significance. She demonstrated the joy of open-hearted giving of oneself, with no selfish clutching for privacy or time of her own. Dawson knew the servicemen saw in Lila an ideal of a Christian wife and mother that they could seek in their own marriages. He could give her unreservedly the verse he knew God had placed in the Bible just for her — Proverbs 31:29: "Many daughters have done virtuously, but thou excellest them all."

Floyd Robertson, looking back on those days, felt Lila fulfilled her mission more favorably than any woman he knew; he attributed much of Dawson's success to her. "He could not afford a drain that so many wives subconsciously create," Robertson said. "Lila not only refrained from that, but she contributed so much encouragement. That doesn't require 100 percent harmony in all areas, but it is an overall attitude and devotion in which none I know excel over Lila. She filled her role in responsibility of the home, the children, and the hospitality, and she was Dawson's strong right arm providing encouragement and support and understanding. Heaven will record how much Lila has been the real source of strength of The Navigators."

"My health is not so good," Dawson wrote to Downing. "Lack of what I want most — pep. Twice in the last three weeks I have steamed up to full power and suddenly sprung a leak and had to almost stop." The six-month seminar combined with other responsibilities had overtaxed him — although only temporarily, for a few months later Downing commented on the thirty-five-year-old Trotman's increased pace: "Your inexhaustible energy remains a continual challenge. Pray I'll receive some from the same source."

But when he found he needed a tonsillectomy in February 1941, Dawson saw God's hand in it. The seminar members could spend a week researching and writing thesis papers. He could get some rest while recovering and use the time for meditation on the Word, for thinking, and for prayer. He took a room offered him by owners of the Southland Hotel across from Biola and enjoyed a profitable ten days of learning and planning strategy.

He thought of the growing servicemen's work and its volume of correspondence, the *Log* to be edited, materials to produce for an increasing demand, and branch headquarters to oversee. But at this moment his burden was to reach high schoolers across the U.S. through Dunamis and Martures clubs, a dream which now seemed nearer fulfillment. He counted some forty-four functioning groups, five of them on ships. But he believed the secret to reaching an entire city or area with the Gospel lay in first reaching its high school students. A further reason to aim at high schoolers was to establish them firmly in the faith before they entered the service as many of them would do.

The lively Dunamis-Martures and Victory-Conquerors rallies were proving that high schoolers and even junior highs could be discipled for Christ. He did not doubt the secret was the Word; they quoted it as basis for their testimony. Highland Park Dunamis Club was one which attracted an unusual group of comers. The club had begun more than a year ago with Dick Soderberg, who now wanted to include his testimony and a Gospel message in his valedictory speech. Dick had recruited his classmate Ralph Winter and his brother Paul, and Charles Fuller's son Dan joined the group. These fellows had set a blistering pace, salting away memory verses by the pound and digging into Bible studies. Daws reckoned it would be hard for an average fellow with only average desire to keep up with this gang, but he rejoiced in the way they were moving ahead with the Lord and determined to keep his eye on them.

Only two summer camps would be scheduled in 1941 — one week for Victory and Martures girls, one for Conquerors and Dunamis fellows. This would mean even less evangelistic emphasis than in previous camps, in line with Dawson's philosophy that a few, more carefully trained, could in the long run reach more in evangelism. The camps would be tied in to fall club work as their follow-up, making the camp week a beginning of something campers would continue weekly in their home localities.

The D&M Seminar had done well in developing materials to help young people get down to business for the Lord, a by-product of its main purpose which was to train the team of four young men and the team of five young women who would travel and establish clubs in high schools and colleges across the country. A Dunamis team and a Martures team had also been formed with members from the clubs who would seek to reach other high schoolers by holding meetings in church and school groups around Los Angeles, giving testimonies and short messages on spokes of The Wheel. It seemed the whole field of high school ministry was about to open wide.

But now that seminar was ending, three of the girls had wedding plans, effectively ending their career as a traveling team before it began. Daws felt the Lord was in it, however, as he wrote Bob Swanson: "God has given Oran Bell and James Downing two of the finest Christian girls I have ever met in my life — precious girls who labor with us in the Girls Bible Clubs." He felt a 'fatherly pride in sending them off to wed these men of God, in' a sense his sons in faith. His secretary Marjory had married Bill Goold at Pacific Palisades during the Life Triumphant in Christ conference when many of their Navy friends could be there to share their joy. Now her successor, Vivian Fusby, was about to be asked "the question" by Vic McAnney. Nadine Simon and John Gillespie, both club leaders, would be married soon and go to an Alaska mission field. Dawson did not see his diminishing female forces as a loss. In fact, he and Lila had promoted some romances as with Jim and Morena. There was still excellent womanpower on deck to lead clubs and train new leaders.

Clearly his priority now was to recruit men for Dunamis ministry — men like Spurgeon's "one," fully yielded, through whom God could show His power. There should be hundreds such men, and women, but they would have to be found and trained one by one. "We must find young men if we have to comb the forty-eight states," he declared to his journal. Next year's seminar should enroll only men — those available for club ministry for several years. He would turn it into a counselor training course, equipping them to train club leaders. One man was available, staying on after seminar to work with the clubs instead of going to teach at Westmont College. Elroy Robinson held three world track records, had been in Dunamis at Wheaton, and had grown in his vision for this ministry.

Robby was quick to take suggestions and act on them, a quality Dawson liked to see.

Another man Daws was strongly moved to call to the work was a first-year Biola student named Lorne Sanny. This young fellow had impressed him from the day he came in September 1940 to inquire about notebook materials he had seen. Dawson had put him off then, explaining Biola's rule against freshmen taking the extra work of Dunamis. But the persistent Sanny returned and found the rule amended to exempt those with a B average and was soon back with proof of his grades. Daws invited him to join the weekly 6:15 A.M. Dunamis Club in his office. He found Sanny poised and confident, a granite block of determination overspread by keen sensitivity. As a pre-law student in Modesto, Sanny had thought of evangelizing the student body by mailing each one a Gospel of John. The college turned down his request for the mailing list, so he arranged to meet with the school board — and got his list. Daws admired that kind of gumption.

Sanny took to Dunamis; he appreciated the value of doing God's business efficiently. He was fascinated by the five Esterbrook pens Dawson kept filled with different inks to mark his Bible and notebooks; by the way Dawson taught punctuality by explaining to a latecomer that his four minutes' tardiness kept ten people waiting, losing forty priceless minutes and slighting the importance of keeping appointments with the Lord; and by the use of a kitchen timer to allow exactly ten minutes in club to check out new verses learned and ten more minutes for the next activity. He responded to the idea of clean-cut reporting of success or failure in TNT assignments, with no half measures or excuses for work not completed. Sanny's competence in club leadership and other things revealed him as a young man with great promise. Dawson summoned him to the hotel and invited him to join the Dunamis staff within the year.

In March, the seminar ended, Daws and Lila made a trip east on short notice, primarily in response to John Prince's plea for help in opening The Navigators work in Norfolk! Prince had recruited a policeman and his wife, John and Louise Midgette, who opened their home to Navy men and needed Trotman's official stamp to make it a Navigator Home. Transportation was assured. They would drive east with a 175 resident being transferred and on the return bring a new car from the eastern factory to California for some Los Angeles friends. With a midnight farewell worthy of the Apostle Paul, a season of prayer in the driveway, and Scripture promises showered on them by those who stayed, they embarked from 175.

After Norfolk came stops in Washington, D.C., Philadelphia, and New York. Then Wheaton and the home of Professor and Mrs. Mortimer Lane, a perennial rendezvous for students and Christian workers. Here also were John Streater, former key man on the *Mississippi,* and his fiancée Carol, a Lane daughter. Streater introduced them to a fellow student, Billy Graham.

"Hi, Billy," Dawson spoke softly, gripping the lanky youth's outstretched hand. Behind the clear blue eyes Dawson saw a porcelain purity of soul. They talked a moment and Daws suddenly asked, "What did the Lord give you from His Word this morning?" Taken aback, Billy thought, what *had* He given him? Anything? He could not be angry with this man whose riveted attention made him feel like the only person in the room. He resolved fiercely that this question would never again find him without a suitable answer.

Many through the years felt this same mixture of pain and gratitude at a brief encounter with Dawson; his distinctive ministry of personal challenge to God's special servants who crossed his path, sometimes at a crucial moment, often led to an altered viewpoint or a changed life. At times it was ludicrous, as when he told the husky (6'4"), unconverted Jim Vaus he was a phony. Other times his word in season brought needed innovation. Jack Wyrtzen, the youth evangelist he had met the previous year in New York, was holding his Word of Life rallies in Times Square. "In our rallies night after night we were seeing quite a bit of success; in fact, in those days maybe a little proud of our success," Wyrtzen recalled. "And one day Dawson came to New York, came out to our home, visited with our office gang. God used him to shake us right down to our faces before the Lord. Daws rejoiced [in the many decisions] but he turned us inside out on follow-up. It was a tremendous help."

* * * *

"D'ya know when I can get in to see Mr. Fuller?" Dawson

held the phone with his chin while he signed the letters on his desk.

"Well," the secretary answered, "I see Monday he has a dental appointment with Paul Dewhirst."

"Good, I need to see Paul too. I'll find out if I can talk to Mr. Fuller in the chair."

Monday found the three convened at the dental office, unfazed by lack of precedent for their meeting place. "Say, Daws," the big man boomed before the dentist's drill made speech inconvenient, "I may have jumped the gun, but Sunday I announced over the radio that any Christian boys in uniform or anyone with a Christian son in the service could write in and we would try to contact them. And I want to turn those names over to you."

Dawson was aghast. "That's just what I wanted to talk to you about!" Soon after the spring trip east he had asked Fuller, Dewhirst, and Moon to act as an advisory council and shared his plans for Army work. "The Army's building up fast," he told them, "and we've got to do something to reach these new men just drafted. Some Army guys come around, along with the sailors, in the few ports where there's a Navigator Home. But we need to get to the men in all these new camps opening up."

He also wrote Downing about it. "We are on the fringe of a tremendous work. Established Christian men are being drafted from every walk of life into the service, presenting quite a different field [but] the same problems. Milo Jamison is carrying out a thorough plan in the Army. I would be content to send all contacts to him, but we see that what is needed is the very personal contact. I could no more drop responsibility at this point than any other part of the work. Most desirable would be men who could go from camp to camp, meet and help establish the men we contact."

Response was heavy from Fuller's Old Fashioned Revival Hour listeners. Letters from servicemen and their families poured in, soon mounting to 1000 a month and requiring another secretary at the Navigator office. Elroy Robinson was sent to Fort Ord and other camps to look up men. With the chaplain's help he located and fellowshiped with several men in a two-day stay. Dawson saw, however, that at this rate a work of any scope would need a number of men traveling to camps throughout the States. In a special prayer time he asked for seven men who would be available for at least a year for Army ministry.

Holy Father, I am asking You to give me seven men for this work. Lord, seven men with special characteristics — one each like Daniel, David, Abraham — Moses — John — Paul, and Peter.

The war in Europe looked no better, and U.S. involvement seemed likely. More and more Christian servicemen awakened to their need of fellowship and help in their new situation. Daws was excited about the volume of answers to letters mailed to them from headquarters offering such help, for each man was a potential recruit in the Lord's army. He was excited, but frustrated. While he wanted to offer each one the complete apprentice training in discipleship that Dunamis gave when personally taught, he had to concede this was impossible.

He must work out a shortcut for the emergency, doing what little could be done for the many while continuing thorough training for the few who could be reached personally. The emergency help for the many would probably be a Bible study which an individual or group could do by correspondence and some instruction in witnessing. What it boiled down to, it seemed, was Bible study and the memory verses. Wherever a key man could be developed in a camp, Bible study groups could gather under his leadership.

In one of his breakfast table inspirations Dawson designed a graphic he called The Hand. Each finger represented a different way to take the Word into one's life — hear it, read it, study it, memorize it — with meditation as the all-important thumb, to combine with each finger in getting a grasp on the Scriptures. Like The Wheel, The Hand immediately became a useful tool, both to illustrate personal need and to gauge the balance of a spiritual diet. Applying it to helping servicemen by correspondence, Dawson reasoned that they could hear the Word preached in church and chapel and could read it on their own, so study and memory were the areas on which he should focus.

Dr. Keith L. Brooks, whom he had recently met, furnished unlimited copies of his question-and-answer Bible study booklets which covered basic truths of The Wheel and Bible doctrine.

His *Young Believers Bible Work* was mailed out from Navigator headquarters by the dozens, then hundreds, followed by letters encouraging the user to "study to show thyself approved unto God. . . ." The forty-nine-verse Scripture memory pack was sent only to those men who requested it and who completed the first six verses as an "Initial Test." Those who finished the question-and-answer study books progressed to the ABC Plan which Dawson had worked out the year before for the high schoolers who needed a simpler plan than Dunamis offered. ABC had also caught on in some student groups not using the entire Dunamis club plan.

Up in Bremerton Jim Forster led a small group enthusiastic about early morning Bible study but bored with Dunamis reporting. Even at headquarters some were beginning to chafe at the drudgery of the written checkup. In the fleet, too, Dunamis fell on hard times as Downing switched the men to the ABC Plan, later dropping even ABC as a group activity when the men became competitive in it, engaging in mental sparring matches at the expense of spiritual profit. Dawson the perfectionist turned down Jim's request to use only parts of the Dunamis system on the *West Virginia,* insisting the plan be used intact and only by those who would do the work thoroughly, keeping up-to-date on the procedures. Failure to complete an assignment was bad for morale, he said, and the men could do memory, review, and study with or without the checkup system. So ended Dunamis aboard ship, except for a few using it individually. The notebook itself, however, survived as important Navigator equipment, in service and out, from that time on.

So remember Jesus Christ. The words of a favorite text from 2 Timothy 2:8 ended the keynote message, as Dawson leaned over the podium to look closely at his audience. "Remember who He is, gang — the Alpha and Omega, your Creator, your Lord, Redeemer, Friend, the Captain of your salvation, your

Commander in Chief. Remember, He wants to show Himself strong in the life of every one of you whose heart is perfect toward Him. Let's pray."

It was a Baptist family Bible conference at Mount Hermon late in July 1941. The denomination had appointed Lorne Sanny, now twenty, director of the conference, and he had invited Dawson as the main speaker. Sanny, spending the summer, except for this week, in a mission to migrant workers, appreciated the help of a nineteen-year-old buddy from his church, Cliff Barrows, who took charge of the physical aspects from mattresses to hot water bottles while Sanny handled meetings and administration. It was an awesome task for the two of them, and Dawson watched with experienced eye for times when they might need help.

Cliff had come to Mount Hermon conferences since age three and had dedicated his life to Christ through Dick Hillis's ministry there. Impressed with Dawson's straightforward manliness and even more impressed that this busy man had time for a personal chat with him, Cliff accepted his challenge to hide God's Word in his heart. Cliff, his sister Mary Jean, and several others with whom Daws spent personal time that week asked for Dunamis and Martures work.

Mary Jean felt that learning to memorize and apply the Word revolutionized her life; she marveled how Dawson "radiated the presence of God. You knew that he knew God," she said. "I never saw anyone live so close to God in practical everyday experiences."

Dawson invited Sanny to meet him at five in the morning for prayer. The two men met down by the stream and prayed, once and again, and Lorne was emboldened to ask the older man's counsel on questions no one had been available to discuss with him before. Daws helped him apply the Word to personal needs in his life, which at the moment was more crucial to Lorne than help in his ministry.

These times cemented a father-son relationship between them which was decisive in Sanny's choice of a career. He considered scholarships to two Christian colleges, a return to Biola where as a freshman he had been nominated for student body president, the possibility of getting a law degree at Berkeley, then chose instead to cast his lot with the man who saw the value of helping people personally with heart needs.

When Sanny arrived at Nav headquarters in September, Dawson knew the Lord had begun to fill his order for the seven men. Others followed. Within two weeks a team of five men left in a 1941 Oldsmobile, a gift from the Fullers, for an extensive trip to minister to servicemen. Dawson wrote in the *Log:*

> *Some of you have been praying for . . . a trip to northeastern U.S. where several Navy ports have never been visited. Hundreds of CHRISTian men have been drafted into the Army or have enlisted who know and love CHRIST . . . yet lack specific training. It goes without saying that the most effective work can be done as men are dealt with in a personal manner. So as . . . the Lord has provided several young men, a car and Philippians 4:19, we are shoving off on this extensive six-week trip which will cover some 10,000 miles. The entire itinerary has been planned in such a way that the men will be contacted in their stations during the evenings.*

John Streater had graduated from Wheaton, married Carol, and accepted Trotman's call to work with men in camps east of the Mississippi. He joined the team for part of the tour, which was billed as having a dual purpose: reaching Army men and introducing Navigator work to the public. Both were fulfilled as the team held meetings in Christian schools and churches, then visited camps where they scattered for one-to-one fellowship with men whose names had been given them. Later the *Log* carried Dawson's report:

> *At Wheaton College, over the air, and in churches, people's hearts seemed stirred to hear and know that business was being done among the Armed Forces of the nation. . . . We were privileged to do personal work in the Boston Gardens at Charles E. Fuller's meetings where some 30,000 gathered to hear the Word of GOD in a single day . . . . Opportunities to serve at Newport, New London, Washington D.C., Norfolk . . . . We were moving at the orders of the "GOD of all flesh." He opened*

> *doors without effort on our part . . . . Real busi-*
> *ness was done at Camp Davis and Fort Bragg and*
> *Fort Jackson . . . . Hearts were challenged at*
> *Columbia Bible College . . . at Fort Huachuca,*
> *Arizona 300 Negroes with open hearts devoured*
> *the Word . . . .*
> *Because of Streater's work, letters turned over to*
> *us by Charles Fuller, praying parents and praying*
> *friends, Christian workers who have sent names,*
> *and because these were followed up with per-*
> *sonal letters, men have written from over 75*
> *camps and forts in the U.S. and Alaska asking for*
> *definite Bible study helps and help in personal*
> *work.*

Bob Swanson booked engagements around New York for the civilian team but noted they were less impressive than the team of sailors. He advised Dawson to "wherever possible have a uniformed Navigator with you. . . . A uniform is a very popular thing today and we must do everything we can to make our witness attractive." At Wheaton, Professor Lane shook his head in wonder at Dawson's perpetual hurry, an image he earned by his compulsion to "get the job done." Dr. Edman again noted approvingly the enthusiastic loyalty of those who followed Dawson, confirming his God-given leadership.

Here at Wheaton a second encounter with Billy Graham included an incident which was rough on the young ministerial student but typical of Dawson's use of the crude tactic of humiliation to make a person think. Invited by Graham to speak at the small church where he was pastor, Daws in his message bore in on the importance of having memorized Scripture ready to use. He compared the ill-prepared Christian to a grocery clerk who assures the customer an item is in stock but does not know where to find it. "How long would that clerk survive? For instance, here's a preacher," and quoting a verse of Scripture he wheeled to ask, "Billy, where's that found?" Flustered, Billy could not say, and Dawson pressed further. "If this is an important verse, you ought to know where it is." Graham was embarrassed but recovered sufficiently to quote a verse for which Dawson could not supply the reference. The congregation enjoyed the volley, but the point was made. Billy's fellow student Bob Evans cringed, recalling his own humiliation the previous summer when in Los Angeles with an evangelistic team he had lunched with Dawson at a downtown cafeteria. "Give that fellow a tract," Daws said abruptly. Finding Bob did not have a tract with him, Daws feigned surprise. "Don't you carry anything to give people who need the Lord? What good is a soldier without any ammunition?"

"A fellow like that you never forget," Evans understated years later. "He was a hard character. But he knew whom to hit with these things and had a purpose for doing it. Probably even in those days he saw something in this young man Billy." Graham — and Evans — did become the closest of friends with Dawson and for years they worked together in their ministries.

T he team arrived back in Los Angeles in time for the 1941 Life Triumphant in Christ conference, which was not the usual uproarious Nav family reunion. Only twenty servicemen were scattered among 140 civilians; the war threat had denied leaves to many and stationed others thousands of miles away. But these twenty men again filled the choir loft at Church of the Open Door for the traditional "Navigator service" after the conference, warming the hearts of servicemen's families with their singing and vital testimony to Christ's sufficiency for the man in uniform.

Most of the headquarters staff of seven now lived at 175 in the distinctive family style Dawson and Lila set as a hallmark for Navigators everywhere. Practical reasons for the community living were to make a home for workers who had come from other cities and to stretch the work's financial resources by pooling expenses. More significant was the training the staff could receive by living in the Home and the contribution they made to the lives of others. Round-the-clock contact tended to destroy facades and open each one's daily life to the others' view. Individual needs could be seen and ministered to in an environment of caring and sharing. Dawson felt the children also benefited from this enlarged family as they could learn more from their lives than was available to most children. And the atmosphere of love and good will warmed the hearts of many visitors and short-term family members who came within its circle.

One such visitor was a debonair young man from Oklahoma ranch country who arrived in Los Angeles planning to go into radio. Asked by a hitch-hiker he picked up where he planned to spend the night, he said he had no plans so accepted his passenger's invitation to the Navigator Home. Thus Daws and Lila extended hospitality on his first night in California to Bill Bright, not yet a believer, but destined to head a world-wide college movement, Campus Crusade for Christ.

Mixed with serious dedication to their mission was the group's continual readiness to play; volleyball games in the driveway, clowning, or practical jokes could break out at any time. Dawson liked planned happenings; he would stage a loud argument on a downtown street with the stocky Sanny and have Hayden appear as a stranger to part them in time to prevent a fistfight. Or he would stroll down the street with Sanny, their shoulders propped together like an A-frame. Dawson's taste for slapstick so evoked his show-off English father that often when Lila watched her husband's corny antics she nudged the person near her and murmured, "Look at Charlie Trotman." The trait was repeated in son Burke, who became a Laurel and Hardy fan and imitator. A newcomer to 175 could sense a purposeful efficiency in the household, but also an infectious spirit of fun that immediately included him in its spell.

The same magic could be felt at the office, now expanded from two rooms to four to accommodate all the workers, desks, and typewriters. Lila brought hot lunch to the office at noon on days when the staff gathered for prayer and fellowship or to hear from a special guest home from a mission field. At headquarters there was a current of excitement about the significance of the work each was doing. At the center of this loyal band of colaborers beamed Dawson, enjoying their devotion and reminding them constantly that "our wonderful Lord Jesus" was author and finisher of all they possessed.

Equipping the four-room office called for Dawson's talent for improvising. With Sanny in tow he toured used furniture places, finding an ancient roll-top desk they could sand and refinish for the newest secretary. Sanny worked at a folding table until the next old desk was found and refinished. Then the arrival of another secretary sent him back to his folding table.

Dawson gave Lorne responsibility for the high school clubs in Southern California, some thirty-five in all. Dropping out of Biola for the semester, Sanny led some clubs and supervised the leaders of others. One he led personally was the showcase Dunamis group in Pasadena with Dan Fuller and the Winter brothers, using what he learned from Dawson to conduct meetings with clockwork precision and a high level of enthusiasm.

Sanny redesigned the Dunamis Bible study plan, calling it AlphAmegA to imply Christ-centered study ("I am Alpha and Omega. . . ." Rev. 1:8). Most clubs became AlphAmegA clubs, using materials similar to Dunamis.

One vestige of early club days provided an amusing vignette: the bus Dawson had used in Long Beach to take servicemen or high schoolers to club meetings and rallies was now sold to the Police Department, which barred its windows and used it to transport prisoners. They did not, however, paint over the lettering, so that on any given day a busload of malefactors might be seen rumbling across Long Beach boldly labeled "Navigators"!

Claiming God's promise to "make a way in the sea, and a path in the mighty waters," Dawson had prayed for a key man on every ship in the Navy. The answer to his prayer and the prayers of the men for transfer to new mission fields was helped along by Congress's 1940 authorization of a two-ocean Navy, which meant many new ships must be manned, their crews salted with experienced men from established crews. McAnney was sent to the *Astoria,* as was Taggart from the *California.* Another key man from the *California* drew the *Chicago.* Floyd Robertson was already on the *Wichita.* Machinist's Mate Jack Armstrong, up for transfer to the *Atlanta,* suddenly felt unprepared; Downing gave him a crash course in leadership, assigning him six new Christians to follow up and guide through the first Bible studies. Jack then went to his new station with more confidence.

Dawson wanted some of these men to colabor with him after their service in the Navy — chiefly Downing, perhaps McAnney, Taggart, Bell, Watters — and some were considering it. *What if,* he suddenly thought, *the Lord gives us the four men who made the trip east last year!* For now, he was delighted to see these mighty men navigating in the fleet, living the life before others, doing their shipboard work a little better, making it their first priority to know Christ and to make Him known. As the Holy Spirit strategically placed them on various ships it seemed like another Acts 6 when the Word grew mightily and the number of disciples multiplied.

Each man was different: intellectually eager like Armstrong or Watters, shrewd and discriminating like Downing, wholly ingenuous like Prince and Bell. But they were strong in the Word and in faith, and dear to his heart. He smiled, thinking how the crew at 175 and the office rejoiced when a Navigator white hat came in sight. They were indeed a close family, as Bell wrote from Honolulu, "All the fellows are homesick for 175." Daws recalled the recent two weeks of great fellowship when the *California* was in and the habit Bell and others had of asking, "What has the Lord spoken to your heart today?" This frequent sharing of the Word encouraged and built the habit of "meditation day and night" that Daws longed to master and teach to the men.

On the ships the bond of brotherhood was evident. Marvin Lokkesmoe, a youngster who had requested duty on the *West Virginia* when he heard Christians were aboard, told how they watched lest any slip from fellowship with the Lord or with the group. When a man failed to come to daily prayer meeting or Bible class, they looked him up. Once Lokkesmoe found a Christian buddy kneeling with some sailors around a dice game.

The buddy looked up sheepishly and said, "Hi, Moe. I only got one dollar left. I'll shoot this and be right with you." "We had real New Testament love for one another," said Lokkesmoe. "Our concern was deep, and it hurt us to have one out of fellowship."

The concern touched all areas. Seeing a Christian wear a T-shirt with a hole in it, Lokkesmoe put his finger through the hole and ripped it off. Just as tactfully, he told another, "Go shine your shoes." The reputation of the group was at stake. As he said later, "The Navy had a lot of guys that the sheriff had chased into the recruiting station, and there wasn't any friendly spirit toward Christians. So we had to be ten times as sharp as anyone."

Bell always wrote of fresh blessings from the Word and of spending time with men: "I was walking around the ship and started by a place but decided to stop in — who did I find? Old Nuckles praying. I had a word of prayer with him and started on my way. Looked in another place and there was James Lewis digging away on his memory. I had a word with him and sat down to write you and along comes old Burton."

Dawson could name the key man and one or two more on most ships, the "faithful men able to teach others also." But he wanted every man they raised up to be that kind of man, for after all, training trainers of men was the only way to get the job done. *What happens,* he wondered, *to those who come after the first two or three men on a ship?* Of course Dawson could not keep up on them personally, but he hoped the key men did and that they were thorough in working with them. Already he had found many did not read the *Log* thoroughly; were they as imprecise in checking their men regularly on their Bible study and memory work, or teaching them the right and wrong ways to present the Gospel, and scores of other things a son in the faith should be taught? He hoped not, but felt uneasy about it, for the solidity of the work done in lives from man to man on down the line was essential if any of it was going to last.

His uneasiness on this point was not helped by seeing the roster of Navigator contacts grow longer day by day. He was leery of The Navigators growing so fast numerically. He would rather have a score of iron men with an eye single to God's glory than a legion made of iron mixed with clay. In fact he did not know how many real Navigators were in the fleet or in Army camps and steadfastly refused to estimate for those who asked. Publicity would be dangerous for The Navigators; he feared the day when the name might become popular. He wanted men to be attracted not to a name or organization but to the Christlike life of a man who worked beside them. If the time came when people gave The Navigators glory which belonged only to the Lord, he decided, the name Navigator would have to go. It seemed distasteful and a discredit to the Lord that any man would want to be identified with The Navigators yet have no desire to get down to business and live the life.

As time went on, he had to work harder at making this principle clear and avoiding publicity. He would not shun growth, for laborers were all too few. What he did intend to fight was the inflation that was inevitable if the movement was popularized. He would bend all his efforts to insure steady, oak-tree growth in the number of men who were known as Navigators.

And happily, there had been little publicity; the main medium was still word of mouth. At mid-year Biola's magazine, *The King's Business*, carried a story on the work titled "What Does Military Life Do to a Christian?" Then on the *California's* April trip to Hawaii, Bell wrote of opportunity to witness to a passenger who was a writer for *Collier's* magazine. Later a *Collier's* photographer came to the office for a picture. Dawson had stalled the request a number of times, sparring for the right to see the story in advance. Finally he consented to a photo in which he would talk to a sailor over an open Bible, a larger-than-life poster in the background shouting, *"Now thanks be unto God who always causeth us to triumph in CHRIST."*

Yet for all the advance warning, it was still a shock. Returning from a week of rich blessing at a retreat with some twenty-five staff and club leaders, Dawson found the September 13 *Collier's* with a lengthy article "Onward, Christian Sailors" by Walter Davenport. There was the picture — sailor, Scripture, and all. The writer quoted a chief bo's'n mate describing the "new Navy," of which one new feature was Navigators.

> We've got about 12 of them on the *California*—maybe 15. You can't tell. Today you've got 12, maybe 15. Tomorrow you've got maybe 18 or 20. They're always working on the wicked, converting sinners, holding revivals, praying with lost souls. Every ship in the fleet's got some—I don't know how many in all and they ain't saying.

Davenport told the Navigator story mainly from his interview with Bell on the trip out. Bell had been unaware he was being interviewed, though he did notice his friend took a lot of notes while they talked.

Dismay was total at 175. First thoughts were that this publicity could lead to restrictions in witness on some ships. The crew prayed, groping for comfort from the Scriptures. Comfort came from the verse that headed the story in bold type. They would claim it for victory — "always" surely meant now — for the Navigators in the fleet whose story it told. Within twenty-four hours Dawson decided it wasn't a blow at all and that quite possibly good would come of it, especially because of the Scripture quoted right in the text.

And good did come of it. Copies of *Collier's* reached every hometown hamlet and the wardroom and library of every ship, bringing contact with many Christian officers and enlisted men. It lent status to existing groups on ships and stations and made friends for The Navigators in countless churches across the U.S. Dawson had realized his vision of raising up a new breed of men, had translated Christianity for them into a whole new way of life; now, as *Collier's* attested, he had also, like it or not, founded an organization, a movement.

It was the organization idea he resisted, feeling it would encourage too-rapid growth and thus dilute the quality of work done in lives; yet he wanted to reach vast numbers of men in the armed forces. This ambivalence and his insistence that men be recruited to live by the Word and follow Christ rather than an organization kept him reluctant to attach the name Navigator to an individual or a local work. "A Navigator is a man who's navigating," he usually answered a query, explaining what navigating meant in terms of The

Wheel. He knew also that a man who truly was navigating would not be likely to so designate himself.

* * * *

The familiar surroundings evoked memories. Here, more than twenty years ago, in the adjoining living-dining rooms of the modest frame cottage the high schoolers had crowded in for Fun and Study Club or C.E. planning meetings. Here Lila had later joined the good times of fellowship and study as an officer in C.E. On this December Sunday in Lomita Daws and Lila were dinner guests of their cherished schoolteacher friends and spiritual counselors, Misses Mills and Thomas.

"Many of my convictions today and the life principles I hold and teach to my men were learned right here in this home," Dawson declared. The women murmured their thanks, passing along the praise to the Lord. Perhaps they discounted some of the credit coming their way as typical of Dawson's expansiveness.

"You'd be thrilled to see the letters that come to my desk every day," he continued, "from men on ships and in Army camps all over the country who are growing in the Word and winning souls to Christ — memorizing and using the same verses you gave me to learn in those early days. And y'know," he added, beaming, "there's nothing namby-pamby about them. They're strong, rugged soldiers of the cross, fit for the battle."

The two listened appreciatively as he told, with the enthusiasm they remembered so well in the youngster they had discipled in his teens and early twenties, of God's working among servicemen and young people in recent months. Absorbed in their conversation, the group was startled by the doorbell.

It was Lila's father, who lived a few blocks away, and his face was tense. "The word just came over the radio," he said without ceremony, "that we've been attacked. The Japanese have bombed Pearl Harbor and sunk some of our battleships. All servicemen have been ordered to report to their stations immediately."

Dawson flicked on the radio. "Did they say which ships were sunk?"

"No, but it looks bad." Mr. Clayton was glum. The group

sat silent, each mentally running through names of friends who might be involved.

"Let's pray," Dawson spoke their unanimous thought.

*　　*　　*　　*

Even as the little group knelt in the Lomita cottage to pray for the men on Pacific ships, questions raced through Dawson's mind. What battleships had been sunk? The *West Virginia?* The *California?* What about his dear brothers? Downing . . . Bell . . . Watters . . . McAnney. . . . Many names and faces flashed before him. He had spoken of them just this morning in his message at the little church where he and Lila were married nine years ago, of their faithful witness aboard the great ships of the U.S. Navy. *Collier's* had referred to Bell as The Missionary. Well, the *Tennessee* had its missionary — Gustafson. Downing had seven or eight solid men on the *West Virginia.* The *California* had several. If any of those ships had gone down, their crews would have heard the Gospel. Not so the *Arizona.* He knew of no key man there, nor on the *Nevada.* Their loss would seem even more tragic.

But the agonizing questions raised by the bleak announcement were laid to rest by an overpowering sense of God's sovereignty and love. Dawson knew the bombing of the fleet did not take Him by surprise and that His eye was on every man who named His name to perfect His good purpose for him. It thrilled him to think how these men schooled in the Word and the love of God would perform in the emergency. He knew they had acquitted themselves well, and this knowledge more than made up for the lack of accurate news.

For weeks, news bulletins revealed little as wartime censorship clamped down. The story of what happened December 7 was gradually pieced together, but until a *Life* magazine photo report appeared a full year later, the public did not know the extent of the devastation. Meanwhile the Navigator story of that day was eagerly reconstructed by those on the home front who swarmed around each new arrival from the Islands. Morena Downing was first, on January 1. Also among dependents returned to the mainland was Bell's wife Arsha, whom Daws and Lila had helped get to Honolulu for her wedding in late summer. Morena and Arsha recounted acts of heroism by

Navigators under siege and unprecedented opportunity for witness to men who were now unusually ready to listen.

Morena had poured second cups of coffee for the men lingering over Sunday breakfast at the Honolulu Navigator Home, some of the thirty who had gathered for Bible study the evening before and who would go back to their bases after church services in town.

Petty Officer Herb Goeldner pushed back his chair. "If you'll excuse me, I have a Bible class at 0800 on the ship." After Goeldner left, they heard gunfire — antiaircraft, machine guns, rifles. The men listened. A sailor twitted the soldiers, "Well, if the island's attacked, good thing it's not up to the Army to defend us."

"Rifle practice," one of them concluded. But Gunner's Mate Downing knew better. He turned on the radio and heard the general alert. The Japanese strike on Pearl Harbor was less than ten minutes old. Goeldner reached the navy yard gate, saw the bombing, smoke, confusion, burning debris, and wheeled back to get the men. They were already in uniform, ready to go. Morena called after her husband, "Deuteronomy 33:12, Jim!" as they roared back toward the action. She saw him little from that moment until Christmas Day when she sailed for home.

Even with war plans brewing, few things had seemed less likely than an air attack on Pearl Harbor. Not only was it poor strategy for an aggressor, but poor judgment; it would immediately mobilize an outraged America to strike back. The Navy's historian Samuel E. Morison says, "On the tactical level, the Pearl Harbor attack was wrongly concentrated. . . . On the strategic level it was idiotic. On the high political level it was disastrous."[*]

There had been a respectable degree of readiness and condition of alert, but military and civilian alike were convinced there was no danger. When war did start, it would be "out there" somewhere. So it was a normal American Saturday night — off-duty officers and men dining out or idling at amusement centers in town and at clubs on base. Many planned Sunday

[*]Samuel E. Morison, *History of U.S. Naval Operations in World War II,* Vol. III (Boston: Little Brown, 1948).

morning golf or swimming. At that moment none of the more than 2400 who would die before noon dreamed of disaster approaching from the northeast at 180 miles per hour. For other thousands, tomorrow would be the first of 1351 days of bitter war.

Inside the main gate the men spilled from Goeldner's car into an arena of incredible destruction. Across at Ford Island where the fleet's eight battleships sat in once-proud Battleship Row, the *West Virginia* was listing heavily to port with fire sweeping her decks. The *Arizona,* blown in half when her forward magazine exploded, was a burning mass of wreckage, showering flaming debris on her neighbors. The *Oklahoma* lay bottom up, and the *California* was sinking slowly. Two destroyers were burning in dry dock beside the *Pennsylvania.* The hangar at the end of the island burned while enemy planes strafed every visible target, human or materiel. Antiaircraft guns fired at the low-flying planes, and firefighting crews were being organized. Oil from damaged ships blanketed the water, much of it in flames.

Some men ran to battle stations they would never reach; others fled their doomed ships for safety. A wounded man shook an angry fist at the sky. Men cursed, prayed, stood dazed, hurried aimlessly nowhere. At the main gate a Marine sergeant took futile aim and fired his rifle at the Japanese overhead. "Well, they were shooting at me," he said.

Downing and Chief Yeoman Watters sprinted to the landing and hailed a boat to Ford Island. Other boats were already picking up bodies and survivors from the water. Rounding the turn, they saw the sinking *West Virginia* moored outboard the *Tennessee.*

"Looks like we'll need both hands, Jim," Watters observed, so they stowed Bibles and notebooks in an equipment box on the dock. The tall, heavy-browed Iowan had transferred with the admiral's staff to the *Maryland,* now tied up inboard the capsized *Oklahoma.* "Glad I'm caught up on my praying," he called back as he sped to his duty station.

Downing too was thankful to be fortified for this day, portions of Scripture rushing to strengthen him even now. He looked across at the doomed *Arizona* where over 1100 men were burned or trapped below to drown. He had known only one man on the *Arizona,* a radioman first class who had been transferred off the ship to Johnson Island. His wife arrived from the States just after he had gone and frankly asked God why. Jim knew she would see why now. God had more work for her husband to do.

The *West Virginia* was one of the first hit, taking six or seven torpedoes in her side which caused the quick list to port. Marvin Lokkesmoe's battle station duty was to counterflood the compartments in such an emergency to help the ship keep her balance. Finding no one to give the order, he opened the valves and counterflooded on his own initiative, at the risk of court-martial for acting without orders. Because the first torpedoes had cut off the power, the officer in charge could not get the order through by telephone to do what Lokkesmoe had done. But his prompt counterflooding and the cables tying the battleship to the *Tennessee* helped correct the list and allowed her to settle to the bottom on even keel instead of capsizing as the *Oklahoma* did. The ship sank to quarter-deck level but stayed upright.

West Virginia's deck officer had seen the first bomb hit the Ford Island hangar, thought it was an explosion on the *California,* and ordered a rescue party. This brought many of the crew up on deck. The early alarm and swift counterflooding were credited with saving hundreds of lives and preventing worse damage to the ship. Only 105 of the crew of 1541 were lost. A dozen or more owed their survival to a wiry, 125-pound Texan, Gunner's Mate Jack Franklin, a Navigator. As bombs and torpedoes pounded the ship, some men were temporarily stunned or asphyxiated by fumes of burning oil. Lying unconscious, these men would drown as the ship sank lower and filled with water. Franklin toured the ship as a one-man rescue party, pulling one after another to safety. He later realized that as he dragged them out one by one he was lustily singing the song "Rescue the Perishing"! Next day he was heard more than once saying, "There goes one of my boys."

Climbing aboard the *Tennessee,* Downing and his shipmates trained a five-inch gun on the *West Virginia* and slid down it to her deck. They pulled fire hoses across with them, since their ship's water pressure was off, and joined the crews fighting flames which now swept the superstructure. One main concern in fighting the fire on the upper decks was to keep the gun deck's store of ready ammunition from exploding.

The *Tennessee* took only two bomb hits, no torpedoes, and was fighting off burning debris from the *Arizona* 75 feet astern while gun crews fired at enemy planes. At noon when the *Tennessee* served sandwiches to both ships' crews, Downing looked for his friend Gustafson with whom he had left his wrist watch before boarding the foundering *West Virginia*. He found Gus handing out Gospel leaflets to the crew, who showed greater interest on this day when many were shaken by a brush with death.

All fires were out by dusk except the *Arizona,* which burned for three days. An expected enemy invasion that afternoon kept crews busy organizing for defense of the island.

"I'll bet you did some hard praying *that* day," someone said to a Navigator after order was restored. "Not really," he answered. "I just reminded the Lord I was there and then trusted Him." It was an outlook common to these men who made spiritual preparedness a way of life. There was a time to pray and a time to give attention to the battle. They called it "living the life."

The *West Virginia*'s crew and survivors from the other ships crowded into quarters at the Naval Air Station, using mattresses spread on the floor. Men wandered around in strange uniforms improvised from parts of whites, blues, khakis, and dungarees. As the ship's postal clerk, Downing felt he could boost the crew's morale by getting the mail moving quickly. He found an abandoned hot dog stand on Ford Island and his friend Lokkesmoe built a mailbox for the new post office.

Sorting the mail those first days, Jim had the sad duty of returning letters addressed to the dead or missing. He reviewed the list of the 105 *West Virginia* men and could account for nearly all having heard the Gospel from their shipmates. In most cases they had said, "Yes, I'd like to make this decision — later." When it was discovered later that some men trapped in the sunken ship lived till after Christmas, Jim hoped that in those dark weeks of waiting they had reconsidered the Scripture and accepted the offer of peace with God.

Men were being rescued as late as Tuesday from the upturned *Oklahoma* through holes bored in the hull. Navigator Joe

Smith had slid off her deck just as she turned over. He managed to swim to Ford Island and had another close call while carrying in the wounded. When the *California* was raised, the body of Shipfitter Francis Cole was found on his bunk with an open Bible where he was evidently talking to his bunkmate about Christ when the attack took their lives and their ship.

In thirty minutes the battle force of the Pacific Fleet had been wrecked, though all battleships but the *Arizona* and *Oklahoma* would be raised to fight again. But thousands of men were gone, many of them without a Savior's promise of resurrection.

The crisis of December 7, 1941 that hurtled the nation and Navigator servicemen into war was adrenalin to Dawson's already keyed-up spirit. He accepted his role behind the lines with all the grace of a disqualified race horse pawing and snorting when he hears the derby's starting gun. He would give plenty to be out there where the action was, out with his men. He saw God's hand in keeping Downing at Pearl Harbor which would now be the hub of troop movements in the Pacific. Bell was there, and Watters usually, as he was attached to the flag admiral's staff. Morris Wilgus from Long Beach Dunamis was with Gustafson on the *Tennessee;* his brother Marshall, after being forbidden to witness at work at an aircraft plant, had joined the Coast Guard. Some men had reenlisted for second hitches for ministry, and now all were frozen in for the duration.

Downing reported that many unbelievers who prayed in panic on December 7 forgot their need of God by December 10. Nevertheless, the Bible classes he now taught seven nights a week in the bomb shelter on Ford Island drew a constant stream of men more receptive than before to hearing the Word. Tony Trevino's class was also well attended, largely by his selective invitation. Downing was amazed at the way Tony could walk through a darkened barracks, stopping here or there to tap someone and say, "Wanna come to Bible class, fella?" with a high rate of response. Jim asked how he did it. "I ask the Lord and He leads me to them," was Tony's matter-of-fact reply.

The bomb shelter classes followed the *West Virginia* format — a character study one night, chapter study another, and evangelistic another — a variety the chaplain endorsed as "dietetic." Though it was impossible to minister in depth to the droves of men passing through, a great many were exposed to the Gospel who would not have been otherwise. If such a mass ministry lacked the thoroughness Dawson could have wished, he was encouraged to hear that Downing had a half-dozen men around him who purposed to give their lives to serving the Lord.

McAnney's reports of God's work on the *Astoria* now reached Dawson secondhand through his secretary Vivian, Vic's fiancée since last summer. Vic wrote, "This digging into the Word to feed the flock is good. The Word becomes more rich as I dig for something for the class. Then too, my own needs are met." Daws noted with satisfaction his reliance on the Word. Walking the decks at night on ships darkened for their safety, the men quoted Scripture from the tables of their hearts and thanked God for using it to speak to them. "More and more I am glad for encouragement to memorize Scripture," Vic wrote. "It has controlled my thinking so that Satan couldn't lead me off. It has enabled me to detect false doctrines. By it I have known how to make quick decisions with precision. Because of His Word hid in my heart, I can be sure at all times what His will for me is. If I get fouled up, it is because I don't follow His leading according to His Word, but let my own desires lead me."

Vic once mentioned some opposition. "We are rejoicing in the knowledge that there is a little conspiracy to put an end to the work. It is evident that old Satan is getting a little nervous at the way some are getting away from him."

Daws was confident Vic and key men on other ships and on shore were strong in faith and would stand, as they had already stood in times of testing. He once pointed out to Vic that he was in an excellent spot for training for his future service for the Lord; his continuing study while he ministered to others compared favorably with a school situation where he would have had more constant study but limited ministry outreach.

Word came also of flourishing ministries on the *Indiana,* the *Pennsylvania,* and other ships, usually traceable to a key man God was using. Except for fellowship with the few whose ships put in at California ports, Dawson's only contact with the men was through the mail, which had become his lifeline. He must be content to stay at headquarters passing spiritual ammunition to those on the battlefront. But his was an effective presence among them, guiding their performance far more than he could know. Like Paul challenging a cadre of Timothys and Tituses by epistle from his Roman prison, Dawson exhorted his men by letter. The familiar "let me give you a verse" of earlier days was now a verse at the bottom of each letter, a ration of strength-building protein carefully chosen for the recipient.

The inspiration his letters gave the men was not the sort to soothe into euphoria but, weighted by their knowledge of Dawson as a disciplinarian, a pacesetter, to call forth their best efforts. He liked to quote military heroes ("Face the other way, boys, we're going back!") as a reminder that discipline in spiritual battle must not be breached by laziness or cowardice. And though he now wrote to many more, his letters projected his personal interest in them that heavily influenced their navigation of unfamiliar waters thousands of miles distant.

Army contacts, now numbering 1500 in less than a year from the start of Army ministry, also profited from Nav systems of Bible study and memory. One of many who wrote to express appreciation was Lars Granberg, a lonely Wheaton graduate stationed at Camp Polk, Louisiana. "It was literally being fed by the ravens to have Dick Hightower drop in on me. Those who love the Lord and speak the language of Heaven are few and far between here, and I was blessed and immeasurably refreshed spiritually. A.B.C. is the grandest way to study the Bible I've ever heard of. I'm getting a great deal from it. John Streater did me a big favor when he introduced me to that course."

When a serviceman did get in for a visit to headquarters, he was overwhelmed by the VIP treatment given him. "Dawson was willing to turn his time completely over to me, a little old sailor off a ship," Gustafson marveled. "When I protested he said, 'What do you mean, man, this is my life.' Like the verse in Philippians he seemed to *naturally care for your state* and how he might help you."

Gus felt Dawson's unpretentious manner was a key to his influence with servicemen, revealing not a superman but one with great confidence in God. His life lived openly before them was an example within their reach. Gus observed this when Dawson shared a room with him at the YMCA in San Francisco and shared in an informal way from the Word.

"He did not seem afraid we would know him so well that he might not command our respect," Gus reflected. "He could let you know anything about him — and be so nonprofessional. And too, he seemed to suffer the same tests and temptations we did; he gave intensely practical advice about things like our attitude toward girls and so on. Even like warning us about the appeal of girls admiring us when we spoke at meetings. And you felt it wasn't just theory with him. . . . He did not let us forget we were in a spiritual war as well as a national crisis and should not be preoccupied, as in 2 Tim. 2:3, 4, '. . . No man that warreth entangleth himself with the affairs of this life. . . .' This complete sharing of his convictions and living them right on our level really had an impact."

The rapport Dawson enjoyed with servicemen made him no less demanding as their coach. And when occasion arose he did not flinch at making an example of one man so that many could learn. One Sunday evening Dawson was guest speaker at a church in Oakland, with the usual line-up of Navigator sailors filling the front pew. To illustrate his message on Scripture memory, he jabbed a long finger toward the man on the end. "Bill, how many verses you know?" "Thirty-six." "How long you been a Christian?" "Four months."

"Ken, how many verses d'you have?" "Fifteen." "How long've you known Christ?" "Six weeks." Daws continued down the row to the man directly in front of him. "One!" the sailor answered defiantly. "Quote it!" Dawson bellowed. The sailor quoted — incorrectly — John 3:16.

Pausing for dramatic effect, Dawson launched the torpedoes. "Friends," he said in lowered tones, "I was going to give a challenge on memory tonight, but the meeting turned out a little different than I expected. Here is a fellow I have prayed for much; I have talked to him about getting down to business in the Word of God. See him? He knows only one verse, and he doesn't really know that one." The congregation squirmed, embarrassed for the poor fellow, but Daws continued. "I'll tell you something else. This man is on a destroyer flotilla based at Treasure Island. And what's God doing on his ship? Nothing!"

Riding back to the base with his buddy, the sailor broke a long silence to seek sympathy. "Boy, Daws sure was rough on me tonight."

Not wishing to blunt the Holy Spirit's message, his friend answered simply, "Daws was right in what he did. God *isn't* working on your ship." That word reinforced the lesson. The sailor began to dig in and soon the results showed on his ship and in his life.

But the church people's reaction was just the opposite of the sailor's buddy. They resented the harsh treatment the sailor had received from Trotman, feeling he did not appreciate the plight of the dear lads in uniform. To Dawson the congregation's sympathy for the sailor illustrated a new element in the ministry to servicemen, one that complicated the task of training warriors for God. Pearl Harbor had unleashed a wave of patriotic fervor and washed through the churches a tide of sentimental feeling for the U.S. serviceman which caused people to shower a sort of mother love on any off-duty serviceman within reach. Thus churches eager to serve the war effort and the kingdom of God sometimes tended to coddle and fete the man in uniform more than was good for his spiritual growth and discipleship.

Another trend was evident in the sudden popularity of religion with servicemen since Pearl Harbor. Previously disinterested men now swelled the attendance at Bible classes. In one Marine unit three of the four sergeants attended the Bible class. An enlisted man holding a class on his ship was congratulated by his commanding officer. Both Army and Navy enlarged their Chaplains' Corps and endorsed a new Service Men's Christian League jointly sponsored by major Protestant bodies.

Inquiries increased from servicemen wanting to "join" The

Navigators. Dawson found it difficult to explain his feeling that the name of Christ was preeminent and becoming His disciple transcended membership in a movement. Corollary to this was the fear that carelessly tagging as Navigators men less than totally dedicated to Christ would do Him no honor and the movement no good. Men who could rightfully call themselves Navigators usually did not, following Dawson's lead, and earning a magazine writer's description, "A Navigator works 24 hours a day as a Christian." So Dawson answered would-be members by explaining that the important thing was to "live the life" and offering any help and materials The Navigators could furnish to make that possible.

The question of membership did arise as Dawson moved toward incorporation of The Navigators, a step he was advised to take to give legal standing to the ten-year-old operation which now handled sizable funds and fielded numerous inquiries about its purpose and function. Incorporation papers filed March 1943 named Dick Hightower vice-president, Jim Hayden secretary, and Harold Chrisman treasurer. Since the by-laws called for a membership, their minimum requirement was met on paper. "Inc." appeared on some of the Navigator letterhead, but Dawson would have his name and title on none of it. He felt a twinge of embarrassment at the need for legal structure of a ministry so personal and informal and so non-secular. And though many items less newsworthy were given space in the *Log* and the new monthly *News Letter* he began publishing about that time, the incorporation was not mentioned in either.

Perhaps spurred by the prospect of naming members of The Navigators corporation, late in 1942 Dawson listed twenty-eight men he considered key in the movement, to whom he would send inner-circle reports and information. He cleared the list with Downing, Bell, and Watters, his top advisers at the time somewhat in the style of David's three among the thirty mighty men. Downing's reply suggested adding three to the roster for receiving general information, but trimming to twenty-four the group to receive financial reports, and to seventeen those to include in consultation.

To Dawson these men were the kind God would use to raise up foundations of many generations. They had proved Him strong in their behalf and influenced hundreds of young men for Christ. They were beloved fellow soldiers, a fulfillment of God's promise to "give men for thee and people for thy life." As Daws now saw it, the disastrous loss at Pearl Harbor was gain for the Gospel, for it dispersed men throughout the fleet much as the persecution in Jerusalem sent the early disciples "everywhere preaching the Word." It seemed significant that the *West Virginia* which had the largest contingent of Navigators had been one of the first hit during the attack. Now these men ministering on new ships and bases were getting priceless experience for the future, their "floating seminaries" superior in many ways to an academic environment where their study could not be matched by such choice ministry opportunities. He wrote to a friend, "With the cream of U.S. young men now in the service getting this kind of training and preparation, we should be able to shake America after the war."

While the war centered in the South Pacific with the Navy and Marines that first year of U.S. involvement, thousands of new Army troops trained in stateside camps to serve in North Africa and Europe. Possibly to compensate for the comparative quiet of his home front duty of encouraging men by correspondence and the bi-monthly *Log* with its challenge and news, Dawson probed other avenues of ministry. Frequent trips to San Diego and San Francisco gave him time with a few key men and a chance to strengthen the work of area Nav Homes. The potential for evangelism among the exploding servicemen population across the country led him to encourage Christian businessmen initiatives to open Victory Centers and to help them find directors. He himself often spoke to servicemen's rallies and held Sunday services at the Naval-Marine Armory.

Early in 1942 Dawson had opportunity to influence a vast new field of ministry through contact with Jim Rayburn of the Young Life Campaign. Joining Rayburn for a series of youth rallies in Texas, Daws shared with his leaders the know-how and materials for establishing follow-up in their flourishing high school clubs. Young Life leaders began to carry the familiar notebooks and memory packs, Rayburn bringing the red leather pack out of a pocket with great ostentation whenever he was in Trotman's presence.

A new idea for Bible study was always worth a try. Dawson wrote in his journal:

> *For the first time we tackle our S.T.S. on a new basis, members of Dunamis club bringing special reports on a given subject, in this case the Blood of Christ, then taking our S.T.S. on an assigned chapter — the 9th of Hebrews. For the next period we decided to experiment, using the S.T.S. topically — the Holy Spirit . . . summarizing the truth of that subject from various places in the Word, taking our Uplifts and Difficulties also from here and there, selecting a passage that we would consider a key to that subject. It seems the S.T.S. will lend itself very well.*

Monthly half-days of prayer were a highlight, when Daws met with his staff men, club leaders, pastors, and other friends for early breakfast at 175, then all went to the park to pray until noon. Consciously or not, he followed Jesus' example of teaching those with whom he worked to pray by praying with them. It bothered him that his prayer time had decreased through the years as activities multiplied.

Pondering the fact that Gospel teams visited jails and rescue missions to reach down-and-outers and hospitals to minister to the sick, Dawson felt someone should be seeking out young men of the "up-and-out" class. Paul was debtor both to the wise and the unwise. As the idea took shape, Dawson called a committee with one member from each area and laid plans for a Triumphant Life banquet at a Hollywood hotel, to which each man would invite a college-level non-Christian. A special speaker would give the Gospel. Hosts would be instructed to carry a New Testament or *small* Bible, to join heartily in singing, make conversation, and not to *Amen* the speaker! They would follow the speaker's message with personal chats with their guests.

"It was most thrilling," Daws reported to Downing after

the first banquet. "About two score unsaved fellows were reached, many of them university men." Even more attended the second, and a new medium for evangelism was launched. These first bimonthly "Andrew dinners" early in World War II predated by twenty years the now-familiar evangelistic banquet.

The year 1942 also saw Dawson involved in a ministry he had scarcely touched to date — getting businessmen down to business. "Navigators are servicemen; we don't work with businessmen," he stalled the lean, serious-faced man who came from the Bay area asking for help in Bible study. Bob Padelford, a new Christian whose pastor had referred him to Trotman, rephrased his request, brown eyes intent as he waited for a better answer.

Dawson was uncomfortable about giving Dunamis to men of this age group; he was used to working with their sons. Whether it was because the leverage of the father-son relationship would be missing with these men or that his job would be tougher without the hero image which made the young more malleable, he did not consciously consider. He knew only that if he invested time and effort in this new avenue of ministry, he would have to give it his best. And how could he add it to his already full schedule? Proverbs 3:27 usually popped into his mind inconveniently at times like this. *Withhold not good from them to whom it is due, when it is in the power of thine hand to do it.* "Okay," he answered, "can you meet my assistant here at 5:30 tomorrow morning?"

"Yes I can," Padelford assured him, passing that further test of his purpose.

Padelford's spiritual hunger helped him endure the hours of Dunamis indoctrination and accept the whole package, the first businessman to follow the rigorous Bible study-memory-discipline schedule. Whenever business brought him to Los Angeles, he stayed at the Mayflower to be near the Nav office, where he spent his spare hours helping print memory cards in the back-room print shop. He introduced to the memory work and to Dawson his businessmen friends Ernie Mintie and Charlie Cooper.

"Sissies memorize Scripture," Cooper led with his broad chin as he and Dawson drove toward San Diego. "Listen, I think *you're* a sissy if you can't memorize five verses by this time next week," Trotman replied with equal subtlety.

"I don't think you can memorize five verses either," was the comfort Cooper got from his wife later at home. Thus he was launched on a memory program he doggedly pursued and later sold to hundreds of businessmen across the country while he was president of CBMC International. In time Mintie, Cooper, and Padelford began meeting with Dawson in an early-morning AlphAmegA group where Dawson's limited success in getting them to stay with it, though difficult for him, was marvelous in their eyes. And their enthusiasm helped get other businessmen started.

The group paid bonus dividends in other ways, such as free trips for Dawson up and down the coast in cars eligible for rationed gasoline. They also went to work on his wardrobe, which had a certain frontier flamboyance, and on his slang-salted vocabulary. Dawson appreciated it all, reveling in the climate of candid exchange among them.

The men also were affected by their contact with The Navigators. "They all thought of Daws as a better businessman than they were," Padelford admitted. "They all recognized his efficiency. They would have been glad to hire him as manager and all his secretaries. Anyone critical of the way Christian organizations handle their business would be impressed with his management of Navigators."

Padelford introduced Dawson to Arnold Grunigen and Harry Smith of San Francisco CBMC, which led to the offer of adjoining office space for distributing Nav materials and handling business in that area. The office opened in summer, and soon there was a servicemen's center on Market Street, where CBMC and Navigators worked side by side. The Triumphant Life Banquet idea, used by the two groups in San Francisco under the colorful name "Christian Business Men From Land and Sea," featured Charles Fuller as speaker and resulted in some decisions for Christ.

Dawson's habit of publicly embarrassing a person for shock effect may have been tamed somewhat by his association with the businessmen. In early spring he had spoken in a Los Angeles church. As the message grew long the pastor's young wife struggled to quiet two small children. "Those your kids, Don?"

Daws asked abruptly. They were. "You better get them in hand." "Amen," agreed the red-faced pastor. "You better do something about that Amen too," the guest speaker added.

Three years later Daws and Lila were invited to the pastor's home for dinner, and his wife recalled the incident. Dawson was aghast. "Did I do that?" Yes, he had done just that. "Wasn't I naughty?" his grin asked forgiveness as he handed his hostess a box of candy.

Padelford and Mintie knew that early in their acquaintance their wives detested Dawson. His extravagant praise of Lila as superstar homemaker and mother drove them to the barricades to defend their own housekeeping practice against his supposedly critical view. "Daws had Lila built up about double her capability," Padelford said. "If I wanted to have him over to dinner there was a real row. He stayed with us sometimes when he was in the area, and when he left my wife would complain, 'He can't tell me how to run my kitchen.' But then when he started the nurses work, that won her heart."

*   *   *   *

The nurses work — another first in that busy year — grew out of a request by student nurses at San Francisco's Mt. Zion Hospital for Bill and Marge Goold to open their home for Navigator-type work with girls. Dawson gave his blessing to the project, provided they find a larger home. Soon Marge's flourishing ministry to girls included nurses from Stanford and University of California hospitals as well, with John and Idella Newman taking over when Goolds were transferred. Across the Bay at Padelfords' another study group of servicewomen and nurses was led by Pat Lokkesmoe, Nav secretary in charge of the new San Francisco office and wife of Marvin Lokkesmoe. With these added ministries and the opening of a San Francisco Navigator Home with Art and Norma Vaughan in charge, Dawson decided to spend every other week in the Bay area, often using the time on the train to dictate correspondence.

On one of these trips he read a letter he might have answered routinely with regrets, an invitation to speak to a score of church young people who wanted "more" from the Christian life. He could not take more speaking dates now, he reasoned, and yet . . . *Withhold not good . . . when it is in the power of thine hand. . . .* He would go.

"It changed all our lives," one of the group, Kent Flygare, recalled. "He challenged us to memory work. About twelve started and found it tremendously prosperous for their souls. I said I couldn't memorize. But Dick Soderberg, who was going to Berkeley, started a Dunamis club with four of us."

And by obeying the Spirit's leading to speak to that youth group, Dawson gained a valuable staff man in Flygare, who came to Los Angeles headquarters more than a year later. Kent supervised the Navigator print shop with a perfectionism matching Dawson's own, turning out printed materials of the extremely high standard both admired. He marveled at the uncanny way Daws could reach into the center of a stack and pull out the one page with a flaw or uneven register. And Dawson instructing a worker on the use and care of the mimeograph would have done credit to a space engineer. Through the years Kent used his unique inventive and mechanical skills to design and build many items for the gadget-loving Trotman. The most far-reaching of these were the dies he designed for the die-cut memory packs to hold the precise number of cards the course required.

*   *   *   *

By June 1942, one year after launching the Army work, Dawson noted that headquarters office was in touch with more Army camps than ships. Yet virtually all Army contact was by correspondence, few bases having a known key man guiding the work as on the ships. Such men could be developed if given enough time with a man like Robinson, but Robby had been on the move trying to cover a number of bases. He had done much good work with men, establishing them in the Word before they shipped out to parts unknown.

Now Dawson thought it would be better to have Robby settle near one base and work with men in depth, training some real laborers, rather than travel from camp to camp. Streater's ministry in the camps had been notable, but he was now an ensign in the Navy. Hayden handled a heavy Army correspondence from the office, coaching hundreds of men in Bible study, memory, and witness. And while this was no match for ministry in person, their reports of victory and blessing from the Word and of fruitful witness gave evidence God was working in their lives. Dawson saw great potential in the Army work and planned to find ways to develop it.

But at this strategic moment the enemy took aim and deftly felled a beloved colaborer, depriving The Navigators of his ministry. Dawson discovered that for several years this man had steeped himself in the literature of a hyperdispensational cult which rejected the Lord's Supper, baptism, the doctrine of eternal punishment, and cast doubt and limitations on the Word of God — teachings wholly unacceptable in Navigator ministry. Dawson hoped and fervently prayed for his recovery of scriptural balance; he needed him desperately in the ministry and valued his fellowship as a dear brother in Christ. But the tentacles of false teaching had firmly gripped the man's soul. With leaden heart Dawson asked for his resignation.

Dawson knew too well the deadening effect of this teaching. He had delved into it years before, finding that "certain portions of Scripture cannot possibly mean you, so you reject them — all but four or five books of the New Testament." Charles Fuller had gently rescued him from embracing these narrow beliefs and had also given him fatherly warning against a critical spirit toward some churches and pastors. "Don't you be critical of any undershepherd God has placed in the pulpit," Fuller said. "He may not have the gift or vision or knowledge you have, but teach your men to cooperate with him."

Though he now endorsed a generally dispensational view of Scripture, Dawson did not hesitate to apply to the here and now some portions indicated for another time. "Israel's job was to get the Scriptures to all the nations, all the families of the earth, to the gentiles," he explained. "That's why God chose them, to bless all the families of the earth, but they failed. Now God has put in the hands of Christ, and of us, the job He originally gave to Israel. Galatians 3:16 says, *Now to Abraham and his seed were the promises given. . . .* With Christ, the seed of Abraham, God started all over, and if any man be in Christ he is a new creature, he is the image of Christ, and the job God started through Abraham must be carried on through

Christ and through us, so that in us shall all the families of the earth be blessed.

"And these hyperdispensationalists give the Gospels and the Acts back to the Jews; they destroy the Great Commission — Mark 16:15, Matthew 28:19, 20, and Acts 1:8. And this is where our guns are pointed: *Every creature* — the Gospel to every creature, a big order. *In every country* — first Jerusalem, and in all Judea, and in Samaria, and then to the uttermost part of the earth. And here's how to get to every creature once we reach every country: *Make disciples . . . teaching them to observe all things whatsoever I have commanded you* — and doing this first in Jerusalem and in all Judea and unto the uttermost part. This command is to us, and if we fail to carry it out we disobey the Lord of glory."

*V*ictor McAnney *missing in action*. The news hit Dawson like a clap of thunder. Lila's letter, which reached him in Mexico, told of Vivian's calm trust in the face of Vic's possible death at sea. He thanked God for this girl who last year had promised the Lord she would give Vic up if He asked for him. Thoughts flooded his mind. "Missing" — but not to God. "In action" yes, as Christ's ambassador in the thick of the battle. He remembered how Vic wrote after going aboard the *Astoria* that he was challenged from Acts 20:26, "Wherefore I take you to record this day, that I am pure from the blood of all men," and prayed he would so fulfill his responsibility as a witness on that ship that he could say the same.

By early 1942 Vic was seeing God answer. "These are great days," he wrote. "This kind of living makes me want to ship over. After almost two years on the ship I see the beginning of the desire of my heart, definite work for the Lord and abounding opportunities to lead others into a more intimate walk with Him." And later: "I have never known such joy, satisfaction, and victory. . . . Men are easy to talk to these days; they are seeing their need of the One Who made them. It is not really fear of death, although it has its effect."

Although McAnney wrote of long, exhausting days of work at his job and ministering to men, Daws noted he had not forgotten the secret of his strength. "I had opportunity to find out just how much good getting up early was doing for me," he wrote. "The fellow who calls me forgot one morning, and I slept in until six. The morning following was not as bright as the mornings when I had gotten up at four and had time with the Lord and in His Word."

For ten weeks Bible classes had continued in the mess hall or on deck under an eight-inch gun turret, sometimes with the chaplain teaching, other times with McAnney or Lenoir or Taggart in charge. Their big problem was feeding the growing number of new Christians, when the continual presence of unsaved men geared all classes to evangelism.

Dawson walked alone in the Mexican sunlight, eyes downcast in thought, eventually looking heavenward to thank God for His sovereign wisdom. McAnney would be the first loss of a Navigator Dawson had counted on for future colaborship. Well, God had a right to choose from His best troops for His own honor guard, all praise to Him. Yet what a vacancy it left in the ranks!

Long afterward the story of the battle off the Solomons that August night would be pieced together. As the *Astoria* headed toward Guadalcanal in a task force support group, all hands knew danger was imminent. "If we come to the worst," Vic said to Tag and Lenoir one evening, recalling his prayer of commitment, "we have been delivered from the blood of all men on this ship." On Sunday, August 2, Chaplain Bouterse had put aside his prepared message and talked to the men of life and death and salvation in Christ. Vic followed him to his room. "Chaplain, let's pray and thank God for the men who will find Christ because of that message." Even as they prayed, a man came seeking to make his decision. Others followed, and the harvest continued.

Later that week they helped the Marines make their landing by shelling the Guadalcanal shoreline and covering the transports with antiaircraft fire. Now as they patrolled the sound, Bomberg chatted with the chaplain on deck, telling of his peace and joy in Christ and a deep assurance that whatever happened would be for the best. After midnight on the quiet tropic night with all asleep except the watch, exhausted from the past two days' action, "general quarters" shocked the ship awake. A task force of enemy ships had roared down from their northwest base through a straight passage called The Slot, the first of many night raids so regular that the disgusted Marines dubbed them the Tokyo Express. Earlier two Japanese scout planes had been assumed friendly or ignored, so the surprise of the weary sailors was total.

In six minutes the enemy had crippled one Allied group patrolling Savo Sound and wheeled around the island to attack the other from the rear, three cruisers and two destroyers incredibly unaware of enemy presence. *Astoria,* the nearest cruiser, was so heavily shelled that fires blazed all over the ship before the crew could mobilize to her defense.

The doughty ship managed to return fire, but the enemy's margin of time was sufficient to finish his deadly work, sinking all three cruisers and steaming safely back up through The Slot to his base. He had won the first battle of a long, desperate campaign that cost the Allies more than 1000 dead and over 700 wounded. The *Astoria* suffered 400 casualties. When survivors of the sinking ship were taken off at daybreak, Vic was not among them, nor was Bomberg. During the battle, word had reached the chaplain that a man lay dead outside his stateroom with a big smile on his face. That would be Vic, as that was his battle station, but the chaplain would have known anyway. Tag and Lenoir survived the attack; three of the nine who had received Christ in the week before the battle did not.

After the ship was abandoned, a sailor held up a small leather packet of memory cards he had fished from the water. "This yours?" he asked Taggart. It was. On the *Astoria,* as on some forty or fifty ships of the fleet, the crew knew who the men were who carried Bibles and prayed.

Chaplain Bouterse pondered why God had not spared Vic. "I have known lots of good sailors, and I've known quite a few Christians," he wrote, "but I have never found one who was so completely both. He was a first-class baker and a first-class Christian. Though I knew him just two months, I count him one of my best friends. His approval meant a great deal to me, I suppose because I knew him to be so close to the mind of Christ. . . . I intend to be with God's help making up for the sermons Vic won't preach, and reaching those he could have reached."

Other Navigators went down in battle, and Dawson felt their loss keenly. But he was proud of their courageous service for their country and their victorious testimony in facing death. He saw these precious laborers as the seed of John 12:24 which must fall into the ground and die and as surely bring forth much fruit. God would multiply them through death, giving men in exchange for their lives.

Jack Armstrong spoke of this in a November letter to a Christian businessman in New York. "What a privilege to give our lives for our country! What a hope a Christian has after death — eternity with the Lord Jesus Christ, and loved ones!

"The things I left at your home, if I don't come back to get them they are yours," he added. The work on the *Atlanta* was going well. "We are still having our Bible classes Sundays as regular as circumstances permit. . . . We always have at least 12 or 15 fellows down; sometimes as high as 25. Numbers don't count so much. It's man to man talks about God's Word that really count. The Lord Jesus Christ continues to become more real and personal to me as the time rolls around."

Later that month the *Atlanta,* part of a task force support group in the sound off Guadalcanal, encountered a twelve-ship Tokyo Express in a post-midnight battle at sea and was badly crippled and scuttled. One of the 169 *Atlanta* casualties was Jack. The chaplain sought to minister to the fatally wounded sailor where he fell, both legs shot off.

"Don't bother with me. I know where I'm going," Jack protested, urging him to spend his time with the unsaved. The same concern was reflected in Jack's letter to his brother a few days earlier. "Soon we leave port for a dangerous mission. If we go down, I'm going to be with the Lord Jesus Christ. I want to see you there, George. . . . He died for you, George, won't you give Him a chance in your life? George, I love you and I want you to come to know my Jesus as your own personal Savior."

An officer from the *Atlanta,* an orthodox Jew, said, "I guess he was the finest man I have ever known in my life." The ship's skipper wrote, "Jack was one of the finest and most popular men attached to the ship. His Sunday Bible classes had much to do with keeping the morale up and our spirit high. He was admired and respected by all from the Captain on down." Armstrong would have been embarrassed by such tributes, but pleased to know that when Jack Wyrtzen told his story and read from his letters on the Word of Life Hour, fifty persons in the audience responded to the invitation, six of them sailors.

* * * *

Reflecting on how God had been fulfilling His promises in the past five years, Dawson could trace a pattern of change in his ministry. His individual work with many young Christians in years when the fleet was in port had given way to ministry at a distance to key men making disciples on their ships and bases. He had moved from intensive practice of follow-up to training others in follow-up, out in locations where independent responsibility helped them grow. The Army work had a healthy start, and the war combined with publicity to cause a contact explosion for The Navigators.

The high school Dunamis work had complemented the Navy ministry; camp and club leadership had proved good training for his men. Ministry with businessmen had begun, as well as work with women through Martures clubs and the nurses ministry. Some progress had been made in establishing area Nav Homes — there were ten official Homes now — though far from enough.

The *Log,* now in its third year of publication, was a vital communications link. Incorporation of The Navigators would put financial matters on a legal footing, and headquarters office was staffed with dedicated workers. And despite the losses to false doctrine and to war, Dawson was grateful for the strong men God had sent to colabor in the work in answer to prayer.

(next page) Casualties of the December 7, 1941 bombing of Pearl Harbor: (from left) the *West Virginia,* the *Tennessee,* and the *Arizona. U.S. Navy photo.*

IV

Sharing the Other Man's Dream

1942-1944

Backyard gathering at "175." Key man John Newman is at Trotman's left, staff men Lorne Sanny, center back, and Jim Hayden, right front.

Wartime Nav rally at San Diego Home included sailors, officers, nurses, and civilians.

One event in September 1942 seemed to surpass all others in significance in a year full of significance. The catalyst was early Navigator John Dedrick, whose modest manner evoked the simplicity of Andrew's delivery of the important invitation to Peter to "come and see." Dedrick, in Mexico translating Scripture into Yaqui under the Pioneer Mission Agency, was convinced its director Cameron Townsend and Trotman should meet. At Dedrick's urging, Townsend invited Dawson as speaker for the annual workers conference in Mexico City.

Each man discovered in the other a pioneer spirit of faith and daring that mirrored his own. Dawson, who since asking God to let him send men if he could not go himself, had firmly held his purpose to steer men to missions after their military service, received new stimulus for his role as recruiting officer. Townsend unblinkingly asked him for 500 Navigators after the war to help do Bible translation in a thousand untouched languages.

That fortnight in Mexico etched new experiences in Dawson's memory. Seeing a heartbroken Mexican woman on her knees confessing to a yawning cleric; hearing about scores of tribes without a word of Scripture in their language; sampling the hot Mexican fare with missionaries on a tour of the city; sadly viewing the shrines to sun, moon, and serpent; visiting an Indian tribe where the Word had gone, transforming the lives of some and even changing their standard of living. What joy it was to fellowship with these fifty brave young men and women at work in the tribes and the thirty who had joined them after summer linguistic training in the States. Dawson entered wholeheartedly into their concerns and problems, his interest in them boosting their morale and opening to him a new theater of combat for the Word of God.

The group, incorporated that fall as Wycliffe Bible Translators and Summer Institute of Linguistics, eagerly elected him to its board of directors. He wore this membership as a badge of honor, feeling close kinship with a group so like his own, who faced hardship cheerfully and enjoyed life to the full.

At the young missionaries' request, Dawson held several sessions on the "value of being down to business in business, memory, study. . . ." Though most had good Bible training and background, they felt a personal hunger for daily spiritual nourishment that responded to Dawson's challenge to "write the Word on the tables of your heart." They liked his home-spun illustration comparing meditation on Scripture to a cow chewing the cud. As bringers of the Word, they acknowledged that their own lives should be powered and saturated with it. Before Dawson left Mexico some three dozen members had asked for the Dunamis setup. He would remember this trip with an exciting sense of accomplishment and of new bonds forged in colaborship, with an increased burden to get the lifegiving Word to tribes in their languages. He ended his journal: "Grand day on the plane with opportunities to witness. . . . Home to my beloved family and fellow-laborers."

Home, too, to catch up on accumulated servicemen's correspondence and headquarters business, to spend a full week ministering in the Bay area, and to leave for a three-week trip east.

In Dallas Daws looked in on Young Life staff members to encourage their follow-up efforts with their high schoolers. He spent time at Nav Homes in Norfolk and Washington, D.C., the latter hosted by a widow, Helen Miller, who resigned a government position to open her home for Navigator ministry. Dawson defended Mrs. Miller before Christian leaders who disapproved of a woman's leading the work, assuring them she was doing a fine job. Furthermore, if God had called a man to that work, where was he?

In Detroit Dawson contacted CBMC men at their convention. In the Chicago area he spoke at Moody Church and spent time with students in Dunamis work at Wheaton. He opened his stepped-up recruiting drive for missions as he spoke to Wheaton's Foreign Missions Fellowship group where John Thorne from the old *West Virginia* was president. Citing the desolate fact of whole tribes without a sentence of Scripture, Dawson threw out a challenge he would use often: why had so few young men, in proportion to young women, volunteered for missions? In the November *Log* he called all hands to pray that God would send hundreds then in uniform to man the thousand unreached tribes after the war.

Again Dawson found his strength depleted as his continuous activity overloaded the power circuits of a substandard physique. This time it disconcerted him; with so much he wanted to do, running out of physical resources was one thing he did not need. But a doctor's humiliating advice to take a quarter-hour nap after lunch began to pay off immediately. So as with any helpful discovery, he was compelled to share it. When journalist Mel Larson was interviewing him for a magazine article, Trotman suddenly looked him in the eye and said, "You better take a thirty-minute nap every afternoon."

He also lectured Roy Robertson and other men he met while visiting the Navy base at Corpus Christi on the value of an after-lunch catnap. He admitted being ashamed at first to be caught napping for it made him look lazy, but it had made his time in the evening so much more effective that he began selling the idea to others. With a typical flash of intuition, on that first meeting Dawson invited Robertson to join the Navigator staff. A fighter pilot and flight instructor, Roy would head the transportation department as Daws envisioned keeping up with future Nav ministries by private plane.

Navigators seeing action in the Pacific made almost casual reference to it. "The war goes on; some days more interesting than others; most exciting were Pearl Harbor, Coral Sea, and Solomons. 'Great peace have they that love Thy law, and nothing shall offend them,'" Jim Willis, transferred off the *Canberra* before it was sunk in the Solomons, wrote to Dawson. "I am still doing Dunamis," he wrote. "Boy, the new truths brought forth in these letters to the Corinthians! They aren't too easy either." As the war ground on into its second year, Dawson and those on the home front prayed for the men's safety, but prayed more that the Word would go forth in power on sixty to eighty ships and stations and perhaps two hundred forts and camps where there was a contact. News of a Navigator killed in battle was passed along with less sense of tragedy than of calm and confident victory: "I suppose you heard of Jack's promotion."

Bible studies, memory card packs, and letters now flowed in greater volume from Los Angeles headquarters and the small San Francisco office to hundreds of contacts. Dawson spent time with key men up and down the West Coast whenever he could and supplemented his personal correspondence with the printed *News Letter* to key servicemen and others, sending it to those overseas on the new V-Mail photo letter form. However, tight censorship allowed little news to filter back to the mainland.

Meanwhile Daws worked toward getting more Nav Homes and servicemen's centers open. Hightower was loaned to direct a center sponsored by businessmen in San Diego. Goolds manned a Navigator Home in San Pedro. When Hightower was sent in March 1943 to answer the insistent call for a New York Nav ministry and to oversee the growing East Coast work, the Jim Haydens and Dick DeLongs took over in San Diego. Chrisman opened his home in Oakland, where Streater's home also was open for work with officers. John and Idella Newman's home in San Diego, where he was now stationed, was the official contact for nurses and officers. A service center opened in Vallejo.

Back in D.C. where Mrs. Miller's home was for Navigators, the Downings used theirs for nurses and servicewomen and Jim taught Bible classes at a downtown servicemen's center. At year's end the Long Beach businessmen opened a center with Dawson's encouragement, then asked for Lorne Sanny as its first director. In New York Hightower began directing the new CBMC Victory Center in addition to the Navigator Home. Dawson continued to pray for headquarters in Portland, Corpus Christi, and New Orleans, and for some facility for servicewomen and wives in Los Angeles. The office now kept seven full-time and five part-time staff busy with various ministries.

An officers ministry in Los Angeles seemed imperative. A

number of Dunamis clubbers would be going into officer training, and Christian officer contacts were increasing. As Dawson
looked for an answer, a home then on the market in South
Pasadena seemed ideal. Twice the size of 175, the forty-year-
old mansion with its luxurious furnishings could house the
growing staff, provide the right setting for an officers work,
and allow hospitality to servicemen and the many friends
Dawson liked to invite as he traveled around the country. God
could indicate His will in acquiring the home by providing
a purchaser, Dawson knew, and this He did when Charles
Fuller offered to have the Fuller Evangelistic Foundation buy
it for The Navigators' use at a nominal rent. So in April 1943
the entire family of six Trotmans and eight workers moved
into "509" as it came to be known throughout the Navigator
world.

Kneeling in an attic room promptly designated the prayer
room, Daws and Lila dedicated 509 to the Lord the night
before they moved in. The Haggai promise seemed appropriate:
*The glory of this latter house shall be greater than of the
former, saith the Lord of hosts; and in this place will I give
peace, saith the Lord of hosts.* Set well back on an acre of lawn
shaded by eucalyptus and avocado trees, a tall palm, and a
stately magnolia, the sumptuous dwelling with its gables and
turrets, stone masonry verandas, wood-paneled and tapestried
walls, mahogany columns, alabaster chandeliers, and wide stair-
cases was in one observer's view the Lord's reward to these
two who had unsparingly shared every previous home with so
many, sacrificially giving themselves to hospitality for the
Gospel's sake.

Yet there was no thought by either of them of slacking off
now. Whenever he described 509, Dawson added gleefully,
"Now I can invite as many as I want. There's plenty of room."
The spacious dining room looked bare with less than sixteen
around the massive oak table and the many nooks about the
place were ideal for tete-a-tetes as the "state" rooms were for
rallies. Now on weekday mornings seven passengers from 509
climbed into the 1941 Olds coupe and rolled down the Arroyo
Seco Parkway to the office next door to Biola. Dawson often
redeemed the twenty minutes in transit by dictating his STS
Bible study to a secretary or pulling over to help a motorist in

need and give him a Gospel tract. Matching bumpers to push a stalled car down the busy freeway was a diversion Daws enjoyed, heightened by the thrills it gave his own passengers.

Though monthly rallies were now fairly crowded out of the schedule, AlphAmegA club work flourished, with new clubs in several high schools and a junior college early in the year. Dan Fuller led a club in Pasadena and the Winters started one at Cal Tech. Dawson's secretary Vivian and the girls led college and high school girls clubs. Daws was glad to have Sanny directing this time-consuming but important club ministry. He still believed it was strategic to get hold of fellows and girls while in high school; so many servicemen had said they would have been better prepared to serve the Lord now if they had begun these disciplines in high school.

Dawson felt God had indeed sent him in the twenty-two-year-old Sanny a Daniel, a Philip — a Timothy. There were at least three areas where he would fit perfectly, for God's hand was on him — but God needed time to build His man and Daws needed patience, he was again reminded. Sanny would be married in June to blond Lucille Brooks, who in high school had maneuvered him to church where he heard the Gospel. They would be ready for an area responsibility when Lorne finished his work at Biola next spring. Meanwhile Lucy assisted Lila at 509, getting from her the kind of training she would need to manage a Navigator Home and fill the special role Lila filled so well.

Lucy found there was more to learn than she had expected. And she also found she learned more just by observing Lila's life as they worked together than by direct instruction. She was amazed to see Lila serve a plain tuna casserole to "company" — such commonplaceness before distinguished guests whom many a hostess would have tried to impress. They were impressed not with a fancy menu, but with the spirit of loving hospitality. Lucy would recall this often when the Sannys served a "beans" type menu to company in their first Nav area, following Lila's example of giving priority to things of the spirit.

"The common touch in any society," Lucy described it. "Lila treated everyone alike. She was no respecter of persons. And she would do anything for anybody."

Dawson occasionally helped with the training of Lila's assistants. "Who scrambled the eggs?" he asked one morning at breakfast.

"I did. What's wrong with them?" Lucy answered.

"They're too hard."

"Well, scramble 'em yourself," she retorted.

But he had another suggestion, which resulted in Lucy's becoming an expert egg scrambler, with a healthy attitude as a bonus. One girl asked Dawson for a foolproof way to avoid burning the toast. "Just don't do it," was his profound formula, thereafter applied to many such jobs in which success depended merely on setting one's mind to do it right. It became a family saying around Nav Homes, repeated by trainers and trainees alike as one of the countless little efficiencies of a Nav operation: "We just don't *burn* the toast at this house."

The whole crew often joined in Saturday softball or volleyball, with Daws as pitcher and captain tailoring the rules for greatest efficiency and always playing to win. "Don't play just for fun; play to *win*," was his dictum. No one dared say so, but some did play just for fun. A few secretly disliked his arbitrary changing of rules and opted out of the next game; others took it in stride. No one could deny that his rules were indeed superior and his strategy did win the game. Through the years, if a man dropped out of the work citing Dawson's autocratic dictation of the ground rules, he would not accept this as the reason. Much as he deplored hurting a colaborer's feelings, he still let nothing curb his genius for devising a better way to do it.

Divine services ended at the Naval and Marine Reserve Armory in Chavez Ravine. Daws, Sanny, and the others talked with the sailors who stayed behind for help. The Navigators held services here most Sundays at the request of the commanding officer and often led men to Christ. Leaving a marked New Testament with these newborn Christians was helpful, but

Dawson still felt the need for a clearly labeled "first bottle of milk" to give them.

"What did you tell your man this morning?" he asked each of the team on the way home. "What verse did you give him?" As they compared notes, the idea was born. A simple one, yet more than mere theory for it was conceived on the battlefront. Why not package the four basic Scripture verses essential to the new Christian's survival — those which would defend him against his new enemy, Satan, and give him vital nourishment from God's Word — and at the same time initiate him to the habit of memorizing the life-supporting Word.

The result was the palm-sized *Initial Rations* packet with verse cards displaying four promises from God to the Christian and a small booklet explaining the immediate effects of the new birth. It showed how to claim the promise of John 5:24 for assurance of salvation; 1 Corinthians 10:13 for assurance of victory; 1 John 1:9 for assurance of forgiveness; and John 16:24 for assurance of provision. And assurance that the packet was a powerful spiritual weapon came in ensuing months when unseen forces repeatedly hindered its production.

Hubert Mitchell, who used *Initial Rations* with servicemen at his Victory Center, suggested the name *B Rations* — *Initial Bible Rations* — corresponding to the Army's K rations. So *B Rations* it was, and the tiny packet assembled for the sailors that spring of 1943 began to cover the earth, going into millions of copies distributed under its later name *Beginning With Christ*. Men in the fleet were enthusiastic. Downing told how gratifying it was to have this material for those he led to Christ. "The combination of spiritual counsel, spiritual food, and a link to further follow-up of the man is unsurpassed." Use of *B Rations* in personal evangelism spread quickly. Dawson promoted it everywhere, happily reporting that even Charles Fuller had memorized the verses. Fuller and other evangelists began using *B Rations* for inquirers at the broadcast and evangelistic meetings. Dawson hoped it would also help fill the follow-up gap left by some hit-and-run evangelists whose practice of giving little or no help to their converts grieved him.

The forty-nine card memory course was also replaced later in the year by a new *Topical Memory System* of 108 passages with three verses on each of thirty-six topics. The first twelve of these verses, designated the *Initial Test*, gave a new Christian or any new memorizer a better chance to succeed, as he first took on the four verses of the *B Rations,* then the twelve of the *Initial Test,* then three larger packs in succession. While he memorized the twelve verses, the *Initial Test* booklet taught him six principles of "winning the battle of memory": 1) get started, 2) keep going, 3) have a system, 4) master references, 5) review, and 6) know what to memorize.

Dawson had asked a number of Christian workers to screen the choice of the *Topical Memory System*'s 108 key passages, which he welded to topics reflecting his practical insights on everyday spiritual needs. Relevant topics like "Be Strong in Temptation," "Endure Suffering and Hardness," "Follow Christ," met a Christian at ground level as no other memory system had yet done. It was pioneering, but in a field where Dawson's footing was sure and the objective clear.

After a memorizer had mastered the 108 he should, hopefully, want to continue learning verses of his own choice. In places where there was Navigator group fellowship, as in Honolulu where Chief Yeoman Kenny Watters was the leader after Downing transferred to Washington, pressure was kept on the growing Christians to continue memorizing. A large chart in the room where Bible study groups met displayed a list of verses to memorize and the names of the men, with squares to check off verses learned. Watters told Charley Myers, a ship's cook he was following up, that every Christian needed to know a dozen basic verses. Charley learned them. A week or so later Ken said, "Charley, a Christian needs at least fifty verses." As Charley neared fifty, his tutor allowed that a man needed a hundred verses put away, at least. Then it was five hundred. "Whenever he thought he had it made, I would raise his sights," Watters said. He was pleased when Charley admonished him sometime after getting his five hundred, "Watters, I was listening to you last night. You could have used this verse, and this one. You don't memorize enough Scripture."

The Keith Brooks Bible study books were mailed out free to servicemen as were the memory materials, their cost partly underwritten by Brooks and the rest by gifts coming in to Nav headquarters. Printing bills for memory packets could run a thousand dollars within two or three months, yet Dawson placed new orders without hesitation as these materials were a life line. The great majority of Navy men were in and out of Honolulu, often giving to the Nav Home there without stopping to think their help might be needed to meet printing bills back in Los Angeles.

Despite the cost, Dawson felt the correspondence ministry was vital at this point. Contacts were increasing too fast to assure many of them of getting adequate follow-up on the scene by a mature key man. The volume of letters and requests for materials showed hundreds being reached, Christians getting down to business in the Word for the first time, or men led to Christ by a fellow serviceman. He saw turnouts of fifty or more for a Saturday night meeting in the San Diego Home and men by the score coming through the new Oakland service center opened by Chrisman in summer 1944. Men who could quote a dozen or twenty Scripture verses were regarded as spiritual giants back in their home churches and by those who heard their testimonies on Fuller's network broadcast or at the Church of the Open Door.

Dawson's aim was to keep in touch with this vast army of potential laborers, following them up by correspondence and any other means and guiding them into fruitful service for the Lord. Their circumstances were ideal for growth, living and working among non-Christians. There was usually spare time available for Bible study, and the Lord arranged transfers to new duty in ways that could develop a man and broaden his experience.

After a Saturday night Navigator meeting at 509 a sailor asked, "Daws, did you hear the bad news?" speaking of the key man's transfer off his ship. Dawson's gaze pinned him to the wall. "I haven't heard any bad news. That's good news. That'll just make the rest of you men get on the ball." The sailor, thus commissioned, would rise to the challenge.

But maintaining contact with this host of men whom Dawson hoped to see join God's labor force in many fields after the war meant feeding them continuous study materials and challenge. When a man finished the first Brooks book he was offered the alternative of further books or the ABC Study booklet containing a supply of 3½"x6" study blanks, prayer list pages, and business pages adapted from Dunamis and AlphAmegA.

Early in 1945 Daws found that contact was in danger of dropping off when a man had done ABC Study for a time and had no urgent need to send for further materials. To bridge the gap at this crucial point he designed the Advanced ABC Study, an inductive chapter analysis including ABC with added features. The student would search for cross references, learning to compare Scripture with Scripture. He would write two applications from the chapter or portion, one in relation to God and one in relation to man. The eminent truth, or doctrinal teaching of the chapter, moved from ABC to Advanced ABC. These approaches along with a summary or outline, a title, basic passage, and difficulties, made Advanced ABC a muscular study for a week's assignment and an effective medium for continued contact with men growing in the Word, though it required more tutoring by mail. The single ABC still had wider use, however, as it was suitable for either a group situation or a man studying alone.

Dawson was amused by a syndicated series of newspaper articles by Navy officer Fletcher Pratt in which he ridiculed "The Navigators, a religious sect founded by some retired salt in Los Angeles" who "have the usual prohibitions of apocalyptic and evangelical new faiths against alcohol, tea, coffee, and even in this case Coca Cola," and "make a nuisance of themselves by asking for a special compartment in which to hold conversion meetings." He took as a compliment Pratt's charge that while claiming his battleship had only three Navigators aboard, he said they caused censors no end of trouble by quoting Paul's epistles so much that "junior officers who do the censoring are acquiring an elaborate acquaintance with Scripture."

This was the first attention the secular press had given The Navigators since the *Collier's* story three years ago — and the religious press had carried little — but it demonstrated the Bible-totin', Scripture-quotin' Navigators were making an impact. Yet as always, Dawson took greatest satisfaction not in their numbers but in knowing God was building men of stature able to lead and disciple others. Men like Kenny Watters, whose mastery of the Word enabled him to teach from any book or doctrine of the Bible, but who knew it was better to get a man studying on his own. Watters, like Downing, had a broad teaching ministry but saw the value of investing time in the individual, imparting his life to a man who would in time become a stalwart for God.

Few had reached the level of maturity to be willing to invest so sacrificially, but Daws knew of about a dozen men well on the way. And maybe a hundred whose single-hearted devotion to the Lord indicated they would spend their lives serving Him, come what may. Eldon Durant, who had won men to Christ on his submarine and seen considerable action in the Pacific, could be characterized by the verse he shared in a letter, "Of Zebulun, such as went forth to battle, expert in war, with all instruments of war, fifty thousand, which could keep rank: they were not of double heart" (1 Chron. 12:33). Blond, softspoken Don Blake, gifted in evangelism, had gone home and led his five brothers to the Lord. A sailor he led to Christ admitted he thought Christianity was only for women and children until he saw Blake and other men living for Christ.

Gustafson, the genial Chicago Swede, had a good ministry going on the new battleship *Wisconsin*. And Charlie Hayes — tall, rangy, with an Airedale friendliness for everyone — had transferred off the *Mississippi* just before she was hit by a suicide plane which killed and injured scores of her crew. God had plans for Charlie. He was assigned to a Farragut, Idaho, base as food service inspector for six camps, a job that took him from camp to camp where he could evangelize to his heart's content. Ordering free tracts, 15,000 at a time, he papered the base.

God had seen fit to call more Navigators Home through the agency of war. Archie Brandt, a top sonarman on the *Scamp* sub, volunteered for extra war patrols beyond his normal tour and on one of these the *Scamp* was lost. Henry Jackson had been missing in action in the Pacific since the end of 1942. John Tinkle, Daws learned later, went down with the *Houston* early that year in a valiant fight off Java. Cliff Holt, early Dunamis clubber and Nav printer, had a fruitful eighteen months in the Navy leading men to Christ and helping Christians on the destroyer *Johnston* before it was sunk in the Battle for Leyte Gulf. "It seems the time just flew by," Cliff said in one of his last letters. "I guess it's because I've been spending a great deal of it in the Word, just studying to my heart's content; so I'm just saturated with it. What a Book! The more of it I absorb, the greater love I have for it, and the more it seems there is to learn." Cliff had witnessed to every man on the *Johnston*, and several received Christ the day the ship went down.

More of His best warriors now Home with the Lord they loved! Yet the eye of faith saw their departure as assurance that the ranks would fill with replacements. In a coincidence unknown to all but Him, two of the men God would give for future colaborship had landed a month earlier with a Marine unit on the tiny island of Peleliu: LeRoy Eims, still unconverted, wondering how to stanch the blood gushing from his wounded leg, and Bob Boardman, tank driver who had read a Gideon New Testament in the hospital and received Christ. Neither knew the other and neither knew of Trotman or any Navigators.

During the war years Dawson gave little thought to recruiting men to The Navigators as a career but much to developing men for missions. Sanny was one exception. He would continue his apprenticeship in a Navigator area now that the idea of nationwide Dunamis clubs for which he had first been called was overshadowed by servicemen's work. Hayden was minded to be a headquarters staff assistant and was gifted for this. For most couples manning Nav Homes in various cities, meeting vital wartime needs by providing spiritual refueling stops, it was an interim ministry or an addition to their regular jobs. Hightower was going to Africa when the war ended. John Thorne in Waukegan, later in San Diego, also looked toward the mission field. So did DeLong as he ministered in Long Beach, San Diego, and San Francisco Nav areas. Dawson encouraged them in this direction and challenged many still in uniform to pray about foreign service.

Cameron Townsend's straight-faced request for 500 Navigators for Wycliffe did not strike Dawson as presumptuous; rather he thrilled at the daring faith of this man with the unassuming manner of a small town shopkeeper, blandly asking the impossible. Townsend's vision of giving the Bible to the tribes also appealed to Dawson's sense of the Word's supreme importance. He vigorously promoted Wycliffe's cause, printing letters and pictures of translators in the *Log*, putting individual Navigators in touch with prayer partners on the field, encouraging men to give to the work and to consider a Wycliffe career. He quoted Townsend's call: "Allied victory must find missionary forces ready for a Final Advance. . . . Now is the time to train pioneers to give the thousand unreached tribes their rightful heritage, the *Bible* . . . ," and added in a newsletter, "Think of it! Mexico has 51 Indian languages alone. . . . Pray that hundreds of thousands in the Philippines, covering 70 or 80 languages not reduced to writing, much less with a single sentence from the Word of God, may some day have it. Then South America with more than this number."

Such enthusiasm gave an aura of importance to missions that was contagious. Townsend saw Daws as a man's man and appreciated the zeal and radiance he brought to the effort. And his visible interest in the members when in Mexico for September board meetings gave a lift to their spirits and sense of team backing. He loved them and they knew it, recalling his taking a gang of them out for late-evening hamburger forays or walks through the city. "Hey, kids, let's try some of this," he would say of some outlandish item on the menu, then try his fractured Spanish on the waiter.

Interviewing prospective Wycliffe members was Dawson's responsibility during the summer of 1943 linguistic training course given some 200 young people — Wycliffe candidates and those of other boards — at Bacone College in Oklahoma. As he had done in Mexico, he sought to help them in their spiritual lives, resulting in a number of candidates asking for the AlphAmegA plan.

Dawson's probing questions helped them pinpoint their need: "How is your prayer life?" "Do you have a daily devotional time with the Lord?" "Can you name someone you have led to Christ who is now living for Him?" Somehow a majority of these earnest young people had finished their academic and

Bible school training for the mission field without ever bringing one person to the Savior or establishing the personal prayer and devotional life lines essential to spiritual health. Though not surprised by this discovery, Dawson later used it in his messages to shock many into recognizing their own needs. The candidates lamely pleaded irregular schedules and lack of time as their reasons but were usually awakened by his next query: "Do you think it will be any better when you get to the field, where you have to boil the water you drink and do endless time-consuming chores you never dreamed of in the States?"

"The important thing is the place you give the Word in your life," he told one candidate. "You don't have to use the Nav system. One method works for some and another for others. But you've got to have this Book in your heart and in your life." At Bacone George Cowan, whom Daws had known since the 1940 gospel team trip, asked him to be best man at his wedding in Los Angeles. Cowan was impressed by Dawson's understanding of the missionaries and his penchant for getting the facts, noting that at conferences in Mexico he showed "he was sympathetic with our problems, and always had a gang with him talking and finding out what was going on. He wanted to know everything about everything."

Added to the AlphAmegA rallies that year were missionary rallies held at 509. Daws wrote that one rally with "five missionary speakers and some sixty down-to-business Christians in attendance saw real work done for the Lord as far as unreached fields of the world are concerned. . . . We expect to go right ahead, challenging key young people to the greatest calling in the world, pioneer missions." Doubtless the challenge was included in 509's Saturday night Navigator meetings, attended mainly by those in Navy and other college officer training programs since ship-based sailors usually put in at San Diego or San Francisco.

Dawson had planned to go on from Bacone to the East Coast for business at Navigator Homes, including time with Dick, Helen, and Garry Hightower at the Home in Brooklyn. But before he left for Oklahoma, word came July 12 of Helen's death and Dick's serious injury in a truck-auto collision, so he went directly to New York. God's provision for his trip in that pre-credit card era had come the day before, a large undesignated gift from a serviceman a year old in Christ.

He found Dick as he knew he would, comforted and strengthened by Scripture he was quoting almost by reflex action, verses acknowledging God's sovereign wisdom in it all. Helen was the first of the Navigator staff He had called Home, and Dawson drew comfort from the way Dick's testimony to His sustaining power was used to reach others for Christ.

While in New York Dawson received word that Lila was ill. As he continued his itinerary to Washington, Norfolk, Chicago and finally Bacone, she was growing worse; surgery for kidney removal was planned. A concerned Charles Fuller called Dawson and asked his permission to change doctors. "Please take charge," Daws quickly consented, "as if she were your own daughter." God had answered his anguished prayer for Lila and, though he did not know it then, possibly spared her life. The Fullers called in their own physician, who hospitalized her to correct severe dehydration and condition her for an urgently needed appendectomy. In his opinion, she would not have survived the other surgery.

Hurrying home to be at Lila's side, Dawson left again when the doctor had assured him she was out of danger. He kept his appointments in Louisiana and Texas, and from there he went on to Wycliffe conference and board meetings at Cuernavaca, Mexico, two weeks of opportunity to challenge and encourage some 100 translators. While there he contracted malaria, landing in the hospital himself for a week after his return home. The Lord allowed this, he felt, so that he could sympathize with missionaries who often fell prey to the disease.

*   *   *   *

Over the years Dawson's prayer patterns had changed. Now that he traveled more, it was difficult to get time for prayer. Consequently, more of his prayer times were alone as it was difficult to schedule periods when a group could meet. He depended heavily on the "world's best crew" to uphold him on the road and was equally conscious of need for their backing when at home. With some alarm he noted after returning from a twenty-one-day trip, during which he had felt upheld by prayer, that his ministry at a small church at home seemed

fruitless. The gang had quit praying! He lost no time in reminding them — and himself — that success in any under-
taking for the Lord came "not by might, nor by power, but by
my Spirit, saith the Lord of hosts."

During one of Bob Padelford's frequent visits Dawson asked
him to join him for prayer in the attic room at 509. Padelford
looked forward to these times whenever their schedules permitted. But today as they waited upon God, the businessman
sensed a solemn mood he could not describe. Dawson prayed
and asked the Lord to really try him. *A daring request,* Padelford thought. "Whatever prompted you to pray that way?
Isn't that pretty dangerous?"

"Bob, I need it," he explained. "It's the only way I can
know. I have decisions to make and have to know whether I'm
qualified to take certain steps that are before me. I have to
know God's hand is on me, and am asking Him to prove me."
He paused. " 'And thou shalt remember all the way which the
Lord thy God led thee these forty years in the wilderness, to
humble thee, and to prove thee, to know what was in thine
heart, whether thou wouldst keep his commandments, or no.' "
Here he had been down with malaria, his beloved Lila in the
hospital twice . . . there was the Hightower accident . . . finances
. . . problems with Nav Home personnel — wasn't that enough
trial for now? Padelford shook his head. Took a lot of courage
to ask that. Dawson did not disagree, but could not avoid or
regret it. Mercifully he was spared the knowledge of two
specific trials that lay ahead, both touching him in areas where
he was particularly sensitive.

In January 1944 Daws was in the hospital again, this time
in Portland. Atabrine had failed to rout the malaria bug, and
his heavy travel schedule seeing pastors and laymen about
service centers and servicemen's work had used up his reserve.
Yet the delay en route did not depress him; he simply summoned those he needed to see to the hospital. He was refreshed
by fellowship with Chief Radioman Cecil Davidson, key man
on the *Idaho* then in port, much as Paul was comforted by the
coming of Titus. Davidson spent all off-duty time with Daws
at the hospital and later at his hotel, gladly buying steak
dinner each night for the two of them for the privilege of the
fellowship. "A lot of guys would have given plenty to get

that time," he said later. Dawson, whose conviction of the value of ministering one-to-one was growing stronger, used such time for building in a life. He also imparted the principle to Davidson, who lamented his meager success in building disciples on his ship. "Pick out one man who is really interested and concentrate on him," Dawson counseled.

Another Portland visitor was a Navy key man, down from Bremerton. Daws had heard little from him the past year and had last seen him before Pearl Harbor. He seemed changed, the old sunny disposition clouded. A recent letter had stated his mission: he was coming to "exhort" his spiritual elder about "backbiting" and discuss some personal grievances. Dawson was nonplused to learn he had caused his dear friend grief. This man had been closer than a brother to him and Lila.

Dawson appreciated his obedience to the Word in coming to him — it must have taken courage — and Daws was anxious to obey the same Word and make things right. The man complained that Daws belittled and criticized him to someone for lack of cooperation in ministry methods and for not using the Dunamis notebook system, a hurt he may have felt more keenly because of his leadership standing with men in the fleet.

Daws earnestly asked his brother's forgiveness. It was difficult to comprehend some of the offenses he detailed, but Daws would not contest them since broken fellowship was at issue. He apologized and cleared the slate. His heart was clear now, and the man seemed satisfied. Daws sent a note with other business to his secretary, who had seen his letter of complaint: "T - - - was down. We got squared away or should I say I did. Humbled myself and asked for forgiveness and surely the Lord was with us. Dear T - - -, sure love him."

"It's a deal, Daws. See you Friday morning." The man's ebullient spirit was reflected in his firm handshake as they parted. Dawson had found Hubert Mitchell an enthusiastic prayer buddy who did not flinch at meeting at five in the morning to pray for two hours before breakfast.

From their first meeting at Mount Hermon in 1942 each had been struck by the other's love for God and ambition for the Great Commission. Mitchell, who had come home from a Sumatra mission field with four small children after his wife died, directed the Victory Center in Los Angeles. The two men's common interest in servicemen's work and in rearing children further cemented their friendship. They met for about a year on Friday mornings in the small "power house" on the roof above the Navigator office or in the cement igloo bomb shelter behind the Mitchell home.

"Here were the two of us," Dawson described it, "and I'm praying in a sort of quiet, conversational tone and Hube's shouting loud enough to get the Lord out of bed."

By spring Mitchell's brother-in-law David Morken, also evacuated from Sumatra by the war, began to pray with them. Like Mitchell, he ministered in churches, camps, and conferences and directed a servicemen's center using Navigator follow-up materials. Dick Hillis joined them in the fall when he came to teach at Biola. He well remembered the time Daws had roared up to Biola on his motorcycle thirteen years ago and nailed him on memorizing Scripture. He had written from China telling of the fine team of men the Lord had given him to train and help in the ministry and had asked to put Navigator material into Chinese to use with them. Daws's reply chilled him: "If you will do it yourself first, then you can use it with your men." He never answered.

Now he dreaded meeting this stickler for pacesetting. When they did meet, Hillis said, "All right, Daws, I surrender. I need to get into memory, and I need the discipline and the study — not for someone else but for myself. When do we start?" "Tomorrow morning at five in my office." Hillis came and began meeting with the Friday morning group, where prayer was interspersed with sharing the Word, usually from "tables of the heart."

Morken had mastered Scripture memory after first declaring he could never memorize, even in school.

"Do you know your name? The alphabet? The multiplication table?" Daws had asked. "You memorized those by hearing them over and over — by review. And you can memorize Scripture."

Morken found it worked. In addition to review, he used Dawson's suggestion for meditation, finding the Word thus digested became part of his life and virtually unforgettable. His wife Helen felt that memorizing Scripture had deepened his ministry and given his preaching new authority.

Hillis's brother Don, home from India, joined them, along with Robert Munger, a South Hollywood pastor. Munger had been speaker for the recent Triumphant Life Banquet held that summer to reach non-Christians or Christians who wanted to grow. He was also keenly interested in servicemen as many from his church were in the war zones. Sanny met with the group when his work at Biola and the Long Beach center permitted. Businessman Ernie Mintie became a regular, as well as Charlie Cooper and Bob Padelford when they were in town.

Their prayer for servicemen centered on recruiting them for the Lord's army as the Matthew 9:38 prayer for laborers came to dominate their requests. Dawson's trips to Bacone and Mexico, besides giving immediacy to the monthly missionary rallies at 509, helped fuel the Friday group's prayer for missions. And the presence of the Hillises, Morken, and Mitchell brought their fields of China, India, and Indonesia startlingly near.

"It wasn't enough for me to pray for China or Bob Munger for South Hollywood or Hube for Sumatra," Hillis explained. "We had to begin with Los Angeles and pray around the world." Daws noted in his journal, "This morning 5 A.M. met Cooper, [George] Cowan, Sanny, Mitchell, Hillis for a precious season of real prayer. These times have been a terrific challenge to all of us and it is thrilling to see Cooper and Mintie getting a world-wide vision." But when Daws said, "Let's pick the tiniest places in the Pacific and pray for them," pointing on the map to unheard-of names, Padelford told him it was a bit far-fetched. To Dawson it was not frivolous but an act of faith. Years later when Padelford said good-bye to Bob Boardman leaving for Okinawa as a Navigator representative, it dawned on him — Okinawa was probably one of the invisible dots on the map they had prayed for those early mornings! He concluded God had given Daws the gift of faith which he used to rally them to pray these things into being.

The Friday morning fellowship had far-reaching effects in the lives of these Christian leaders whose mutual encouragement and influence they would long remember. Dick Hillis noted the wartime hiatus spent praying for missions, in addition to bearing the hidden fruits of intercession known only to Him, sent most of them back overseas to serve Christ. He also found a personal benefit. "During those times I realized the great pulsating force of Daws's heart was love, expressed in a desire that every one of God's children be conformed to the image of God's dear Son. If they weren't, and God told him to put his finger on that nonconformity, he would do it. This gave a deep love in my own heart for Daws. No one has ever personally hit me harder in relation to my spiritual life, and no one has loved me more."

This personal ministry of help to God's servants who were leaders in their own right was increasing. God was answering Dawson's earlier prayer for wisdom in counsel similar to that seen in mature saints without waiting for their years. God would trust him with this gift and with that other badge of early maturity: suffering.

Servicemen's centers in large and small places around the U.S. filled a vital wartime need for ministry to GIs, sailors, and Marines. Rev. George Bostrom probably opened the first one, in Tacoma. ("You can tell a Navigator as soon as he walks in," he told his sons. "They know the Word.") Hightower had helped open one in San Diego and later directed the Victory Center in New York, where he could bring key servicemen from the Navigator Home to train them in personal evangelism. Morken was in Santa Ana, Mitchell in Los Angeles, DeLong now in Long Beach. On his northwest trip cut short by malaria in Portland, Daws spent time with several directors of service centers. He felt a three-day conference would be extremely profitable, bringing these directors together to fellowship and share their experience, to consider ways to improve their ministry, and to learn more about follow-up.

Men from thirteen centers in western states accepted The Navigators' invitation to the conference held at 509 in April. Its success was reflected in their enthusiasm for planned future meetings. Hubert Mitchell's sessions on personal evangelism and Dawson's on follow-up, messages from Charles Fuller, Louis Talbot, and others filled the days. A second conference called for late July in Chicago was hosted by CBMC, with fifty men sharing their common concerns in servicemen's work and taking back ideas and helps, including a stiff Trotman challenge on follow-up. Daws had found most of these men enthusiastic in evangelism but needing vision and know-how for establishing a new Christian in the Word and in living the life.

It disturbed him that in many centers springing up around the country men were led to decisions through inept "coffee-and-doughnut evangelism" — a fifteen-minute message over breakfast, a raised hand into which a *B Rations* was thrust, a pat on the back and God-bless-you-soldier. For these lads, spiritual survival would be a miracle. The practice went against his feeling that a job so important should be well done; more, it must grieve the Lord who wanted *every* Christian to grow to full stature in Christ. Nor was Dawson cheered by a survey showing that only three of 200 men who received *B Rations* at service centers finished the four verses and asked for more, contrasted with 65 percent who finished among contacts, new and older Christians, made through Charles Fuller's broadcast.

When a key man, Charlie Hayes, visited Los Angeles, a sailor hailed him on the street. "Hey, look what I got." It was a *B Rations!* Charlie was aghast. "Daws, he's the worst enemy of the Gospel in our camp." "Look into it and report to me, will you?" Daws asked. The sailor had stopped into a hospitality center and had been cornered in a gospel meeting where the speaker said they had something to give anyone who raised his hand after the meeting. "I raised my hand and that's all they gave me," the disappointed sailor told Charlie. Daws resolved to declare a personal war on such misuse of Nav materials, knowing patient education of the users was the only way. He considered an hour-long interview reasonable for explaining the *B Rations* to an individual.

Dawson's crusade for thorough evangelism and adequate

follow-up was just beginning. He repeated the challenge often: "Remember, making a decision is 5 percent; 95 percent is following through. God is not glorified by a raised hand unless the decision is confirmed by a Christian life that follows it."

His dim view of an evangelist's or pastor's interest in "souls" which ended with a raised hand or a prayer at the altar was becoming known, and he did not modify it though some thought his criticism too harsh. He often cited the Los Angeles tent campaign where 400 registered decisions for Christ but were not followed up, and not one came to a follow-up meeting later planned for them. Speaking to a Navigator conference he shouted, "What God wants is men born into his family who are conformed to the image of His Son and show forth the savour of His knowledge in every place. You lead a man to Christ. You tell him he's saved. You get him to join the church. You leave him. You let him go along living his worldly life. When does he do the most damage, before or after? You *know* it. And preachers know it, and evangelists know it, and they go right on winnin' more souls and leavin' 'em and winnin' more souls. Does it make sense?"

*   *   *   *

Navigator Homes and contact points increased during the war and so did Dawson's problem of manning and supervising them as military orders kept key men on the move. Hightower helped greatly on the East Coast until his accident. Bob Suttie stood by for Dick in New York, then later came to Los Angeles and was sent on to open a downtown Nav office in Seattle. Louella Dyer's home was still a rallying point for hospitality there, but a contact man was needed. Four months later Suttie was called into the armed forces, and Dawson again faced a manpower need.

Sanny was the obvious choice for Seattle. Graduating from Biola, he was ready to take on an area work. His boyish appearance at twenty-three might keep some from taking him seriously as a representative of a Christian work, but Daws knew he would make it. He was confident, meek, a man of prayer and solid in faith, tenacious in his purpose to please God.

Suttie, a popular speaker and evangelist, had not been as conscientious about follow-up as Sanny would be. Dawson had schooled his Timothy in this and hoped Seattle would become a showcase area work. His parting word: "Sanny, no matter how many Sunday school classes you teach or Gospel team meetings you have, or whether five or a hundred come to Saturday night meeting, when I come to Seattle I want to meet your men who are down to business in the Word. Find some who have made decisions but haven't had any help and spend time with them, stick with them, and get them digging into the Word." Sanny arrived in Seattle June 1944, armed with promises from Scripture, assured he and Lucy were heavily backed in prayer, and challenged by the instruction to "stick with your man."

Dawson believed he should be flexible in the demands made on different areas and the degree and kind of direction he gave colaborers, considering their backgrounds and capacities. He would keep core objectives in view, giving them priority over nonessentials. Even with Hightower, his first trained man sent to an area, he would not differ again over his policy of making financial needs known. Floyd Robertson observed to someone that though Dawson's ideas were definite, he did not require one to agree with him on every point. When a key man reported with alarm that John Midgette of the Norfolk Home did not teach the believer's permanent security in Christ, Daws replied he was aware of this and that another Navigator had unfortunately tackled John on the subject.

"Every other phase of Johnnie's life and ministry is strong," Daws wrote. "Some men he produces are stronger than some of our leaders who are straight on this subject produce. I refuse to allow John's lack of understanding on this subject to take him out of the work. I don't think it will be long till the Spirit of God reveals the truth to him." Rather than embargo a going ministry because of its flaws, he would encourage and help it improve.

As administrative travel to the areas cut into Dawson's direct ministry, he tried to redeem the time it required. He still used train trips to San Diego or the Bay area for study and dictation. The secretaries who went along could broaden their own ministry by spending time with nurses and other girls in the areas. Work on memory and Bible study materials was often done en route, though one such Bible study course modeled on

The Wheel was drafted in a secretary's notebook that was later lost.

When Dawson did have opportunity for ministry to groups or individuals along the way, his dynamic interest which bored in like a magnifying glass in the sun's rays made the encounter memorable. On the train to San Diego he fellowshiped with a man going as a missionary to India. More than ten years later the missionary said of that chance meeting, "I learned in that one hour some things I have been trying to apply to my missionary work ever since."

A sailor at the San Diego Home, a new Christian, was awed and a little frightened at the sight of Dawson, much younger than the sailor's image of a Christian leader, slight of stature but big-jawed and tough looking. Nevertheless the sailor, Ken Swan, who would one day direct a Nav area, remembered his message. "He spoke on 1 Corinthians 16:13, on those four things, and made us all memorize it. I never forgot it." He also remembered the next message he heard from Daws — at Louella Dyer's in Seattle — on Scripture memory. Dawson himself was not as convinced of the permanence of his impact. Late in 1944 he wrote:

> *When I write my journal I usually back up, taking Sunday, Saturday, Friday, etc. By the time I got to Friday night I could hardly remember what I had preached about, Thursday the same. If I forget what I speak about, what about those who hear? Again I face the fact that the most real thing in all our labor for the Lord is to speak so simply, so definitely, with attention focused so clearly on the thing God wants to say to His people that there is no confusion regarding what He has said.*

For Dawson, having too many irons in the fire at all times kept things exciting. All his activities, however, pointed to the growing purpose to raise a mighty army of trained soldiers for Christ and for world missions. The urgency was reflected in a rare magazine article, probably his first outside the *Log,* in *The King's Business* for November 1944:

> *America has everything, including the greatest responsibility of any country in the world. The richest of all nations and the most enlightened, she has the best in science, education, transportation, production, and unlimited resources. Above all, the Gospel of Jesus Christ has been allowed to spread throughout our nation by preaching, evangelism, personal work, the printed page, and radio.*
>
> *If all this is true, what are we going to do at the end of World War II? From the commercial and political standpoints, the national leaders of America realize their job in a post-war world and that it involves millions of people and billions of dollars . . . .*
>
> *But Christians! What of our job, the greatest one of all? . . . National Geographic told of 2700 nations, countries, or tribes of the world, each having a different language . . . . The job of world evangelization is to be done by individuals. God has always done His greatest work through a man. The Lord will use us if we are willing.*

Viewing the Great Commission, he felt The Navigators' two main contributions would be men and specialized emphases such as follow-up. But the job indeed called for a many-pronged attack and the efforts of agencies with differing visions and goals, some of those differences represented in his own circle of friends. Two years earlier he had written Downing: "The *Lord* is doing some wonderful work in the States through other agencies. With many there is the closest cooperation. They are covering the field that we will not be able to reach. On the other hand we are able to follow up some of those who profess to come to *Christ* through their ministry and which would otherwise be neglected."

Daws could wholeheartedly encourage and help these other works. For one thing, whatever he could do for the leader of a work would contribute to an entire ministry for Christ in an area he would not otherwise reach. For another, by providing the emphasis and perhaps materials for follow-up or Scripture memory or Bible study, he could add a needed dimension to that ministry. And too, it was personally rewarding to Dawson to see the other fellow's dream fulfilled. Sometimes he described a man's work or plan to a third person in such glowing terms the originator scarcely recognized it. David Morken ventured to share with Dawson his idea and burden for a certain ministry and was overwhelmed by his immediate understanding and enthusiastic offer to help. Morken also appreciated the fact that though his friend was a perfectionist, he did not try to fit everyone into a perfectionist mold.

Frequent contact with West Coast CBMC groups came about as Dawson traveled with CBMC President Charlie Cooper on his business trips. Cooper and Trotman challenged CBMCers to memorize Scripture as a necessary part of their own emphasis — personal evangelism. Back in New York Bob Swanson still promoted memorization with Christian businessmen.

At Bacone that summer Dawson again ministered to missionaries of twenty-eight boards, especially Wycliffe candidates, signing new users of AlphAmegA. He went on to The Firs, a conference center in the Northwest run by his Biola friend Grant Whipple. Here Young Life and Navigators combined their 1944 staff conferences, with Jim Rayburn and thirty workers from around the U.S., leaders of five area Navigator Homes and Los Angeles headquarters staff. The two groups had enjoyed close ties of fellowship in the Lord, and adapted AlphAmegA notebook and memory materials were being successfully used by Young Life staff and their high schoolers. Daws was most thankful for Young Life's actual and potential outreach to the nation's high schools, which he felt would far exceed what he had originally planned for Dunamis and Martures clubs.

Another important movement was launched that third year of the war through the vision of Navy pilots Jim Buyers and Jim Truxton to band together Christian pilots and mechanics who would volunteer to fly for missions. Daws was impressed with their plans and offered them office space and the names of Navigators who might wish to join them. He was able also to give periodic counsel on personnel and administrative policies. Their first full-time worker, Women's Airforce Service Pilot

Elizabeth Greene, came to live at 509 and staff the Missionary Aviation Fellowship office until the next year when she became the group's first pilot on the field, serving Wycliffe in Mexico. MAF grew solidly, expanding into new countries and programs only after careful surveys and planning with the mission boards they would serve.

An invitation to speak an hour each day at a seminary where twenty-five to thirty men were studying for the ministry gave Daws another investment in the work of others. "It thrills me to touch the life of a man who will touch a great host of men," he wrote Downing. "Our best investment is with faithful men who shall be able to teach others also. The president asked me to shoot straight and hard on being down to business, following through, memorization of Scripture, etc. Hearts have been open and business is being done."

During the fall the men meeting Friday mornings for prayer crystallized a plan to present the challenge of world missions to teen-age youth. The Hillises had been working with high schoolers, Navigators had AlphAmegA clubs, and the others often spoke to youth camps and conferences. But Hubert Mitchell returned from a visit to Wyrtzen's Word of Life ablaze with the idea of starting a Saturday night rally with direct missions appeal to young people. The men immediately named themselves as a committee to launch the weekly rally, for which Dr. Talbot offered the Church of the Open Door auditorium and Dawson began preparing a counselor follow-up corps.

The rally, with Mitchell directing, would replace AlphAmegA rallies, Dawson decided, and he would hold Saturday night Navigator meetings in his office an hour earlier so that Navigators could counsel and take part in the program. Chicago Youth For Christ had just started, aimed at evangelizing youth, in part as a counter to the big city sin problem. In Pasadena Pastor J. Vernon McGee had held a successful rally in May. Young Life had been well received. Kids were listening.

So the Saturday Nite Jubilee the first Saturday of January 1945, with the well-known musicians Rudy Atwood and Lorin Whitney at piano and organ, caught the trend and from the beginning drew large crowds of young people. Morken followed Mitchell as Jubilee's director, till both returned over-

seas, demonstrating the missions message they had been bringing to youth. The Jubilee became Los Angeles Youth For
Christ, joining YFC International organized in Chicago the
same January the Jubilee had begun, with Billy Graham its
first field representative and Pastor Torrey Johnson its first
president.

*   *   *   *

While stationed stateside, the key man who had confronted
Daws in Portland was now ministering at a servicemen's center.
He felt he must meet with Dawson to say he would not be using
Navigator follow-up methods there. Daws quickly assured
him he would not be expected to do so. They fellowshiped
again a few months after Daws had asked his forgiveness for
past slights. The man's wife had replied to his apology by
asking to meet and discuss all past misunderstandings, so Dawson made the trip to see the two and hear their grievances.
Again he asked their forgiveness and was given a new list of a
dozen persons he had wronged by criticism or by criticizing
others to them.

"I am sure that through the years while noticing the trait in
others and condemning it, I myself have become very critical,"
Daws wrote Downing. "I praise *God* for my brother's faith-
fulness in coming because he came with nothing but the Word
of God and a desire to fulfill the will of *God*." And to Watters:
"The *Lord* has very graciously brought home to me with force
a lesson I should have learned long ago. . . . Although I am a
firm believer in exhortation, have preached the same and have
done much of it, and also am a firm believer in going directly
to a person instead of to another about that person, I have
apparently slipped and now this has been straightened out."
Having written letters to those on the list, Daws was glad to
see the slate cleared and fellowship restored all around. A note
from the key man's wife said, "You have won my husband's
confidence and deep love in a greater way than I can express
by your complete obedience to His Word."

He did think of one more person Daws should write — a
sailor — to finish clearing things up. Daws said he would do
this if he knew what he should write about and would also
mention the wonderful fellowship which now existed. *Strange,*
Daws thought, *after three face-to-face times together in the*

*last half-year and the considerable anguish of getting all ac-
counts straight to the minute, that his brother should only
now bring up another name, and with such a vague idea of the
offense.* Well, he would think nothing of it, for he intended to
go the tenth mile if necessary to have a conscience void of
offense toward God and men. This was worth whatever it cost,
and it was good to have the case closed.

At the Navigators-Young Life conference at The Firs the
ministry of the Word by Dr. Jack Mitchell of Portland and
Dr. Wilbur Smith of Chicago was especially timely for Dawson, depleted after the heavy summer of travel and ministry.
"God sent them and they fed us," he wrote. "We did not
realize how empty we were and how much we needed the
Word. We came home with new spiritual vigor and determination and vision to fulfill the job He has given us."

One need he saw was to organize headquarters office, which
had expanded too fast for orderly growth. Addie Rosenbaum
and Millie Hopkins, Biola students looking toward foreign
missions but obedient to God's redirection to serve in the
Navigator office, solved the immediate problem and met the
continuing need for swift efficiency in a rapidly growing ministry. Some jungle trail would have to wait for other footsteps
bringing Bibles to a waiting tribe, but on the heavenly books the
contribution of these two who went into battle armed with
typewriters might well earn the tribute given Marconi's tele-
graph — "What hath God wrought!"

His faith and courage bolstered by fresh infusions of the
Word and the "world's greatest crew" standing by, Dawson was
ready to plan big. He was fighting under an invincible Commander on a world-sized battlefield for the mighty cause of the
Great Commission, and victory seemed certain. He was undis-
turbed that the budget edged steadily upward. There were
printing bills for ever-larger orders of study and memory
materials, though the Christian printer who liked the work
priced jobs at a minimum. New office staff could be housed
sumptuously at 509, with room to spare for guests Daws loved
to invite from wherever he went. Added office space and equipment he could usually get at bargain rates — still they cost
something. But the Lord had provided so unfailingly that

Dawson could view the present financial squeeze almost with detachment.

A number of servicemen had allotments from their pay sent to The Navigators, and an occasional large gift came in time to meet a special need. Dick Hightower, now remarried and back in New York, telephoned that he had received a settlement from the car accident and wanted to send part of it to the work. When this came it would clear all current bills and leave a sizeable sum to invest in new printed materials. A five-dollar gift from an officer and $100 from another serviceman came in time to pay the November office rent, important because the landlord had answered an inquiry about The Navigators saying they always paid right on time! It was evident Hudson Taylor's axiom that God's work done in God's way will never lack God's supply was alive and well.

Daws made decisions about travel and other ministry activities on the basis of whether it was God's will for this time, not on the basis of available funds. He saw a trip to visit the Honolulu work as an immediate need, as DeGroff was unable to come to the mainland. And Chrisman would make a circuit up the eastern seaboard and back through Chicago and Wheaton, taking care of business in Daws's stead.

In mid-October another letter from the man who had exhorted him brought disappointment to Dawson and a sinking feeling that something was wrong. The letter contained solemn warnings of disobedience — and the name of yet another sailor to whom Daws should apologize. T - - - again protested the Dunamis — AlphAmegA disciplines. ("To me your notebook system is a weight.")

For the first time in these months Dawson reacted; he was hurt, but tried to answer the letter in the right spirit. He defended the Dunamis plan, pointing out that many who used it properly did profit from it. And he promised to write the sailor. But T - - - rejected his explanation and called for a face-to-face meeting. This was perplexing to Dawson, reopening a once-closed case.

Fabulous "509," Trotman home and center of Navigator hospitality from 1943-1953.

V

Toward Producing Reproducers

1944-1948

Dawson on personal prayer retreat at California's Acorn Lodge.

The crisp December air felt good on his face as a light breeze swept through the trees on South Pasadena's rolling hills. After dinner Daws had taken jacket, Bible, and a Navy blanket and bounded up the winding street behind 509 to a favorite knoll where he could look down on the town lights or see the stars overhead. Here he spent precious hours alone, praying aloud, singing praise to the Lord, quoting Scriptures of promise and challenge that flooded his mind — now wrestling in urgent prayer, now pacing the hillside in silence.

He had had similar time with the Lord here last evening after the airline canceled his space to Jacksonville at flight time. He had thanked the Lord for the changed plan; then the mail brought evidence that it would have been the wrong time to go. He never doubted that God led in such changes in travel and ministry, as it was all committed to Him in advance.

There had been much recent activity — trips to San Diego, to Oakland to get the service center going, launching the Jubilee, reorganizing the office, holding Navigator meetings and AlphAmegA rallies, helping MAF, Young Life, and CBMC, attending Wycliffe board meetings, and more. And the Nav work in areas across the U.S. and in Honolulu was having the normal problems of a work of God battling the forces of darkness. In the time here on the hill last night the Lord had given him strength to make some hard decisions — decisions made for eternity.

Tonight he reviewed his commission from God and was moved to make a request. *Holy Father, I'm asking You to begin working now in the hearts of high school and college kids and business people You will give us from across the U.S., topnotchers, for the work You are going to do through The Navigators in years to come.* It was as good as done. "Might as well put it down in my book now," he noted later, "for the *Lord* accepted my request. It is on *His* books and on the way."

As he waited on God to search his heart, Dawson wondered why the battles became heavier farther on in the Christian life. It would seem as he grew closer to the Lord and was entrusted with more responsibility, the "schooling" should ease somewhat — but it had been just the opposite. Personal victories he had won, even the simplest kind, had to be fought for again and again. He concluded that the closer one pressed into the enemy's territory the harder he fought. Even as now when it seemed the war should be ending, both Hitler and Tojo were fighting desperate rear guard actions to delay an Allied victory they must know was inevitable.

Dawson was glad 1 Corinthians 10:13 never wore thin; he would always need to keep it handy. And 1 John 1:9. His protracted experience of receiving reproof and making things right with those he had wronged convinced him of this. It was painful, but worth it to have perfect fellowship restored with the Lord and with His children. Dawson knew he had needed to recognize the sinfulness of his careless criticism of others, and he felt he had profited from the experience of humbling himself before these men.

And again this week the Lord had sent, through a new staff member, a gentle but timely reproof. Dawson thanked God for Addie's quiet discernment and courage to point out his neglect of the very thing he preached — applying the Word to his life in practical ways. Surely if his life could be affected, Satan could undermine the entire Navigators work. Daws acknowledged that he had been roughshod in his treatment of people, particularly those working close to him, finding fault with them in the presence of others, being insensitive to their feelings and sometimes to their convictions. He purposed by God's grace to be more considerate of others and to avoid trampling some less able to charge forward in the Christian life at the velocity he thought necessary.

He was grateful for the young men and women of the headquarters staff — each a special gift from the Lord — whose pictures he showed on trips along with those of his family, relating their abilities to all who would listen. He gave thanks now for the world's greatest crew and swellest family, dwelling longest on Lila, his priceless helper through the years, still growing in grace and Christlike beauty. She had been so patient in frequent illnesses the past year and a half — the latest her thyroidectomy last February. She had loyally encouraged him during his recent difficulties, careful not to interfere with the work God was doing, yet unwavering in her support. They were both almost foolishly happy now to learn their fifth child was on the way. They prayed for a boy.

Grace Wallace, Stanford graduate nurse in charge of San Francisco nurses work since last December, had answered Dawson's call to come in June to assist Lila. Besides caring for Lila, Grace had managed the home with its some twenty residents in superb fashion, swiftly preparing delicious dinners and serving the crew with a self-effacing spirit. Grace's coming was another of the Lord's choice blessings to the work.

If Daws's prayer of last year for the Lord to try him came into his mind this night on the hill above 509, he may have concluded God had done just that, and that He was sending the little one to comfort him and dear Lila as part of the "afterward" of a Hebrews 12:11 chastening. But if the Lord in His wisdom had more trial in store, Dawson would cast himself, as David did, on His mercies. Whatever flaws He exposed would be submitted for His forgiveness; this would not mar the reality of their relationship, Daws knew, or deny him answer to the prayer he had made in faith tonight for future workers. What God had promised, He would perform.

Three days before Christmas Daws telephoned home at midmorning. "Dear, remember the money for the hospital that we decided to put into the general fund for the crew?" Lila remembered. In fact, more than once, with her full approval, money given them for personal needs had been so used. "Well, in this morning's mail there was a personal gift of $100 for us."

"Good," she laughed, "it's just in time. I'm having pains seven minutes apart." "What!" Dawson yelped and sprang into action. With $20 Lila had salted away, they now had the exact amount the hospital required on admission.

In the waiting room Daws passed the time dictating to a nervous secretary stories of how God had in the past supplied funds or food at the precise moment of need. Early in the afternoon Charles Earle Trotman was born. Pausing to thank the Lord, Daws opened his Bible to the verse he believed the Lord gave him for Chuckie — Luke 2:40, *And the child grew, and waxed strong in spirit, filled with wisdom: and the grace of God was upon him.* Later when talking with Lila, Daws picked up her Bible which opened to the same verse. When Chuckie was six days old Daws noted in his journal: "An exceptional child — so say the nurses, the mother, and the father, and there is no doubt about it."

Getting passage to Honolulu in January 1945 took some doing as space priorities went to war-related passengers. Dawson had prayed he could go by troop ship, as he wanted to share the men's experience of crowded conditions, studying the Bible in noisy, smoke-filled compartments, and witnessing by acts of kindness which opened the way for the Word. Troop ship it was, though he was given officers' quarters and shared a compartment with only seventeen men. The ship zigzagged for six days across waters that had seen enemy action.

Finding that divine service had not been held aboard for some time, Daws suggested it to a Navy officer who forthwith announced one for Sunday morning. Under sunny skies more than 400 men turned out for church call. A portable organ and a cornet soloist supplied the music before the guest evangelist climbed to the improvised podium, silently claiming Joshua 1:9 for courage. He stuffed his scribbled notes into a pocket, held the microphone with one hand and his Bible with the other, grateful for memorized Scriptures he could quote as he flipped the pages of his Bible presenting the Gospel. The 100 New Testaments he had brought were claimed in minutes, with more promised those who wanted them at the ship's office. A more attentive audience Daws had never seen, and when he saw many scattered around the ship reading their Testaments that afternoon, he knew they had heard his message on the unity and power of the Word. The spiritual hunger of these men was a preview of what he would find in Honolulu.

Once there, he exploded into superlatives. "What a spot! Opportunities are tremendous." Though well aware from the mail and from visiting other areas that Navigator contacts had grown from hundreds to thousands, he still was amazed at the milling squads of men in uniform here in this largest Nav work anywhere — men hungry for the Word, eager to learn of Christ and to be used by Him. "Imagine the problem DeGroff faces," Daws wrote to Sanny, "attempting to get to these fellows individually." Seventy men out to the Home one Sunday and sixty the next, with only about twenty of them repeats. DeGroff, who had faithfully ministered year after year amid the changing scene, now also taught four civilian clubs, preached somewhere twice on Sundays, had a different group of twelve to fifteen servicemen in the Home every afternoon, and in addition handled correspondence and business connected with being a missionary.

Dawson plunged into such a steady stream of meetings at bases and at the Home, with individuals, twos and threes, having to shout to be heard on a wild ride across the island in a Navy bus, that he soon gave in to a sore throat and insisted others talk for a few days. "I've had more time with fellows already than in an ordinary month of Sundays," he said of the first three days.

The highlight was hours of fellowship with Watters and other men, some he had not seen since the war started, others in from battle areas whom he met for the first time. He spent mornings in long individual sessions with DeGroff and key men, afternoons ministering to groups at the Home, and evenings with Bible classes on bases. He visited officers and nurses groups, some "regular, rugged Navy guys" at Camp Catlin led by Storekeeper Maurice Denham, soldiers at Fort Shafter and Schofield Barracks, Navy men at Barbers Point, Marines at Aiea, a class Cliff Holt had started at the receiving ship at Pearl Harbor. Some chaplains attended the meetings, and Daws met others by appointment, including an interview arranged by Lt. Ed Phillips and Yeoman 1/c Ray Stedman with the Chief of Navy Chaplains then in Honolulu en route to the war area. To Daws this public relations contact alone would have warranted a trip to Washington.

He preached every Sunday in local churches. "The Lord has used these church services to further cement relations between churches and Navigators," he wrote. "Almost everywhere I preach a third or half of the audience is servicemen."

Wherever he spoke, Daws hit the same theme with variations — The Wheel. At Camp Catlin after Denham had saturated the class with scores of Scriptures, Daws said, "Well, guys, I'll give you just one verse. You've already had too much tonight." With that verse he showed them the value of meditation and how to meditate on a verse for personal profit. And always there was exhortation to continue in memory and to follow up new Christians.

The Honolulu experience was adrenalin to Dawson. In 1940 he had seen the thousands of men there as an ocean-sized fishing pool; now he saw a mature harvest, much of it wasting unreaped. It was an emergency. "Big things are in my heart," he wrote the Los Angeles crew. "I'm amazed. My vision is getting more world-wide and is beginning to expand first with USA. Pray, gang!" He added *please rush* to his request for laborers. "I am asking the Lord to give us a half-dozen men for the Navigator work as soon as He can possibly muster them," he wrote Sanny. "I have extended invitations to Dick and Don Hillis and Lyman Wendt and Norm Crider." He also asked Lorne to consider a transfer from Seattle to Honolulu: ". . . 5 to 10 or 15 times as much work and opportunity here as where you are. . . . I laid this before DeGroff and he is more than thrilled. . . . Your abilities would complement each other, I know. If it wasn't for all my responsibilities at home, I would pack up and bring half the office crew and head this way."

But what Honolulu — and the whole Navigator work — needed more than manpower was a course correction. This fact emerged as Daws met with Watters, Phillips, and Denham for nearly four hours to analyze needs and discuss possible answers. True, DeGroff did need help with the tremendous work load. But the diagnosis they made seemed so obvious and right it must be from the Lord. Both at the Home and in the groups on base, too much had been left to meetings; and meetings were so frequent that man-to-man time for either leaders or led was crowded out. Watters recalled that Daws's message in Honolulu five years before had been "Feed My sheep"; now he was preaching "Teach the sheep to eat." Watters asked Daws to critique the Bible class after Charley Myers had preached

for ninety minutes. "Too much meat. Too much heavy preaching," was Daws's verdict.

A few, including Watters, were helping men individually,
with telling results. Myers, Don Rosenberger, Dave Rohrer, and
others, products of man-to-man ministry, were fast becoming
equipped to help other men. But the main product of Bible
classes was more Bible classes, with the leaders who studied and
taught also getting most of the benefit. New leaders who came
up were usually men who would have surfaced in any case,
trained or not.

Somehow the tide must be turned from so many meetings
toward committing things learned to faithful men; and many
"things learned" were best imparted from life to life. The few
gifts required to teach one man made it possible for any Joe
to have a ministry. And a man who was trained through individual help would likely use that method — such was the
uncanny power of pacesetting — in building another man and
equipping him to "teach others also." That was it: *producing
reproducers.* A man would reproduce after his kind, reproduce
both man and method. Classes produced classes; faithful men
produced faithful men.

Daws had practiced the 2 Timothy 2:2 principle all along,
training his men with the idea that they would so train their
men. But he was an able juggler of many activities and perhaps
had never been so impressed as now with the excellence of the
one-to-one approach. The war boom had sidetracked this emphasis while he tried to meet the needs of so many, hiding its
true significance: that man-to-man was not only the most
effective but the *fastest* way to reach the greatest number of
men. His advice to Sanny to "stick with your man" was this
principle in essence; a carefully trained man would double and
multiply his ministry. But now the budding idea unfolded to
full bloom and promised a quiet revolution in the work.

Dawson's report of the revolution was just as restrained:
"All key hands have been made to see that for the most part
meetings, meetings, meetings have practically robbed all of
them of time alone with men. Remedies are being made gladly."

It was clear to Daws now that this was the principle he had
searched for, to apply purposefully throughout the work. He
would begin immediately to preach *Produce Reproducers —*

which in terms of the Great Commission he and many others would come to regard as a golden key.

✻   ✻   ✻   ✻

Though the largest of Nav areas, because of its distant location Honolulu was the least supervised or informed on operating policies. Thus much of the time Dawson spent with DeGroff was toward closer alignment with headquarters. The financial policy of meeting current needs with funds currently received in answer to prayer was virtually unknown in Honolulu. Understandably, a sizeable bank account had built up at this nearest Navigator base where a man could draw off and hand in all the surplus he had on the books when his ship was in.

DeGroff felt he had followed a prudent course in saving for future needs, but readily agreed this balance should be transferred to Los Angeles headquarters where all printing and correspondence expense was borne for study materials given free to all servicemen. The 2 Corinthians 8 principle applied here: "He that had gathered much had nothing over; and he that had gathered little had no lack." Daws was especially glad for this provision for headquarters bills and some needed refurbishing at 509, whose rich interior was over forty years old, its fabrics threadbare.

At one point during Dawson's four weeks in Honolulu T - - - suddenly appeared to "deal with" him again about backbiting and using "the ungodly methods in the notebook system." Daws pled with him, "Why do you keep bringing up these things long ago confessed and forgiven? It just makes a new wound where one was healed. I believe you're off on a tangent in this, brother." Before leaving the Islands Daws told Watters, Phillips, and one or two other key men of the past year's exchanges with T - - -, expressing sorrow over his seeming preoccupation with the matter.

Flying home on the *Honolulu Clipper* was great adventure; Daws managed to get up to the cockpit and work with the navigator, with boyish delight watching the powerful machine move through the Pacific night and home to that special praying group ("You're a precious gang. I love you all.").

Lila and Vivian met him in San Francisco, the placid Viv bursting with excitement. Daws had asked Watters in their time together in Honolulu, "How many items do you have to discuss?" "Ten," Kenny answered. "Well, before you start, I have one." "Shoot." "I wish you would fall in love with my secretary." Without a word Ken held up his list. Item one was Vivian.

She had been on his list four years ago, and he had prayed for direction. Then his buddy Vic McAnney proposed to her. Vic never knew of Ken's interest, nor did Vivian. God had given her a victorious testimony in Vic's death and healed her heart. That God's hand was on this new romance Daws was certain. He had sounded out her feelings before the trip, characteristically enjoying his role of go-between as he had with Downing and would with scores of others. "It will not be long until KW comes to the States," he had written in a letter to the office. "I hope the Lord plans to put him near headquarters if we are going to do our best work. He is one of the Lord's first-line officers." Viv got the message.

In Oakland Dawson spoke to a rally of 250 friends at the opening of the Nav service center at 606 Grand Avenue, striking the revolutionary theme which emerged at Pearl Harbor. "The one big challenge before The Navigators is to produce reproducers." With stabbing forefinger and narrowed eyes he asked, "Who, because of you, is carrying on the Gospel of Christ?" And in his *News Letter* reporting on Honolulu: "Business was done for eternity. It was most gratifying to see the fellows accept with open hearts . . . the big job before The Navigators — to *produce reproducers*." He told of spending much time with the key men, stressing the need for "spending time with individuals, strengthening them, through the Word of God and fellowship, that they in turn might do the same with others."

Back at headquarters he called the crew together, with Dick and Don Hillis and MAF's Betty Greene, to "lay before them what we really mean now when we speak of *producing reproducers*." He began to pray they would be saturated with this doctrine.

Meeting Lila and some of the crew in the Bay area had made Daws more eager to get home to the rest of the family, especially his new son, after six weeks away. On leaving, he had written in his journal: "Dine with my darling Lila. We have a precious time of fellowship and how I love this girl — mother of my five. Haven't seen a more beautiful creature in all the world than Chuckie lying in Lila's arms. Oh, how I love this little guy!" But before they reached home, word came that Chuckie was ill. Seriously ill, they soon discovered, as the convulsions which racked his body could be stilled only with barbiturates.

*   *   *   *

Within days the verdict was in: Chuckie would never be normal. No medical possibility they explored offered any hope for his development, and though some friends felt God would heal him by prayer, Daws and Lila somehow knew He had sent Chuckie to them just as he was. Often in the past when he had seen a retarded child, Daws had felt God would never give them such a child, for he could not bear it emotionally. Now here was this beautiful baby who would never walk or talk, never know more of the world around him than the face above his crib of one who bathed and fed and dressed him, never speak the name of Jesus till he stood whole in His presence. Was this God's answer to Dawson's prayer for trial? He could not be sure, but he knew beyond doubt it was from God.

But what of the promise He had so clearly given at Chuckie's birth? *And the child grew, and waxed strong in spirit, filled with wisdom: and the grace of God was upon him.* Daws resolutely turned back doubts as he faced the sure prospect that the child would *not* grow and be strong in spirit, filled with wisdom. *Lord, I can't doubt, so I will leave it with Thee to show me.* Romans 4:20, 21 came with force to reassure him. God was testing his faith as he tested Abraham's — also regarding a son. *He staggered not at the promise of God through unbelief; but was strong in faith. . . .* Here was his answer. He must not waver in unbelief. Perhaps "filled with wisdom" had a higher meaning — Chuckie would not grow in human intellect but would be a channel to minister God's wisdom to them.

Dawson knew God had not mocked them with that promise. The undergirding conviction of God's sovereignty cast him and Lila wholly on the Lord. They acknowledged His ways and thoughts as higher than theirs and clung to Psalm 115:3

— But our God is in the heavens: he hath done whatsoever he hath pleased. They had said "Thy will be done" and meant it.

Coincident with the news of Chuckie came a conciliatory letter from T - -- , followed by a barrage of letters quoting warnings from Proverbs, citing real or fancied slights by Dawson and dismissing his apologies as insincere. Watters, now on the mainland, had tried to reason with T - - - and give him the facts.

In a desire to be scrupulously fair, Watters also faced Dawson with a candid review of facets of his teaching which seemed to produce spiritual pride, his conduct among associates, his careless and ungenerous words about some of God's servants, and the intimidation of some by his demanding presentation of the claims of discipleship.

Many hours alone on the return trip from San Francisco where he met with Watters and two or three other Navigators brought Dawson low before God in contrition. He saw how he had offended brothers dear to him and precious to God. With broken heart he again wrote the brethren in Honolulu: "I am guilty." To an associate he confided, "I thought my heart was going to fall apart. Lila too suffered. . . . I'm still stunned. The Lord is cutting deeply into my heart regarding my methods and preaching and handling of cases. It will be necessary to re-think a lot of things. I've been so sure I was carrying out His orders and with an eye single to His glory. I must in all this willingness to be broken also remember that I serve the Lord and must please Him at all costs."

By this time the situation had become confused by hours of talk and a blizzard of letters explaining, accusing, defending, apologizing. Finally, a mimeographed open letter to "The Church" asked the reader to call on Dawson to repent. Mailed to hundreds of people, from prominent Christian leaders to apprentice seamen, it presented "proof" of Dawson's guilt of misdeeds and words in personal conduct and handling of Navigator funds, and expanded versions of previous charges.

Daws was stunned. Even before this letter went out, he was anguished that his guilty plea could be construed to cover almost any offense an accuser or hearer imagined. Now he thought of the hopelessness of separating truth from falsehood in the minds of more than a few . . . the disruption of the singular unity and fellowship among Navigators . . . the potential harm to young believers . . . the shameful blot on the name of Christ.

Charles Fuller said, "Daws, you should never have started writing letters about this. I have been accused of such things in my ministry. Others have; it's a common occurrence. The best thing to do is trust the Lord and don't waste time answering charges. Go on with the ministry and God will take care of you." Fuller and four other leaders drafted a public statement of confidence in Dawson and the Navigator work to answer the many who wrote in response to the letter.

Dick Hillis and Navy Chaplain Arthur Glasser, whom Daws had met months earlier, chose to rebut T - - - by mail, as Watters and Rosenberger continued to do. Daws found himself restraining his loyal defenders from a backlash reaction which would not please the Lord. "I'd like to get hold of him and shake his teeth loose," Lila said in a candid moment of hurt. "Now wait just a minute, Buddie," Dawson warned. "He is your brother. An attitude like that toward him is sin." He urged the crew to heart-searching application of 1 Peter 3:8-17. *"Finally, be ye all of one mind, having compassion one of another, love as brethren, be pitiful, be courteous: not rendering evil for evil, or railing for railing; but contrariwise blessing. . . ."*

Daws could not deny the stabs of pain each day's mail brought to his heart. Messages of support poured in from friends who had no inkling of what had happened. Letters also came from those — including seamen out in the fleet — who took the letter at face value and called on Daws to repent. But he fought hard to heed Mr. Fuller's advice and use his time for the ministry instead of defending himself. His times with the Lord were rich. "He is doing a work . . . that will have a bearing on all the future," he wrote in his journal. "One passage brought home repeatedly is: *Every branch in me that beareth fruit, he purgeth it, that it may bring forth more fruit.*" Many Scriptures came alive in those days, causing him to see as Paul did in prison that "things which happened unto me have fallen out rather unto the furtherance of the gospel."

Wycliffe's September conference found Dawson more usable in God's hand. "The events of these months prepared my heart for the time in Mexico," he wrote Watters, who with Vivian headed the New York Navigator Home since Hightowers had sailed for Africa. "There seemed to be evidence of business done for eternity in the hearts of many missionaries. . . . I am reviewing old verses in 2 Corinthians and picking up new ones. I am amazed; the Lord has never spoken to me more clearly than through this Book."

In October Daws made one more effort to clear the air, inviting T - - - to meet with him and the five Christian leaders who had issued the earlier statement. But the meeting was never held. The affair slowly wound down, with a man coming now and then to present a grievance, ask explanation, or express regret.

Convinced the Lord had allowed the twin trials of Chuckie and this experience, Daws actually welcomed them as essential to his personal retooling for days ahead and as part of a general retooling of The Navigators if the Lord planned to do great things through this work in the future. The personal renewal had to come first — getting down to bedrock in his own life — before The Navigators could prepare for the post-war expansion that was inevitable. He had already seen change in his attitudes, in understanding and tolerance of others' feelings and burdens. Friends also noticed he had mellowed. Morken's wife Helen saw gradual change in Dawson over the years — a certain hardness of spirit, which she attributed to hard striving to do God's will, giving way to a "beautiful gentleness which comes from walking with the Lord. . . . the sweetness and mellowness of God's grace permeated his heart."

Not that he would never again stoop to the sin of criticism or of riding roughshod over those less dominant than he, but a lasting work had been done. Doubtless with God's chastening in mind he wrote one of the men, "1945 has been one of the greatest in my entire life, and I have nothing but praise to my omnipotent, omniscient and omnipresent Saviour." In Washington for the East Coast Conference, Daws shared with the Downings a personal interpretation. "Back when I asked the

Lord to give me the maturity for godly counsel that Charlie Fuller and Daddy Moon have before I get older, if I had any reservation, it was that He would spare my family and my reputation." God had spared neither.

That God's hand was moving to use The Navigators in a larger way was evident to Dawson by His provision of choice men. Now they must find His plan for a broad financial policy, continue to clarify ministry principles, and survey the regions beyond in preparation to carry out His orders to possess the land. Daws was increasingly certain that follow-up, Scripture memory, the disciplined life pictured in The Wheel, and the vision of producing reproducers were largely lacking in Christian work, and he felt God had made him responsible to spread awareness and practice of these truths throughout Christendom.

A further thought electrified him: had Satan seen the awesome potential of person-to-person multiplication and moved to suppress it as it came into focus? Daws felt that if producing reproducers rated so much attention from the enemy, it might well be the atomic bomb of world evangelization.

W ith the war ended and men in all the services getting out, Dawson was in a strategic position to help many who were seeking God's direction for their lives. In touch with men on 800 or more ships, stations, and Army camps during the war, The Navigators now offered through the *Log* a Personnel Classification and Allocation Program to counsel men on schooling and possible fields of service.

Besides his link with the men, Daws knew firsthand the work and leaders of a number of foreign missions, churches, and other works for which he could enthusiastically recruit. Many would be challenged by Townsend's call for Navigators for Wycliffe. To others Daws recommended Orinoco River Mission in Venezuela, where Prince was going; Africa Inland Mission, chosen by Harris and Hightower; Gospel Recordings, headed by that plucky woman of faith Joy Ridderhof; other missions known to be given to the Great Commission. There was the young Missionary Aviation Fellowship, and high school and college ministries of Young Life and Inter-Varsity to which men could give themselves at least during their period of schooling.

These other works were promoted in the *Log,* now edited by ex-Navy Chief Yeoman Don Rosenberger, as post-war service opportunities for Navigators. The first real Navigator conferences in several years, engineered by Downing and Watters on the East Coast and Trotman at Forest Home for the West Coast in spring 1946, rallied 120 men in or just out of uniform. Here also men were encouraged to steer toward the best use of their talents in serving Christ. The West Coast Conference with Tom Olson, Daddy Moon, and Dr. Jack Mitchell teaching the Word had the flavor of pre-war Life Triumphant in Christ conferences. More than one conferee came forewarned of Dawson's famous "airplane test" — a vigorous shaking of loose papers out of a fellow's Bible or notebook — and of his grabbing a verse pack from a pocket to demand correct quoting of a verse picked at random.

Daws was amazed to find fifty men at Biola that fall who had done Navigator work in the service or in the clubs, many of them led to Christ by a Navigator. He felt sure other Bible schools and colleges had similar groups, though perhaps smaller, and that many more than he knew of or had counseled would go into foreign missions or pastorates. Several Nav nurses also were joining Wycliffe, where linguistic training added to their nursing skills would make them invaluable.

He was grateful for top men God had directed to the Navigator work. Don Rosenberger and David Rohrer, former admirals' aides, used their gifts at Nav headquarters as they absorbed training for future ministry. Ex-Navy pilot Roy Robertson reported in and enrolled in aircraft mechanic school, remembering Dawson's idea for an airborne staff and gospel team to work while traveling between headquarters cities. Cecil Davidson signed on, his skills in radio to contribute to possible radio connection with Navs world-wide. Howard Davis of the *New Mexico* took over the Army Department. Army Captain Lee Sundstrom came to help with the radio project and later head the San Diego Home. Daws considered all these men potential area directors. He recruited more secretaries from as far away as New York and as near as Pomona to handle increasing civilian use of the *Topical Memory System* — the year brought over 2100 enrollments — and Bible study and notebook follow-up materials.

In thirteen years of work with servicemen Daws had seen the image of the American serviceman change from the hard-bitten tough of the thirties to the wholesome boy-next-door doing his duty for his country, hoping to get an education and a job when he was out. By war's end many thousands of these young men had been faced with the claims of Christ and many recruited to discipleship, often one by one on the after deck of a ship, in a mess hall Bible study on a base, while cruising dark waters in a submarine, or crossing Europe with Patton's tanks.

Dawson knew the Navigators had helped to bring about this change in the serviceman's image — and indeed in changing the image of a soft and permissive Christianity to one of virile and vigorous commitment. Yet he was more determined than ever to suppress the Navigator name, to take none of the glory from God who had promised to make a way in the sea, a path in the mighty waters, and to raise up foundations of many generations. This was partly behind his charge to Navigators going back to home churches and to schools: "Don't go back there as a Navigator. Don't hang out a shingle. Just live the life, throw your weight into helping your pastor, your Inter-Varsity group, win hearts and set the pace. God will give you a ministry."

A Nav Home in every port city was no longer needed, though a few places were strategic. Watters went to Wycliffe, leaving New York without a full-time man. Jack Wyrtzen served as a point of contact for Navigators. Chaplain Glasser took the Long Beach servicemen's center, turning it over to Goold when Glassers sailed for China with CIM. Maurice Denham, former Navy key man, became Chicago representative. DeGroff went into civilian ministry full time in Honolulu. Howard Davis enrolled at Wheaton and served as Nav man there. Norm and Marge Crider, who had hosted the Jacksonville Home, considered a ministry on Guam. The Floyd Robertsons opened their home to Navigators in D.C.; Downings had been transferred to Brazil. The Oakland service center closed and Chrisman led a concentrated study program for Navigators just out of service. Norfolk had Chaplain Robert Evans and Petty Officer Ed Gray standing by, then ex-Navy man Jake Boss. Businessman Bob Crawford was the contact in Philadelphia. Sanny closed the Seattle office and worked from the Home, ministering to civilians and servicemen.

Servicemen were still high priority, but Daws was drawn into full-scale civilian ministry as nearly all his Navigators got out into civilian life. Headquarters office readily geared into correspondence contact as it had long done for servicemen. But civilian situations were varied. Instead of the shipboard Bible class led by a key man, it might be a church group or Sunday school class, a home Bible study or a college campus where a key man helped Inter-Varsity, a Bible school or seminary with ex-servicemen enrolled. Daws soon found that apart from on-the-spot leadership of a local Nav representative, little could be done from a distance but furnish memory and study materials, encouragement, and occasional counsel by mail.

This vast dispersion of men to Bible schools, colleges, and mission fields was a class graduated, a task finished. But it also meant the opening of wider fields for recruitment of laborers, a realization of Isaiah 54:2, 3; *Enlarge the place of thy tent . . . spare not, lengthen thy cords, and strengthen thy stakes. . . .* The cause of producing reproducers would be helped by this scattering of laborers to every corner of the harvest.

* * * *

Most significant in transition from wartime to peacetime navigating was the change precipitated in financial policy. Income had declined immediately as servicemen's allotments ceased and gifts from men now going to school on the GI Bill were curtailed. The $11-a-week allowance for the office crew (with more for married members with households to keep) was regularly prayed in, becoming $6 some weeks, and some weeks only $2. Printing, grocery, and travel bills were not paid promptly. Then a $500 gift from a man's mustering-out pay would relieve the pressure. Three such gifts in January 1946 raised morale considerably, paid the bills, and helped buy a much-needed company car, and similar windfalls came mid-

1947 from sale of the Jacksonville and Oakland properties. But it was clear months before this that the Lord was keeping the budget afloat by these special infusions while He signaled a change. Dawson was slow to acknowledge it because he disliked giving time or thought to the subject of money and because it seemed to threaten his conviction that God would always supply if His conditions of faith were met.

Dawson's first response was deep heart-searching. He called the crew together and warned that the Lord could be withholding His blessing due to sin. If there was an Achan in the camp, the work was in trouble more serious than financial. The search for disobedience ended, he then sought guidance in possible new directions for supporting the work. There was Paul's example of using his craft of tentmaking for self-support in the ministry. Daws could make mottoes, he decided, as in the early days. In fact, he enjoyed art so much it was difficult not to pursue it as a hobby. He decided to look into screen process and airbrush work and make some motto masters to be reproduced in quantity for retail outlets.

In the fall Davidson had opened Reliable Radio Repair near the office to help support the work. Superior Sign Service soon followed. Rohrer found employment in Pasadena. Rosenberger represented a Christian publisher in western states, also marketing Dawson's mottoes to bookstores. Rod Sargent, ex-Navy man led to assurance of salvation by Rosenberger, replaced him on the road while Don managed the business in Los Angeles. Hayden taught and coached at a Christian high school. Other moneymaking schemes surfaced — ventures in rubber-base paint and mining gold from mine tailings proposed by friends as a source of handsome support for Christian works and missions.

But the paint and mining businesses were stillborn. And results of the other tentmaking projects were mixed. Dawson felt this avenue had been fairly explored and that he and the entire crew had proved their willingness to pitch in and support the work. The Lord must have a better plan to fuel the worldwide outreach ahead, for which Daws sorely needed the manpower now occupied with earning daily bread for the crew.

Recognizing that he was both opinionated and open-minded, Daws knew he must be open to the Lord for possible change in financial policy. Through The Navigators' fifteen years he had believed the supply or withholding of finances was God's checkrein on proposed moves in the ministry — and an excellent way to keep them in prayer for needs. Yet Downing was right: Daws should be trusted after all these years to find God's will apart from the gauge of money supply. It was good discipline for a man just winning his spurs, as Sanny had done so well in Seattle. Daws did not want any to miss these precious lessons he and Lila had learned by trusting God for necessities from one day to the next.

He consulted businessmen on the new Navigator Council and their advice was ready. "Daws, hundreds of people who can't give their time to Navigator ministry would be happy to give financially if they knew about it, and these fellows with you could give *their* time to ministry." Daws listened, wondering if this was true.

The financial slump continued, relieved only by an unexpected large gift or sale of property. After deliberation, prayer, and discussion with the board of directors he concluded the Lord was indeed leading to change the policy and make needs known. With potential demand all over the world for what The Navigators offered, Daws knew it was no longer a matter of asking the Lord to supply food for the table, but to supply for a growing army of laborers, for hundreds of thousands of *B Rations* in other languages, for transportation and equipment to work in many countries and areas. It was reasonable to assume God might establish a supply corps of hundreds of saints who would give and pray for the work around the world. Daws had not hesitated to ask colaborers to give their time and talent, in effect their lives; yet he had a block against asking people to give their money. It was not consistent, he concluded, and he would have to do it.

With this resolved, he purposed to present the idea to six individuals and let their response indicate how God would lead. With uncharacteristic timidity he approached Mrs. Alexander Kerr, head of Kerr Glass Corporation since her husband's death. She had been so blessed by the *Topical Memory System* that she enrolled dozens of people and encouraged them to memorize. Dawson's diffident presentation of the need was sheer torture for him, ending in amazement at her sympathy and eagerness to help.

"I had no idea," the good lady said. "I thought your work was underwritten. Why didn't you let anyone know? You deprive others of the blessing of sharing in this ministry." From that day on her contributions were regular and generous.

The other test cases were also encouraging. Convinced God was in it, in December 1948 Daws sent a letter to Navigator friends appealing for their support for the projected world-wide expansion of the work. The response was small financially but gracious in many expressions of thanks for the privilege of taking part. Though he himself had always been blessed in giving, Daws was startled by the thought that his adamant stand against sharing the financial burden with others had deprived them of that blessing. The staff concurred in the new policy, with evident unity of heart.

Faith would certainly not be eliminated. It would always be necessary to trust God to supply and to prompt those who would give. He could still regulate the amount of income as a stop-and-go signal for projects; and there would be opportunities to venture out by faith in His forthcoming supply. The following fall a survey found only thirty-two giving monthly to the work, mainly those who had personally benefited from Navigator ministry. A California businessman whose Christian life was revolutionized by personal help in Bible study and Scripture memory visited the office, saw a need for offset printing equipment, and promptly supplied it. He then sent out a letter asking others to join those thirty-two regular contributors.

*　　*　　*　　*

Another part of retooling for post-war advance, in addition to personal and organizational, would be philosophical. Principles distinctive to Navigator ministry would be defined and clarified. Some needed no definition, only statement. The Wheel, depicting essentials of a life centered in Christ — the Word, prayer, obedience, witness — had stood the test of time. All hands knew The Wheel and the importance of the devotional life, of regular memory of Scripture, of personal Bible study, basic to Dawson's ministry from the start — and the 2 Timothy 2:2 principle, long practiced but little preached until Honolulu. Now Rosenberger, Robertson, Davidson, Rohrer, and Davis began systematic study of these principles, eagerly digging into the

Acts and Epistles, finding more than Daws knew was there to corroborate them.

At a 1947 staff conference at Wrightwood, Robertson presented a masterful study on the "key man" principle from the Old Testament and from Paul's ministry. The conference became a seminar as men shared their studies of Nav principles in Scripture, with illustrations from their experience. Sanny, down from Seattle, presented his thesis that 1 Corinthians 3 indicated building in another life by the one following up a babe in Christ, rather than the accepted idea of building in one's own life. A session on ABC Bible study showed how to teach someone to make his own discoveries in the Word and apply them to his life. A discussion of the principle and practice of pacesetting was revealing, and an attempt to get to the heart of the implications of 2 Timothy 2:2 helped unify the staff on what they believed and taught. Daws felt the week was strategic.

Back at headquarters the search went on, placing in scriptural setting such emphases as redeeming the time, pacesetting, meditation, multiplication. Their study of the latter convinced the men the term "producing reproducers" was a valid scriptural concept. But it could not be pictured on an organizational chart, as Daws forcefully assured them when he found one had tried it, for spiritual reproduction involved much more than the transmission of materials or a system of teaching.

At the 1947 Navigators Conference Daws stressed to sixty men gathered from across the country the importance of close cooperation with other works besides The Navigators. Afterward he wrote:

> *In the light of Phil. 2:3, 4 and I Cor. 12:14, 21 the Lord would be honored and glorified through . . . cooperation among His various works. It is our privilege to have close fellowship with Inter-Varsity, Youth For Christ and Young Life Campaign. God favored us at the conference with speakers from three other outstanding works — Wycliffe Bible Translators, Moody Institute of Science and Missionary Aviation Fellowship. It is our purpose to familiarize ourselves with Christian works which honor the Lord . . . to learn of their*

program and stand by in prayer, and to serve them
in other ways.

Even as the Lord's special commission to The Navigators
became clearer, Daws promoted other works more vigorously,
doing all he could to help them carry out their own vision.
Concern for other members of the body of Christ was biblical,
but he also made it part of the Nav credo to assist other works
in fulfilling their ministries, and in addition sharing any Nav
principles with them that would forward their cause. This was
often best done by sending them men, for he sought to instill
in the men he trained a compulsion to practice the unique
Navigator emphases they had learned, whether they did so
through The Navigators or in another context.

On a six-week trip east after the conference Daws ministered
to Wycliffe people in summer training in Oklahoma, Word of
Life Fellowship in New York, several churches, and Inter-
Varsity's staff at Canadian Campus in the Woods where Director Stacey Woods asked him to present Nav principles to his
leaders with specific plans for their use. Daws spent time individually with many, a method he felt most effective for "getting
real business done" in the life of a servant of God. In one or
two cases the head of an organization made the *Topical Memory
System* mandatory for his staff, something Daws did not favor;
he preferred to give a strong challenge and let response be
voluntary, having long since learned that excess pressure could
sour a person on something even clearly in his best interest. He
was later proved right as some workers resented being required
to memorize and eventually dropped it.

Daws had spent summer 1946 with the staffs of Wycliffe
in Oklahoma, Young Life in Colorado, Youth For Christ in
Minnesota, and Inter-Varsity near Toronto, stressing the need
for a strong devotional life for the Christian worker. He was
happy to note at summer's end that Inter-Varsity staff members
and Youth For Christ directors were in the TMS as Young
Life staff already were, setting the pace for young people they
reached. "Pacesetting," he wrote in the *News Letter*, "is always
a prerequisite for those in places of leadership who would
challenge others."

Pacesetting was the lever he had pressed the previous January when officers of the year-old Youth For Christ International met in Los Angeles to plot future strategy. At a meeting at 509 after all had enjoyed one of Lila's outstanding dinners, Daws spoke to them in hard-sell terms on the need to follow up young people who found Christ in YFC rallies in some 300 cities and to get the Word into the hearts and lives of these newborn Christians. This implied the local rally director would first have to be in the Word, which in turn meant each of these men present needed to set a clear pace in his intake of Scripture.

Daws grinned as he told of it later. "Rosenberger, Denham, Davis, and Sundstrom gave testimonies; then I plowed in on follow-up and the memory work. Billy was there, and all the YFCI leaders, Chaplain Bob Evans, Torrey Johnson, Chuck Templeton, Chuck White, Cliff Barrows, all of them. About nine-thirty Hube Mitchell interrupted, 'Daws, these men are tired, and we've got another big day of meetings tomorrow. Maybe we should bring this to a close.' Then Torrey jumped up. 'Sit down, Hube. Go ahead, Daws. We haven't had the altar call yet!' Unanimously they refused to quit just when we were getting down to brass tacks. The meeting went another hour and we decided to continue the next morning." Evans and Barrows were already in the TMS and could testify of benefit to their lives. Remarkably, nearly all these leaders accepted Dawson's challenge to get into it, fully convinced that they must do this. Neither they nor he thought his compelling pressure on them incongruous.

Don Hillis had written while Daws was in Honolulu telling of follow-up plans for Los Angeles Jubilee and reporting that follow-up was the known weakness in most of the 300 rallies.

Dawson replied, "Why have we been so long realizing this need? . . . I have an idea or two how we might get at this. Can we not, as America did December 7, 1941, begin to lay plans to turn the tide of battle. Once we realized we were being defeated we still had to give ground — Guam, Wake, the Philippines — but we started to train men and gather material and equipment for a push to come. It was not immediate but had to be dealt with by a long range vision."

Traveling about in those heady post-war years when youth interest in the Gospel was high and evangelism was coming alive, Daws had increasing contact with leaders of other works, most of them his contemporaries or younger. God gave unusual opportunities to speak a word in season that a more timid ambassador would not have dared — exhorting a leader to forsake his grudge against another, later urging the other man to be reconciled to the first. The Lord used this unseen ministry of godly arm-twisting, as Daws with boldness and humility probed little-known differences between brethren and brought the authority of the Word for healing. On a single trip his stops in the southwest, midwest, and east included a ministry of reconciliation with leaders of different works. High regard for each of them made it easy to exhort them to appreciate and encourage one another. Through the years he was pleased whenever he could get heads of parallel organizations together for prayer, when each could bolster the other's ambitions in Christ.

This ministry to leaders was heavy on challenge. Robert A. Cook, one of the core group of early YFC evangelists, observed that Daws "had a built-in radar that figured what you needed most and emphasized that. He had a spiritual inner ear that told him what the person needed and often what the person was thinking about." His perception was aided by seeing the man not in the aura of his position as Christian leader, but as an individual of unique value to God's kingdom.

Conversely, but in the same vein, he saw great possibilities in the ordinary lad, the serviceman or civilian, who thought himself insignificant. Daws was able to communicate to this average Joe a belief that God could use him and guidance in how to prepare himself as God's servant. A young man or woman of modest talents could hear Dawson tell of his or her abilities and accomplishments and wonder of whom he spoke. Nonetheless, his belief in what God could do through them was convincing — even to them.

VI

"Let's Finish the Job"

1948-1956

(right) Daws and Lorne Sanny with their wives, summer 1952.

(below) With Misses Thomas (left) and Mills at farewell before his China trip, March 1948.

Peking, March 6, 1948. For the threatened city of 3,000,000 souls — as many as Los Angeles on a fraction of the land area — it was one of the first Saturday night Youth For Christ rallies and one of the last. Communist artillery crackled in the distance as they neared the city in their bid to sweep the entire land. The American waiting on the platform to speak experienced "my first big scare," caused not by Communists but by culture shock. As Dawson looked out over a sea of eager Chinese faces, he felt as if this were his first sermon ever, and his memory left him. Then topics began to flood his mind and were as quickly rejected; he decided to give his testimony. Beside him the warm-hearted Andrew Gih, evangelist beloved throughout China, interpreted. A few responded to the invitation to receive Christ. "Oh how I wanted to take one aside after and explain 'the way' more perfectly, but my tongue was tied," Daws wrote his praying crew in Los Angeles.

Dick Hillis had come back to China after the war to make a survey of churches in Honan for CIM. Returning home for his family in 1946, he tried to describe his burden to Daws. "Man, there's a harvest in China, and either you've got to go or send your best man," he declared, surprised at his own ultimatum. Dawson prayed often about it. Early in 1947 Hillis with Andrew Gih saw continued good results in Chinese evangelism. And Dave Morken and Bob Pierce, in five months of YFC evangelism all over China, witnessed more than 17,000 decisions for Christ. Morken reported this to Daws in October and laid it on the line. "Daws, this is the hour in China. Thousands are responding to the Gospel, and the one thing needed most is Navigator follow-up. I talked to Dick about it, and both of us feel your going to China now is imperative. We will each give $100 toward your trip." It was God speaking. Daws decided he would have to go.

Morken helped plan the trip and raised funds at Youth For

Christ rallies. The YFC-sponsored trip drew enthusiastic support from Church of the Open Door, First Mate Bob's Haven of Rest broadcast, and others interested in missions. Daws planned blocks of time to hold conferences in Peking, Shanghai, Chengtu, and Canton, strategic centers of China accessible to the greatest number of missionaries and Chinese Christian leaders.

First to meet him on landing in Shanghai were CIM missionaries Eber and Anne Hazelton, friends since lumberyard days more than twenty years ago. Also in China were former Navy chaplains Arthur Glasser with CIM in Canton and Dan Carr with the Baptists in Chengtu. Streater was there with Scandinavian Alliance Mission. Bill Blackstone, Presbyterian missionary in Hong Kong, had had exposure to Nav work at Berkeley where Robert Munger had been pastor since leaving South Hollywood. In Peking Daws met Clyde Jowers, who said he became a missionary because of Daws's challenge to the *West Virginia* gang.

Daws and Andrew Gih enjoyed the warm hospitality of Oriental Missionary Society's Rolland and Mildred Rice, the four fellowshiping late over hot chocolate after full days of meetings. "I surely love Andrew and everybody," Daws wrote. "They're such dear people. Andrew's so interesting, good sense of humor, loves the Lord." The spirit of love and common cause among missionaries of different boards was gratifying to Dawson. The Great Commission was their one objective. The Salvation Army made its hall available for Dawson's long morning sessions with 125 missionaries and Chinese. He spoke to 100 high school Christians in afternoons and preached Gospel messages on alternate evenings with Gih, wedging in personal time with many between sessions and at meals. At a university where he spoke to thirty students, other students in the next room were hearing Communist propaganda and singing its praises.

Symbolizing Dawson's mission was the ingenious fifteen-inch-square aluminum gadget he used as a visual aid, a hollow white-on-black circle painted on the metal, lettered in Chinese, "The Christian Living the Life." A button he pushed brought a white hub into the center of The Wheel, bearing the Chinese symbol for Christ; other buttons made spokes spring into place as needed when he was speaking. "The Chinese love it," Daws wrote of the magic gadget. But his joy was that they grasped and accepted its message, for talks with them and the missionaries revealed his trip was most timely. No one had seemed conscious of the need for follow-up and for teaching Chinese to witness. Bringing one to a decision for Christ seemed the only goal. Some did go to Bible schools to train as pastors, but the vision of training lay witnesses and of teaching individuals their responsibility to reproduce other Christians was notably lacking.

"Oh such interest shown in the memory plan," Daws wrote. "I find practically no Chinese Christian had caught the significance and value of memory. Only Andrew Gih seems to know many verses. He knows the Word." Daws estimated a hundred university students in Peking would start the TMS, which had been translated in Los Angeles by two Chinese Christian scholars and would now be distributed from Peking.

The fact that the Communists were closing in could only enhance Dawson's message of teaching Chinese Christians self-propagation. "Sunday I spoke to a hundred missionaries," he wrote Chrisman. "Each is praying, 'Shall I flee or stay?' Communism is moving in with speed and force. Peking, a city of 12 universities with 50 percent of students sympathetic, will be next." Hillis, writing from Honan, underlined the urgency:

> I have no idea whether you are in China or U.S.A. or whether this will reach you ... we have been living through the most dangerous days of my life. The army is dug in one mile from here and almost every day they send over some big shells.... Daws, my heart has been thrilled at the way the Lord is using Navigator material here. This group of young men are really growing; this is doing them more good than a Bible school training for they are learning how to get things from His Word. Wish you had pushed me on this ten years ago.... Daws, the Chinese church has done almost nothing in the way of *missions*. That is why all western Asia is without the Gospel. I am praying the Lord will use Navigator materials to make them see they must *go*. If West Asia is to be reached for Christ the Chinese church must arise and do the job. The Christians of India must catch a vision too, thus I am praying the Lord will open the way for you to go to India.

In Nanking, David Adeney, CIM man assigned to Inter-Varsity, arranged meetings with student group leaders for Dawson's two days there. "I feel you have a message greatly needed here," Adeney wrote. "I am so glad you have material in Chinese which we can introduce to fellowships throughout the country."

Shanghai was next, after eleven days in Peking. Due to uncertain mail service Daws felt more TMS distribution centers were needed besides the one in Peking serving north China. "It's now on my heart to pray God will give us a Nav full time for China," he wrote. "Perhaps India, Africa, a man each." Judging from response in Peking, he could foresee calls for Navigator follow-up in countries yet ahead. But the magnitude of China overwhelmed him. One-fourth the world's people — with missionaries being forced out, the job of evangelizing China would be up to the Chinese, as it should have been anyway, he thought.

The crux of the problem was illustrated in Peking and evident in Shanghai also. Scores of missionaries and Chinese pastors admitted that few lay Christians were active witnesses, probably because they lacked personal intake of the Word. Missionaries tended to plant churches like those in their homelands, with the pastor teaching and the people sitting and an occasional young person volunteering to study for the ministry. Thus the concept of "every Christian a witness" was revolutionary to both shepherd and flock. But the task was not to challenge Christians to win souls; they must prepare to do so by hiding God's Word in their hearts. This meant missionary and pastor should memorize and set the example, and Daws was encouraged by their eagerness to begin. "This is the need," missionaries of many groups agreed.

Morken had done effective advance work for the trip, urging Navigator follow-up as the answer to China's present need. Andrew Gih also conveyed his depth of conviction as he preached and interpreted. And the wholehearted acceptance of the memory work by even senior missionaries would give a healthy start here in China, Daws felt, where individual reproduction of Christians might prove crucial to future survival of the Chinese church. Gih said years later, "The Navigators fill a need not only in China but the Church all over the world. That is a weakness of the churches. The Christians are not doing what they need to do. The Navigators not only just memorize the Bible verses. That's only one side of it. The other side is to reach out to get Timothys."

Three weeks into the mission Daws wrote Morken:

> *Meetings here are as good if not better than in Peking — 30 pastors and 30 other workers besides another 80 or so attend morning meetings. They are eating up The Wheel, The Hand, the Word. . . . I'll never cease praising God for His leading through you for China — dear, wonderful, dirty China. The Lord has been [Eph.] 3:20ing right along. My brother, Dave, now is the time to strike — we cannot lose an hour. . . . All of us believe you should come out to take over Youth For Christ China full time and Hillis would take over follow-up entirely.*

Daws was fighting loneliness for his family and crew. "I love you all so, and honest I have to keep from thinking about you all too much because it hits me like a ton of bricks in view of three months to go," he had written from Peking. Later: "Surely miss my family, my crew, but think! Nearly a month is gone. I'm in a strait betwixt two. This trip, however, was eternally planned." The two days in Nanking followed Shanghai, then far west to Chengtu. Daws battled a cold and sore throat and a heavy schedule but could not afford to miss any of these strategic opportunities. He snatched a little rest when he could and took his pills; this and the prayer of his gang at home kept him going. "Andrew is tired but fighting on," he wrote of his teammate who had endured a similar bout in Peking.

But Daws forgot his own discomfort when he saw the suffering Chinese, tens of thousands of refugees pouring into Nanking, Shanghai, and other centers in the chill March of 1948. His heart was torn as he saw their pitiable faces, saw them shivering in tattered clothes. Homeless women and children huddled on sidewalks. And someone had thrown a dead baby into a missionary's yard.

Flying to Chungking in a two-engine plane, Daws reported "one of those little prayer meetings aloft. The weather changed suddenly and six or seven planes turned back. Ours was so ordered, the captain told me later, but he kept on, just hoping.

I could see we were overdue for a landing and felt led to pray for a break in the clouds. Just over a little town our pilot saw a break in the clouds and dove through. There was the field. It's treacherous country so we were not a little relieved. We refueled and went on to Chungking."

One day of meetings there, then on to Chengtu. He was again amazed at the hunger and receptiveness to the Word. Thirty-five Chinese came forward the first night he spoke. He invited them to come early next evening for follow-up help, when he taught them John 5:24 and John 1:12. All thirty-five returned the third night, plus ten new ones to get the same help. "Now I've got the three groups coming tomorrow," he wrote. He was touched to see missionaries standing by to observe and learn what to do for a new Christian. Why didn't they know these simple things? Why had their training not taught them this? he wondered. Here was the real need, and he believed some recognized it.

On the fifth day in Chengtu he was downed by a lacquer poisoning similar to poison oak, left helpless while Gih finished the meetings. Knowing he must not miss the weekly flight out, Daws pulled his body together with its "100,000 blisters" for a painful trip back to Chungking by motor scooter, bus, plane, and chair, only to end up in the hospital. When the doctor told him he would be there a week, he thought, *There go the Canton meetings — but God can work it out.* God did, sending Hillis to Canton to take the meetings till Dawson was able to come and finish the series. "My heart is strong, my faith has soared," he wrote April 15 as the two sailed down the Pearl River to Hong Kong. "I feel I was following an itinerary planned from the foundation . . . only the grace of God permits me to be His ambassador. . . ."

"So much China needs," he wrote. "Pray I'll find out what our *Lord* wants." And to Sanny, left in charge in Los Angeles, "This trip is really an Isaiah 54:2,3 and I believe God is ready to supply both means and manpower to enable us to supply men the world over . . . as Nav representatives." After China, Daws would never be the same.

Hubert Mitchell, now directing Southeast Asia YFC, had urged Dawson to come on to India, as had Don Hillis, also back on his field. Mitchell was in Calcutta when Daws arrived by one of those special arrangements with the Lord that were becoming the norm. He had missed a flight out of Hong Kong and would have arrived three days late in Calcutta, too late for the connection to Bombay. Daws asked the Lord to get him to Calcutta if it was necessary to His program, even if it meant adding a special flight. Sure enough, the weary flight crew landing at Bangkok was ordered to take the plane on to Calcutta instead of going off duty as scheduled. Grudgingly they took off with their four passengers, three of whom Daws learned did not have to be in Calcutta for several days. The crew never knew they had a Jonah-in-reverse aboard.

Calcutta — and all his brief India stay — further illustrated needs he had seen in China, where leaders seemed to agree the job was not done and that he had somehow touched on the answer to their problems in principles of The Wheel, pacesetting, and 2 Timothy 2:2. It was sobering and humbling to think God may have sent him to see and take action to remedy these conditions prevailing in the church in vast areas of the world even as he had seen in the States. Yet here it was; he could not escape the evidence of it.

On that sweltering April Sunday in India's hot season he preached four times in three of Calcutta's largest churches, standing with deep respect in the pulpit of missionary pioneers William Carey and Adoniram Judson of a century and a half ago. The sight of crowds pressing in everywhere was beyond the comprehension of the man from the spacious American West. It was staggering to come from China with its quarter of the world's population to this land with another one-fifth. Flying with Mitchell across the subcontinent to Bombay he could look down on thirty to fifty villages at a time. There had to be a way to reach these millions; Isaiah 43:19 assured him there was a way, a new way.

"Hube, d'you realize this guy Karkat Man could be the key to getting the Gospel into Nepal, a country closed to missionaries," Daws exclaimed. Karkat Man, a dealer in musk who traveled to Calcutta had happened into a meeting where Daws was speaking. Afterwards Daws led him to Christ. Now Mitchell was pledged to spend personal time with him in follow-up. "Daws," the expansive Mitchell declared, "this week has revolutionized my thinking. I'm going to put some main strokes into these four — Karkat Man, a Chinese, an Indonesian, and an Indian. I see it. If I can stay with these men, give them time on the side while I go on with the big meetings, we'll see them go back and do the same with men in their own countries."

Daws was delighted. How he admired this man who was willing to change his whole approach at the suggestion of a guy who had barged in seventy-two hours before. But he knew Hube's conviction was from the Lord and the Word, and he would follow through. He knew he would have to send him help; a Nav man for India was a must. If even half the missionaries since Carey had followed the simple pattern Paul set with Timothy, teaching him personally, training him to commit to faithful men who would teach others also, where would India be now? Sending Indian missionaries all over the world! But the mid-twentieth century prevalence of bigger meetings to reach more masses of people was already being sensed by missionaries as futile.

After a meeting in a large Bombay church they journeyed by train, bus, and jeep to Mahableshwar, a mountain retreat where westerners went to escape the heat and study language. Daws looked forward to much prayer time with Mitchell and Don Hillis and fellowship with some eighty missionaries to whom he would speak during three days of sessions. The spiritually drained missionaries sought him out at all hours for private chats. It wrenched his heart to hear their stories of failure and discouragement, all seeming to stem from common roots: weak personal prayer and devotional life, lack of feeding on the Word for their own spiritual health, neglect of personal soulwinning, and consequent failure to build the same things into the lives of Indians. The result was a discouraged sense of fruitlessness.

Here again he wondered that their training for foreign service had omitted two things most needed: the know-how and importance of discipling those won to Christ and of maintaining their own fellowship with the Lord. He tried to encourage these wilted warriors in the battle and press upon their sagging spirits at least one aid to recovery — the *Topical Memory System*. Many did enroll and take heart in setting a new course toward more meaningful spiritual life and more fruitful ministry.

Flying homeward over the Middle East, Daws looked down with awe at Acts country. "Naturally my heart throbbed as we stopped at Damascus," he wrote. "Here Paul was commissioned through Ananias and later let down the wall in a basket. . . . I take hope when I remember I have the same God and am in the same identical program, indwelt by the same Spirit, have the same Word of God."

Europe fascinated him, the time in Belgium, Holland, Switzerland, England, and France affording new sights and language riddles, strange money and customs, with every detail absorbing his interest and relating inevitably to what was nearest his heart. From Nimes, France, he wrote, "As I passed many ruins yesterday on the train I was impressed. Then I thought, older than these were the very words in Isaiah I was reviewing. But these were not seared or worn with time but alive, fresh as the moment the ink was drying on the parchment."

He spoke at meetings — a Bible school in Doorn, Holland, Youth For Christ in Paris and other cities, and groups gathered to learn about follow-up — with the mechanical Wheel flashing spokes freshly lettered in the local language. But most exciting was his discovery of individuals he felt were strategic to God's program: a Dutch war widow who wanted to translate and distribute the *Topical Memory System* for Holland; a keen young Frenchman burdened to reach all France for Christ; former British army corpsman Joe Simmons in Manchester, whose wartime contact with Hightower in New York launched him in memory and Bible study and led him to see the need for this in England. These were key individuals, Daws felt, keys to unlock whole countries for ministry if they could once grasp the significance of 2 Timothy 2:2.

Alone in Paris with a free evening, Daws decided to spend time with the Lord. Slipping up to the roof of the George V Hotel, above the gaiety and wickedness of Paris streets, he stretched on a blanket under the May sky much as he would in Southern California and enjoyed several hours of fellowship with the Lord he loved. His prayer ranged far, from his loved ones at home to the vast lands of China, India, and Europe. The enormity of the need God had allowed him to see was frightening — it seemed 1 percent had been done with 99 percent left to do. Calls for follow-up help, already more than he saw how to answer, were mounting. Yet, he reflected, God loved the world and sent out twelve apparently ill-prepared disciples to the world as their parish. It could be done, by His grace *must* be done. First priority was to mobilize all resources and men around the U.S. and get them to think and aim toward answering these calls in many countries.

Looking up at the stars, he reviewed aloud some of the great Isaiah promises of God's power and His certain plans. *Lord, what do You want us to do that would please You more? What are we doing that we should drop . . . or what are we omitting that we should begin to do?*

Basic to the job, he reaffirmed, was the objective of building The Wheel into the life of every one who would be Christ's disciple. This was a minimum goal: the Christ-centered life with the Word and prayer, the intake spokes, balanced by the outlet of obedience and witness. Then there was the Hand, the outline for teaching one how to get God's Word into his life and know why he should do it. The Wheel, the Hand — pondering what he felt the Lord was impressing on him there in the darkness, he chose in lieu of pen and paper a mnemonic device, associating his points with the Big Dipper hung in the northern sky. The pivotal star where the Dipper's handle joined the cup would be The Wheel, for it was indeed pivotal. Drop the Word spoke down to the star below it and call that the Hand. Four ways to take in the Word, and the meditation thumb to combine with each of the four for a better grasp.

Another important emphasis would be evangelism. He hung this on the star off to the right, forming a scoop — that was it, a scoop to bring people into the Church. Then follow-up came naturally after evangelism. That would complete the four stars of the square, turning the scoop into a cup — good! A cup to hold the results of evangelism, conserving them against loss.

What else? He was thrilled with the way God seemed to confirm to him these basics, clarifying the course for the future. Pacesetting was vital, for the servant of Christ must be able to say with Paul, *Be ye followers of me, even as I also am of*

Christ. Teaching a young Christian to "do as I do" gave leverage to the teacher and hope to the learner, who could see his instructor was an ordinary guy presenting reachable goals man to man, setting the pace by doing himself the things he was teaching. The learner knew he could make the grade because he followed the steps not of a spiritual giant like Hudson Taylor, but of his own friend. Daws would call the star on the handle nearest the cup the Pacesetting star.

The Other Works emphasis must be included — the laborer for God encouraging and showing genuine interest in others whose work might differ from his own. How else could the Body's members fit together to complement each other? Somehow at this moment Dawson's belief in the Other Works principle became a strong conviction, though he had always practiced helping and encouraging others in their vision. Now God rooted it deep as part of his philosophy. *Look not every man on his own things, but every man also on the things of others.* He would remember Other Works by making it the next star out on the handle.

Reaching farthest out to the tip of the handle, the last star had to be World Vision. A vision for the *whole* world, the world God so loved. Daws had heard that Napoleon's men carried with them a map of the world to remind them their leader wished to conquer it. God's men must get on their hearts what is on His heart and never forget for a moment the whole world: *Go ye into all the world and preach the Gospel to every creature . . . make disciples of all nations . . . in Jerusalem . . . Judea . . . the uttermost part of the earth.* Counting back through the stars, reviewing each point to test its validity, Daws suddenly saw another symbol in his new course of navigating by the stars. The Dipper pointed always to the North Star and revolved around it; the life of a disciple would constantly point to the Lord Jesus Christ.

* * * *

Hume Lake, a rustic camp just opened in the California High Sierras by dedicated Christian laymen, was the site of the 1948 Navigators, Staff, and Girls Conferences. Here Dawson unveiled the challenge of the Big Dipper, presenting the familiar principles in a new package, with the added impact of making it official dogma. The trip had so fired Dawson's spirit that he electrified this gang of young men and women with his description of the part they could have in the world harvest. He issued a direct challenge to the 100 men to help fill the gap by taking Nav emphases to fields of the world. The Great Commission could be fulfilled in this generation if these missing links could be supplied.

The job had three phases, he said. First, giving a tribe or nation the Bible in their language as Wycliffe was doing and Morrison had done in China. Next came the work of the evangelist and missionary, preaching the Gospel and winning converts. The third phase was follow-up, bringing young believers to maturity in Christ, enabling them to reach others in turn. The need for laborers to major in follow-up was becoming known, and Navigators could help most in this third phase, he said. "Missionaries in China and India professed ignorance of much God has entrusted us with, and they're begging for help." Daws felt it was a big step to have missions and other works expressing sufficient confidence in The Navigators to ask for help. Now to find and prepare men available to go, and get them out.

But what kind of men? Much as he wanted to send out scores in all directions, Daws was convinced the quality of the laborer was vastly more important than the number, as God had proved by reducing Gideon's small army even further. Paradoxically, Daws held out to everyone there the hope of being one such laborer. *"Get a world vision,"* he roared, with jutting chin and clenched fist outthrust. "God can use you to get the Gospel to the ends of the earth if you never leave Minneapolis, if you are asking Him for that. I don't care how small or insignificant you think you are, it's who God is that counts. He's the God of Daniel, and He said 'Call unto Me and I *will* answer thee and show thee great and mighty things which thou knowest not.' Not one of you is too small or insignificant to reach *one* and help him until he can reach another, and if that goes on you *can* reach the world."

Having thus put the world within reach of the least of his brethren, Daws proceeded to hammer on the musts of quality in work and worker. He spoke powerfully on faith and obedience, showing how the contexts of familiar Scriptures invariably linked faith with obedience to God. He gave messages in depth on points of the Dipper; a sober warning of hindrances to being used of God — sin, prayerlessness, lack of courage, busyness; and an exhaustive list of advantages of systematic Scripture memory. The new *Search The Scriptures* plan was presented to conferees, analyzing a chapter or portion by four separate approaches, along with a strong scriptural plea to appreciate, encourage, and join the other fellow in *his* work for the Lord.

One eager student asked Dawson how he could "grow real fast. Boy, I hope when I'm your age I'm half as far along as you!" Daws thought of territory now clearly mapped that had not been before. "When you are my age," he said, "if you're not twice as far as I am, I will be very disappointed." The conferees left Hume Lake fired to reach the world from Minneapolis or Seattle starting with one person, meanwhile digging into the Word and preparing to be the kind God could use anywhere to stand in the gap. They had seen an example of multiplication in the group from Seattle: Charlie Riggs, an Army officer Sanny had trained, who in time reached George Clark, who reached another man, who reached another. All were at the conference. Sanny had kept his charge of four years ago to "stick with your man."

Dawson felt it was time to start beating the drums. Go all-out to propagate these principles proven by experience yet lacking in so many ministries. Two things he must do: train and send men as specialists to supply these missing elements in other ministries, and begin to expand Navigator work itself to more areas. He should find potential leaders who could be developed to top capacity in reaching others, at the same time encouraging *every* person to teach one other in discipleship. Hume Lake offered an ideal spot for a summer leadership training course for a few dozen men. They could start by building a lodge which would house them for an intensive training program while they ran boys camps as a means of outlet. Dawson assigned the lodge project to John Crawford, just out of Navy uniform and living in the Oakland Nav Home, whenever the way opened to start building.

Before his China trip Daws had been asked by Torrey Johnson, YFC president, to speak at Beatenberg, Switzerland, in August to 400 delegates coming from twenty-seven countries to the first YFC World Congress on Evangelism. He would also accept the invitation of Inter-Varsity's Stacey Woods to address an expected 300 student delegates to an international conference in Lausanne. These would be unprecedented opportunities to communicate the message that burned in his heart. He had written Hillis, Mitchell, and Morken:

> *To say God has done something in my heart is putting it mildly. I realize the past 15 years God has been preparing me for this hour and I must work and fight and press toward completion of the task at hand . . . the spread of the Gospel in this generation and giving every soul an opportunity to hear it.*
>
> *I saw in China, in India, in Holland, in France, in Switzerland, in Belgium a thing I suspected all along but now I have seen it and talked to the missionaries and workers: they do not have adequate follow-up or even the beginning of it; they have neither been fully conscious of the need nor taught how to go about the job, and are ready to see something done. The people they reach are not getting down to business in personal work and would have no idea what to do with any who came to Christ through their ministry. Suppose even a few of the ten to twenty thousand missionaries to China in the past 150 years had understood what the Scriptures teach on follow-up, propagation and multiplication . . . each generation in the past hundred years would have heard the Gospel. No, the cry today is "Send more missionaries," as though that would do the job. The thousands haven't reached the hundreds of millions in many decades — how will additional thousands remedy this situation?*
>
> *The secret of fulfilling Mark 16:15 is in the last verses of Matthew — making disciples. My heart is set on this . . . . I verily believe within five to seven years we can double the number of souls won, to*

> *say nothing of the succeeding few years. . . . There
> are two billion people in the world and a big, tough
> job ahead — not too big, however. I believe we can
> get the Gospel to the ends of the earth in this gen-
> eration.*
> *It thrills my heart to remember those early morning
> prayer meetings when all of us fellows prayed to-
> gether and asked God to touch the whole world.
> Though spread apart by the diameter of the earth,
> we are working together with one heart for this
> thing that is upon the heart of our wonderful
> Lord.*

Dawson was encouraged that the message had already gained
some attention. CIM's Dr. Ford Canfield had asked Arthur
Glasser to teach Navigator follow-up methods to candidates
for China two years before. And the dynamic young go-getters
of YFC International had responded in a great way to the
word given at 509 that night. Daws had been with them at
their Medicine Lake, Minnesota, convention and often at local
rallies. Lunching with Torrey Johnson, Daws boldly asked for
an hour every day at Beatenberg to present these things. Johnson agreed, indicating there would also be time with key men
on the *Queen Mary* going over.

Not everyone was so receptive. Before leaving for Europe,
Daws with Lorne Sanny, now at headquarters as vice-president,
received a distinguished Christian leader from Budapest. Eager
to talk with him about Europe, Dawson outlined his mission,
spreading the *Topical Memory System* out on the floor to illustrate it.

"Hah, don't spend money to send this to Europe," the good
doctor sniffed. "Send the money instead. They won't accept this
in Europe." This dash of cold water made Daws tingle with
determination. Afterward he said in firm measured syllables,
"Sanny, we will see people in Europe memorizing Scripture if
I have to move over there myself. . . . Did you hear what I
said?" "I heard you." Sanny's faith matched his own that it
would be so.

At Beatenberg Daws felt great freedom in communicating
with his audience and was grateful for the generous allotment
of time even though many notable speakers were present. Not

surprisingly, all during his association with YFC men and Word of Life's Jack Wyrtzen while he plied them to consider the individual, Dawson found his own esteem of mass evangelism was growing.

A foursome meeting for prayer on a Swiss mountainside was a high point of the week. Hubert Mitchell recalled it: "Daws had called us together for prayer and meditation. Billy was there, and Bob Evans. We had kind of a time of confessing our needs, our shortcomings, our lack of power and effectiveness among people. And we made a covenant that we would know much more of the Bible by heart — dig in. We shook hands four ways and covenanted to really get down to business in the Scriptures, not know about the Bible but know the Bible."

Graham asked the three friends to advise and pray with him about the presidency of Northwestern Schools, Bible school-seminary-liberal arts college in Minneapolis, a post bequeathed him by the venerable Dr. William Riley though he felt neither qualified for nor called to that ministry. The others encouraged him to accept it, but Dawson asked some searching questions. "Billy, what would you do with a Bible school if you had it?" What would anyone do with one? "Do you think any Bible school in America is doing the job it should do?" More food for thought. "What do you think should be done?" Graham asked.

"Billy, one of the *first* things a Bible school should do is teach the fundamentals of leading a man to Christ and following him up to the point where he could win a man and follow him up. And basic as that is, there's not a Bible school in America that has this in its curriculum." Graham's response was hearty. "Daws, you're going to have a key to the school and come in and give them this!"

"I can't do it," Daws replied. "Well, why not? What do you need? Money? Men?" Billy was puzzled. "First, I need you," was the unexpected answer. "If you get this on *your* heart and dig in and set the pace, we won't have any trouble getting it across to the students." "All right, I'm willing," Graham consented, unconsciously revealing his own greatness.

He did accept the post at Northwestern, determining to make it a base for evangelism world-wide. He slated Evans and Trotman to speak to the 1000 students and faculty at a two-week missions conference in February. "Billy's beginning to see what has to be done in his heart if it's going to be done in the school," Daws told Evans as they spent time together during that conference. Daws had stipulated that Graham and the faculty attend his daily sessions. A dozen years his junior, Graham marveled at the discipline Trotman demanded of himself. Knowing that in his forties he still memorized new verses to add to hundreds on the tip of his tongue and took a hard line on keeping spiritually fit when discipline was not easy for him and he could have gotten by on talent and ingenuity, gained Dawson the evangelist's deep respect. He saw that this man's heart, like his own, longed to know God and to move heaven and earth to bring others to know Him.

Bob Evans shared his burden for Europe, a continent few saw as a mission field, either vaguely considering it Christian or dismissing it as having "had its chance." Evans planned a Bible school in France where he could train young Europeans to evangelize Europe. He would give Nav emphases prominence in his school, having come to appreciate the work as a Navy chaplain and through frequent contact with Dawson. The impression deepened as Daws expounded the Big Dipper when they were together in Paris.

At Graham's urging Daws sent Don Rosenberger to teach three Nav courses at Northwestern in fall 1949, though the school's board was not ready to accredit them. No other schools offered such courses with or without credit; why go overboard? But Rosenberger's classes were immediately popular, with a respectable enrollment of those hungry to benefit from them even without academic credit, learning practical things they would use in their service for Christ for years to come.

After speaking to a conference of a large mission society that spring, Daws had written Art Glasser in China: "Our hearts are sick as we run into these young prospective missionaries who have gone through Bible school and seminary training without learning some of the basic principles . . . and by the grace of God this is going to change. We could almost say, 'This one thing I do!' While we pray the *Lord* will give us balance, one of our major emphases, we are keeping our guns trained in the right direction."

Rosenberger took with him to Minneapolis several ex-service Navigators who were with him in Oakland where he had filled in as Nav director following Chrisman. They enrolled in schools of the area, forming a team for ministry to fellow students. Another Oakland ex-sailor, Bill Fletcher, was already there in school, training several students individually. Rosenberger's gift for teaching enhanced his courses in personal Bible study, Scripture memory, and follow-up, while his bent for analysis and outline packaged them in graspable form.

Daws was wary of much outlining or systematizing of any of these emphases, however, and they had clashed on this point, Daws fearing outlines might short-circuit the living reality of a truth in the heart of the learner. A neat outline of a principle could too easily be passed on to a man as "training" and become instead only a page in his notebook, without freshness or spontaneity. Too, outlines reminded Daws of the very "Bible school approach" he had criticized as inadequate, quoting the axiom, *Telling is not teaching; listening is not learning.*

Robertson, Rosenberger, and Rohrer had pursued their exegesis of Scripture on Navigator principles, outlining each major and minor topic and grouping all in a syllabus to follow in training a key man, with time frames for each item. This Dawson watched closely, not wishing to dampen their initiative but fearful lest they go about propagating truths they did not yet fully own. Sanny had rightly grasped Dawson's insistence on flexibility and freedom in the Spirit when he moved to Los Angeles headquarters before the China trip. "Daws," he had asked, "as vice-president what are my duties?" "We don't do it that way," Daws answered. "We don't give a man a title and a list of duties. We give him a job to do. Then if he needs a title to clarify it, fine."

Dawson's devotion to free form often frustrated Rosenberger and other young assistants, and they felt his experience-backed ability to think more deeply and see farther down the road stifled their ideas and initiative, causing friction. An intuitive leader and forceful exhorter, Daws did not often curb his domination of affairs in favor of developing the young leadership; hence, some promising juniors eventually felt squeezed out. Others — like Sanny — quietly endured, committing any feeling of suppression to the Lord while recognizing the larger truth that Dawson as God's man had more to give than he could possibly take away. Sanny, for his part, settled this out alone at Hume Lake, getting God's direction from the Word to stay at Daws's side regardless. Once this was done he could ride out any future rough weather on the basis of simple obedience to God.

"You have a New Testament tonight, gang, because the apostles believed in follow-up. Paul's letters were follow-up letters — Corinthians — Thessalonians, the first book written. I found twenty-four places that indicate Paul felt responsible to follow up the Thessalonians. Why didn't I see it before? Nobody told me. That's why a lot of us don't see anything. Everything we know of the Bible is what somebody told us was in it instead of what we have searched out ourselves."

The crisp air of the June night carried the scent of pine and spruce into the big tent auditorium at Hume Lake. Daws gripped the front of the lectern, seeming ready to spring at his audience. "Did Peter believe in follow-up? Hah, he'd better; he had a special message on it from the Lord Himself. 'Peter, do you love Me?' 'Yes.' 'Feed My lambs. Do you love Me?' 'Yes.' 'Feed My sheep. Do you love Me?' 'Yes.' 'Feed My sheep.' And Peter got the message. Whether or not it was *agapao* or *phileo* — the point of His message was to *feed the sheep*.

"When Paul wrote to the Colossians, was he satisfied for just a few in the church to be out and out for Him? *Christ in you, the hope of glory* — that's for *every* believer. *Whom we preach, warning every man, and teaching every man in all wisdom; that we may present every man* perfect *in Christ*. Where does damage to the church come? Not from outside, but from those *in* the church who are not bringing glory to His name. That's what we preach now: *every* man a victorious Christian, *every* man a producing Christian. God isn't glorified in raised hands, but in lives trained and taught the Word of God. . . . And that's the responsibility of the spiritual parent."

Daws liked to illustrate from nature this responsibility to feed, protect, and train the young. "Why does a hen hatch only fifteen chicks? Why does a bird hatch only four eggs at most instead of a dozen? Because it keeps both parents busy bringing enough worms to feed four hungry mouths. And those little birds are protected and fed constantly until the day when they are pushed out of the nest and learn to fly off and find their own food. That's normal. Here's a hen in the chickyard taking her little brood around and scratching for them and uncovering nice worms for them to eat. And pretty soon they see how she did it, and they start scratchin' up worms for themselves. And that hen that is selfish by nature will stand back and cluck to show her chicks where the food is instead of gobbling it up herself. That's normal: the parental instinct to provide for the young."

The mood of the 1949 Navigators Conference was expectant. The 165 choice men, including a few key high schoolers from the clubs, showed seriousness of purpose that made them a stimulating audience; they seemed to sense anew their own strategic importance to the Great Commission. Later in Los Angeles, the six-week Navigators Seminar enrolled thirty-seven men and seven girls invited for indoctrination in New Testament "Navigator" principles long neglected in the church but now stirring the consciousness of Christian leaders here and there.

Dawson had hit the ground running on return from China last year, his job clarified in the Big Dipper illustration and urgent requests received from missionaries and pastors in almost every place for "a man to teach us these things." In December he sent Roy Robertson as the first Nav representative overseas to help Dick Hillis establish follow-up in parts of China and train a few men as quickly as possible before the impending Communist takeover forced missionaries out. Robertson had only five months to work before Shanghai fell, but he prudently arranged for the *Topical Memory System*'s distribution from four centers across China and stayed to train seven men in 2 Timothy 2:2 methods designed to carry on person to person even when no church meetings were allowed.

Mitchell, faithfully training his four men in Calcutta, was waiting for the Navigator God would send to help in India.

In the May 1949 issue of the *Log*, the first in almost three years, Dawson wrote:

> *About 17 years ago we began to ask our Heavenly Father, as did the Lord Jesus, to give us the heathen for our inheritance and the uttermost parts of the earth for our possession. Not long afterward we were permitted to start the Navigators work, reaching men from every state in the Union. Some of these men have gone . . . a host of them are preparing to go. In the last two or three years we have specialized in certain phases of work God has given us to do, so in addition to providing manpower to established missions for regular missionary and translation work, we are training chosen key men who will go to foreign countries as representatives for The Navigators.*

These men, he said, would impart and demonstrate the multiplication idea as they worked alongside missions and national churches, supplying the emphasis of working with individuals to supplement group and mass ministries. They would seek to change the pattern of missionary practice by eventually making themselves unnecessary.

Noting calls from twenty countries for Navigator materials and methods, Daws explained that these would be ineffective without men trained to use them. Robertson was the first man sent out and more must follow soon. "I'm glad we're under way in China now, even though it is late," Daws wrote to Rohrer. "A delay of one year means that seven years later we have accomplished only six years' work. And we haven't lost the first year, but the seventh, which could be crucial."

He had regained his balance and confidence briefly lost in the 1945 ordeal and could now boldly present multiplication as a missing link in world missions, key to "reaching the greatest number of people in the most effective way in the shortest possible time." He hit it hard in this summer's conferences and seminar. "I believe now this mimeographed letter and the whispering campaign it set off in 1945 was Satan's first attempt to stop this thing we were teaching: follow-up and the 2 Timothy 2:2 principle. I believe he saw we were coming close to the very key to carrying out the commission of Jesus Christ and put on his main attack to try to destroy the work.

"In the early days of The Navigators we spent lots of time with one man. Then the war brought hundreds of contacts in on us and everything was Bible classes; we lost sight of the necessity of man-to-man training in making disciples. Then in Honolulu I found Navigators teaching forty Bible classes a week. I should have rejoiced, but I didn't. I said 'Fellows, something's missing.' And we began to see it. The word I used was producing reproducers. It was just the gray dawn beginning to appear. . . . and the day I left Honolulu this attack came that threw even some leaders off balance who had begun to see this principle. For almost a year the work suffered.

"So we've been emphasizing man-to-man about three and a half years — spending lots of time with one man. Also the need to teach a man that no matter what else he does, he should ask God for an Isaac, a Timothy who will be faithful to reproduce a man who will in turn be a reproducer.

"Now let me warn you, fellows, Satan tries to corrupt any truth or make you misuse or get it out of balance. And because man-to-man is effective, don't start thinking it's the *only* ministry. One fellow in this room wouldn't go to a Youth For Christ meeting where I was speaking because he didn't believe in mass meetings — even though the very fellow who taught him man-to-man was speaking at a mass meeting. Now that's going out of balance. Even if you do major in man-to-man, group work is tremendously important. You can have precious fellowship in a group that you can't have just one with another. And there's a challenge in seeing others down to business and hear them sing the praises of the Lord. What a big thrill it was when I first heard 3000 young people at Christian Endeavor convention sing 'Since Jesus Came Into My Heart'! I felt I was in heaven hearing 3000 voices united in praise to the Lord.

"A group also gives balance to your life and keeps you from being just one man's disciple. Members of the group rub off on one another as each contributes something different. This may be one reason the Lord commands us in Hebrews 10:25 not to forsake the assembling of ourselves together. So it's obeying the Lord, and we have plenty of examples of this in Scripture.

"One thing about group ministry is that it redeems the time.

If I can put a point over to twenty of you at once, it's a time-saver, isn't it? Right now in this group I've got your attention. Some of you may be glad your neighbor is getting this message and some may be hurt because I'm drivin' too straight in your direction — but I do have your attention. Later when I work with you I can start from here and build on what you already know. So it's redeeming the time.

"Now let it be clear that man-to-man is not the same as the 2:2 ministry. By 2:2 we mean continuing propagation — any chalk around?" He placed the blackboard where all could see it. "Paul to Timothy to faithful men to others also. Joel to the old men, your children, their children, another generation, in Joel 1:3. They were concerned that the chain not be broken. And when we work with a man we're concerned to know what he does with *his* man. And it takes time and patience, seeing the work go on to third and fourth generations. If *this* man is being reached, I can die in peace. Because you cannot see this man reached" — stabbing a bony finger at the fourth man in line — "without knowing *your* man passed on the idea to faithful men able to teach. It's the system God inaugurated at the beginning, creating every living thing with the seed within itself for propagation. And when through the Gospel He makes a new creation, He fully intends him to be self-propagating. The entire world was populated as a result of God's command to Adam and Eve to be fruitful and multiply; it makes sense that if Christians would be fruitful and multiply the entire world could be evangelized.

"So the 2:2 principle as we refer to it is the Christian reproducing after his kind, and man-to-man is more the idea of father and son, parental nurturing and training up in the faith. They are interwoven. Man-to-man is basic to the 2:2 ministry but won't reach the uttermost part of the earth; 2:2 will. And I hope none of you fellows will be satisfied until you see your great-grandchildren in the Lord. It's a goal every one of you could aim at. I'm no longer concerned about accomplishing a lot for God. If I can see my great-great-great-grandchildren strong, in the Word, reproducers, that's all I want.

"When I visited Sanny in Seattle he introduced me to ten men, one of them Charlie Riggs. Charlie had caught this vision and was spending time with nine fellows, one of them George

Clark. Clark worked with eight men and one was Bostrom. Bostrom had four, one of them Leierer. You saw them at Hume Lake last year, all going on and producing. We counted back on one chain and it averaged six months from the time a man started until he began to work with his man. If we extended that figure so that at the end of each six months each man took on a new man to help, in a year there'd be four, in two years there'd be sixteen. And in fifteen and a half years we'd reach the world — we'd have over two billion!

"Where are we now on this basis? I don't know, and I don't care. The question isn't how many we have but how strong, how virile, how pure, right? This method *looks* slow and it is, at first. After it gets going there'll be the numbers. Suppose you decided to make your whole ministry personal work, winning souls day in, day out all your life. If you won say three a day or 100 a month, that's 1200 a year — in fifteen years you'd have 18,000. Or suppose you were an evangelist and held the biggest meetings America has ever known, getting 1000 decisions for Christ in a three-week campaign. If you could hold twelve campaigns a year you'd have 12,000 decisions or 180,000 at the end of fifteen years. You'd go down in history, wouldn't you? But this way, through multiplication, it would be 2,174,000,000.

"But *please,* don't use this six months' deal on a mechanical basis — it'll get us in Dutch. This is only an idea, a blueprint, showing what would happen, and we have a few examples. We *don't* say 2:2 is reaching a guy in six months and getting him to get another. It may take five years to get his first man — or he may get him in three months. So lay off trying to keep score. It takes more than six months to bring a spiritual child to maturity, and it takes help from the grandparents. Don't push your babes or contacts out to get more contacts and get a weak, anemic heritage — does that make sense? We don't want any high-powered reports of great-great-grandchildren, so don't worry. Just pray — believing — and wait God's time. Obey God. He gives the harvest."

The seminar, characterized by experiment, was counted a success. Time between classes and discussions was filled with team projects, enjoyable fellowship, and merciless critiques. At the end it was clear that next summer's seminar would be different. But the caliber and response of the young men and women only spurred Dawson to expect a greater session next year at Hume where the lodge would be ready to use, away from telephones and other distractions of the city.

With Robertson working under handicap in Shanghai in a ministry he hoped would continue when his time ran out, Dawson pursued plans to get a man to India. His sense of urgency to plant the flag of 2 Timothy 2:2 in other parts of the world was quickened by ominous moves of world Communism threatening to close doors to missions. Thinking in terms of "If we lose the first year, we really are losing the seventh year," he was exceedingly eager to launch the *Topical Memory System* and multiplication vision in first stages in as many countries as possible. During the summer he knew the Lord was moving him toward Europe and Africa. "I am sure the trip will take not less than six months," he wrote the staff. He would hold conferences in Britain, Holland, France, and three parts of Africa, perhaps returning through Asian countries.

After seminar Dawson spent a week in Oklahoma interviewing candidates for Wycliffe, charging them to add to their translation work an investment in one life they could disciple for Christ. In Los Angeles he helped Daddy Moon recruit personal workers for Billy Graham's tent campaign coming in September and, leaving Sanny to throw the Navigator staff into this effort, departed for Europe just as the tent meetings opened.

Africa had been cut from his itinerary, but Daws still planned up to six months for Europe, to learn what the church was doing in each country and find the best channels for Nav emphases. He would make contacts through Youth For Christ, Inter-Varsity, and friends of Mrs. Alexander Kerr, now an avid Scripture memorizer eager to see this introduced in her ancestral Germany. Daws would go in largely unknown and seek audience with local groups, watching always for the individual who might be a key person in that country. Such individuals naturally drew his attention and in them he saw greatest potential for getting the job done — Gien Karssen of Holland whom he had met last year at Beatenberg, Joe Simmons in England, and others the Lord would bring across his path. Large meetings seemed of dubious lasting value, but the one or half-dozen who stayed afterwards to ask for more loomed important to him.

Paris was first, where Bob Evans's European Bible Institute would soon open. Meetings Evans had arranged with Christian leaders, evangelists, and missionaries enabled Daws to promote the cause of EBI. He would also find prospective students for the school as he traveled.

The possibilities of Paris astounded him. There were always 75 to 100 missionaries studying French for service in Africa. Those Dawson met were most receptive to the truths he presented. Paris also had a half-dozen places where thousands of students ate subsidized meals every day — an international fishing pool beyond imagining! Here he found an Indochinese student who showed immediate interest in the things of Christ. He felt sure many a Cornelius or Lydia was right in this spot.

"Gang, I am amazed at the lack of initiative, productive thinking, and planning on the part of the church to carry out our Lord's last commission," he wrote home. "I feel as though we had been going through the Dark Ages in Christian work. Everybody immediately responds to our message. All acknowledge the lack. What could have been done if we'd all known the simple rules and followed them. They're ready to respond if we'll help."

He could wait no longer. No matter what he found in other places, a Navigator must start work in Paris now. He wrote Rohrer a firm call to Europe, to headquarter in Paris and help Evans in EBI, launch the TMS, and minister to men available on every hand.

Germany would affect him too. On October 26 he wrote, "Who am I going to send to Germany? It must be as soon as possible. Pray." And Holland, November 4: "Did I ask you to pray for a man for Holland? Isaiah 45:11. Let's find him soon, Sanny, and get him learning Dutch." In Naples he would devise a plan for the Nav man to meet an Italian student in Boston who would teach him language while learning Nav principles. England would be different, for Joe Simmons was under way teaching a few men to memorize, study, witness, and have a quiet time. Daws had written Joe, who assumed he was coming to hold meetings, "No, I want to spend time mainly with you."

A military permit for Germany was arranged by Europe's chief of chaplains, Col. Paul Maddox, who invited Trotman to his home. Maddox was deeply impressed by this layman's contagious sense of mission, his deep insight into Scripture and practical way of imparting it. He offered Dawson valuable help, not the least of which was a German secretary to write letters inviting Germans to a series of meetings Daws would hold. The secretary's concept of church as a place to christen, marry, and bury changed when she learned that reading and memorizing Scripture and helping others spiritually was for church members as well as ministers. She soon found Christ as her Savior. Maddox saw this as one of many results of Trotman's having "so permeated his heart and life with the Word of God that it overflowed into every action and contact — a living example of the Bread of Life."

Daws tried to convey his feelings to those at home. "My heart is getting a continual conditioning. Everywhere I look I see need and opportunity. We all know need in general, but seeing the people, the look on their faces, begins to burn into one's heart." Missionaries, chaplains, servicemen, German Christians attended his Frankfurt meetings, fourteen or more coming back each night, some from Wiesbaden where he had spoken at Youth For Christ. Two Germans especially interested him — a godly woman he had met at Beatenberg, now translating the *B Rations* into German, and a young YFC convert eager to grow, Traugott Vogel. Dawson planned a February seminar in Paris for one or two key persons from each country to learn more Nav principles and perhaps be interested in EBI. Traugott must certainly be included.

Holland and Scotland and England varied greatly in schedule and contact — faculty and students at Netherlands Bible Institute; a banquet with eighty-five evangelical leaders in Glasgow; Anglican and Plymouth Brethren congregations and a YFC rally of 400 in England; extensive time with individuals. But results were strikingly similar: awakening hunger for the Word;

vision broadened to include discipling and the prospect of multiplying; recognition that Christ's promise that "greater works than these shall ye do" could literally apply to the Great Commission.

Daws spent hours across a table from Joe Simmons sharing the Word on 2 Timothy 2:2 and Big Dipper principles. Joe's eyes were opened to things he would now impart to his young men. He later recalled, "Dawson made you feel you were a key to evangelization of the world."

The earnest response of Europeans added poignancy to the need of this continent which, in contrast to the Orient, had centuries of Christian heritage but had somewhere missed the point. The enormity of the challenge reflected in Dawson's letter home: "I realize history is in the making. Why should He let me have a part in this? We're in this up to our necks, there's no retreating now. Gird on thy swords, beloved crew, and remember your Sword is invincible. What's the biggest thing each of you has asked for yourself lately?"

His times with the Lord were richer for being hard to get, often taken while walking under the night sky. Such fellowship was also a weapon against loneliness. Visiting the Isle of Man, his father's birthplace, he spent a free evening out on the breakwater leading to the lighthouse. As he walked he sang and prayed for many by name, the Big Dipper visible in the north reminding him of his mission. "Asked big things," he wrote. "Sang a score of songs to my wonderful *Lord*."

Italy was next, and the pressure grew heavier. "I can't tell you all that's going through my heart and mind," he wrote from Naples. "I hardly get to think over the problems of an area before I'm in another area facing a completely new batch. Already I'm dreading Rome, where I'll have three three-week-olds in the same meeting with the leaders and three nights only." He had met with the Rome YFC committee and discovered the meeting's purpose was to find a way to help three new Christians present to grow. So his Rome conference would combine an audience of Christian leaders and babes in Christ!

In Naples he was moved as he watched a holiday crowd shouting petitions to a religious statue being paraded through town. Later he walked out to pray alone. "Tonight I prayed for Italy. Short, but strong. The first time· I ever felt the real burden," he wrote. "I wonder why we can't get a burden sooner. Pray He'll give it to all of us. Please all of you get one of these 50¢ Hammond atlases and pray through it over a period of time and do it again and again and again. Soon The Navigators will be giving tests on where certain countries are, what's been done, do they have the Word etc., so get a running start." The incredibly strong loyalty and solidarity of the Navigator staff had often been remarked by Christian leaders. Here was one of its secrets — Dawson compelled to share with his gang by the next air mail the heartbeat of his concerns and experiences and to bring them actively into the cause at hand. Part of the charisma of this team leadership was its spontaneous immediacy, light years away from the concept of a "report to members."

On the first day in Naples he had met a dozen young men age nineteen to twenty-seven, none over thirteen months old in Christ. His heart sank. Who would help them, and how? All he could do was bring them into his meetings geared to leaders, with added hazards of a language gap, an unknown interpreter, a culture gap, their lack of Bible knowledge, and the prevalence of superstition. As the meetings progressed, eleven hours one day, twelve hours the next, the problem increased. "This really took it out of me," he wrote. "I'm worn to a frazzle. Ground has been covered and two or three possible fellows spotted. But warfare is rugged, dear ones, and if ever I was in it I am now."

These twelve lads and countless others they symbolized lay heavy on his heart. "If we had an Italian-speaking Navigator I would get him over here immediately. What a crime we didn't start 16 years ago getting our Navs ready to produce reproducers, learning languages and Big Dipper principles. If so many of God's servants hadn't followed the traditional approach and had done a little investigation of the biggest assignment ever given man we'd not be so unprepared at this most strategic hour of earth's history."

What Daws had seen during ten weeks in six European countries overwhelmed him, with three months more of it before he would board the *Queen Mary* in March. He wondered if he could bear what he would find in countries ahead — crushing famine for the Word, spiritual hunger, pitiable ignorance of the remedy. The task seemed hopeless — until he recalled the motley dozen who tramped over Palestinian deserts with the Galilean, starting to spread His message "unto the uttermost" with ever so much less in resources. The thought encouraged him.

He knew the answer to needs he had seen so far was men — Ezekiel 22:30 kind of men to make up the hedge and stand in the gap. A host of these were in preparation, but who was ready now? The more he prayed about this, the more inclined he was to drop everything and go get some men ready to send to Europe. No point in going on to eight more countries and seeing needs he could not meet, when his heart could hold no more. The Lord confirmed his decision, and days later, surprising all but Lila and Sanny, Daws landed in Los Angeles.

February 1950 — when Dawson would have held the Paris seminar for key Europeans, he set out instead with Sanny to tour the U.S. in search of potential area representatives, some of the "topnotchers" he had specifically prayed for on the hill just over five years ago. With the priority of finding men for Europe as well as the Orient, they would survey manpower resources and help men plot courses of training to best prepare them for assignment anywhere. Dawson was torn between desire to get men out at once to start laying foundations in other countries and the prudent alternative of taking time to complete their preparation.

The Los Angeles area ministry had thrived under Sanny's leadership, the key men in touch with some ninety men who were growing. Dallas, an early stop on the circuit, brought ninety contacts to a two-day conference and fruitful interviews with seminary men. Over 400 turned out for meetings at Bob Jones University, with a warm reception from many whose lives had been touched by Nav work in the service. The school's evangelistic emphasis made Dawson's message on followup timely.

At Columbia Bible College were more Navigators planning

for missionary service, among them Gordon Gustafson and his ex-Navy Timothy, Cecil Hawkins. The speaking and interview schedule was heavy in Columbia. Here also Daws and Lila were invited to the governor's mansion where the Billy Grahams were guests of Governor Strom Thurmond. Graham was finishing a campaign in Columbia with some 35,000 at his closing meeting, a sharp upturn in attendance having followed his Los Angeles meetings in the 6000-seat Canvas Cathedral while Daws was in Europe. That campaign stretched to eight weeks, the conversion of some notables and sudden national publicity making Billy and the Gospel page-one news.

Dawson reveled in the opportunity to minister at Annapolis and West Point, where eager audiences of midshipmen and cadets asked for more, and four West Pointers came to Christ after his evangelistic meeting. In Boston he spoke to a follow-up rally instructing 1000 inquirers from a seventeen-day Graham campaign held in January.

In Chicago and Wheaton, Daws and Sanny found more laborers in the making. But a weekend conference near Minneapolis outshone in significance any event of the trip. Here were over 140 students and young working people from the Twin Cities moving ahead in the Word and evangelism, most of them getting help individually. Bill and Jeanette Fletcher's contacts and some from Rosenberger's Northwestern classes had asked for help in discipleship and discipling others. In his few months in the area Rosenberger had emphasized evangelism and the key men had led twenty-five to Christ in their various schools.

He held a high standard for those looking for a challenge. An ex-Marine student he invited to join the key man group asked how much time it would take. "The rest of your life," Rosenberger replied in terms the Marine understood. He joined. At the weekend conference he met Dawson and was impressed by his love and genuine interest. "It wasn't fake," he said later. "I'm a schemer and conniver, and I can detect it in others." From that time LeRoy Eims, the Iowa kid who survived the Peleliu invasion realizing he needed to know God, committed his life to bringing others to know Him. At conference he tried to understand Dawson's explanation of "seven weeks' back review" of memory verses and concluded he must review all his

TMS verses seven times a day! The technology did not come through to him, but the message of the life did.

Many conferees sensed Dawson's confidence in their potential and had a persistent feeling he spoke personally to them in his messages. Daws was indeed thrilled with this group, yet ambivalent about seeing a work grow so obviously Navigator. Last fall he had warned Rosenberger, "No big rallies. Go back there and throw your weight into the school and the established works. Help Inter-Varsity. Don't promote Navigators or build an empire." Yet in spite of it all, here was a gang so biased toward Navigators it was frightening. Daws did want to leave the door open for those God would direct to work with The Navigators, but he wanted to see them prepare to labor with many mission groups and churches.

As it turned out, this Twin Cities group would yield an unusually large contingent of laborers in home and foreign missions and church ministries — and of future Nav representatives, wives, and girls workers. Daws met Waldron Scott, who had given Eims the *B Rations*. A lad with strong Bible background, Scott had seen in this group a vitality he admired and ways to make stand-up application of the Scripture he knew. And the vision of reaching the world through multiplication appealed to him as revolutionary. There was Doug Sparks and his ex-service buddies Bob Seifert and Bob Glockner who had brought him to Christ and started him growing. And dozens more, each Exhibit A of what God could do with a fellow or girl who began getting into the Word and obeying it.

＊   ＊   ＊   ＊

Rosenberger brought a busload of girls to Girls Conference at Hume Lake that summer and another bus filled with men for Navigators Conference, which registered a record 240 men from points east, southwest, northwest, and both service academies. Conferees came only by invitation from Nav headquarters, as did 100 men and 20 women for the four-week seminar in July.

Daws felt the seminar this year accomplished far more, going beyond the experiment of last summer, analyzing the year's ministry in the areas, the mistakes and results. Greater emphasis on evangelism marked this summer's sessions, with a veering away from notebook and hour-a-week training of men toward more training by influence of life and the "with him" principle. Multiplication was again stressed. Daws's uncomfortably keen insight into lives, redeemed only by his deep love and desire for their success, made seminar personally memorable for all and added up to near exhaustion for him. He was overjoyed to appoint the first Nav reps for Europe — David Rohrer, back from Europe to teach at seminar and return with bride Jean Campbell of the Los Angeles staff, Bill and Jeanette Fletcher to work in England, George Clark and Bob Hopkins for France and Germany. The GI Bill would pay their tuition for language study in Paris, with a little left to live on.

To the seminar crowd Daws laid on the line the Lord's all-or-nothing call to discipleship in Luke 9. "Ninety percent of you won't be around five to ten years from now." His tone dared them to prove him wrong. "You'll wash out, join the ranks of the also-rans. You make big promises, big talk. But you're not willing to pay the price to follow through and carry out His orders." Among those for whom it was a memorable time of commitment was Doug Sparks. Canny, analytical, goal-centered, Sparks vowed he for one would not be an also-ran. Alone in prayer by the lake he dedicated his life to fulfilling the Great Commission. Another was Waldron Scott. Out under a pine tree that day he searched his soul concerning whether he would be one of the 10 percent or the 90 percent and got a firm promise from God to sustain him.

The spring manpower survey trip and the heavy summer training program had kept Daws away from headquarters too long. He began turning down all engagements for the latter part of the year to give his time to tending the store. Some 550 each month were enrolling in the *Topical Memory System* and correspondence had increased both from the U.S. and overseas. Only one staff bulletin and three issues of the *Log* had gone out this year, edited by Sanny in the *News Letter* format and printed on the new Multilith. There was the business of dispatching the first Nav group to Europe and of deciding how long Robertson should stay in Communist China. Other missionaries were dispersed or fairly immobilized in Shanghai. Robertson wanted to stay, feeling he could discreetly carry on his ministry. He reported 800 Chinese were progressing in the

TMS, thirty in one province having finished it. The course needed to be translated into three European languages and possibly others. Daws also sent men out to such places as West Point, Oklahoma City, and Seattle for further training as they assisted the area man or worked as Navigator contacts with a few men who had asked for help.

There were meetings with the YFC committee and Wycliffe board, coordination with Young Life conferences, and production of Bible study and notebook materials in the office print shop, supervised in detail by Dawson to the silent dismay of some who thought his standards of workmanship extreme. There was his businessmen's club with Mintie, Cooper, and others, a ministry Daws greatly enjoyed. And there was strategic time with individuals. One of these was Bill Bright, who had made a decision for Christ on his own five years before and had had no follow-up. He began coming around for time with Daws and Sanny, "very hungry to learn anything I could about the Lord," he said later. "Daws influenced my life by the warmth and dynamic of his life and the challenge of his person, his vision, and how God used him, more than any teaching." Daws was mightily impressed by the soft-spoken, brilliant young man who seemed to have an insatiable appetite for God.

It was good for Daws to be home for a season with his family and the crew, including several fellows who worked around headquarters mainly to get time with him. He often played chess with one of his children during dinner, so engrossed in the game that neither he nor his young opponent knew — or cared — what they had eaten. And there were unforgettable Tuesday night prayer meetings on the hill above 509 with the fellows — Jake Combs from Minneapolis, ex-Navy officer Bill Michel, wounded ex-Marine Bob Boardman, Cecil Davidson, and others. Their vision grew as they quoted and claimed promises and prayed, as his had grown in those early prayer times in the hills and later with Hillis, Mitchell, Morken, and Munger. Jeremiah 33:3, Isaiah 43:4 and 58:12 were more real now than ever — he had seen them partly fulfilled. But he could sense that these fellows did not yet believe God *could* and *would* do what He promised. In fact, they asked for peanuts when they should be asking for continents.

"Wait a minute, guys," he suddenly interrupted one of their low-budget prayers. "You're not really asking things for the world. Your vision is limited. You need to *ask big*." Rather than continue, he sent the fellows down the hill to spend the rest of the time listing things that could enlarge their vision.

Certain God would use anyone whose heart was perfect toward Him, Daws kept up the challenge to believe God and pray for big things. When he could not be present at a staff prayer meeting, he asked Sanny to "make a note of what they ask for and tell me. I want to know if they're asking big."

The need for more office space was urgent by mid-year 1950, with every facility strained at the downtown Biola building. After searching the area for months, Daws and Sanny recognized God's spectacular answer to prayer in the place they found — a small one-story factory building, minutes from where the staff lived at 509 and the Sanny home in Pasadena. John Crawford, who had finished the Hume Lake Lodge with a hardy crew of Nav volunteers, would remodel the office building, to be ready for the staff by November.

During the fall when Dawson had determined to cut back his activities and catch up, one more idea clamored to be implemented. He thought of promising young disciples in college who might end their four years with purpose cooled and vision for serving God dimmed unless they were helped to grow in discipleship right in their school environment. His idea was to have them reduce their course load by two or three hours and enroll in Navigator courses off campus, subjects designed to help them witness on their campus mission field and provide a sizable amount of training by the time they graduated. So in September the UCLA Project was launched with twenty-seven enrollees taking two classes one evening a week, taught by Lorne Sanny at the new Nav girls headquarters opened near the campus with graduate nurse Leila Elliott in charge.

There was one last diversion from Dawson's plan to stay home — another trip overseas. Hillis strode into his office in September and came right to the point: "Daws, God is sending several of us to Formosa. Who are you going to send from the Navs?" He told of the unlimited freedom for evangelism Bob Pierce had found among the 3.5 million Chinese refugees from the mainland, including the 600,000-man army and the

Chiang government, which combined with resident Taiwanese to double the island's population. Madame Chiang wanted a half million gospels for her troops. Hillis was assembling a team to distribute them and do evangelism among the soldiers, refugees, and Taiwanese and wanted someone to provide follow-up for the expected decisions. Wheels spun in Dawson's mind, bringing the swift decision that he himself would go. He telephoned Robertson in Shanghai to meet him in Tokyo in November and proceed to Formosa.

They spent a week in Tokyo where Morken now labored with Youth For Christ. Daws had long wanted and been urged by others to get a Nav man to Japan. He found that missionaries he had known from Peking were also praying he would go to Korea. As he saw it, Tokyo would be strategic as an Orient headquarters from which Robertson could reach out to the Philippines, Indochina, and other Asian countries — a goal more urgent now that China had fallen to the Communists. In Tokyo alone Daws noted forty universities with 180,000 students — what an opportunity!

But Formosa was the challenge of the moment. While the team evangelized and distributed gospels, Dawson held conferences with national pastors, church laymen, and missionaries in different parts of the island, in cities and back in the mountains with the tribespeople. He felt a strange joy in the rough living conditions, enduring cold and sleeping on floors — a rare privilege to bear something for his Lord's sake. Robertson's task was to find a way to follow up the decision slips piling up in Taipeh and provide a Bible study correspondence course to meet the needs of these thousands of new Christians. Daws left him in Formosa to finish this job and returned through Tokyo, reaffirming his choice of this city as Orient headquarters. Roy would move here as soon as he could be replaced in Formosa. Daws arrived in the States January 1951. With over 5000 decisions recorded in the two and a half months, Hillis also returned for 1.5 million more gospels.

In his work with pastors and churches on Formosa, Daws had found the same lack of understanding of the individual's responsibility before the Lord that so hindered the church in other lands. A simple awakening of the lay Christian to his role as witness would be a great victory for the cause of Christ in Formosa as it had begun to be in some other quarters. A Navigator for Formosa was imperative, and within days he was chosen. Doug Sparks, majoring in history at Macalester College in St. Paul, was recommended by Rosenberger and given a call. His commitment at Hume Lake tested sooner than he expected, Sparks promptly accepted the call, leaving his completion of college for another day.

Flipping through his Bible, Daws read from the back fly-leaf an inscription datelined London, Westminster Abbey, 5/2/48: *Seeing marble statues erected to the memory of men. Is this what You want, Lord? Or do You want living men dedicated to the glory of God? Oh Lord, help me build men, strong, holy, prepared men to go to the four corners of the world who will do the same. Daws.* Slim, whitebarked trees stood like sentries guarding his hillside prayer spot. A light breeze felt fresh on his face. Small fleecy clouds floated by, as rare in the blue California sky as these priceless times alone had become. It was a time to soak in the Word and hold consultation with his Commander in Chief, and to do as David did, *remember the days of old . . . meditate on all Thy works. . . .*

Some had speculated that changes brought on after the war and sudden demobilization meant The Navigators would fold up. Daws remembered calling staff men together in Los Angeles to assure them this was only the beginning. "God is going to push us out in new areas," he told them. "I believe He has not begun to show what He's going to do through The Navigators." Now he could look back on nearly six years since the war and see the retooling God had brought them through in preparation to share in the great task of reaching the world in this generation.

Retooling was first of all personal for him. He had been mellowed by the unthinkable experience of Chuckie's illness, made more considerate and understanding. The T - - - affair combined with this to humble and soften him. But he had felt then and did now that God prepares for His great moves through trial. A friend who had studied mission movements was convinced this development was part of the pattern.

"Daws, this movement is of God," he had said. "There's the matter of the challenge of your authority. When God raises up a man and proposes to do something with him, early in his experience his authority is challenged by a member of the group who is a key man.

"For another thing you are creating your own language — expressions like 'down to business' and 'hiding the Word.' When a movement is going to do something it starts creating its own language because the concepts that have served before are not adequate to cover it." The gift of talented staff men and women was further indication, Daws felt.

Another important factor was the redirection of financial policy, the Lord's clear leading to allow many more of His servants to share in supporting the work. Tentmaking had been given a fair trial but was clearly not the answer — yet another token of His intent that the work be no longer a small family affair. Funds were still short, but the new policy had broadened the base of support in a manner suggesting future expansion.

It was significant too that Nav — or New Testament — principles had been defined. Producing reproducers had emerged, its survival of attacks on it confirming God's leading to preach the multiplication principle. Especially since it revealed a universal neglect of the truth that the sheep, not the shepherd, bear the lambs. If the church could only be awakened to this fact, the effect would be explosive. The 2-4-8-16 idea had been criticized, the enemy's attempt to discredit a weapon he knew was powerful. Daws had countered with a warning to the fellows to use this projection only as illustration, not as actual theory.

The Wheel had also come under fire. Where was the Holy Spirit? The church? The answer was simple enough: the Holy Spirit was present in every spoke. In fact, The Wheel could as well be called The Christ-Centered, Spirit-Filled Life. As for the church, The Wheel represented the individual Christian who along with others made up the church. Fellowship and teamwork were indeed essential.* If any doubted it, Daws reminded them that a wheelbarrow operated alone on a single wheel but it had to be pushed!

The Big Dipper graphically summarized the Navigator task, a rememberable guide to these main truths Daws felt had been too long neglected.

In his four trips overseas he had found the need in other countries identical to that in the U.S. and the untapped potential of the ordinary Christian the same there as here. His burden to provide follow-up help for these countries and instill the vision of multiplication had begun to materialize. He had hoped to send men to implement the Nav vision in context of regular missionary work with established groups, but this did not succeed. Though he would still recruit hundreds for other missions, it was apparent the Navigator job must be done by men sent wholly under Nav auspices. They would be able to serve other missions best by adding the dimension of Nav emphases to the work of those missions. It would be necessary also to remain independent of the church, overseas as in the U.S., in order to serve the whole church with these needed emphases. The Navigators would send their men to plant on foreign soil such concepts of lay discipleship as follow-up, the importance of every Christian reproducing, the necessity and the how of getting into the Word and establishing a fruitful prayer life.

Thus, sooner than he expected, The Navigators would go international. Roy had shown what could be done in his short time in China, and he would open other countries of the Orient. The fellows had a toehold in Europe. There was no man yet for India. Many men were coming up, but he wished more were ready now to do the job overseas.

The pieces were fitting together now — the early promises from Isaiah, the unfolding answers, the trials and testings, the expanding opportunities. Never had it been clearer than at this moment that God had given him this special mission for this time, a unique part to play in the total picture.

Lorne had said once on their trip last spring, "Daws, you seem almost like a man of destiny." "I never thought of it

*The Wheel later included a Fellowship spoke.

that way," he had answered. "But I do know this. God has given me certain promises. Some I have seen fulfilled, some are being fulfilled, and I know He is going to fulfill the rest."

"Gang, I know you're all carrying a load — every one of you. We've got more than we can handle, and the work is growing fast, but I know this: we've got to help Billy Graham. After being at the Fort Worth campaign, I have no choice but to go all out to work with Billy. And that means every one of us will have to dig in and ask God to enable us to produce twice as much." Just back from Fort Worth, Daws had called all hands together on the shaded flagstone patio behind 509. "I'll be giving half of my time to the Team, and I'll be calling on some of you to give at least that much. We'll all have to work harder than ever and trust God for the resources. Remember, with Him *all* things are possible."

The relaxed scene did not suggest a call to action, the patio overlooking a rolling expanse of green lawn stretching toward the three tall avocado trees at the edge of Monterey Road. But the staff sensed a momentous change in store and rallied as always to Daws's challenge. He reviewed Graham's urgent invitation to join the Team and design a follow-up program for the growing number making decisions for Christ. The evangelist would not take no for an answer.

Daws had wrestled with the decision as he paced the beach on Formosa last fall. At 44, senior to most of the Team, he had wondered if he could fit into their style of operation. But his main reservation was the increasing demands of the Nav work. Roy was ready to open headquarters in Tokyo as soon as Sparks was under way in Formosa. The Europe team in Paris and Manchester would need help. He must think of reinforcements for both continents, and men for South America and Africa. A Nav training center was needed to prepare men to go.

Meanwhile, a few could be trained in Los Angeles or placed with Rosenberger or Riggs, whom Sanny had left in charge in

Seattle, or with Lee Sundstrom in San Diego. With only three area directors in the entire U.S., not much cross training could be done.

Servicemen's work claimed high priority as the armed forces built toward three million by summer for the Korean War. Unlike the ministry during World War II, Dawson proposed to concentrate on producing reproducers while doing whatever possible for the greater number of men. Finances also had priority because of rising ministry expense, purchase and remodeling of the new office building, and purchase of the home at 509. The Hume Lake Lodge, a project of great benefit in building and great joy in using, would now be sold to help provide funds. Sanny would be giving much of his time to finance contacts. The important 1951 summer conferences and seminar would be in Santa Barbara on Westmont College campus. New stateside areas should be opened, others strengthened.

All these things crossed Dawson's mind as he prayed over Graham's request. His top men also questioned committing The Navigators so massively to a ministry almost opposite of their own. Yet the Lord was clearly leading to accept the responsibility for campaign follow-up, and the Fort Worth visit clinched his decision.

There were many points in its favor. Hundreds of converts were entitled to help. Follow-up team men could be developed and trained on the job. Sparks and Robertson could learn from the experiment for their follow-up of mass evangelism in the Orient. And the link with Graham would give The Navigators publicity and exposure virtually shunned before but now a definite need. It would also answer the criticism that The Navigators were not interested in mass evangelism. In fact, with foresight that hardly showed indifference to mass evangelism, Daws had long since mapped out a plan for following up inquirers from evangelistic meetings and was ready to tackle it — though he approached the campaigns as an amateur. "I have tried to tell Billy and the others this is really a new field to me but they just laugh," Daws wrote the staff after his first campaign in Shreveport, Louisiana.

He had called Rosenberger to join him, sending Navigator Joe Noble to replace him at Northwestern Schools. Daws assembled a small follow-up team and found housing for them with local Christians. He then concentrated on training those who would care for the new Christians after the crusade was over. He held no illusions about the task, for his experience in getting lay people to work in evangelistic meetings had shown that not one in ten could use his Bible to lead another to Christ, much less follow him up. Leading Shreveport laymen met with him each morning for follow-up instruction, the women in afternoon sessions. Pastors met twice a week for counselor and follow-up training, some declaring afterward that the classes changed their entire ministry. Lay church leaders undertook soulwinning with new enthusiasm, delighted to see scores of people each week from the Graham meetings uniting with their churches.

A half-dozen or more Navigators worked in each crusade, some becoming regulars, such as Sanny, Dawson's deputy in this as in the Navigator work. Riggs helped in various cities, transferring from Seattle to open a Nav area in Fort Worth six months after the crusade. From each city the follow-up team sent detailed reports home, involving the staff deeply in prayer for the crusaders.

Daws wrote that Graham was "truly a man of *God*. I marvel at his poise, his growth, his humility, his level-headedness, his flexibility and his eagerness to find the right way to do things in order to have a conscience void of offense toward *God* and toward men." He also wrote the staff glowing descriptions of each team member and his ministry — Cliff Barrows, Grady Wilson, Jerry Beavan, Bev Shea, Tedd Smith, Paul Mickelson, Willis Haymaker. "I love every one of these people, have confidence in them and consider myself most fortunate to be working with them."

After Shreveport came a Memphis crusade in May, Seattle in August, Hollywood in September, and Greensboro, North Carolina, in October. Dawson worked out procedures to give each inquirer a trained counselor of the same sex and age group who could see that his decision was clear, give encouragement and help in Bible study, and get him into a local church. Observing problems in the system led to solutions at the next crusade until the counseling-follow-up program was fairly complete.

A series of classes before the crusade taught prospective

counselors to determine an inquirer's need and meet it from the Word of God, then leave an accurate record of the decision. Counselors were selected individually if they qualified and were issued badges authorizing them to serve.* After praying with the inquirer and starting him on the *B Rations*, the counselor introduced him to an advisor, usually a pastor, who asked what decision he had made. This allowed him to give his first testimony and get further help on the spot if his decision was not clear. The advisor system, originated in Dr. Jack Mitchell's counselor training in the Portland crusade, helped the counselor do a thorough job and gave the inquirer extra support.

In Seattle, Daws added young women to the follow-up team to help in the office and work with women counselors and inquirers. By mid-year Daws and his staff had designed an *Introductory Bible Study* based on The Wheel for inquirers to use along with the *B Rations* memory work. Tested and revised for later crusades, the IBS was much in demand for the help it gave new Christians. Richard Halverson of Hollywood Presbyterian Church was among the pastors who used the IBS in special series of classes for church members.

Beginning that first year, an inquirer's decision card was referred to the church of his choice for pastoral contact and follow-up. Volunteers processed cards late into the night, getting them to the pastor's desk within forty-eight hours of the decision. Counselors were asked to telephone or visit those they counseled and ease their transition to the new way of life. The follow-up office arranged meetings for special groups of new Christians, provided Bible study material to those requesting it, and served as a link between inquirers and churches.

Daws gave his best efforts to ensure that every person who came forward was individually shepherded to clear understanding of his faith in Christ through the Word. Beyond this, he was elated to see progress in pursuing his long-range concerns. Perhaps most rewarding was training lay Christians who learned by "bunting in" their first soul in the counseling room that God

---

*This led to a ludicrous *faux pas* when a follow-up team member questioned the presence in the counseling room of a voluble woman wearing a flamboyant hat and pounds of jewelry, only to find the badgeless counselor was the revered Dr. Henrietta Mears of Hollywood.

could use them after all, learned how to study and memorize Scripture and see it make a permanent difference in their lives.

Daws's rule of life to seek to invest in every person who crossed his path found good outlet in the crusades. He often wrote to share with his gang the tremendous qualities and possibilities he saw in some new friend. He watched always, and taught his men to watch, for potential Timothys in whom to invest in depth, establishing that relationship of spiritual building and impartation of life which had become the cornerstone of his ministry philosophy. His own Shreveport Timothy was a businessman, Dan Piatt, who took hold and began to grow as if force-fed, dogging Dawson's steps everywhere to learn more.

Not least of Dawson's rewards was the blessing received by young pastors like the Reverend Ken Smith of Pittsburgh. Attending early morning follow-up instruction meetings, Smith confessed Dawson's presentation of The Wheel and the how of devotional life spoke to his personal need. "Something I had never heard before," he said. "It began to get through to me that ministry depended upon life. I hadn't seen this as a *principle*. I wanted an effective ministry and had prayed for three years the Lord would show me how to lead someone to Christ.

"I knew Daws was giving the logical application of the inspiration of the Bible. We hold the Bible to be the only infallible rule of faith and life. Daws was the first to show me the two embraced as a principle. From then on my problem was not theological but applying what I knew. My devotional life began to have meaning. I began to see God do what He said He would do."

Work in the crusades produced "accelerated growth for our men under proper conditions, opportunity to work together, pray together, and be under direct supervision," Daws wrote. They could learn valuable lessons handling the myriad details of chairs, traffic, counselor classes, and materials, speaking to groups, dealing with problems of spiritual birth and growth — a range of activity broad enough to reveal a man's strengths and weaknesses and guide in giving him further responsibility. Daws often corrected them in direct, blunt terms with the rest of the follow-up team present. From this crucible some came forth as burnished gold and others did not emerge at all. Working with Graham, Daws assured his staff, was a "great and effectual door to . . . broaden our own vision, teach us new lessons, enable us to supply ideas to churches and groups for growth and follow-up . . . a shot of spiritual adrenalin along lines so much upon our hearts, including evangelism in every phase."

As Daws designed improvements in procedures, he depended on Sanny to implement them. During the Chattanooga crusade Sanny remarked, "Daws, it's easy to lose the vision of training one man when you're involved with details of a crusade like this."

With calculated shock effect, Dawson told the man who had worked at his side twelve years, "Sanny, I wonder if you really have this vision to the point that it's burning in your heart and occupies your thoughts morning, noon, and night."

Daws was delighted to see the joy and personal satisfaction the Graham Team and wives found in memorizing Scripture and counseling inquirers. Even Billy carried the Nav memory pack in his pocket and labored valiantly to quote portions of the TMS word perfectly — an example Daws was glad to use in goading others to memorize.

Weeks before a crusade Graham and Dawson met with pastors of cooperating churches to outline plans and present the counselor training and follow-up phases. Daws heard the evangelist declare that "decision is 5 percent, following through on the decision is 95 percent," and that "there is no such thing as mass evangelism; we bring people under the sound of the Gospel and to a place of decision. The real evangelism takes place in the inquiry room." Daws knew Billy, unfailingly gracious, was quick to give credit to others. Yet he was thankful for this powerful endorsement of the importance of follow-up to Christian leaders across the country. And for the way God meshed the person-to-person emphasis with crusade evangelism. "It is amazing to see how the *Lord* took us, so keen and bent on individual contact," he wrote, "and threw us into the largest mass effort in the States today and caused it to fit in perfectly."

The two ministries obviously contributed to each other. History would judge the far-reaching effect of the alliance on the church at large — perhaps a watershed — but surely larger than either dreamed at the moment. For in city after city as hundreds, then thousands of counselors were trained, spiritually dormant laymen and women began to realize their potential for bearing fruit for God. Other evangelists and churches adopted follow-up systems in their campaigns. Follow-up became a household word in evangelical Christendom.

Daws began to shift to Sanny's broad shoulders more responsibility, trailed at an unsafe distance by authority. Sanny coped with it by much prayer, careful organization, and endless patience, running interference for Dawson and many of the Nav staff. The two were often at the same crusade, seldom at Nav headquarters at the same time. Coordinating both ministries was difficult as Daws insisted on making all decisions personally, down to the color of paint for storage shelves and the choice of paper and ink for every printing job. The remarkable bond of love and loyalty among the Nav staff allowed for such idiosyncrasies, but they exacted a toll in physical and emotional strength, demanding long hours and flexibility from everyone.

Sanny understood his position as executive officer for an exceptional man of God and devoted his considerable faith and capacity, unnoticed only because he stood in Dawson's shadow, to doing the most thorough and competent job possible. Without fanfare he managed the successful 1951 finance drive to "Anchor Home Base," making possible the purchase of the new office building and 509. During the school year he again headed the UCLA Project with good response from the collegians enrolled.

It was also Dawson's busiest year, involving him in a wide spectrum of concerns with no slacking of intensity toward any; the chart showing hours his children spent in piano practice was as absorbing as the chart of Bible study enrollments and evangelism by students in Formosa.

He had shared with the 100 contacts at seminar the goal to plant Navigators in 200 countries, "every nation of the world," a goal he saw inching toward reality one country at a time. Robertson was now in Tokyo, where an initial supply of 10,000 Japanese Bible studies was in the hands of seekers, mainly from Morken's YFC evangelism. In July Daws dispatched Gene and Dean Denler, just graduated from Northwestern

Schools, to Formosa on the first leg of a round-the-world musical evangelistic tour sponsored by Graham. But when ten weeks of evangelism brought 10,000 decisions for Christ, they asked permission to stay on the island and follow them up rather than go on with the tour. Korean War servicemen contact combined with civilian and crusade use swelled the demand for Nav memory and Bible study materials. Enrollments in the TMS reached toward 9000 annually. Boardman was sent from headquarters staff to direct a service center in Yokosuka, while George Bostrom from the crusade follow-up team went to assist Robertson in Tokyo.

As if trying to perfect his juggling act, Daws during the first year of Graham crusading also stepped up his help to other works. Jim Vaus, finally converted in the 1949 Graham meetings, was out in evangelism with Nav men assigned to help him. Sharing Jim's interest in winning his former boss, underworld figure Mickey Cohen, Daws once entertained him at dinner at 509. He gave Dick Hillis's new Formosa Gospel Crusade office space in the Nav building and took its first secretary into the 509 family as he had done for MAF. As the Hollywood crusade ended, Dawson's calendar included time with Bill Bright to help with formative stages of Campus Crusade for Christ; with Bob Finley launching a ministry with international students; with Young Life's Jim Rayburn; with Jack Wyrtzen; speaking to an Inter-Varsity group at USC; speaking at Biola; an executive committee meeting for Los Angeles YFC; and board meetings with MAF and Wycliffe. Then he was off to meet Graham in Houston and then to look in on the start of the Greensboro crusade and speak to pastors.

Finding Greensboro follow-up preparations expertly managed by Sanny and his Nav team of seven, with instruction classes being taught in the churches, Daws was delighted and a little sad to know they had done it all without him. "It was great to be in Greensboro," he wrote the staff. "I had a very strange feeling there, however, for . . . I felt about as necessary as an appendix. They were gracious to say it was nice to have me around. . . ." But he assured them it was a goal fulfilled to see his men taking over. *Never do anything someone else can or will do when there is so much others cannot or will not do.* He could now confidently leave most of the crusading to Lorne Sanny and the men and women he would train.

The Greensboro follow-up office remained open three months after the crusade at the local committee's request with Bill Michel, just graduated from Fuller Seminary, in charge. Washington, D.C. churches also asked that the office there stay open. Pastors met to work out ways to nurture new converts sent to them and to keep lay members active in winning and helping spiritual babes of their own. Similar things were done in Pittsburgh, Detroit, and other cities with good effect. Riggs's move to Fort Worth for Nav student ministry was timed also to permit work with churches absorbing converts from the earlier Graham crusade and help in crusades planned for the South and Southwest. Rosenberger likewise transferred to Washington to reopen a Nav East Coast work with collegians, servicemen, and professional men and periodically help with crusades in the East.

Counselor training and follow-up for mass evangelism now seemed firmly established; normal demand should ensure its continuance and wider use. Thousands of babes in Christ were getting important first help in the new life and being channeled into the local church. But more significant to the Great Commission, thousands of church people were being awakened and trained as laborers in God's harvest.

"Everybody's face looks sad. I've been realizing how little the future holds for these precious souls. Oh, we've got to get to them with the message of God's love. How could Christians have so loused up the job!" Dawson's sudden outburst as he wrote Lila from Zurich summed up his burden for the lost and joyless people and the compulsive sense of his mission. Europe, possessor of the Light for nineteen centuries, seemed least excusable for letting it flicker to its present feeble glow. If a handful in each generation had obeyed Paul's command to Timothy, Europe would have been a citadel of missionary strength and would have reached the world.

Graham had encouraged him to make this trip — had at first planned to go himself to enlarge his world vision, observe needs, and minister to Christian workers and missionaries. Leaving in February 1952 at the end of the Washington crusade, Daws purposed to strengthen the hands of his men in Europe and the Orient and survey new territory — including part of Africa. He would also meet Christian leaders on Graham's behalf to discuss possible future crusades. He shrank from the thought of nearly four months of travel, but with Isaiah 54:2, 3 ringing in his ears he could go in the Lord's strength, sharing with the gang the challenge to "ask big."

The night before he left Graham presented him with a suit-case, asking the crusade audience to come up afterward and fill it with money for the trip. They did — generously — many of them convinced by attending follow-up instruction classes that these truths were needed in other countries.

He landed in Europe sick; reaction to the shots, he reasoned, and accumulated weariness. Unable to eat or sleep well and too weak to stay up, he crept off to a corner of Switzerland to rest, and in two or three days had recovered his strength.

"Oh it feels so wonderful to feel good!" he wrote. "More than invigorating my body the Lord has done so to my soul. Have read Matthew, Mark, Luke and John and some of the Psalms. . . . It has been many years since I have thus devoured the Word by the hours and I'm amazed at the results to my thinking, vision, planning, outlook. How could one become so busy? I trust this is just the beginning of new power and clarity of vision."

Later from Manchester: "I'm as far as Galatians and watching for moments to get in a few more chapters. Of course I stop to make notes and cross references and meditate. It's just great." He asked that a book be sent airmail — Edman's *Light in Dark Ages*. It would stimulate his vision for Europe and he would leave it with Rohrer. When it came, however, it took second place to his New Testament reading, now in Hebrews 11. "Boy, is it ever thrilling. Last night I couldn't lay my Bible down until nearly one-thirty."

He wanted to get more days alone with the Lord, and his crew must do it. "How about each of you getting off alone for *a day each month*. Take a lunch, have a whole day of prayer, read a challenging book and the Word. You could keep a journal of things the Lord showed you or laid on your hearts. When I'm back we could get together and share these."

His own sharing of the trip was most competent. He sent vivid descriptions of events and feelings by swift, fluid handwriting or the typewriter of a willing scribe, in almost daily letters headed "Dearly beloved Lila and those my helpers in Christ Jesus" or "Dear Lila and Crew," enclosing an occasional love note for Lila.

He rejoiced to find the Europe Navigators under way, piloted by Dave Rohrer, a wise man for one so young in Christ. Rohrer accompanied him through Europe and profited from hearing the 2:2 message reemphasized. He admitted a need "to have our sights pointed again toward the goal of reaching the individual man." As usual, Daws was intrigued by individuals he discovered. Daws concluded that one amazing twenty-year-old Norwegian who spent hours a day in the Word on his own could well be a Timothy, Tychicus, or Aristarchus. He would gladly spend hours with such men — yet give a curt rebuff to others who asked for time, hoping to shock them into action.

"I've *got* to see you," a GI said after a servicemen's meeting in Frankfurt. "Are you in the Book?" Daws asked. "No." "Did you ever spend an hour with Bob Hopkins here?" "Yes." "Did he tell you to get into the Book?" "Yes." Then the verdict: "You don't need to see me. You need to start crawling."

England was pure joy — many hours with Bill and Jeanette Fletcher, Joe and Marie Simmons, and a core group of disciples. Joe's planned emigration to New Zealand would mean a good start for the Nav ministry there, Daws felt, and Joe could in time branch out to Australia.

Norway was new territory, with large turnouts for Daws's meetings — up to a thousand — probably because they had heard of his link with Graham. His enthusiastic interpreter was Hubert Mitchell's wife Rachel, home from India. Rachel was godsent; one who knew and believed in his message made all the difference. He noticed the contrast when a stranger interpreted for him. "I cannot describe the agony of my soul and brain," he wrote from another city, "when I drop in among new people of a different culture and in one hour try to put over eternal truths through the voice and words of another man.

Of all tasks God has given me this is hardest, from which I find greatest temptation to run. Three more months of this. . . ."

A group of ministers met with him to ask about getting Graham to Norway, their desire whetted by hearing of the thorough follow-up program. He found similar interest by Christian leaders in other cities, from London on. The follow-up element removed widely held honest doubts about sponsoring a city-wide evangelistic campaign, but many were unaware of other facets of revival. Cooperation of various denominations in a city was a strange idea. And the vital place of prayer was often ignored. In a city where a revival twenty years earlier had increased one church's membership 600 percent, they pled for another revival.

"From what I have heard," Daws wrote, "they are oblivious of approaching revival from the standpoint of 2 Chronicles 7:14. Tonight when the pastor came by to say howdy, he joined us for ice cream. Then we asked him to the room to pray but he said he'd had a busy day and was too tired. Yet this man is among those most urgently pleading with God for revival."

At the Paris Nav Home a conference with staff and key people from six countries sent Daws's spirits soaring. Here in Paris just over two years ago he had been moved to get Rohrer to Europe; now work had begun in several countries. As young Europeans were recruited, they could be brought to Bob Evans's EBI, where Nav men now taught some courses. The TMS was ready in three languages besides English. There was a feeling much would be happening in Europe.

One Paris conferee observed the spirit of the group. "The love and consideration for one another among the Navs had made an indelible impression," she wrote. "You know, something of the spirit of the Lord Jesus when He said, 'I came not to be ministered unto, but to minister.' This has spoken to my heart."

With the instinct of God's recruiting officer, Daws singled out two young Frenchmen at the conference. "You two are all France needs," he declared, "and if you won't do the job, we'll ask for other young men who will." Before he left, they responded, "We're with you." He wrote, "If ever eternal history has been made in the Navs it has been in Europe these last weeks."

Holland, Belgium, and Italy held further challenge. It was painful to see so many urgent slots for Nav men with so few ready to send. In Naples Daws found Floyd Robertson still in the Navy and spoke to the Christian Activities Committee, some thirty missionaries and servicemen, at Floyd's apartment on the familiar themes of devotional life and investing in one man. When the group asked for a Navigator to direct a servicemen's center in Naples, Dawson's first choice was Dan Piatt, the Shreveport businessman who had dropped everything to join the follow-up team in Washington. Piatt accepted the call and with his Timothy, Pete George of Texas, arrived in Naples by June. Daws commissioned him to add to his work with U.S. servicemen some "contact with Italians and begin the slow process of producing reproducers."

In Switzerland with a few days to rest and ski, Daws was again absorbed in the Word, thinking, praying over ideas that seemed too big. Yet . . . "I think of the power of the Lord, the greatness of the task, the clearness of His leading, the promises He has given, the precious band of colaborers, of Billy's eagerness to tackle big things, and I am encouraged. Pray that impressions from Him may be lasting, His orders understood and carried out to the letter." He spoke of ideas for crusade follow-up by churches and for training men in Nav principles, which he would discuss with Rohrer and Robertson and share at staff conference. But lest the gang sit back and wait for July he cautioned, "Meantime, let us hope and pray none of you people will let your brain cells lie dormant on these important subjects."

His compulsion to train, often by sharing what he himself was learning, was not hindered by being an ocean away. He wrote from Frankfurt how Jerry Beavan's diligence in correspondence challenged him. Beavan, in Europe on Graham Team business, used spare moments to write cards to friends. "Remember, gang," Daws relayed the challenge, "emotion is no substitute for action. Every time we are stirred to do a job and fail to follow through, we not only immediately fail, but lessen our drive and weaken our prayers of resolution. I guess you all know 2 Cor. 8:11, *Now therefore perform the doing of it; that as there was a readiness to will, so there may be a performance also out of that which ye have.*"

He also charged one of the staff to be observant: "I trust the Lord is giving you wide open eyes to see those extra little things that need to be observed or done or thought about. I believe even the strongest of the Lord's servants lose much precious time because they have not disciplined their minds to action and trained themselves to be observant in moments when they do not sense they need to be. Along with this, I am 100 percent in favor of recreation and relaxation that entirely dissociates one from his regular work."

Nor did distance prevent his slight annoyance at his staff's failures. He misplaced his passport and later retrieved it at the Manchester airport. "Have you stopped praying, you people, about those little things?" he complained.

*   *   *   *

Tracing his Lord's footsteps through places he had read about for twenty-six years — the Mount of Olives, Gethsemane, up Calvary's hill — Daws could not describe his emotions. "I expect to walk through these places about every day," he wrote from Jerusalem, "read and pray and *listen*." In this land where the Son of God gave His life a ransom for every person, he saw hundreds who never heard, "who have no idea the predicament they're in or the marvelous means of escape which came through The Great Event.

"Sin abounds on every hand. Stealing, cheating, lying. Hatred and bitterness are on faces. Such bitterness from both sides (Arab and Jew) is seldom seen the world over. . . . I've given a coin here and there to blind beggars along the streets where He saw the blind. Would I love to take them by the hand and lift them up."

His heart bled for a group of people, old and poor, who probably spent their life savings on this Easter pilgrimage. "They're here to get that final touch at the place where Christ died. Kiss statue's feet and stand in awe as though awaiting a miracle. Kids, we've got the truth, the light to dispel this darkness. We've got to get it *out, out, OUT*." Local workers held little hope. "Older missionaries here and in Lebanon and Syria have a gloomy outlook. They don't expect anything in their lifetime, feel they're laying groundwork for the next generation. The idea doesn't hold water. Bill Antablin, teaching at the university in Beirut, has hope and feels Navs have the best approach. We may send a man to Beirut or Jerusalem."

The thrill of setting foot on a new continent was all the greater because it was Africa. For years Daws had looked forward to this. Now that he stood on Egyptian soil he was as unaware of what lay ahead as Joseph had been when he arrived with the Midianite caravan, but as sure that God had purposed it and "meant it unto good." In conditions not as bizarre as Joseph's but seeming almost as futile, he traveled the length of the continent and left twenty-five days later with little guidance for the next step but certain that God had worked.

In Cairo as in other key cities — Frankfurt, Athens, and Hong Kong yet ahead — he looked up contacts referred by International Christian Leadership, a Washington group ministering to officials and prominent leaders. Two such men here were eager to learn about Navigators and enroll in the TMS. While in Cairo Daws worked out the idea for a new memory pack, one urged by Miner Stearns of Belgian Gospel Mission to bridge the gap between the *B Rations* and TMS. The eight-verse packet would be twice the size of the *B Rations* and cover truths a young believer needed most.

In Tanganyika Dick Hightower and another missionary were ready to initiate Dawson to the African bush. They made a four-day safari in the worst rainy season that nearly marooned them behind several swollen rivers. Then in Johannesburg Daws found arrangements for his time had broken down completely. He gamely admitted in a letter that "our old standby Romans 8:28 is working full speed. I keep wondering what I am doing way down here." The ultimate snafu was an airlines' failure to book his flight out, so the weekly flight to India took off without him. This meant missing a long-planned meeting with some 700 missionaries in South India.

Acknowledging his time was in God's hands, he stayed on to discover the extra days here were worth the whole trip. South Africa YFC leader Denis Clark lined up meetings almost non-stop with groups of Christians. "In all my travels I've not talked to a gang more open-hearted, eager to learn," Daws wrote. "I couldn't help feeling this is why I came to Africa and but for a missed plane I'd have missed it." This surprise blessing and those yet to come more than offset his feeling after the Middle East lap: "I keep hoping this is my last trip, but who but God knows that I may have to do a lot more."

"I've really come to love this great country," he wrote of Africa. "It's indeed fabulous; it's made a lifelong impression upon me." He purposed to learn more about places, their history and people. "When I see how much there is to learn, how little I know after 46 years, it frightens me a little when I think of the kind of men we need. Oh for a large band of spiritual Calebs, men like Moses and Paul and David. 'Who is sufficient for these things?' *He* is!"

Daws reached India sick and exhausted, having battled transportation problems and climate changes for several sleepless days and nights. But at Landour his spirits rose as he went into another marathon of meetings with 225 missionaries. He was held together physically by their prayer. The five YFC men planning follow-up for all India felt his visit was most opportune, and he arranged on the spot for them to begin distributing Nav materials from Bombay. "This four days in India was as strategic as South Africa," he said. "The roughest trip yet but the most blessed."

He found Taipeh a spiritual boom town. Here only eighteen months earlier he had pondered how to follow up thousands whose decision cards were already cold and thousands yet unreached. Hillis had combined his efforts with other missions to reach the entire island. Sparks directed sixteen workers handling correspondence courses from a follow-up office impressively named Bible Investigation Training School, with 28,000 enrollees. The Denler twins were busy teaching follow-up classes and training men. "We've decided to cancel Denlers' world tickets and leave them here another year," Daws wrote. "Doug and the Denlers have been mightily used of God, have won hearts and grown tremendously and are still the humble, yielded men we all have known.

"I'm talking to the boys about how to screen out and find their gems and polish. Dick Hillis also has chosen a man with whom to spend two hours a week in the Word. Imagine it — 28,000 have finished the first lesson and asked for more. In a sense this whole thing is backward. Jesus prepared the 12, the 70, the 120 before 5000 came. Is His strategy to be overlooked or forgotten or improved upon? He has the masses on His heart more than we." Daws exhorted his Nav men to use balance, doing evangelism while they trained individuals, and Hillis and his men to do man-to-man training along with their evangelism.

Wide grins on the faces of Robertson, Boardman, Bostrom, and Morken greeted Daws at Tokyo's airport. Morken's YFC evangelism was garnering many seekers and some 5000 had completed one of his Bible studies. The studies and Japanese TMS were handled by the Nav follow-up office from head-quarters shared with YFC downtown. The Nav men had gone out under Youth For Christ's name and sponsorship.

It was great to be in another country where work was under way. "What marvelous attitudes these men have," Daws wrote. "What a joy to work with them. Like those in Europe and Formosa, they needed their sights corrected and were happy to get down to facts, exhortations and charging. But they're doing a terrific job." He found Robertson had saved problems and plans to discuss in person. "Lots of important ground is being covered, policy made, areas surveyed, manpower needs reviewed and no doubt Navigator history is in the making. The fellows have big plans for the Orient which will involve sending more Navs."

After Daws spoke to a servicemen's rally in Yokosuka, Baptist missionary Joe Gooden appealed for financial support for a Navigator to help Boardman in the new servicemen's center. The response was enough to provide for two men — one for servicemen's work, the other to help in Japanese follow-up. Daws wrote, "It looks like the Orient will get four or five men before the year is over. Boy what days to be serving our King, the King of Kings." He would have to conclude later that in his zeal he sent some men overseas before they were ready.

*   *   *   *

It was a proud moment for Daws at staff conference when he presented six men selected to go overseas as Nav representatives. Besides the two promised for Japan, there were men for Hong Kong, Cyprus, Formosa, and India, with leeway for the Lord to change their direction. This He did as Doug Cozart was refused a visa for India and went on to fruitful ministry in Korea, first in follow-up for YFC, Pocket Testament League, and Hillis's Orient Crusades, later for Bob Pierce's World Vision. He found great opportunity for evangelism in schools and among refugees, the ROK army, and Red Chinese prisoners of war. Thousands of POWs did the Bible studies, which were shuttled by air freight to the Formosa follow-up office for checking. A spectacular sequel to the Chinese POW ministry was that of the 14,000 who later chose repatriation to Formosa rather than the mainland, 10,600 had found Christ in Korean POW camps and been followed up by OC-Navigator Bible courses.

Warren Myers, in charge of a Nav study program at First Presbyterian Church of Berkeley, was posted to Hong Kong; Jake Combs, then in Washington, D.C., to Formosa; Waldron Scott, Minneapolis area key man, to teach at American Academy in Cyprus and disciple Greek, Turkish, and Armenian high schoolers.

Overseas routes would be heavily traveled in later years. But for Daws no later appointments would match the thrill of Sending the Six this fall of 1952. He knew now the Navigator mission of building foundations of generations must be undertaken by men trained and sent by The Navigators with no strings attached.

W hile Daws was in Africa, an urgent appeal had come from evangelist Edwin Orr in Brazil to "send a Navigator leader or, better still, come down yourself." Orr saw Brazil, called by some the world's greatest mission field, verging on revival. Thousands were coming to Christ in united campaigns; churches were filled. But the great weakness was follow-up, he said, and Christians were not in the Word — strong reasons for The Navigators to come. His plea added weight to Daws's burden to get a work started in Latin America, as did the knowledge that multiplication, slow in beginning stages, would be much set back by loss of the first year. So in October, scarcely reacquainted with his family after the world trip, he headed south for seven weeks to survey the land.

Coincidentally, Clyde Taylor of Evangelical Foreign Missions Association planned a South American trip, and they would travel together, their schedules in some countries matching that of mission executive John Savage of England. This added dimension of fellowship greatly enriched the trip.

"My son, wife, and daughter were counselors in the D.C. crusade and they warned me about you. They *said* you'd have me doing the memory work," Taylor said, shuffling his TMS cards. "But this stuff really gets in your blood, doesn't it?"

The tour cemented their friendship, each coming to appreciate the other's life and vision. Taylor said he got so sold on the Nav program he had to preach Trotman's message along with his own in two countries where Daws was not with him.

Missionaries and national Christians immediately responded to the concepts of follow-up — though Taylor was unable to find a Spanish word for it — and one-to-one training of Christians in the Word. Here and there a sparkling Christian showed almost pathetic eagerness to start now. In Chile, Daws found no one working among the 12,000 university students in Santiago. One mission with some forty workers scattered through rural areas had not considered that using their resources to evangelize and disciple literate collegians could give them a pool of potential new laborers for work in the countryside. Daws's strong suggestion that they change their strategy was humbly accepted by the mission's leaders.

Daws spent more than a week in Peru seeing his Wycliffe translators in action and listening to their concerns. Giving them his message on the three phases of ministry — Bible translation, evangelism, and making disciples — he proposed they engage in phases two and three without losing sight of their own job of translation by finding and training one person, perhaps their translation helper. As one of Wycliffe's official family, Dawson went by mission plane to visit the Piro tribe, where a polite exchange of gifts left a Piro wearing his shirt and Daws carrying away a pottery vessel. He found it a most practical gift when two lady passengers on the trip back were seized with airsickness.

Finding former Navigators John Prince, Eldon Durant, Ken Watters, and others on missionary duty was a special treat. Daws was touched to hear that Prince, unable to get the language, was about to be sent home when the mission gave him another chance on an island where three missionaries had failed to establish a work. Not knowing his limitations, Prince had turned to and built several flourishing congregations. "He proves 1 Corinthians 1 better than anyone I've ever seen," Daws wrote.

In Quito Daws was surprised to see on his reception committee George Sanchez, briefly a high school Dunamis clubber in the forties. Dawson's time there awakened Sanchez to his need to get the basics into his life and to invest in men along with his missionary radio work at HCJB. He began at once to train three young Ecuadorians. In an unusual step, Daws told George and Florine he felt they would some day serve with The Navigators.

In three countries Daws asked Christian leaders to serve on advisory committees for The Navigators. The Nav ministry would be heartily welcomed in South America partly, he thought, because word had spread of the work in Europe, in the Orient, and in the States with Billy Graham and such groups as Campus Crusade and Youth For Christ. The time was ripe to send three Navigators: one to Brazil, one for the three southernmost countries, and one for the northwest. "I know you will be praying," he wrote the staff, "that those He has foreordained to pioneer will be chosen and on their way as quickly as possible. A year saved now getting established on this fabulous and spiritually hungry continent will mean much later on — or could mean the difference between open and closed doors."

But the year would pass, and other years, and he would never see this dream fulfilled.

Summer training seminars had grown shorter by about a week each year since 1949. At Young Life's Star Ranch in Colorado space limitation to 100 people meant holding two 1953 seminars, each two weeks long. The thought of covering all necessary ground in the brief training periods was only one of the pressures Dawson faced as his beloved gang assembled from across the U.S. He had asked the staff — especially those overseas — to suggest subjects they felt were neglected in their own training; the resultant list was long, and he must select. Manpower needs had snowballed the past year — not only those he saw in South America, but in the Orient and Europe, in Graham crusades, in Campus Crusade's college outreach, and as support personnel in U.S. areas. Girls workers were needed both in Nav areas and in the crusades.

Here at seminar was a select corps whose élan reflected his own. He was impressed by their unity and love in a family tie that stretched across the world, and their dedication to the Lord. He needed no proof that these top young men and women were ready to give their all in any way God led. The warning jokingly circulated was to come to seminar "with your heart open and your bags packed."

A few were ready for independent responsibility, and Daws could think of several places for each man. Others were in stages of preparation, but a shortage of top leadership to finish their training was a problem. Sanny was doing three jobs: carrying the crusade ministry, raising funds for a new head-quarters property, and preparing to make a ministry trip to Costa Rica. Sargent was rapidly growing into responsibility at headquarters, taking much of the load off Sanny. Rohrer, Robertson, and Sparks were overseas, while Rosenberger was in D.C., seemingly drawn more into youth evangelism than train-ing men as he had done so well before. Daws had been traveling more than ever and would spend much time in crusades. It frustrated him to see this wave of keen young leadership coming up, men with several hundred to several thousand verses, and be unable to groom and develop them further. An alternative was to send them to assist overseas and U.S. leaders and train on the job. It was, Daws felt, a risk worth taking.

Perhaps to give them a personal prayer list, Daws spoke on qualities God's man most needed. Among them were drive, the will to think and to set the pace, a strong devotional life, a heart for evangelism, and know-how to follow up a new Christian. God's man would need balance, an interest in other works, and a good report of the brethren. High standards — but weighed against causes of first-term missionary failure and against things Daws knew of which had made dropouts of men, they were crucial.

While naming strict requirements for a Nav representative, Daws reminded the group in the rustic Star Ranch meeting hall that *every* person could reach and train one disciple. He challenged them to believe God and use His gifts to the utmost.

"Our ultimate goal is to fulfill Christ's last command: preach the Gospel to every creature and teach them to observe all He told the Twelve. Ye shall be witnesses *both* in Jerusalem *and* in Judea *and* Samaria *and* uttermost part. Here we have key contacts in a few places in the U.S. Last year when we marked on the map those who had learned 100 or 500 verses or more, pins were clustered in about five states. I looked at the other states and thought of all the young people, intelligent and all-out for Christ, who have the Gospel but that second part of the Great Commission has not come to them: *teaching them to observe all things.* Wouldn't it be wonderful if we could spot them all over the U.S. I'm thinking of seven places I could send one man. Wherever the Lord leads him, he will touch a life who will touch a life, and in two or three years 150 kids will be at an area conference and know the thrill of hiding God's Word in their hearts."

He reviewed the moves into China, Formosa, Europe, Japan, the calls from other works, and the need for men in South America. "Will you pick up the burden of every major country in the world? I hope you have a world map where you can see it at least once a day and get on your heart what's on His heart. In many countries people burn little candles and worship stones. The Gospel brings light to this darkness. People have gone and preached the Gospel but have not taught them how to dig into the Word and do all He told the disciples to do, so there's a vacuum. The need is desperate. Oh, we need the blessing of God to keep from making mistakes. We need financial provision. We need manpower and womanpower. Oh, begin to pray as you have never prayed before."

Daws gave a series on Navigator history, hoping a review of his past mistakes and successes, and the principles involved, would arm his listeners with material for self-development. He added some hard-hitting messages from the first chapters of Deuteronomy on commands to "go up and possess" the land and to hold the ground gained "by little and little" (Deut. 7:22).

The days filled with interviews, as many as seventeen in a day planning and praying with Dawson about possible assignments. Tension built as decisions were kept secret so that he could be first to announce them. By the last day, suspense crackled in the air. Savoring his role as commanding general of a highly motivated army eager to go anywhere he ordered, Daws read the names of "those whose status is changed or who are being moved to new areas." There were no men for Africa or South America but a few new assignments and many for on-job training in established areas.

In the hearts of two or three at seminar, however, was a growing rebellion against Dawson's leadership as dictatorial, a trait he would have stoutly denied, pointing to his respect for each person's wishes and leading from the Lord wherever they differed from his own. But the intensity of his burden and conviction and the velocity of his impact on those around him doubtless alienated some and stepped on toes as in earlier years. His deputy Sanny understood this ego-bruising tendency and had no problem with it, though he frequently administered first aid to the hurts of those who did.

Navigator activities that year were as diverse as a circus, with some performers in double roles and Daws vigorously directing the action in all three rings. If thoughts of his own mortality intruded, he dismissed them. He would prepare — sometime — to turn the job of world conquest over to others, but for now the tight-rope balancing act was too fascinating. Here was Robertson overseeing work in six countries; Cozart had a booming ministry in Korea; Sparks reported 8000 decisions for Christ in a single month in Formosa, 6000 of them from the witness of the students. Gene Denler was doing follow-up work for Hillis in the Philippines; Myers was under way in Hong Kong; Boardman was in Okinawa. In Europe, Dan Piatt had answered the call to begin work in Holland. Work in France,

Germany, and England progressed, and Simmons was ready to start in New Zealand. Waldron Scott had some young disciples in Cyprus.

Across the U.S., men in a dozen Nav area headquarters ministered on military bases and college campuses; there were six Graham crusades a year, more service centers manned and personnel loaned to other works. The Los Angeles office produced more Bible study materials than ever and enrolled 1000 people each month in the TMS. If Daws had not already seen the need for a training center for the growing cadre of Nav workers, the 1953 seminar and the annual Nav conference with 350 eager young contacts at Forest Home would have proved it.

The ideal arrangement would be a place in the heart of the U.S. which could serve as headquarters, manpower training center, and year-round conference grounds. What better place for the gang than the healthful Colorado high country Daws had come to love from spending time at Young Life's Star and Frontier ranches? "Keep an eye out for a ranch for us, will you?" he asked his friend Jim Rayburn. It would be good to be neighbors with Young Life.

Before Daws left for Latin America in October 1952, Rayburn had asked him to come to Colorado to see a property. It looked good. The Navigator board and the businessmen approved, and Sanny was charged to raise funds for the project, preferably from sources not already supporting the ministry. Bill Bright, an expert on ranches, was enthusiastic. If Navigators moved to Colorado, he would consider moving Campus Crusade there. But when the $5000 option payment was not on hand in time, Daws took it as a caution light from the Lord. Funds had still not come in by February. He asked the staff to pray God would give them Pine Valley or a place as good or better.

Late in February Dawson was to meet with pastors in three crusade cities and stopped in Colorado to see how Pine Valley looked in winter. Realtor Guss Hill asked him to look at an estate he had in mind for Billy Graham as the site for a future academy. Glen Eyrie, a 700-acre valley of incredible natural beauty with a score of buildings, secluded yet nearer the post office than twenty-eight-acre Pine Valley, sent Daws into flights of description Graham could scarce believe.

"If you don't get Glen Eyrie," Daws enthused, "The Navigators want it." Back in Los Angeles he pictured this Garden of Eden. "Why gang, I'd rather pay *half a million* for Glen Eyrie than the $212,000 they asked for Pine Valley. And the owner is letting us have it for $300,000 since it'll be used for religious purposes." He spoke with the assurance of one who could write the check right after dinner; his staff mentally pondered the bargain — $300,000 compared to $212,000, both much more than the nothing on hand! But to Daws it was no problem. This promised land must be possessed.

Graham did want Glen Eyrie and signed a purchase option readily underwritten by thirty businessmen sponsors. He wanted The Navigators to maintain the property and use it for their own purposes as well. Dawson met Graham in Colorado in May to make a promotional film and discuss plans. Graham envisioned a unique role for Glen Eyrie in the Great Commission. He spoke enthusiastically of prayer and Bible study retreats for international students, personalities from the sports and entertainment world, government leaders, men from industry. And he felt Glen Eyrie was ideal as an international home and year-round training facility for The Navigators.

But as news spread of Graham's interest in Colorado property, it was questioned by some who felt this was too far afield from evangelism. Protest rose, and by mid-August he was forced to abandon his Glen Eyrie dream. With heavy heart he relayed his decision to Daws, who numbly replaced the phone on his desk and called in a half-dozen of the staff. "The Glen Eyrie deal is off," he announced, his face ashen. It was as though he said the holy city, the New Jerusalem, had burned to the ground. They had all toured Glen Eyrie while at seminar and keenly anticipated moving there soon. This was incredible.

After hours of staring at the gray ashes, they saw the phoenix rise full-grown — The Navigators could undertake the purchase themselves! Leaping intuitively to a decision he knew God would ratify, Daws wired Graham: "FEEL MOST DEFI-NITELY THAT NAVIGATORS MUST ATTEMPT PUR-CHASE GLEN EYRIE."

Phones began ringing, typewriters humming, and soon a brief was ready to present The Navigators' case at a Kansas City meeting with Graham and the sponsors. Could The Navigators raise all that money — in only six weeks — for the down payment? Yes, Dawson declared on naked faith. Could they maintain the buildings and property, the private water system and other features of this self-contained community? "We can do it," Daws assured them, tapping the dossiers of Nav staff men and trainees who had the necessary skills. Glen Eyrie, the nineteenth century estate of Colorado Springs' founder, was a coveted property for which many ideas now bloomed, including using it for profit as a luxurious private club. But Graham believed God wanted The Navigators there and, laying his own faith on the line, turned the option over to them alone. Daws took his dossiers, his faith and rekindled spirit back to report to a waiting crew.

*   *   *   *

The news exploded them into action. Hearing God had given them the option to buy Glen Eyrie, their response — reinforcing Dawson's conviction this was of God — was like Caleb's: "Let us go up at once, and possess it; for we are well able to overcome it" (Num. 13:30). Two fellows gave their cars. The fiancée of one, not knowing of the car, gave the $100 she had saved for their wedding. Two men cashed bonds in order to give, while other staff members borrowed sums large enough to make repayment a test of faith. The office staff turned to on writing and printing materials, including a four-color, thirty-one-page display book on Navigator work world-wide, to use in presenting "Glen Eyrie — Venture With a Vision" to friends around the world. A Los Angeles printer produced and contributed two beautiful color brochures depicting Glen Eyrie. Daws summoned a dozen of the U.S. staff and Dave and Jean Rohrer from Europe to work on the project. Area directors came to pray and plan for mobilizing the gang in their areas.

Daws marveled that the Lord would give him, who suffered torture asking for money, the task of raising over a hundred thousand dollars in just six weeks — an amount larger than The Navigators' annual budget! Yet never in his life had he been more sold on a project or more eager to enlist all hands to tackle it. Stopping at Glen Eyrie after the Kansas City meeting, he had climbed to the top of a ridge overlooking the valley to make a covenant with God. *Lord, if You entrust this all to us, I want to dedicate it now to You as David did, to be used for Your glory, to make known Your holy name in all the world*. With Bible open to 1 Chronicles 29:10-13 he scratched the reference on the sandstone rock face to witness his pledge.

Once he believed God would give Glen Eyrie, Daws was bold to ask everyone to give. He raced from checking a printing detail on the promotional material to phoning a friend for advice on mapping strategy for his amateur fundraisers. He grinned. "Gang, some day we'll say we thought Glen Eyrie was a big project!" For some reason, probably his perfectionist desire to do it right and equip them properly, he waited till September 2 to send a four-page letter to the world-wide staff telling them the Graham situation had changed. "I am so convinced this project is of the Lord and that every dollar invested will bring dividends now and in years to come and in eternity that I want every one of you to have a part." He called for sacrifice and for asking "those to whom you minister, regardless of nationality, to share, if only a mite, a yen, a franc. . . . Let them have the joy of investing in this place . . . the focal point of a work which by His grace is to lay foundations for many generations."

The first deadline came less than halfway through the six weeks — $10,000 to pay on the furnishings contract must be in hand before bank closing September 4. Materials and information had not yet reached overseas Navs and U.S. workers had just begun to make contacts. On the morning of the 4th the staff prayed for $2000 needed to complete the payment. A $500 gift from a widow in Arkansas, $100 wired from Washington, and $100 a young housewife brought in helped make up the total just ninety minutes before the bank closed. The crew was ecstatic, feeling God had done it as a token that He would take them the rest of the way.

That payment cleaned out the cash; next day only $4 came toward the $100,000 due in twenty-four days. Daws had momentary doubts, quailing at the win-or-lose venture of faith into which he had led the Navs. If they didn't make it, the disaster was unthinkable. Gifts made sacrificially would have to be returned to disappointed friends. The $50,000 option money would have to be repaid to the Graham Association. Thousands invested in travel, printing, and postage would be lost, plus months of time taken from the ministry. All this, plus regular running expenses, would put finances too deep in the hole to fathom. Worst of all, failure would give the enemy room to taunt the staff, Christian leaders, and friends who had gone out on a limb in faith: "Where are your promises of God now? Let Him get you out of *this!*"

Three weeks into the project, with the headquarters crew moving at top speed, Daws was puzzled that the overseas gang did not respond at the same fever pitch. Involved in their local ministries, such as following up over 22,000 Japanese decisions from World Congress evangelism, some simply missed the urgency of his message. But his follow-up letter did get their attention, galvanizing the Navigator world to action and to prayer.

Only a handful of area Navs demurred, feeling the Lord's work did not require a plush estate in the Rockies. Dawson sought to reassure them but charged ahead, encouraged by the enthusiasm of the others. He saw in the project a reenactment of Nehemiah and the united effort to rebuild the wall of Jerusalem. It was clear that "the people had a mind to work" and were ready to rise up and build. As days passed he saw striking parallels with the book, including discouragement by those who doubted the effort would succeed, other hindrances and delays, even a call by the owner for a meeting to reconsider the purchase. He now regretted his decision to sell and wished to break the option. Daws replied much as Nehemiah had: he was too busy working to stop for a meeting.

On September 11 Rod Sargent, making contacts on the East Coast, phoned that a Nav area man had told him Glen Eyrie would be useless to The Navigators as the purchase contract did not include water rights. "That's not true," Dawson shot back, "but if this has shaken your confidence and you can't push this with your whole heart, come on home." No worker could succeed with less than total sense of victory; he could go out again with his faith refueled. Reassured, however, Rod stayed on the job.

Mid-September was the crucial point for Dawson. Harassed by the tempter, he was for a black moment in his hands. *What if we don't make it?* Two-thirds of the time was gone. The office crew, Daws with them, had subsisted on the prayers of others through long days without letup. The bookkeeper bringing him the daily report found him with head down on his desk. He looked up, wiping some tears. "I'm at the end of my own effort," he said quietly. "I know now that whatever is done, God will do it." The ridiculously low bank balance she showed him substantiated his conclusion.

With that battle won, Daws did not again lose heart. When one of the inner circle wavered, another shored up his courage and faith. Daws allowed no one to entertain a doubt or give in to fatigue lest it cause a leak in the dike of team morale, which was high. It was not win-or-lose now, only *win*. "The deadline of the 29th is upon us," Daws had written the gang. "All of us must wage all-out warfare in prayer and hard work. This is more than a 'venture' — this is *it*!"

On September 16 Graham's business manager George Wilson called. With thirteen days to go there would be time to take action if The Navigators fell short, to protect the option money.

"How're you coming, Daws?"

"Great! We're gonna make it," he shouted cheerily.

"Good. How much do you have so far?"

"What's that?"

"How much do you have?"

"Oh, I don't know exactly, George, it's coming in from all over. Our people out in the areas have a lot they haven't sent in yet," he said. "But we'll make it." He had stepped into the Jordan now. The well-guarded secret bank balance was $3183.

Nor did he release day-to-day figures even to key area workers and risk discouraging them. He was cheered by the perseverance of his colaborers and beloved friends in other works who set aside their own programs to help The Navigators. Bill Bright's action was typical; he not only gave sacrificially, but wrote 5000 friends of his new organization asking them to help. Sanny and Sargent and the area teams were out making calls — Daws too when he could get away. Asking the Lord what he could give, he thought of the white Pontiac Lila had bought for him with her inheritance. He determined to sell the car for Glen Eyrie. Later he secretly hoped it would not sell or perhaps would not be needed for the deadline, then hated himself for wishing it; how many others were sacrificing much more than this!

A professional fundraiser dropped in, looked over the campaign. He was amazed. "You're doing all the right things," he said. "But for a drive this size you need a large challenge gift of around $35,000." The largest gift had already come, $4000 from a couple who mortgaged their home in order to give. Their gift had helped in the early $10,000 payment.

On September 17 Sanny phoned that a $40,000 loan had been offered. Daws felt this news, one day after he had assured Wilson all was well, was God's provision of an answer for those who asked for figures, though he did not intend to use the loan. The Lord would be honored by giving total victory without borrowed money.

Indeed the word coming in daily with gifts showed He was doing an unprecedented thing. As workers went out telling the story, people at once felt personally involved and even responsible for the success of the drive. "We have about eight men in the Nav work here at the Academy," a midshipman wrote. "Some of us can write to our home churches. Thanks for the privilege to share." A Louisiana banker wrote that his son in the Navy asked him to send $100 from his account. "My wife and I are [also] giving $50 because we are convinced it is greatly needed." A government employee: "I have just lost my position due to reduction in force but I must send you a check for $10. I realize how vital it is Glen Eyrie be purchased *now* . . . for the sake of unsaved ones around the world."

Whether large or small gifts, in cash or donated labor, a note of joyful sacrifice ran through them and a strange urgency that could only be from God. A coed at Baylor University sold her tennis racket and radio and sent the proceeds. A woman sold her parrot and sent $30. A six-year-old gave his birthday dollar "for that house." A student nurse in San Francisco sent $2 — "a small amount but I just pray the Lord will honor it." More than $900 came from a young lady in Seattle who had won a battle with cancer. A Chattanooga schoolgirl sent $2, a man of eighty-three with no retirement income a check for $10, saying he wished it had been $1000. Two small boys gave their jar of 902 pennies.

What had begun as a misting rain was now a steady shower of gifts, some coming from overseas. Cozart in Korea and Boardman in Okinawa said to use all their September income for Glen Eyrie. From Italy, Pete George sent a month's income; Piatt, moving his family to Holland, gave the money from sale of their furniture. Gien Karssen, The Navigators' Lydia, sent a thousand guilders from herself and Dutch contacts. In Formosa an old Chinese woman sold an heirloom painting and walked across Taipeh to bring a thank offering to the Lord for Doug Sparks's ministry to her family. Her gift was included. And fifty dollars from Thirza Skoff, the Austrian girl Dawson had led to Christ in Peking. He winced at seeing gifts from meager allowances of missionaries of other groups, American and European. These along with the yen, the francs, the pesos of believers of many nations were far more significant to him than their amount, sizable as that was. Their labor of love would forever stamp Glen Eyrie as the place where God would fulfill the promise He had given from Deuteronomy 28:12 of men to lend to many nations.

The Japan Navigators, with the World Congress and financial problems themselves, nonetheless came aboard. On September 20 Robertson cabled "SERVICEMEN IN JAPAN RALLYING WITH SEVERAL THOUSAND" and asked that all September income for Japan staff go for Glen Eyrie. Roy prayed the servicemen would give $10,000. They exceeded that.

On September 22 with one week to go there was $22,000 in the bank, the next day $28,000, and the next $33,000 — less than one-third of the money needed. Some had pledged to give later, but the $100,000 must be in cash; postponement was impossible since the owner would cancel the sale on any pretext. Another hurdle was finding two co-signers suitable to the seller. Though dozens of men of means were available when Graham was the buyer, few were willing to risk it with the unknown Navigators. Finally two Christian businessmen agreed to co-sign and were accepted.

The balance climbed to $41,000 on the 25th, to $60,000 by the 27th. Western Union clerks, aware of the race against time, phoned excitedly of money coming in by wire. The special delivery postman asked, "How's it coming? Are you going to make it?" When Daws left on the 28th to sign the papers in Houston the total was $78,000. Part of that day's receipts was from the sale of the cherished white Pontiac.

He asked Sargent to meet him in Houston for the signing; Sanny, in Detroit for a Graham crusade opening, could not come. The Los Angeles bank would wire the funds to Houston at the last moment — but the last moment was near and the goal not reached. The 29th dawned on the office crew making trips to post office and Western Union and posting tally sheets in the manner of election returns. In Houston a businessman told Daws, "When you call your office, find out how much is still needed and I'll raise it at my club luncheon." Daws called — $8000 to go. The man raised that amount among his friends and returned to hear that Los Angeles had gone over the top, with $100,300 in at 1:15 P.M. Dawson said apologetically they wouldn't need the $8000 now; his friend cautioned him to wait and see.

They did need it — for fire insurance and closing costs. The Lord had provided on an Isaiah 65:24 basis. But the suspense was not over. When Dawson called at the Houston bank for the $100,000, it was not there. Discovery that it had been sent to the wrong bank came after that bank had closed. The man who raised the $8000, however, was its board chairman, so was able to reopen the bank and get the money.

This series of miracles ending with a photo-finish race would surely glorify the Lord before those who trusted and those who doubted. A thrill of celebration ran through the Navigator world among more than 2000 in fifteen countries who had worked, prayed, and given with abandon to "build the wall," including even the attorneys who donated part or all of their fees.

"The Lord did it!" Graham shouted when he heard the news. He had told Daws he believed God led him to withdraw from the purchase because He intended The Navigators to have Glen Eyrie all along.

Wealthy businessmen who had withdrawn their backing were now amazed to see what God had done through the small and sacrificial gifts — the majority twenty dollars or less — of those who believed God's promises. One who did help was jolted. "I have read of such things in the Bible but had never seen it in my day. I didn't believe they could do it; I told them so and told others they couldn't, but now I see it was the Lord's will." In Taipeh where missionaries and Chinese Christians had prayed all night the 27th Hillis said, "By one o'clock I knew the Navs had Glen Eyrie."

Every gift counted. Those who were part of the holy conspiracy of conquest would never be the same after the miracle of Glen Eyrie. Days before the deadline Dawson wrote, "On the lips of thousands will be praise to the God who has shown He can do the impossible. The world will see what can be done by a band of Christians whose hearts are united, who know how to trust their God and how to roll up their sleeves and work. Many will get their first glimpse of this kind of faith in action."

Engrossed as he was in the six-week marathon, Dawson was amazed how the Lord enabled him to take part in other works. He had helped Bill Bright with incorporation of Campus Crusade, to which a half-dozen Nav men were loaned. He had attended Fuller Seminary's dedication as a Foundation member, spoken to San Diego YFC, met with MAF's board, and launched a plan for systematic giving to other works by any-one interested. Now after signing the Glen Eyrie papers, he was off to Chicago to speak to an EFMA convention, drop in on the Detroit Graham crusade, and meet with the board of Inter-national Students in Philadelphia, stopping first in Colorado to map plans for the crew getting Glen Eyrie ready to be Nav headquarters. Then to London for meetings with British pastors and key laymen in ten localities, preparing for next spring's crusade at Harringay Arena.

He knew the meetings would be crucial, for he would meet head-on the critics of this unknown evangelist who wanted to attempt what no one else had done in Britain. And among clergy who did know of Graham's evangelism there was much skepticism about its lasting effect. Daws went into the series with fear and trembling and saw prayer answered as he had great freedom in describing the follow-up program. He spoke from Colossians 1:28,29 and Ephesians 4:11-15, presenting what God expects of a believer as a measurable objective for each one making a decision in the crusade.

The ministers were pleased, their questions answered, and cooperation was assured. Methodist minister Joe Blinco felt Dawson saw clearly "the apostolic place of the consecrated layman in extending Christ's kingdom. His passion to communicate and to make communicators sprang from that." He did not feel Trotman's lack of education limited his genius. "Daws was in tune with one of the greatest movements of the Spirit of our time, re-emergence of the place and purpose of the dedicated layman, putting the Bible in the hand and heart and mind of the individual."

Daws returned home to direct the men working on Glen Eyrie and encourage John Crawford's team of seven men raising funds to finish paying for the property. He himself worked on projects for which he had long seen a need: writing an evangelistic Bible study course and preparing a booklet of selected Scriptures to give inquirers in place of the Gospel of John.

*   *   *   *

It was a dream come true. As Dawson's eyes swept the living room, a crackling fire on the hearth highlighted faces of some forty of his colaborers. One was reporting what God had done in his area and sharing a nugget from the Word. It was Christmas week 1954, end of the first full year at Glen Eyrie. Back from another trip to England, Daws had issued a short-notice invitation to "come to Glen Eyrie if you don't have other plans." The result was an impromptu conference of staff and key people from the Midwest, Pacific Coast, and Texas — Ed Reis with some from Minneapolis, Bob Foster from Los Angeles, Skip Gray from Portland, and others — such a blessed time that Daws decided the staff must come this same week each year. At last there was space enough to invite as many as he wished.

There had been great fellowship around the Lord and His Word, fun in the snow, and yelling in the stands at a collegiate hockey game. The office staff cut their hours and joined in meetings. Lila listened from an adjoining room where she was recuperating from surgery and long illness. Daws was sorry the rest of the Nav family was not there; he wished he could have sent them all funds to come.

Times like this had been part of his vision for Glen Eyrie — closer fellowship for all the staff, those from both U.S. and overseas coming in to be renewed and to impart from their experience to those coming up. Here Daws, Sanny, and other leaders could also be in daily contact with increasing numbers of men in training for future colaborship. Leaders of other works could come together as he and Jim Rayburn and Bill Bright had done, riding up into the mountains on horseback for extended times of prayer, or meeting as YFC International and Jim Vaus's Missionary Communication Service had for executive board business.

Daws reflected that it had been the fullest year of his whole life. At the Glen all hands had worked harder than even in the purchase drive. By mid-year Sargent had moved headquarters office and staff from Los Angeles and installed them in the sturdy brick building that had been Glen Eyrie's powerhouse, its rough interior transformed into modern offices for Nav international administration. The crew under Crawford's direction also built bunk beds and dining room furniture and prepared housing for Glen Eyrie dwellers numbering about sixty by midsummer — office staff, maintenance crews, trainees, and summer helpers. All pitched in evenings on chores such as cleaning rooms of the stone Tudor castle, largest building on the thousand-acre estate.

Wearing the embroidered western shirts that became his hallmark, Daws enjoyed touring the Glen with the men, issuing endless instructions and ideas that they jotted in pocket notebooks. Bill Michel, recalled from International Students, acquired several responsibilities as these tours progressed — managing food service, the greenhouse, public relations, and upkeep of grounds.

Momentum had been strong to finish paying for the Glen once the down payment was out of the way, and Crawford's men working on the Ten Month Plan made good progress. But their ranks dwindled as some were needed elsewhere and available funds went into Glen Eyrie's operation. So by the end of September 1954 the required $60,000 payment was made and the balance refinanced for smaller annual payments. Amazingly, Glen Eyrie had been the scene this first summer of six week-long conferences and two three-week seminars concurrent with them. One conference was for businessmen and one for pastors. Roy Robertson came in time to add an overseas dimension to the programs. The coming of the new Air Force Academy was to Dawson a further seal of God's approval on the acquisition of

Glen Eyrie, especially since the academy site would include Pine Valley which The Navigators came so close to getting.

The Glen had fulfilled its promise in versatile ways. Special dinners at the sumptuous Pink House, now the Trotman family home, were occasions to present the Gospel to community leaders and military commanders and inform them about the Navigator work. And Daws was delighted to honor his father at an eighty-second birthday banquet in the Castle's Great Hall. The spruce-dotted lawns and rocky slopes of wild grass, yucca, oak, and juniper offered places to get out alone or with another for meditation in the Word and prayer, where eternal business could be done in lives in a setting conducive to hearing the voice of God.

There was close esprit de corps on the Glen, plenty of fun and laughter amid the work, and unsparing heart-searching as one or another learned a tough lesson. Dawson's habit — and Lila's — of dropping a word of appreciation in passing to one of the crew with the assurance, "Sure love you," encouraged and spurred them on. Daws brought the gang together Wednesday and Saturday evenings at the Pink House for fellowship and instruction and Thursday mornings at six for united prayer.

One purpose of the Glen was demonstrated over and over as men joined the crew to be trained while they worked. A lesson of faith could be learned by a lad in the print shop. "We can't do that kind of job on a Multilith, Daws," one protested. Dawson's eyes penetrated the printer. "Never say can't! *I can do all things through Christ which strengtheneth me.* We have the Master Teacher on our side, and we're going to show the world some new things in printing." And the job was done on the Multilith.

The core of Glen Eyrie's potential, Dawson felt, was the building of skilled spiritual craftsmen for the Great Commission. The program was under way with thirty trainees in classes and on work projects where their needs could be observed and met. A few came from other countries and there would be more. It would be strategic to send men back to their own lands with this vision and to recruit and send from areas of the world most readily productive of disciplemakers. Scott, home from his Cyprus assignment, was doing a good job helping Robertson train the men. Roy's course in missions principles symbolized what was happening — men with overseas experience coming back to invest in others who would go out in turn. This facet of Glen Eyrie's ministry was exciting to Daws. Three Glen trainees had already gone overseas; more would follow to work with Navigators, Wycliffe, and other groups. God had begun to fulfill the promise that Glen Eyrie would lend unto many nations.

Daws knew he was considered harsh in his dealings with some. Once while rebuking a man severely for moving ahead of the Lord in seeking a wife, he paused and said, "I've had fellows leave the work because I talked to them this way." *I don't doubt it one bit,* was the miserable fellow's unspoken thought. Daws had, in fact, been hardest on those he loved most, and especially intolerant of their refusal to deal with minor but crippling faults. If they would only resolve to learn the lesson and go on from there, priceless ground could be gained for Christ. He so desired to build foundational truths into lives that he was at times led to excess by his thoroughness and persistence.

Trivial incidents could be used to teach valuable lessons. He recalled a truck trip from Los Angeles with Cecil Davidson when Cec had "fixed" a loose taillight connection only to have it go out again. Daws pointed out to Davidson in unforgettable terms that this illustrated a life habit of carelessness. Another man, engaged to one of the secretaries, asked during the Glen Eyrie drive to see Daws about setting a wedding date. Daws withered him with a look. "Now we talked about this a year ago. Why can't you just commit it to the Lord until he leads? Here we've got a world to reach for Christ and you're thinkin' about a wedding date!" With the man's perspective restored, Daws assured him the wedding was very much in his thinking and he even hoped it might be at Glen Eyrie in the rose arbor.

Though it could be hard, Daws felt drastic surgery was often kinder in the long run. If his violent temper of earlier days at times resurfaced, he did not recognize it. For one man, whose inner core of obstinacy needed complete excision, he called a meeting of a dozen men to testify against him in forthright candor; then they prayed together for his repentance and growth. Another man, equally strong-willed, he handled with exceeding gentleness lest he crush his spirit or alienate him. To still another who asked for help in a weak area he showed endless patience and understanding.

Dawson's heaviest heartache now was that he had indeed lost some men. In January after the Glen Eyrie purchase, two Nav representatives had come to accuse him of not backing one of them while he was overseas, of allowing him to suffer financially while headquarters had plenty. Dawson was taken aback. He knew the little gang had had their faith tested severely. In fact he had recently sent a circular letter asking those who could to contribute to them and their work. He felt it was vital, however, that new headquarters in areas or overseas learn to trust God for daily provision; without this they would miss precious lessons. Sanny's experience in Seattle had proved this, building his faith and that of others. But the man would not be dissuaded; he resigned to form his own evangelistic organization. His colleague took on other ministries, leaving the Nav work in his area to be resumed by others.

To this day Daws would welcome both men back to the work and had let them know it; he prayed fervently they would return. He rejected the notion that they had really resigned because his domineering through the years and squelching of their initiative had mortally wounded their relationship. He was convinced he had been objective with them and all his staff, aiming only to accomplish desired results for the Lord's glory. And his love for them and their precious wives was still strong, God knew.

He was amazed to realize now, six years after the first man went to China, the Navs had a beachhead in twelve countries besides some thirteen areas of the U.S. Key people from six countries had joined with Americans for a Nav seminar in London last spring during Harringay. Here in the States men were growing in vision and skill. Most were ordinary fellows whom Daws knew God would use because they were willing to get into the Word and get the Word into their lives. With Glen Eyrie established as a base at the crossroads of the Navigator world, Daws felt all the pieces were in place to press the battle to the gates. The most important of these was so basic to all the ministry that it was taken for granted: a man like-minded, a Timothy to whom he had committed all he had learned for thirteen years — one who would naturally care for the state of the Nav work world-wide and had been his backup man in virtually every situation.

This principle, which some men of God discovered too late in their ministry to apply, had been fingered by Fuller Seminary's president, Dr. Edward Carnell, at lunch in Pasadena last month. "Have you made provision for the perpetuity of this movement? What would keep The Navigators from going liberal after you leave the scene?" Daws reached for a paper napkin to draw a diagram of the 2 Timothy 2:2 principle. "I have given my life to provide the answer to that question." No constitution or by-laws could guarantee the purity of a work, only faith in promises claimed and a faithful man to carry on. Sanny, he explained, was that man. He recalled his pleasure in telling Bob Evans in London during Harringay that "people are asking for Lorne now instead of me." This was evidence the job had been accomplished. Carnell listened, struck by the implications of the Timothy principle.

Suddenly in mid-January Daws knew he was exhausted. It was as if a tightly wound spring within him might snap, a tension built so steadily for so long it had gone unnoticed. Driven by zeal and exuberance to set what would be a killing pace for most men, he had not taken as much as a week's vacation in four years. He had spent a third of his time in Graham crusades and, at perhaps greater cost, had given Sanny and other experienced staff to that ministry.

He had gone to London for the pastors' meetings immediately after the Glen Eyrie drive and went back again in February '54 for the crusade. He and Sanny had handled Nav administration from London while overseeing follow-up for the mammoth three-month crusade. With 2900 trained counselors and follow-up instruction classes for church leaders, follow-up was provided for an incredible 34,560 inquirers, seven times the number in any stateside crusade. Meetings and teas planned for nurses, professional men, and other special interest groups were among means used to help the new converts. But Daws's greatest joy was in seeing Britons leading others to Christ in the counseling room and diligently following them up.

Then came the exhilaration of setting Glen Eyrie in motion and the first summer of conferences. In July and August Daws had 300 conferees, guests, staff, or trainees for mealtime fellowship or interviews at the Pink House, where college-trained Floy Moody and Helen Stafstrom did yeoman duty as hostesses, managing the home and caring for Lila during her illness the rest of that year. There had been a Wycliffe board meeting in Oklahoma and a crusade in Nashville; a missionary conference in Wisconsin where he spoke on follow-up in the national church; six weeks in England gathering material for a book Graham asked him to write on Harringay converts. There were trips to Los Angeles and other areas, and at the Glen more time with individuals, an indispensable part of his ministry.

The administrative work load, decisions to buy a new oven for the Castle bakery or to produce Nav Bible studies in Tamil, increased as work budgets grew larger. Still Daws did not feel overloaded; his intense interest made him tackle each matter with uncommon verve. Added to this was the physical factor. The doctor who attended Lila examined him and discovered what Dawson had called leakage of the heart was actually coarctation of the aorta, which resulted in excess blood supply to the upper part of his body and less to the feet and legs. This could flush the face, speed the brain, and generate more ambition than the body could match in strength.

When Daws finally recognized he was tired, he was impatient with the fact. He noticed he could not face some of his daily work or go through his mail. The aversion seemed temporary, yet deep down was a gnawing realization he would have to relinquish personal control of some things and delegate them. What taxed him most was counseling and building in the lives of those at the Glen, helping them hurdle major hindrances to becoming fruitful servants of Christ. Alone with Lila in their room one Friday, he fell across the bed sobbing, clear evidence of emotional fatigue. His doctor told him he had narrowly missed nervous collapse and must give up all responsibility for at least a month. He phoned Graham to ask if he might drop out of crusading for a time, then left for California to bask in the sun at Mrs. Kerr's home while he oil-painted landscapes.

The month lasted two weeks, with Daws able to forget his work except for planning to send a Navigator to South America. Sanny was in Glasgow for five months for the coming crusade. Sargent handled headquarters administration, Robertson the Glen training program. Addie Rosenbaum, Dawson's trusted secretary, took care of correspondence for him. The next few months he spent between California and the Glen, trying desperately to relax. By spring he was allowed limited return to work and spent part of his day on business, the rest on oil painting or shooting magpies, which he explained were the vicious criminals of birdland. He also liked to chug around the Glen in his Model-A Ford which sported three horns — an ah-ooga, a blaster, and a ding-dong, the latter triggered by the clutch pedal. A sight to remember was Daws, looking like a mischievous schoolboy, chauffeuring the portly Dr. Theodore Epp around in the tiny car.

But his valiant effort to disinvolve himself was unsuccessful. After a few days' exile he would plead loneliness and return. Doubtless a source of his struggle during those months was reluctance to give up any of the work God had given him which he felt, correctly, he could do better than others. It seemed at every turn he saw work done or decisions made which showed need for correction or improvement. His compulsion was to see every job done right and to personally train the one doing it. Whether this stemmed from his perfectionism or his staff's need for maturity, or both, it contributed to his refusal to quit — and to frequent shortness of patience with those nearest him. So while his fatigue lessened, frustration built from the inner battle that he alone must face.

From San Diego to Boston the ministry in seven full-fledged areas and numerous contact points was thriving. Personal evangelism and discipling moved ahead on campuses, military bases, and among working people. Area Navs did follow-up for Youth For Christ and worked with other campus organizations and churches. As Daws spoke to spring '55 area conferences and heard reports from Robertson, Sargent, and Foster on their tours, he was convinced the area work had never looked better.

Top fellows and girls were showing up at the Glen for training, and a third series of classes had finished in time to put everyone to work preparing for summer conferences. Dawson's delight in the Glen never flagged. In a staff bulletin he quoted a Colorado old-timer: "It was a great pleasure to see the old Castle and surroundings truly come into their own. There is a new light about the place, the dignity of being wanted, of usefulness. The community is very proud to have one of its most famous pioneer possessions taken over by so worthy a cause, so appropriate for it."

Over in Europe Piatt was teaching church follow-up classes and training counselors for the summer Graham meetings on the continent. Bob Hopkins and George Clark also taught in German and French and met with pastors' committees. Though this took them from their main work of man-to-man disciplemaking, Dawson felt it was the right investment of manpower for the time and would pay dividends in God's total program. The fellows in the Orient were helping with Morken's coming crusades in Taipeh and Saigon and continuing follow-up and other help to YFC, Orient Crusades, and World Vision. Daws was glad for their availability to serve other works, something he had painstakingly built into all his men. He also appreciated being able to send Nav men out nominally under other missions as this spared The Navigators some of the administrative machinery of a conventional mission board. It was thrilling to know Nav materials were used increasingly in other languages and that discipling was under way in many countries.

Though all available men were either following up others' evangelism or engaged in Nav man-to-man ministry, Daws dreamed of Navigator evangelistic teams going out — to Latin America, for instance — to do both evangelism and follow-up, a more complete ministry as Denlers had done in Formosa. Urgent needs had been met by Nav men helping other works in follow-up, but Daws felt it would be healthier if those works learned to follow up their own converts. And the Nav program would be better balanced if it included direct mass evangelism, at least in some areas.

At that moment when it seemed the entire work was enjoying God's blessing, a phone call to Tokyo brought bad news. Tipped by a traveler from the Orient, Dawson called the man Robertson had left in charge in Japan and found virtually all the Nav staff enmeshed in strange doctrine taught by visiting speakers. It was unbelievable, a blow on his blind side. Navigators, known for strong devotional habits and continuing study of the Word, should be the last to fall before such basic tricks of the enemy. His heart wrenched by a feeling of betrayal, Daws dispatched Robertson to see what could be done.

Robertson was aware of Japan's reputation as the most treacherous field for the psyche of the Christian worker, but he could diagnose the situation apart from that. Staff members had ignored his instruction to busy themselves with language study, had unhappily neglected their devotional time, Bible study, and memory, so were vulnerable. Their longing for something special, something more in their Christian experience, which Roy saw as a result of this neglect, made them accept hungrily any magic answer offered at the right moment. Saddened, he labored to restore the group to spiritual sanity, and in midsummer asked Daws to come to Tokyo.

Daws took Bob Foster along for an all-Orient staff conference in September, with Hillis also present. Spending days in fellowship in the Word, in prayer and patient persuasion, in demonstration of his love for them, Daws felt sure the Lord had won the victory. It was a heartrending experience, but worth it if these errant members could be restored.

They were not. Within months all had left the Navigator work, a heartbreak to Daws, no less to Robertson. The workers would be replaced, but what of the dear ones themselves? Times like this showed, as did the happy fellowship at Glen Eyrie and among the staff around the world, the special bond which held the Navigator family together in mutual love and caring.

R esponding to Graham's request that he be in London for the 1955 crusade at Wembley, Dawson arrived in May to find

Sanny had the most efficient follow-up procedures ever. He and Riggs had trained 5000 Scottish counselors and provided help for 19,200 who made decisions in the six-week Glasgow crusade. Sanny's recorded counselor training classes had also been held in cities throughout Britain where the crusade was later relayed by telephone land line, thus counselors in every city were ready to help inquirers. Here in London he had 100 volunteers processing some 3000 decision cards nightly, getting them out to ministers along with a follow-up letter to each inquirer in the next day's mail. That was one of Sanny's strengths — organization. And the British loved him. Daws was delighted to see God's hand upon him.

Wembley was unforgettable. An average of 60,000 people poured into the stadium daily for eight days, with 3000 coming out onto the turf to register decisions and get individual counsel — usually in the rain! What a joy to see many one-year-old Harringay converts serving as counselors and leading others to Christ. One couple who between them had counseled 118 inquirers at Harringay could six months later account for 114 going on with the Lord. A physician and a businessman converted at Harringay told Daws they had many invitations to preach and the Lord had allowed them to win at least fifty souls. He wondered how many new Christians like these men might also grow and bear fruit if given the same important help in the early hours of their new life. Graham's evangelism and that of others who copied his follow-up system had proved that recorded decisions were more than statistics; they could be the beginning of productive ministries. Daws was grateful for Billy's vision and insistence on adding follow-up to his ministry in those early years.

Now Sanny had trained Riggs and others and would soon be free, Daws hoped, to give more time to the growing Nav work. Riggs showed great capacity and could take over much of the crusading; he would soon go to set up meetings for Billy in India. Piatt now coordinated Graham's meetings on the continent along with directing Europe Navigators, a position Daws meant to make official as soon as the board could meet. During the five years of heavy manpower investment in the crusades, Dawson had seen the Navigator work and vision advanced greatly in the church and in many quarters because of Graham's generous endorsement of Nav follow-up and training.

Glen Eyrie's second summer of ministry almost doubled the first: eleven conferences instead of six; a special training program for some eighty-five summer staff, office, and Glen crews; special visitors; board meetings of other works; improvements made on the property and increased work at headquarters. Pastors conference alone held great potential, Daws felt. Last year the pastors had embraced enthusiastically the principles of man-to-man and small-group training of their laymen. Indeed this summer's speaker was a Michigan pastor who had applied in his church the things presented at that first conference. It was staggering to think what this could mean if it caught on with ministers and laymen across the country.

As always, Daws loved the fast pace. He felt stronger now, able to keep his hand in it all and spend time with people — though he could not face certain paper work, preferring to ride his horse into the hills for prayer with someone or shoot arrows at an archery target on the lawn.

One responsibility he could not face was finances. But in November when overdue accounts reached $35,000 and income lagged, he knew he must. He was preparing a Bible study course for Dr. Epp to offer his Back to the Bible radio audience and was hard put to buy paper to print it. Support for eighty-five staff, crew, and trainees at the Glen and other costs of the expanding work had mounted.

It was time for united action, and Daws called in some key area men to discuss it. As they prayed and talked over ideas to solve the financial problem, Daws knew the Lord was going to work it out. Relaxing in that anticipated victory, he said abruptly, "Hey, y'know what we oughta do? Put up a cable car from the top of Razorback over here to Echo Rock as a kind of skyride! Wouldn't our guests love that? And the crew?" *Yeah, sure,* thought the nonplused area reps who were still down under that $35,000 debt. Daws understood, and with effort came back to the business at hand. He knew God could solve the financial problem the same way He had given Glen Eyrie, through faith and hard work, so he was no longer fettered by it. Daws talked about his plan to dedicate Glen Eyrie debt free, as he had promised the Lord. He also wanted to see the day when he could sign large checks contributing monthly to Young Life, Campus Crusade, Inter-Varsity, and other works.

In the fall training program Daws thought he at last saw the format — flexible of course — for building the men Glen Eyrie would lend to many nations. It was the same training he had given men in Nav Homes through the years, only given now to larger numbers. His standards of excellence for his men had been criticized by some as based more on works than on grace. The charge was sincere, as was the complaint that he gave more time to the gifted man than to the weaker brother. Daws felt neither charge was warranted, for Christ's call to His disciples was a call to discipline, a life "unto good works," and he must expect no less than his Lord asked. And by investing most in those with fewest problems, he would have more men ready sooner to minister to the weaker brethren than if he had given all his time to them.

This year he found men from thirteen denominations, seventeen states, and four foreign countries were in the program. Its five phases included classes, with assignments and grades; character training on the job, lessons of attitude, dependability, teamwork; outreach among servicemen and in local churches; training in vocational skills such as plumbing, carpentry, or cooking; and man-to-man counsel. Classes planned by Sanny were courses in Bible study, evangelism, follow-up, disciple-making, as well as skill and perspective courses in message preparation, leading groups, church history, and current events. Daws enjoyed teaching some classes, his unorthodox teaching methods compelling students to stay alert and think. He also took time to counsel with individual trainees.

Glen Eyrie Night, now a Thursday tradition, was Daws's special province. It was a variety time for fellowship with the Glen family, for singing and sharing the Word and prayer. Announcement of an engagement or overseas assignment added excitement and suspense, with it understood that only Dawson made any announcement, small or large. The playful warning to listen well lest you miss hearing of your engagement or transfer was nonetheless valid. On a spring night in 1956 Bob Howarth, British trainee who had found Christ at Harringay, heard he was to join the first Nav landing party in Kenya. Noting surprise on Bob's face, Daws asked, "Hadn't I told you about that, Bob?" Skip Gray, used to short-notice assignments, recalled a January Glen Eyrie Night when he heard "along with the rest of the staff that we were moving to Texas, which we did in March."

Daws was overjoyed to see Lila in radiant health again after long confinement to bed. Married twenty-three years and still sweethearts, neither could converse with friend or stranger long without telling of their love for the other, a love readily seen by any who entered their home. Now that she was stronger, Daws could realize his long-time wish that she travel and minister around the U.S. He asked her to take a team of two or three girls and visit the work in various areas, sharing her life with area Nav staff and contacts as well as with a different team on each trip. Lila was reluctant, but after her first trip in January 1956 to several east central states she gained courage and was soon looking forward to her next foray.

During these months Dawson seemed to drive inexorably toward an objective he had to feel was nearer now. The world loomed large in his thinking, yet smaller as its myriad sentry posts were being manned by God's servants. Last September at conference with the Wycliffe group in Arkansas he had poured out his heart on reaching the world — together. Renewed fellowship with Watters, Dedrick, and Newman stirred him to send more Navigators for the translation phase of the task. On return from Tokyo in October he had a week at Fuller Seminary to challenge these future leaders to know the Word and to invest in individuals who could multiply their ministry. Days later in Lincoln, Nebraska, he sought to convince Back to the Bible conferees that Christians were "born to reproduce." In Chicago he spoke to Moody Bible Institute student body and promised to write a course in Scripture memory for the correspondence school; then to Los Angeles to speak to an MAF banquet and meet with the board, deeply moved by the martyrdom of pilot Nate Saint in Ecuador.

He felt compelled to strike a blow wherever he could to get his main message out. His goal, by whatever means, was to get every Christian around the world into the Book. At home he exhorted the Glen staff to believe God's promise of His sovereignty in their lives and obey His command to give thanks in everything. In a "Dear Gang" letter he told the staff how he prayed Romans 15:1-7 for them and charged them to memorize it. Spoken or written, his message impacted in a way that could make each individual feel singled out as its target.

Analyzing needs in the work, Daws felt the most urgent was to raise up men who would think — men gifted in leadership, who could form area teams of some of the assistant-type faithful men now available. There were many places he could use men of this caliber with drive, vision, and ability to mobilize others, to take responsibility for all phases of the ministry in an area. He also saw a need to develop many "sub-Homes" where couples would use their homes for ministry under supervision of an area rep.

He believed these needs would be filled and that God was going to do great things with The Navigators. His own main work had been accomplished. He was sure of his men — principally Sanny, but also Robertson, Sparks, Scott, Sargent, and others — keen young men maturing and showing remarkable capacity. They were his guarantee that his commission based on God's promises had been and would be carried out. Secure in that knowledge, he went on preaching his message as widely as opportunity allowed. But his strength was running short again, and he was unwillingly taking to bed for days at a time. He knew he continually overran his strength, but felt if he stopped unless obviously ill he would be guilty of laziness and of pampering himself. He had often asked God to let him die with his boots on, so was determined never to be caught with them off.

A trip east in February 1956 resulted in assigning Waldron Scott to reopen the D.C. area and LeRoy Eims the Omaha area. Daws then traveled west to speak to the Eugene, Oregon, CBMC and to a rally in Fresno, California, where Bob Seifert represented The Navigators. At a weekend conference at Mount Hermon he gave a memorable message on "Love" and another on "Why Men Fail," a catalog of seemingly small things that spell disaster to the life of faith.

In April he visited D.C. and the Richmond crusade. In May, Dallas and Houston, where he met Lila and her team of girls. He and Lila visited their son Bruce and his wife in Waco and held their first grandchild, David, one week old. Back at the Glen to speak to pastors conference late in May, Daws was thoroughly spent, like a thoroughbred who had punished himself in the stretch to win one more race. He shared with Jack Mayhall, a youth pastor he was recruiting to The Navigators, his dream of bringing together heads of evangelical groups, missions, and schools to pray and plan toward reaching the world for Christ and strengthening each other's hands in the task. Aware of the need for flexibility and of the danger of getting out of balance on some emphasis, he felt close contact among such leaders would benefit all and provide balance, as Graham had strengthened The Navigators' position on evangelism.

He spoke to the pastors with power and conviction, and once slashed too keenly with the blade of sarcasm in illustrating a point. The point was a worthy one: that denominational differences must not hinder fellowship among Christians. But he learned afterward that his words wounded some, and he was deeply sorry. Out alone in prayer he confessed and wept over it, and at the evening meeting offered a humble apology. Having done so and been forgiven by God and man, he dismissed it and went on to preach with great freedom on "The Need of the Hour." Some saw in this a pacesetting lesson: since forgiveness is instant and complete, the enemy should not exact a further toll of remorse from the one forgiven. The case was closed, and he would go on with his message.

> *What is the need of the hour? For a beggar on the the street it's a dime. For a woman going to the hospital it's a doctor. In Christian work we often feel the need is a larger staff. Many a minister would like to have an assistant. Better facilities and equipment. A training center. Communications — radio, literature.*
>
> *We may think the greatest need is entrance into closed countries. We'd like to see doors open to Nepal or to China. Paul found closed doors, but*

they weren't a problem — God used them to show him other doors that were open. And God could open the door to China in forty-eight hours. Many in the South Pacific are hearing the Gospel today because China is closed.

Some think they need more time. Or money, the biggest of all needs. Frankly, I don't believe the need of the hour is any of these. What is the need of the hour for Kenya? Two or three men. If the men are ready, God will supply the money. He isn't looking for money; He's looking for men.

I believe the need of the hour is an army of soldiers dedicated to serve Jesus Christ in getting the Gospel to every creature — who believe not only that He's God, but that He can fulfill every promise He has ever made, and that there isn't anything too hard for Him . . . .

One verse I rest upon is 2 Corinthians 9:8; "And God is able to make all grace abound toward you; that ye, always having all sufficiency in all things, may abound to every good work." Based on that promise I'm asking the Lord to somehow let us serve every good work in America and the world. Years ago I didn't know how we could help some of the brethren whose hearts were closed to us. I'm seeing it today. I see young men in seminary getting a vision of these — not Nav principles but New Testament principles — by their own searching of Scripture, and they're applying it. I see a time not far off when it's going to permeate right down to every group in the world. . . .

The need of the hour is to want what Jesus Christ wants and to believe He's given us the power to get it. Then nothing can stop us. Do you believe that? You can have a part in it, but you've got to ask. Call and He will show you things you can't even comprehend. Back when I prayed for Formosa I wasn't thinking as big as I'm now seeing in Formosa. Because He said to call and He will answer and show things you don't even think about to pray. So when you call, ask big!

If Daws was sure because of his men that he had accomplished his God-given mission, there was one point on which he could not yet relax. There remained very much land to be possessed, with no toehold yet in Africa or South America, no number one man planted on either continent. And now God was providing men for both major areas. George Sanchez, home from Ecuador due to his wife's ill health, would be able to spearhead in Latin America. His perfect command of language and culture would greatly enhance his usefulness there. Daws was elated. At this stage of the Navigator work he had been asking the Lord for some mature men like Sanchez, Downing, and others to give stability and leadership for the many young men coming up. He had issued a strong call by letter and in person to Downing, who would soon retire from the Navy. Jim was praying about it. "If Jim Downing comes into The Navigators," Daws confided to the gang at Glen Eyrie Night, "you will know *God* sent him. Jim makes no move until he is 200 percent sure of that. But all of you pray hard that God will send him."

Hightower, having brought his family home from Africa when his youngest son contracted polio, was available to help launch the work on that continent by making periodic trips to place and assist workers and by raising funds for the venture. Daws had sent George Clark from France to accompany Clyde Taylor on an African survey at Taylor's request. A warm invitation followed from Pocket Testament League and other missions in Kenya, encouraged by the colonial government, to do evangelism and follow-up in Mau Mau detention camps. Daws felt it was the Lord's open door and asked Hightower to go with the first workers to Kenya in June 1956. Sparks, just back from the Orient, would also go to set up correspondence Bible studies similar to those in Formosa.

It was a small step, a tiny spot on a huge continent, but along with the start in South America it was highly significant to Dawson. He wrote Graham: "We believe this push into Africa will be as fruitful if not more rewarding than the tremendous opportunities in the Orient the past few years."

Dawson called an all-hands meeting in the Great Hall the morning of June 12 as a fitting send-off for the travelers to Africa. Hightower and Sparks would fly out next day; Daws would leave a day later for the East Coast Nav Conference at

Word of Life's Schroon Lake in New York. In a charged atmosphere he told of his long-held desire to enter Africa and his regret that he could not go with the first party. He spoke emotionally, intensely: "I don't know what to say, gang. This is rough for me. *Me,* stayin' home, livin' in the Pink House, while these guys go! That bothers me. There's nothing I can do about it. God is making room for young fellows to take the place of some of the older ones." In Mosaic terms he went on: "I hit fifty a couple months ago and realize I don't have the drive I did at forty — and thirty — much less at twenty-five."

Probing the depths of every soul in the room, he made each one responsible for the success of this mission. They must prove their willingness to lay down their lives for the Gospel by pouring out their hearts in prayer for these men and for Africa. "You have all this energy, and you're letting Satan rob you of it — minute by minute, hour by hour, day by day. What will you do? You can't go — but you . . . can . . . pray." To breathe the weighted air of that hour was to accept the burden of making disciples in Africa and the rest of the world. No one could go out free or pose as a bystander. Each left the meeting taking the world with him.

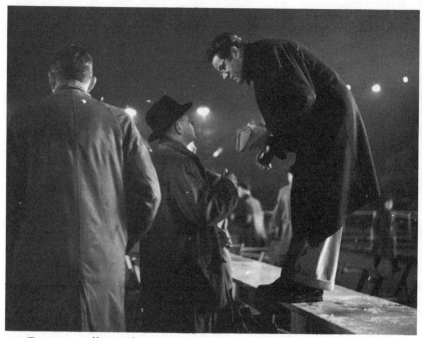

Dawson collects decision cards from workers after Wembley meeting, London 1955.

Christmas at Glen Eyrie, 1954. From left: Bruce, Daws, Lila, Faith, Ruth, Burke.

VII

The Legacy

The bracing, clear air of the Adirondack noonday was scented with fir. Schroon Lake sparkled a brittle sapphire blue, its glacier-fed depths not quite ice cold. Dawson sat in a wooded spot not far from the beach, one finger marking his place in a paperback copy of Bounds's *Power Through Prayer*. If he could only hear the voice of God with a fresh, authoritative word for now, for his own heart, a word of intimate communion with the One he had known these many years and longed to love more deeply. He prayed now, expressing this desire in short, unstudied phrases, stopping to read a paragraph and meditate and pray again.

"Hi, Daws," his friend Jack Wyrtzen called as he sauntered up, having arranged to take him water-skiing. Wyrtzen observed his thoughtful mood, asked what was on his heart.

Daws told of his desire to hear in a new way the voice of God. "I need more of this," he gestured with the book he held. Wyrtzen concurred. They talked of things they wanted to see God do. In their years of colaboring in the Gospel, He had brought them both through many challenges and triumphs and through deep waters, with ensuing victory. Today their faith was strengthened, as always, as they fellowshiped together.

Then the two took off with the boat with boyish abandon for several laps out and across, Jack at the helm towing Daws on water skis until he dropped off at the pier winded and ready to quit. Wyrtzen wheeled back to the dock where they filled the boat with conferees for a roaring ride on the deep blue.

"Isn't this great!" Daws exclaimed to the other passengers. Minutes later they unloaded at the pier and filled the boat with more conferees. Daws turned and called to the lifeguard, "Go get Lila. Tell her I want her to come with us." He arranged a signal so the boat could swing back to pick her up if she was coming. Lila seldom got to come with him to these conferences, and he wanted her in on the fun of the boat ride. She was

Billy Graham gives Dawson's funeral message in the Castle's Great Hall.

away, however, so the lifeguard waved to the boaters to go on.

Skimming powerfully across the choppy lake, swerving and turning into their wake for the fun of it, they laughed and shouted above the throaty roar of the motor.

"Can you gals swim?" Daws asked the two beside him on the front seat, perched on the backrest with their feet on the seat. Floy Moody nodded yes. The other girl said no, she could not, so Dawson sat between them, locking arms across the width of the boat for stability.

Suddenly the boat wheeled in a fast right turn and just as suddenly smacked a wave. The combined effect catapulted the nonswimmer and Dawson off the boat on the wide side of the turn into the water. Daws still gripped the girl's wrist, steadily holding her up, treading water, and the boat was swinging back around to pick them up. One boater dove into the water, then two more. Dawson's grip on the girl was firm, and he was able to keep her head above water; it would be all right. His legs pumped the cold water, and he felt tired, spent. The boat was coming; they were yelling directions and a swimmer reached them. The girl released her hold on him and grabbed the swimmer, pulling her under. They had her now, were pulling her into the boat. Good. He could not have held her up a moment more. It had taken all his strength just to keep her head above water, and he couldn't hold his own head above the surface. *Thank you, Lord, for helping me hold her up until. . . .*

Could this be—— Lila had told him of her conviction that God would take him Home soon. Was this it? Well, if it was, *precious Lord, I'm ready. . . .* "Get Dawson!" they were yelling now. "I've got him by the hair. . . . He knew the girl was back in the boat now. *Thank you, Lord. . . .* "Help me, somebody," he heard a distant call, "I can't hold on to him. . . ." Cold, icy water . . . he felt heavy . . . he was sinking, sinking. . . . *Lord, Lord Jesus! . . . My Lord . . . and My God! . . .*

A balmy June breeze wafted the happy chirping of birds and the fragrance of blue spruce in through the gothic windows of the Castle. Bright sunshine patterned the valley floor with shadows, the massive red sandstone formations silhouetting their strength against a blue Colorado sky. On the main floor and balcony of the Great Hall more than 300 family and invited friends sat listening, remembering, rejoicing. The flag-draped coffin — the flag from Bill Goold's casket seven years before — seemed curiously out of place, for death was an impostor in this scene of triumph.

Billy Graham was speaking in conversational tone. "We have come here today not to mourn and to weep, [but] to share in the triumph of a man who touched all of our lives. I think he touched more lives than any man I have ever known. We today represent thousands of people of many races and languages and cultures touched by this great man. . . . He has outstripped us in the race; he's pulled anchor and set sail. And I think today he would say with Paul, *For me to live is Christ, to die has been gain.*"

Graham pictured from Scripture what death is for such a one — a coronation . . . a rest from labor . . . embarkation on a voyage . . . a move into a new house . . . an exodus to freedom . . . and the transcendent thrill of being ushered into Christ's presence. For his listeners suspended in the summer afternoon the sad sense of loss was overpowered by joy. In that hour hands could easily reach across the narrow border between Glen Eyrie and heaven.

When Graham recounted his early contacts with his friend, it evoked ripples of laughter across the crowd, in no way incongruous with the spirit of the occasion. He told of the time at Wheaton when Daws asked the eager freshman what the Lord had given him from the Word in his devotions that morning.

"Well, I hadn't had my devotions. I hadn't been with him five minutes until he was challenging my life and probing to the depths of my life," he marveled. "Many times we bared our souls to each other as only men do who have fullest confidence in each other. And I sought his counsel often. I haven't made a major decision in the last few years that I didn't seek his counsel." The evangelist drew eight lessons from Dawson's life that he would commend his hearers to follow.

Sanny had been in Tulsa with Graham for a rally on Monday, June 18 when Rod Sargent called to tell him Dawson had possibly drowned at Schroon Lake. He was stunned. Here in Oklahoma two weeks ago Daws had casually asked him, "Sanny, what if the Lord took me Home — would you be ready to take over?" He had answered that the Lord wouldn't make any mistake like that. Now he went to Graham's room to tell him. "I can't believe it," Billy gasped. "Oh God, help me to rededicate my life!"

Other Christian leaders were equally shocked; more than one broke down and wept at the telephone when he heard. "He was my best friend," one said, "one of few people a man meets in his lifetime in whom he can have complete confidence." "An era of evangelical Christianity has just passed," said another. "I feel somewhat lonely as I think of the fellowship and strength Daws has given us." "No man in America has so vitally affected my life in the last ten years." "Word of Daws's death is like a solar plexus blow."

Reactions by some of stunned disbelief, by others of pre-cognitive acceptance as God's will, characterized Navigator staff and friends around the world. Arriving in Colorado Springs on Tuesday, Lorne held up his New Testament and asked with a rueful smile, "You still believe this is true?" He knew they did. There was a strange serenity among the crew, deep sorrow but a feeling of rightness that did not question God's wisdom. For Dawson, an expert swimmer, to drop instantly from sight when within the grasp of his rescuers could have only the explanation of the chariot of Elijah: God had sent for him.

The Nav family looked unquestioningly to Lorne for leader-ship, as to an eldest son in the loss of a father. After setting in motion necessary business at Glen Eyrie, he took Burke and Faith, the youngest Trotmans — Bruce, an Air Force officer, had come from Texas — to Schroon Lake on Wednesday morn-ing. Here too was a sense of peace and victory. Lila had in-sisted the conference go on. Her radiant testimony at the evening meeting, scarcely four hours after the accident, showed faith and committal.

"God prepared my heart for the news I received today," she said in calm, steady voice. "Heaven gets richer all the time, and it's richer tonight. Praise God for almost twenty-four of the most blessed years of my life with this man of God." She then read A. M. Overton's poem, "He Maketh No Mistake."

Ruth, whose engagement to staff man George Wortley Daws had planned to approve this week, played piano for the meeting.

Waldron Scott, directing the conference, had mobilized prayer that continued all night as conferees prayed name by name for Nav staff and friends around the world; this doubtless helped account for the incredibly tranquil aura about the camp, the acknowledgment here as at Glen Eyrie that God had prior right to intervene. Some had noticed that even Dawson's last message to the conference Monday morning was different. "The only message of his I could ever take notes on," said Air Force Lt. Bob Stephens. "He went down all twelve or fifteen points on his notes without digressing to illustrate. It was a powerful message on Why the World Isn't Being Evangelized, but he seemed preoccupied." Walking to the meeting with Daws, George Wortley had noted a determination in his manner; he seemed unusually burdened.

Jim Downing arrived early Tuesday morning, ready to tell Daws of his decision to leave the Navy and come into the work. Wondering at the unusual atmosphere of the place, he soon learned he had missed Daws by a few hours. His presence lent strength to Lila and leadership to the searchers who had spent many hours in the boats. They feared they might not find Dawson's body; the lake was deep and there had been others never found. The search was continuing next morning when Sanny arrived. He went immediately to comfort Wyrtzen and help shield him from the enemy's accusing darts of guilt. He had steered the boat, making the sudden turn which caused the accident — only because God could trust him to bear this agonizing memory.

Late Wednesday afternoon Dawson's body was found at a depth of fifty feet by a skindiver who came to help after his mother up in New England heard radio reports of the search. The coroner determined drowning as the cause of death, rather than heart attack as some had speculated. Undoubtedly the combination of cold water and faulty circulation caused his leg muscles to tire and give out in a short time.

It seemed the Lord had allowed them the fifty-hour hiatus in order to plan and regroup. Meanwhile the news had traveled swiftly, clattering out over Associated Press wires. Radio stations WMBI Chicago and KTIS Minneapolis were scarcely ahead of

HCJB Quito and DZAS Manila in relaying it to distant corners. Messages of comfort and of personal loss began pouring in.

Reactions were surprisingly strong from some who were more remote. Cowboy singer Stuart Hamblen, a casual acquaintance, said, "I have never had anything so shake me as this has. I can't understand it." Some felt as they would in losing a parent. A staff member's uncle, who once heard Dawson speak, wept for an hour on hearing of his death. Business magnate C. Davis Weyerhaeuser of Tacoma wrote, "Words fail to express the feelings which accompany the loss of so great a leader as Dawson." Gambling czar Mickey Cohen and his wife wired, "WE KNOW THAT DAWS IS OK, ALTHOUGH WE ARE QUITE UPSET BY THE TRAGEDY."

A soldier in Tacoma, memory verses in hand, heard the news by radio and thought, *That's the guy responsible for my growth in Christ, and I have never met him.* A teacher in the Los Angeles Nav work said later, "My first thought was that Dawson Trotman wouldn't want me to sit around and mope, so I said 'onward and upward' and went down to finish my wash. I just couldn't believe it. I wept through the wash."

Time magazine devoted almost a page to his biography. Evangelical magazines and radio programs gave tributes — Wyrtzen's Word of Life Hour with Charles Fuller speaking, Graham's Hour of Decision, Dan Fuller on the Old Fashioned Revival Hour, Epp's Back to the Bible Broadcast, and First Mate Bob's program among them. Al Sanders produced a moving memorial program on Biola radio and *The King's Business* published a memorial issue.

At the core of memorial services in London, Hong Kong, Los Angeles, and other places were Daws's lifelong friends and innumerable persons whose lives or service for God had been affected by an encounter with him: an hour at the airport in Okinawa; a chance meeting on a train; a word after a meeting — living answers to his frequent prayer that eternal business might be done even in such fleeting contacts. In the words of YFC's Bob Cook, Daws "by the sheer weight of his devotion to Christ and the Word challenged thousands to become something for God."

Wycliffe dedicated the Dawson Trotman Memorial Base at Limoncocha, Ecuador, Word of Life a new Dawson E. Trotman

Memorial Auditorium at Schroon Lake. A California business-man wired $500 to start a memorial fund to perpetuate Dawson's vision. It was decided the fund, promoted by Jim Vaus, Graham, and others, would best fulfill that purpose by helping to finish payment for Glen Eyrie.

By June 27, the day of the funeral at Glen Eyrie, the Nav family had dealt with its grief. As guests began to arrive, the occasion took on the air of a celebration, which indeed it was — a time to rejoice for one who had finished the race. There were warm greetings, joyous handshaking, and fellowship in the business of God's kingdom among Christian leaders whose busy lives seldom afforded such time together. Henrietta Mears exclaimed over the Glen's beauty. Bob Pierce and Frank Phillips of World Vision, Dr. Edman of Wheaton, Hubert Mitchell, Pastor Roy Laurin, Jim Rayburn, Jack Wyrtzen and Carlton Booth, Bob Cook, Bill Bright — Daws had been thrilled to think of bringing such friends here for prayer and fellowship and their enthusiasm did him credit.

Jim and Morena Downing, John Streater, Mrs. Kerr, Dave and Jean Rohrer, Charlie Riggs, the Dan Piatts, all long-time colaborers. With the Grahams came George Beverly Shea and Paul Mickelson of the Team and George Wilson from the Minneapolis office. Dick Hillis, with whom Daws had planned to meet this very day to plot Orient strategy. Irene Mills, his schoolteacher-counselor from early days, his sister Mildred, the Walt Stantons, Jim Vaus, William Nyman of Wycliffe, many others dear to him were at the private funeral in the afternoon. Friends huddled over matters they needed to discuss, making the buffet lunch in the Castle more like a family reunion than a wake. Daws would have enjoyed this day more than anyone.

In the evening about 2800 persons attended a memorial service held in two Colorado Springs churches. Rayburn and Pierce gave eulogies. Shea sang, with Mickelson at the organ. Faith and Ruth Trotman sang "He'll Understand and Say Well Done," and Lila gave a clear testimony of victorious submission to the will of God. Graham's message was as always a presentation of Christ, after which dozens of hands were raised to indicate personal decisions. This, too, Daws would have cheered.

Later that evening a score of the Christian leaders gathered to dedicate Lorne Sanny for leadership of The Navigators, a commission obviously given him by the Lord and heartily endorsed by Navigator staff around the world. The qualms felt by some in the group gathered in prayer that June night were those of a trembling faith, wondering who could emerge from the shadow of Dawson Trotman and successfully guide the Navigator ship of state. But their confidence was rightly directed to the God of Dawson Trotman — and of Lorne Sanny, 35 — as Dr. Edman read the first chapter of Joshua and charged the new director to lead with courage, faith, and obedience to God and His Word. The Paul-Timothy, Elijah-Elisha, Moses-Joshua principle had worked in Scripture, and it would still prove true.

A small plateau on the ridge overlooking the Glen, near Dawson's favorite prayer spot, was chosen for his burial. There a bronze plaque commemorates with the words of John 15:13 a man who gave his life for others: *Greater love hath no man than this, that a man lay down his life for his friends.* It has remained a place for prayer and reflection.

Reflection, perhaps, on the qualities of discipleship Graham reviewed that sunny June afternoon in the Castle:

> Dawson *loved the Word of God.* I think more than anybody else he taught me to love it. He always carried his Bible around and always had it marked. And he could turn to it quickly. He would say, "Billy, have you seen this?" or "Here's a little nugget I got from the Lord today. I want to give it to you." The Word of God was sweetness to him; he meditated in it day and night. *The law of his God is in his heart; none of his steps shall slide.* How many times he told me that!

> Dawson was a *man with a vision.* When our God is small, the world looks big; but when our God is big, the world looks small. And Dawson saw the world as conquerable for Christ. No project was too big to tackle if he felt God was in it. To Daws, God was big and the world was little. The day he went to be with the Lord, some of his men arrived in Africa. One of his great visions was to open Africa. He was always dreaming, planning, and scheming about new methods and means of reaching people for Christ. He seemed to have a sanctified imagination which would look beyond handicaps and circumstances and barriers. He was a general — a strategist. God gave him that ability.

> Dawson was a *man of prayer.* Many times he slipped away to pray with you. He would tell me about times of prayer he had with Jim Rayburn or Stacey Woods or Jack Wyrtzen. I remem-

ber in London Dawson would slip into my little room when things would seem impossible, and we'd get down on our knees and pray. When we first came to Glen Eyrie, Ruth and Daws and I walked up on that little knoll and knelt and prayed up there on the rocks as we looked out and visualized this whole thing for God.

He was a *man of discipline*. His life seemed a rebuke to this undisciplined, loose-living age. He disciplined his own life, but he demanded discipline in others. He was organized. He believed the highest calling required the highest quality of living. He wanted the Lord to have the best of everything. He wanted us to be our best for God. His room, if you went to see him at a hotel, was always neat. His whole life was that way. And that's the way a Christian should be.

He was a man of *complete dedication*. He could say with Paul, "This one thing I do," not "These forty things I dabbled in." He was everlastingly at it.

Dawson was a man with a *consuming passion for souls*. His love for the lost coupled with his boundless energy took him to the ends of the world to encourage, train, and strengthen laborers in Christ's vineyard. I remember seeing him in these meetings talking with individuals, making appointments all day long to help people grow in the grace and knowledge of Jesus Christ. Over in London, many times in the counseling room he and my wife would be the last ones dealing with people. A passion, a love for souls.

Next, and this is very important, Dawson was the *master of the soft rebuke*. He quoted that verse in Proverbs 27:6, *Faithful are the wounds of a friend*. . . . He would come to you and say, "You know, I believe this ought to be in your life. You're not keeping up with your memory work; you're not keeping up with your prayer life," or this or that. He had courage and did it in a sweet, humble way and quoted so many Scriptures you knew it came from God. He could rebuke you and make you love it. I learned something from him that way.

Lastly, Dawson *lived for eternity*. His sights were trained on heaven. He died as he had lived, bravely. There was no hysterical shout for help, no frantic gesture of desperation. He died courageously, selflessly. And having saved another, he slipped out of this life. What a reception there must have been last Monday a week ago in heaven!

* * * *

Thus did Dawson Earle Trotman at age fifty depart the planet with as little ostentation as marked his arrival in an

Arizona mining town early in the century. He left an organization of modest proportions — he had not given himself to building an organization — no more than 140 staff members in the U.S. and a dozen other countries. He had served on boards of several mission groups and worked with the Graham crusades. Other men had done as much — some far more. What, then, would emerge as unique or distinctive when his spiritual will was probated? It would be difficult now at midsummer 1956 to assess the significance of this life and its impact on its times. True assessment could be made only in the total hindsight of eternity: but as time passed some would attempt to define and measure his contribution.

Controversial he was, as some detractors fervently attest. Loved, admired, sometimes followed blindly, resented bitterly he was also. Catalyst of the best efforts and achievements of some who had been afraid to try; unwitting represser of others who felt their best efforts would not please him, no matter what.

He left no legacy except that held in trust in the lives of men. His investment in countless men and women throughout the world would be the evidence of his influence on his times. What did these see and emulate in his life? He epitomized many things, varying with the eye of the beholder:

— an awesome respect for the promises of God and the power of the Word, seeing it not as a treasure held on deposit but as a limitless fortune to spend for the benefit of many.

— a vigorous, sensitive love for Christ that jealously guarded His glory and sought much time with Him in solitary worship, a relationship which sustained his drive to carry out the Great Commission.

— intense interest in the individual, a concept of a person's potential that could boost his self-image and fire his expectation that God would use him.

— an inventive genius combined with an inquiring mind that enabled him to devise methods any Christian could use to study and memorize the Word, to pray, to witness, to grow in Christ.

— a love of beauty and appreciation of God's artistry in nature; the belief that His lavish gifts were for His children to lavishly enjoy.

— an expansive generosity which could empty his wallet or wardrobe for a friend's need on a moment's impulse.

— a desire to excel and insistence on excellence in any endeavor.

— fervent love, even though expressed on occasion in contradictory form if Daws was disappointed in one's attitude or actions. His displeasure could be most severe with his family or closest associates, for whom his expectations were highest.

— keen discernment which could swiftly touch an open nerve of individual need and counsel a course of action based firmly on Scripture.

— a penchant for practical reality in contrast to theory or assumption, and courage to ask others to "face the facts." He asked "How is your memory work?" and "What verse are you working on now?" when some were better prepared to answer the theoretical question, "Do you believe Scripture memory is important?"

— an active, moving vision of the world he was commissioned to reach and of ways to do it more effectively.

— an unshakable and contagious faith in God's sovereignty and power.

— a habit of applying the Word in practical terms to every facet of living, a practice given a third dimension by continual memory and review of hundreds of verses of Scripture.

— empirical rediscovery of man-to-man ministry as a viable scriptural principle.

— a revival in practice of the Hebrew idea of training the whole man, in contrast to the Greek discipline of intellect alone.

Over the span of a generation Dawson influenced many through these life qualities and convictions, inspiring one to be a man of prayer because Dawson was a man of prayer ("Ask big!"), another to discipline his life, another to purity of dedication or to a spirit of wholeheartedness and "can-do." His influence will extend through them to others in many cases; in others, it will not.

What, then, will endure to become a permanent page in church history and in fulfillment of the Great Commission? What would prompt a Christian leader to call him the prophet of the twentieth century? Or evoke such superlatives as "one of the truly great men of our generation," "a Christian hero," "few men of this or any generation influenced more lives for God," "his outreach shall endure through all eternity," "a truly great leader . . . what he started will never die"? Or lead a mission executive to call The Navigators the great movement of the century?

Undoubtedly the answer lies in two distinctive contributions which many believe God gave the church through Dawson Trotman "for such a time as this." The first is follow-up. Not that Trotman was the first since the apostles to promote parental guidance of new Christians toward spiritual maturity, but he came at a time when the prevailing idea was that a soul won was a mission accomplished. He began to preach and practice follow-up and to call the servants of God back to their responsibility for the 95 percent — nurture of the young in Christ. To help in this task he designed how-to-do-it follow-up tools and methods.

After Graham adopted systematic follow-up in his crusades, other evangelists and churches followed his lead and follow-up became the norm. Churches began holding special classes for new Christians using The Wheel as a teaching guide. Question-and-answer Bible studies, popularized by Dawson along with card systems for Scripture memory, proliferated for church and home study and individual use. Some contend that these practical methods of follow-up helped stem the increasing drift away from the church.

The second contribution is rediscovery of the multiplication principle. This, too, Dawson demonstrated in his own ministry, boldly claiming the Great Commission could be fulfilled, the world reached in a generation if the principle were taken seriously. A corollary to this was the implied value and useful-ness of every Christian, for in this ministry every layman, talented or not, could participate.

Those who doubted the effectiveness of multiplication or asked why, when the "each one reach one" idea had been around for a while the world was not yet reached, Daws answered that it was the same principle by which the world had been populated — yet the secret lay in multiplying *disciples* rather than merely adding members to the body. When spiritual parents imparted to their spiritual children the wisdom to train their own young in Christ, reproduction of disciples as the Lord meant in Matthew 28 would be assured.

Dawson's pioneer role in reviving these principles of discipleship also helped to spark the laymen's movement of recent years. Laymen have discovered they *can* memorize the Word and equip themselves to disciple others and have tasted the joys of personal, direct ministry on their own. The Bible study tools Trotman devised with the young Christian in mind have worked for them and stimulated them to serve God. Graham crusade counselor classes have steadily built this lay ministry concept into the fabric of the church in many countries.

The concept of follow-up has been widely accepted; that of disciple multiplication has not. Yet within the Navigator movement its fire burns bright. The results Dawson did not see in large numbers are increasingly seen now in many areas of the world. And — by faith — he left knowing his Isaiah promises would be fulfilled. *I will give men for thee, and people for thy life. . . . And they that shall be of thee shall build the old waste places: thou shalt raise up the foundations of many generations; and thou shalt be called, the repairer of the breach, the restorer of paths to dwell in.*

Dawson traveled around the U.S. in 1950 with Lorne Sanny in search of potential Navigator representatives. He found them at this Minneapolis conference. Twenty-five of this group later joined Navigator staff.

The Castle at Glen Eyrie.